Early Historic Settlements at Shetrunji River in India

Early Historic Settlements at Shetrunji River in India

Ashit Boran Paul

AGAM KALA PRAKASHAN
DELHI

First Published 2017

ISBN : 978 -81-7320-156-1

Published by:
Dr. Agam Prasad, M.A., Ph.D., Diploma in Museology
For **Agam Kala Prakashan**
34, Central Market, Ashok Vihar
Delhi - 110 052
Tel.: 91-11-27212195, 65688806-7
Fax: 91-11-27212195
Email: agambooks@gmail.com, agambook@yahoo.com
www.agamkala.com

Composed by:
Aman Printographics
Delhi - 110 052
Mobile: 9891395309

Printed by:
Chawla Offset Printers
Wazirpur Village, Ashok Vihar
Delhi-110 052

Printed in India

Dedicated to my parents

Contents

Foreword

I am extremely glad to write this Foreword for the book entitled Early Historic Settlements in Bhavnagar District with Special Reference to Padri. The Bhavnagar district was important right from the beginning of the early settled life going back to 4000 B.C. It has yielded a large number of Harappan sites some of which were studied in great detail. The elements and characteristic features of the Harappan culture in Bhavnagar district were properly identified during the course of excavation carried out at the site of Padri from 1990 to 1995. However, the cultures prior and after the Harappan period were not studied properly. This is, therefore, the first systematic effort in documenting Early Historic settlements in Bhavnagar district.

Dr. Paul undertook systematic village to village survey in the entire Bhavnagar district, discovered and studied more than 100 sites from the point of view of understanding the exact reasons for the locations for these sites. He studied the determinant factors for the establishment of these sites and arrived at the conclusion that the locations of most of the sites were governed by the arable land. The settlement pattern studies on Early Historic Culture is not carried out in great depth in India and therefore this work assumes greater significance. This can serve as a model for future researchers for planning to work on similar model. Efforts have also been made to categorize sites in different hierarchical levels and relationship between different sites from the point of view of trade and economy. In future some of the important Early Historic sites need to be subjected to site catchment analysis to understand the subsistence strategy and level of economy of this people. The research carried out by Dr. Paul have demonstrated that Bhavnagar district was an important region for the Early Historic people where they mostly subsisted on agriculture and carried out hinterland and international trade. Some of the sites located along the coast may have played important role in overseas trade of the Early Historic people. Dr. Paul was not able to identify the roles of some of these sites but this could be an important topic for future research. Some of the sites in this region have produced Roman and Iranian pottery indicating trade contacts with those regions. However, more research is required on this aspect.

Overall, the research carried out by Dr. Paul is significant and has added new dimension to the Early Historic archaeology in India. I congratulate Dr. Paul for his immense contribution to the relevant field which might serve a model for the future researchers.

Deccan College Post Graduate and Research Institute, Pune
Date: 18th October, 2016

(Prof. V.S. Shinde)
Vice Chancellor

Preface

The present work is the revised version, which earned the author Ph.D. degree from the Deccan College Post Graduate and Research Institute, Pune in India in 1999, of the detailed study of the settlement archaeology in the lower Shetrunji river basin of Bhavnagar district in Gujarat. The Shetrunji river basin and coastal part of Bhavnagar district in Saurashtra played an important role during the Early Historic period (1st century B.C.-A.D.) as is evident from the excavations at Padri, Bhavnagar District, Saurashtra. An extensive survey was carried out on both sides of the lower part of Shetrunji river basin on foot during the field seasons of 1996-98. In all, twenty-two Early Historic sites have been studied along the coast and the lower part of Shetrunji river of which eight were already reported by the earlier scholars from the point of view of settlement pattern.

The author is express his deep sense of gratitude to Prof. Vasant Shinde, his research supervisor for his constant encouragement, guidance, extending maximum facilities and allowing him to use the excavated material of Padri. Without his help and valuable suggestions at various stages, it would not have been possible to bring this book to its present form. Besides, the author is also grateful to Prof. V. N. Misra, the then Director, and Prof. K. Paddayya of Deccan College who always encouraged him on various occasions.

Dr. Mahesh Bhai Pandya and his family of Padri village for their warm hospitality. It is because of their co-operation that the author could complete his field survey in the Shetrunji river valley in Bhavnagar district Gujarat. The Ford Foundation grant of Jahangirnagar University in Bangladesh extended substantial financial support for this work. The author is also grateful to his teacher Prof. Abu Imam who inspired him to study archaeology in Post Graduate level at Jahangirnagar University. The author also acknowledges his wife Pallabi and daughter Dipanwita who were with him at Deccan College while completing this work.

Ashit Boran Paul

List of Plates

Pl. XII-a: Iron objects: Nos. 1-4-Nails, No.5-Chisel, No.6-Knife, No.7-Hoe, No.8-Pick, No.9-Fish hook.

Pl. XII-b: Iron objects: No.10-Knife, No.11-Pendulum, No.12-Arrowhead, No.13-Door chain, No.14-Knife, No.15-Bangle, No.16-Clamp(?), No.17-Dagger.

Pl. XIII: Bone objects: No.1-Arrowhead, No.2-4-Points, No.5-Arrowhead.

Pl. XIV-a: No.1-Terracotta Lajjagauri figurine, No.2-Lajjagauri figurine in stone, No.3-Vishnu figurine in stone, No.4-Lower portion of a deity, No.5-Sand stone head of Lord Ganesa, No.6-An unidentified stone figurine, No.7-Terracotta female figurine.

Pl. XIV-b: No.1-Terracotta bull figurine, No.2-An unidentified stone figurine, No.3-A terracotta yoni portion of Lajjagauri figurine, Nos.4-7-Terracotta bull figurines. No.8-Terracotta figurine-shaped spout, No.9-Terracotta bull figurine, No.10-Terracotta head of a bird, No.11-Terracotta bull figurine, No.12-Terracotta head of a elephant.

Pl. XIV-c: No.1-Terracotta head of a bird, No.2-A hand made terracotta torso. No.3-Terracotta bull figurine, Nos.4-5-Terracotta dog figurines. No.6-Terracotta ring fragment, No.7-Terracotta horn fragment, No.8-Terracotta bull figurine, No.9-A miniature terracotta bull figurine, No.10-A fragment of terracotta human figurine.

Pl. XIV-d: Nos.1-2-Terracotta boat-shaped motifs.

Pl. XV-a: No.1-A small clay toy pot, No.2-Black jasper weight, No.3-Dolorite weight. No.4-Pottery lamp, No.5-Pottery lamp, No.6-Basalt potter's dabbar, No.7-Fragment of columellar, No.8-Basalt mullar, No.9-Rubber stone.

Pl. XV-b: No.1-Terracotta incense burner, No.2-Terracotta lid finial, No.3-Terracotta crucible, No.4- Fragment of terracotta incense burner.No.5-Fragment of a terracotta gamesmen, No.6-Terracotta circular base of a goblet, Nos.7-8-Terracotta wheel, No.9-Fragment of terracotta incense burner, No.10 Ground shell.

Pl. XV-c: No.1-Used shell, No.2-Terracotta stopper, No.3-Terracotta ball, No.4-Stone ball, No.5- Fragment of hammer stone, No.6-Terracotta ball, No.7-Chert flake, No.8-Fragment of white glass.

Pl. XV-d: Terracotta tablet with Brahmi inscription.

Pl. XVI: No.1-Shell pendant, No.2-Terracotta stopper, No.3-Shell pendant, No.4-Shell pendant, No.5-Terracotta stopper.

Pl. XVII-a: Nos.1-5-Terracotta discs, No.6-Stone disc.

Pl. XVII-b: Nos.1-7-Terracotta discs.

Pl. XVIII: Nos.1-7- Terracotta ear-stud.

Pl. XIX-a: Early Historic site at Bandi-Rohil.

Pl. XIX-b: Early Historic site at Begali.

Pl. XX-a: Early Historic site at Bhalar.

Pl. XX-b: Early Historic site at Bharapur/Juno Timba.

Pl. XXXIV-a: Red-Slipped Ware: Nos.1-3-Jars, No.4-Pot, Nos. 5-6-Jars, Nos.7-8-Pots, Nos.9-10-Cups.

Pl. XXXIV-b: Red-Slipped Ware: No.1-Pot, No.2-Dish, Grey Ware: Nos.3-4-Basins, Nos.5-6-Jars, No.7-Pot, No.8-Jar, Red Ware: No.9-Saucer, Red Polished Ware: Nos.10-11-Jars, Nos.12- 13-Bowls.

Pl. XXXV-a: Red-Slipped Ware: No.1-Pot, Red Ware: Nos.2-3-Jars, Red-Slipped Ware: No.4-Jar, Grey Ware: No.5-Dish, No.6-Jar, Nos.7-8, Dishes, Nos. 9-10-Jars, Red Ware: No.11-Bowl, No.12-Dish-on-stand.?

Pl. XXXV-b: Red-Slipped Ware: No.1-Pot, Nos.2-3-Jars, No.4-Pot, No.5-Jar, No.6- Pot, Nos.7-8- Dish, Red Polished Ware: No.9-Jar, Nos.10-11-Bowls, No.12-Jar-No.13-Sprinkler.

Pl. XXXVI-a: Red Ware: No.1-Pot, No.2-Jar, No.3-Pot, No.4-Bowl, Nos.5-6-Cups, No.7-Bowl, Nos.8-9-Uncertain sherds.

Pl. XXXVI-b: Red Ware: No.10-Uncertain sherd, Red-Slipped Ware: Nos. 11-13-Jars, No.14-Pot, No.15-Jar.

Pl. XXXVI-c: Red-slipped Ware: No. 16-Bowl, No.17- Jar, Nos.18-19-Uncertain sherds, No. 20-Lid- No. 21-Jar

Pl. XXXVI-d: Red-slipped Ware: No.22-Uncertain sherd, Grey Ware: Nos.23-24-Jars, No.25 –Pot, No.26-Handi, No.27-Pot.

Pl. XXXVI-e: No.28-Amphorae handle sherd.

Pl. XXXVI-f: Red Polished Ware: Nos. 29-30-Jars, Nos.31-33-Spout/ basins.

Pl. XXXVII-a: Red-Slipped Ware : Nos.1-2- Jars, No.3-Dish, No.4-Pot, No.5-Cup, Nos. 6-7-Jars, No.8-Pot, Red Ware: No.9-Jar.

Pl. XXXVII-b: Red-Slipped Ware: No. 10-Conical spout, Nos.11-12-Bowls, No. 13-Spout, Grey Ware: No. 14-Jar, No.15-Pot, No.16-Jar, Nos. 17-18-Pots.

Pl. XXXVII-c: Grey Ware: No19-Pot, No.20-Dish, No. 21-Dish-on-stand?, No.22-Lid, No.23-Spout.

Pl. XXXVIII-a: Red Ware: Nos.1-6-Jars, Red-Slipped Ware: Nos.7-8-Pots, Red Ware: No.9-Cup.

Pl. XXXVIII-b: Red-Slipped Ware: Nos.10-11-Jars, Nos.12-13, Pots, No. 14-Basin, Grey Ware: Nos.15-18-Pots, No.19-Dish, No.20-Bowl/dish, No.21-Bowl.

Pl. XXXVIII-c: Red Polished Ware: Nos.22-26-Jars, No.27-Bowl.

Pl. XXXIX-a: Red Ware: No. 1-Lamp/lid, Nos.2-3-Cups, No.4-Dish, No.5-Pot, No.6-Jar, Red-Slipped Ware: Nos.7-9-Jars, No.10-Dish, No.11-Jar.

Pl. XXXIX-b: Red Ware: Nos.1-2-Jars, Nos.3-4-Cups, Red-Slipped Ware: Nos.5-Dish, No.6-Pot, No.7-Jar, No. 8-Bowl, No.9-Painted sherd.

Pl. XXXIX-c: Grey Ware: Nos.10-12-Jars.

Pl. XXXIX-d: Grey Ware: Nos.13-14-Pots, No.15- Jar, No.16-Pot, No.17-Dish, No.18-Bowl, No.19- Conical spout.

Pl. XXXIX-e: Red Polished Ware: Nos.20-21-Bowls, No.22-Sprinkler, No.23-Jar.

Pl. XLVI-b:	No.12-A perforated terracotta disc found at Phulsar, No.13-A circular terracotta disc found at Gorkhi, No.14-A circular potsherd disc found at Ichhora, No.15-A circular terracotta disc found at Piparla, No16-A circular terracotta disc found at Shilavadar, Nos.17-18-Unperforated potsherd discs found at Saltanpur, No.19-A circular terracotta disc found at Bhegali.
Pl. XLVII-a:	Sand stone muller found at Bhegali.
Pl. XLVII-b:	Nos.1-2-Fragments of shell bangle found at Hathab, No.3-Shell bangle found at Piparla, Nos.4-6-Fragments of shell bangle found at Hathab, No.7-Fragment of Shell bangle found at Pavti, No.8-Shell bangle found at Bhalar.
Pl. XLVIII-a:	Shell dibatage found at Hathab.
Pl. XVIII-b:	No.1-Used shell found at Hathab, Nos.2-3-Used shell found at Chopa, No.4-Used shell found at Piparla, No.5-Used shell found at Saltanpur.
Pl. XLIX-a:	Terracotta animal figurine found at Bhegali.
Pl. XLIX-b:	No.1-Terracotta lamp found at Saltanpur, No.2-Decorated terracotta bell found at Pavti, No.3-Stone ball found at Saltanpur, No.4-Fragment of terracotta bell found at Piparla, No.5- Terracotta stopper found at Saltanpur, No.6-Terracotta stopper found at Saltanpur, No.7-Fragment of unidentified figurine found at Katva, No.8-Agates flake found at Piparla.
Pl. L:	No.1-Vitrified clay found at Devalia, Nos.2-3-Vitrified clay found at Hathab, No. 4-Iron slag found at Saltanpur, No.5-Unidentified stone object found at Shilavadar, No.6-Fragment of iron object found at Bharapur, No.7-Iron slag found at Phulsar.
Pl. LI- a & b:	Punch marked copper coin found at Hathab.
Pl. LII:	Nos.1-3-Punch marked copper coins found at Hathab.

List of Figures

List of Tables

Introduction

The Shetrunji river basin and coastal part of Bhavnagar district in Saurashtra played an important role during the Early Historic period (1st century B.C.-A.D.) as is evident from the excavations at Padri, Talaja *taluka* of Bhavnagar District, Saurashtra (Shinde 1992a, Paul 2000). However, this region was not surveyed systematically for antiquarian remains. To understand the Early Historic archaeology and its settlement pattern, the lower Shetrunji river basin and coastal areas of this region were selected for a detailed study.

The area of present study is the lower part of Shetrunji river basin i.e. in and around Padri and Hathab in the Bhavnagar District of Saurashtra, Gujarat.This river is the second largest river of Saurashtra, has a total length of about 180 km of which about 92 km of its course is through the district (Trivedi 1969). Thus the total area under study is around 1000 sq. km. The sites of Padri (Ghosh 1989: 206; *IAR.*1972-73) and Hathab (Schoff 1912: 39-40; *IAR.* 1980-81) have been treated as index sites. The region around these sites has been thoroughly investigated. Padri is located in the lower part of Shetrunji river basin which was systematically excavated (Shinde 1992a; 1992b; 1992c; 1994a; 1994b; 1996 and 1998). The Early Historic phase is confined to the upper three layers. The other site at Hathab, 23 km east of Bhavnagar town, is located on the Gulf of Cambay. It represents ancient *Hastavapra* or *Hastakavapra* (Trivedi 1969), which was rendered as *Astacampra* in the Greek literature (Schoff 1912: 39-40). The site may have played an important role in the socio-economic organization of the Early Historic period.

The archaeological potential and importance of Bhavnagar district was established by some important discoveries in the field of Prehistoric, Harappan and Chalcolithic culture. Prehistoric research in Saurashtra began as early as 1884, when Fedden investigated the geological features of the Peninsula belonging to the later part of the Trappean and sub-recent times (cited from Chakrabarti 1977: 10; Jairath 1986: 1). On the other hand it was Bruce Foote (Foote 1916: 146-155) who was amongst the first persons to collect Palaeoliths in India and carried out an exploration in some parts of Peninsular India and report his finds as "Neolithic and pottery of later date" in early part of the twentieth century. Since then, Saurashtra has received much attention by archaeologists. In the early fifties R. N. Mehta discovered early Palaeolithic artifacts for the first time from the Amreli district in Saurashtra (Jairath 1986: 1). In 1962 Sankalia (Sankalia 1965: 327-340) discovered Early and Middle Palaeolithic artifacts from the stratified deposits in the river valley of Bhadar. In the late seventies Sundarrajan (*IAR*.1967: 86) brought to light some Early Palaeolithic implements in the Sherdi Valley in Junagadh district of Saurashtra. After wards, Lele (Lele 1972) discovered a good number of Early Palaeolithic sites in the Bhadar river valley. Similarly, the evidences of Middle Palaeolithic artifacts were collected from various parts of Peninsular India by Pandya in 1952, Rao in 1959, Lele in 1970-71, Marathe in 1975 (cited from Chakrabarti 1977: 12). Apart from this, in late eighties Chakrabarti (1977) discovered many Early and Middle Palaeolithic sites in the Kalubhar valley. Besides, Possehl (1980), Suman Pandya (1973) and Jairath (1986) brought to light some Palaeolithic sites in Bhavnagar district.

The research on Harappan culture started in 1930, in Gujarat in general and in Saurashtra in particular. It was Father H. Heras of Bombay who first carried out an excavation at the vicinity of Valabhipur, Bhavnagar district in Saurashtra in 1930's. The excavations have yielded few objects like knob-pot, knob-jar-covers and terracotta calf. However to the excavator these materials belong to the Mohenjo-Daro-Harappan period (Heras 1938; 1990: 56). In 1935 M.S. Vats of the Archaeological Survey of India had conducted an excavations at Rangpur in Limbdi Taluka of Surendranagar district in Saurashtra. On the basis of his findings from the excavations, Vats assigned these to correspond with the late period of the Indus Valley sites (Vats 1936: 38). Since then, Rangpur was subjected to excavations which were successively undertaken by Ghurye in 1937, Sankalia and Dikshit in 1950 and Rao 1953-56 (Pandya 1973: 82).

After the Independence of the country, all the Harappan affiliated remains went to the geographical boundary of modern Pakistan. In accordance with this situation the Archaeological Survey of India carried out an extensive exploration in Gujarat, Rajasthan, Haryana and Punjub (Ghosh 1952; *IAR*. 1953-54: 6-7). Rao, Pandya and Nanavati discovered as many as 88 Harappan sites in various parts of Gujarat during 1950's (Koiso 1994: 13-14). Subsequently, excavations at Lothal have brought to light Harappan culture. Rao conducted an excavation at this site for over eight seasons during 1954-1963 (Koiso 1994: 17). At the same time Subbarao and Pandya jointly carried out an excavation at Prabas Patan (Somnath). It has yielded Harappan Pottery associated with other local wares (*IAR*.1955-56: 7-8; 1956-57: 16-17 and Subbarao 1958: 132-34). In 1957 and 1958 Pandya conducted an excavation at Rojdi, now known as Srinathgadh, and later Dhaky also carried out an excavation at the same site (Koiso 1994: 21). During 1970's and 1980's district-wise explorations were carried out in Saurashtra by the Department of Archaeology, M.S. University of Baroda in joint collaboration with Archaeological Survey of India. The surveyed districts were Panchmahal (Sonawane 1974; 1976) Banaskantha (Parikh 1977), Kheda (Momin 1974; 1976a; 1976b; 1979 and 1984), Jamnagar (Bhan 1983; 1986) and Bhavnagar (Jairath 1986). Along with these surveys, the works of S. Pandya (1973), Possehl (1977; 1980), Chitalwala (1979) and Shinde (1991b; 1992a; 1992b; 1998) on Harappan aspects are very important.

On the other hand archaeological exploration and trial digging have brought to light Chalcolithic culture on the river valleys of Ghelo, Kalubhar and Shetrunji in the district (*IAR*. 1957-58: 18-20). Besides, two important excavations at Valabhipur (*IAR*.1979-80) and Padri (Shinde 1992a, 1992b; 1992c; 1994a; 1994b; 1996 and 1998) have established the archaeological potential of the district. The systematic and large scale excavations carried out at Padri by Dr. Vasant Shinde and his team of the Department of Archaeology, Deccan College, Pune, have thrown light not only on the various aspects of rural life of the Harappan culture in Saurashtra, but have also produced evidence for stratified phase of the Early Harappan as well as Early Historic periods. There is also proper evidence, particularly in the ceramic assemblage, of the cultural transformation from the early to mature phase of the Harappan culture. This phase yielded a huge structure complex having a number of rooms of varied dimensions and functions. The Early Harappan phase discovered at Padri is characterized by the Padri Ware which is coarse in texture, slightly ill fired and treated with a thick coating of bright red slip. Some of the fossil types of the Saurashtra Harappan culture such as convex-sided bowl with stud handle, dish-on-stand and perforated jar were introduced by the Early Harappan people in this region. The Mature Harappan Phase, dated between c.2400-2000 B.C. at the site, yielded four structural phases. All these phases are characterized by mud and mud brick and either squarish or rectangular domestic structures. The Mature Harappan people most probably undertook the occupation of salt farming as their main livelihood. This phase is characterized by the typical Harappan painted Red Ware. The Early Historic phase at Padri dated between 1st century B.C.-A.D. is known for the discovery of the possible temple of *Lajjagauri* (Shinde 1994). This phase is characterized by two main wares -Red Ware and Grey Ware, both coarse in fabric and slightly ill fired. The former is represented by wide-mouthed cups and small globular pots and the latter is dominated by the large globular pots. Besides, the discovery of tortoise-shaped copper lamp at the site in Early Historic level suggests contact with Rome in the 1st century B.C.-A.D. (Shinde 1992a: 81).

The main aims and objectives of the present study were to reconstruct the settlement patterns in and around Padri and Hathab during the Early Historic period. The settlement pattern studies in archaeology started at first in Europe, Middle East and New World, but began only in recent times in India. It should be mentioned that no work on Early Historic archaeology has yet been undertaken in this region so far. Therefore, the present study of the settlement pattern is the first of its kind along the coast and in the lower Shetrunji river basin. The present study is also an attempt to deal with the following aspects of the Early Historic period:

1. To discover the sites,
2. Patterns of their distribution over the landscape,
3. The function of each settlement and its role in the international and hinterland trade,
4. To reconstruct the life style of the people in this region during the Early Historic period,
5. Size of population of different sites from the archaeological remains and
6. Finally to propose the chronology of the explored sites in relation to the systematically excavated site at Padri.

In order to achieve this task, an extensive regional survey was carried out during 1996 to 1998. For locating sites the present author used different survey methods like village to village survey on foot and relying on local information, survey along the coast and both banks of the lower part of Shetrunji river, and the study of the survey maps of India. Besides, studying the already reported eight sites by the earlier scholars, the author has discovered fourteen more sites in this region. During the course of exploration, the sites were examined from observable surface remains and exposed section checked to obtain information about the thickness of deposit, stratigraphy and cultural sequence. The data from the fieldwork was interpreted by using different archaeological methods and the present work is based on Trigger's (1968) third level of settlement pattern studies i.e. zonal patterns.

Besides the introduction, the study is divided into seven chapters.

Chapter I (Environmental background) gives a brief account of geography, topography, drainage system, geology, climate, soil types, vegetation and present settlement pattern in this region.

Chapter II reviews data available on the Early Historic culture in Gujarat with special reference to Bhavnagar district.

Chapter III deals with the Early Historic Phase at Padri including structures, stratigraphy, pottery and minor objects.

Chapter IV gives the detailed description of the sites found during the course of exploration including their location, size, site typology and material remains.

Chapter V is an important chapter that deals with settlement patterns. It discusses origin and development of settlement pattern studies, size and distribution of the sites, function of each settlement and demographic analysis of the Early Historic period.

Chapter VI deals with the chronology of Early Historic settlements in relation to the systematically excavated site at Padri.

Chapter VII contains the conclusion of the present study.

Chapter I

Environmental Background

Introduction

The modern Bhavnagar district especially lower Shetrunji river basin has been selected for the present study. Bhavnagar district is located between 21°18', 22°18' N latitude; 71°15', 72°18' East longitude. The Arabian sea on the south and the Gulf of Cambay, on the east are the two distinct ecozones of the region. The district of Surendranagar and Ahmedabad lie in the northern horizon whereas Rajkot and Amreli districts are located to its west (Fig.1). The Bhavnagar district covers an area of 12,048 sq. km. Three sub divisions, seven *talukas*, 5 *Mahals* and 894 villages are the various political entities of the district (Trivedi 1969: 3). This chapter deals with a detailed outline of the present environment of the Lower Shetrunji river basin, which includes the Bhavnagar district. Besides, it also discusses topography, drainage, geology, mineral resources, climate, vegetation, soil types, agricultural pattern and present settlement pattern of the district. The main body of the data of this chapter comes mostly from the published sources (Trivedi 1969; Despande 1948; Foote 1916; Wallace 1888; Govindal *et al.* 1965; Lele 1972; Fedden 1884; Wadia 1970; Chakrabarti 1977 and Jairath 1986).

Topography

The components of the topography of Bhavanagar have preserved a varied form of geomorphology (Trivedi 1969: 5-13). It may be divided into three subdivisions:

1. The coastal plain and the adjacent sand bank; 2. The Inland plain and 3. The hinterland and the Kathiawar hill ranges.

1. The coastal plain and the adjacent sand bank

Islandish terrain with flat surfaces are the major features of the coastal landscape. The deltaic and eroded surface with swampy and sandy soil is the other aspect of the coastal land form. low reefs, foot hills, plain with occasional creeks, low muddy foreshore lined with mangroves, partly rocky or sandy surfaces are also encountered with the coastal littoral of Bhavnagar district. The total coverage of coast lines is 144 km (tentatively). The coast lines overlook the Gulf of Cambay and Arabian sea through a muddy foreshore which can be divided into three sections:

I. Muddy foreshore of marsh and swamp and mangroves partly sandy and rocky which extended from Sonrai creek to Gogha; II. The sandy coast which extended from Gogha to Gopnath points and III. The rocky coast from Gopnath to Gadhada.

I. Muddy foreshore – Gogha

From the Sonrai creek to Gogha is a 30.4 km stretch of low muddy foreshore of marsh and swamp lined with mangroves, which is at places sandy and rocky. The coastal plain extends about 5 to 6 km along the river courses and at places (for example the landmass between the Sonrai creeks and the Bhavnagar city) the tract extends to about 19 km.

II. The sandy coast which is extended from Gogha to Gopnath points

From the Gogha to Gopnath point, the coast covering a distance of about 52 km presents a diverse topography and is more sandy. For a distance of about 34 km from Gogha to Morchand, the sandy coast is comparatively broad and high, broken by ravines and trees. South of this, up to the mouth of Shetrunji, the sandy coast narrows down but it is fringed with sand hills. Beyond the river Shetrunji the coast widens out again and lastly merges with the marshes of Saltanpur and Tarsara.

III. The rocky coast from Gopnath to Gadhada

From Gopnath to Gadhada the coast covering an area of about 51 km is rather rocky and strewn with offshore islands. They are moderately high and sometimes hollowed by the sea into caves. This coastal belt with bold headlands, continues up to Diu.

2. The Inland plain

The Inland plain occurs in stretches to the broken hill ranges. Taking two sections, the inland plain could be divided into two dissected landmasses. One across the plain from the north-west highlands to the Cambay coast, another across the district from Sonrai creek in the north-east to the district boundary in south-west. The landmass across from the depositional plain in north-west high land to the Cambay coast, which cuts through the Shetrunji river, has an average height of 152 m. At the Shetrunjaya hill, the land abruptly rises to about 498 m from the sea level, but it sinks to a plain of 76 m with a few broken detached hills rising to about 244 m. Thereafter the land gradually slopes southwestwards and maintains a height of 152 m for a short distance off the district border and near the sea. The hills of coastal region are characterized with medium height and cut abruptly through the alluvial deposits. The coastal deposits are determined with denuded materials carried out from the high lands through the fluvial domination (Trivedi 1969: 8-9; and cited from Chakrabarti 1977).

3. The hinterland and Kathiawar hill ranges

Two parallel ranges of hills running north-east and south-west dominate the north-west and the central south regions of the district. These hills belong to Kathiawar group and possess a varied physical character. The hill range which comes under Kathiawar group in the district runs parallel to a the coast in a southwest-southeasterly direction. As a result Kundla, Palitana and Sihor form hilly landscape with a range of elevation between 305 and 458 m. These hills are barren and rocky with a few lenses of low brush wood and some others have an abundance of grass. To the south of the Shetrunji the Moidhar hills or the lesser Gir present a continuous range of grass covered hill slopes which rise abruptly on the north side end in long spurs running to the south-west (Trivedi 1969: 9-13).

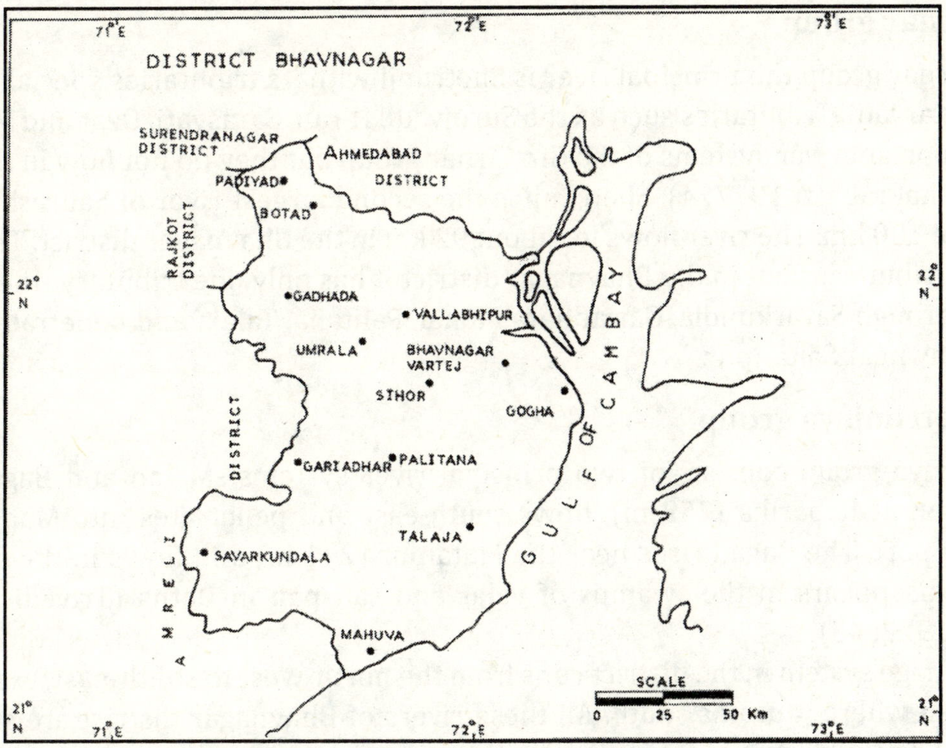

Fig.1: Political boundary of Bhavnagar District.

Drainage: River system

The district is characterized by a well developed drainage system (Fig.2). The rivers along with their tributaries form three groups of drainages such as

I. The Mandav group, II. The Gir-Girnar group and III. The Shatrunjaya group.

These three groups are cut across the landmass in between the two hill ranges of the peninsula. The drainage in Saurashtra has a perfect radial pattern. The north flowing streams meet the Gulf of Kutch or little Rann, whereas the west flowing streams meet the Arabian sea and the east flowing streams terminate in the Gulf of Cambay (Trivedi 1969: 9-13).

I. The Mandav group

Ghelo, Kalubhar and its tributaries Ranghola, Padala, Keri, Goma and Utavali are the main river systems of the Mandav group. Ghelo has a total length of 89 km which includes 72 km of its length in the district. The river flows eastward and penetrates the tidal creek which opens out to the Gulf of Cambay near Bhavnagar proper. Kalubhar (91 km) enters the district near Padapan and runs about 65 km parallel with Ghelo. It bifurcates into two channels near

Chamardi and then flows in the tidal creek near Bhavnagar along with many of its tributaries and streams such as Ranghola and Meleshari.

The less significant rivers of the district are Keri, Padala, Goma and Utavali. Padala flows southeast through marsh and swamp and terminates near the Sonrai creek. Goma flows northwest and meets the river Bhadar at Rangpur in the Surendranagar district. On the other side Utavali, partly flowing in the District, disappears in the swamp of Dhandhuka.

The Gir-Girnar group

In the Gir-Girnar group the principal river is Shetrunji with its tributaries specially the Shel and the Dhattarvadi. Tributaries such as the Surujvadi. Hiran, Sarasvati, Ozat and Vrajani are the other important river systems of the Gir-Girnar group but they do not flow in the district (cited from Chakrabarti 1977: 4). Shetrunji is the second largest river of Saurashtra with a total length of 180 km. The river flows for about 92 km in the Bhavnagar district. This river is fed by many tributaries but in the Bhavnagar district it has only one tributary -the Shel. The river flows through Savarkundla, Gariadhara Mahal, Palitana, Talaja and penetrates into the Gulf of Cambay near Saltanpur.

III. The Shetrunjaya group

The Shetrunjaya group consists of two principal river systems -Malan and Bagad. Malan takes its origin at Rabarika (252 m), flows south-east and penetrates into Mahuva creek near Mahuva port. The Bagad rises near the Matalpur (241 m) and flows in the south-east direction. It disappears in the swamps of Valar and salt pan in Datha (Trivedi 1969: 13; Chakrabarti 1977: 43).

The drainage system in the district runs from the north-west to south-east, except in the Mahuva taluka where it drains south. All these rivers of Bhavnagar district are sluggish in character and dry up during summer. During the rainy season they swell into a considerable size and carry large volume of water.

Geology

Geologically Bhavnagar district comes under the greater peninsula of the Indian sub-continent with basalt as the main rock formation. Numerous dykes and wide range of younger rocks with aeolian and alluvial deposits are other geological formations of the district (Wadia 1970). All these rocks and alluvial formations occur in Deccan Traps and are associated with lateritic rocks, Gaj beds, Miliolite limestone and conglomerates. Deccan Trap is noticed in the major portion of the district except the eastern and southern coastal tracts. The two ecozones are formed with tertiary and post-tertiary sediments. The traps are formed due to lava flows emplaced from fissures and are oriented in the horizontally bedded form through a gentle tilt towards south. The thickness of the traps varies but maximum is about six hundred meters. The basaltic flows are occasionally filled with chalcedony, agate and calcite. Agglomerate, tuffs and ashes are also seen in the inter-bedded portion of the traps. The various layers of lava flows include basalt, dolerites, felsites, granophye, obsidian, pitchstone, rhyolite, soda felspar rocks, trachyte, diorite, agglomerates, breccias, tuff and ashes. The dykes of the district which are mainly concentrated around Talaja, are composed of compact greyish-green to dark grey in colour and micro-crystalline, sub-ophitic in texture. Lateritic is concentred in Adewada and Budhel, Thoradi, Badi, Morchand area of the district in the form of continuous band and varies from 1 to 3 km in the width and 32 km in length. Besides laterite isolated patches are observed at places. The rock is formed of soft variegate concretionary ferruginous clay of red to lavender and grey colour containing a fairly rich proportion of iron (of?) and passing into haematite and red ochres. The average thickness of laterite in the district is 5 m.

Gaj Bed

Gaj bed occurs extensively in the stretches toward the southern side from Akwada to Mathwada in a continuous chain of the district. Later, the chain is covered by the alluvium plain. The beds are horizontal and thickness ranges in between 12 and 15 m. Gaj beds consist of conglomerate grit, sand stones, clays and marls. Gypsum is associated with clays and marls and belongs to the Upper Miocene period. Fossils are also reported from the Gaj bed belonging to the genera of *Pacten, Ostres, Voluta, Bchinns, Arca, Cardium, Sclaria, Venus,* and fragments of the molar of Masto don does not occur in India. Apart from these, tertiary fossils of several varieties belonging to the families Proboscidea, Ungulate, Crocodylia, Chelonia and Pisces are recovered from the Piram Island. They are of *Brahamatherium, Dinotheriumindicum* and *Collossochelys atlas.*

Conglomerate

Outcrops of conglomerates are also noticed at places in the district with maximum thickness of about 15 m at Jasapara, a village located 20 km south of Bhavnagar city. The conglomerate disconformably rests on the laterite and the trap at an elevation of 8 to 10 m about mid sea level, half a km inland from the Gulf of Cambay (Lele 1972). It is made of quartz, chalcedony, chert or agate, pebble (20-25 mm) well cemented with siliceous and ferruginous cement (Lele 1972). The conglomerate found from Alang, Mittivadi and Bhumbli are either ferruginous or agatiferous (Fedden 1884).

Miliolite and Alluvium

Miliolite and limestone are noticed around Gopnath and Mahuva towns of the district. These rocks also form the bluff and cliffs on the south-eastern coast. At places, it extended sheeting the surface of the country (Fedden 1884). The maximum thickness of miliolite of the district is not yet known but from other places such as Veraval and Dungarpur in Junagadh district it varies from 46 m to 50 m. The formation shows a variation in vertical as well as lateral textural characteristic (Govindan *et al.* 1965).

The alluvium deposits of the district are concentrated near the coast. The deposit constitutes sand dunes, tidal mud flats, raised beaches and fresh water alluvium. Sand dunes are common in the vicinity of coasts whereas fresh water alluvium is observed along the river valleys and forms a thick blanket near Gogha, Bhavnagar, Vartej, Sihor, Sanosara, Talaja and along the southern coastal tract.

Minerals and Rocks

The Bhavnagar district is poor in metallic minerals but other natural minerals are available in the district, namely agate, chert, flint and ores, ochres, clays, etc. are available in large quantities near Lakhanka between Badi-Chhaya and Rampur. A few horizons of bauxite

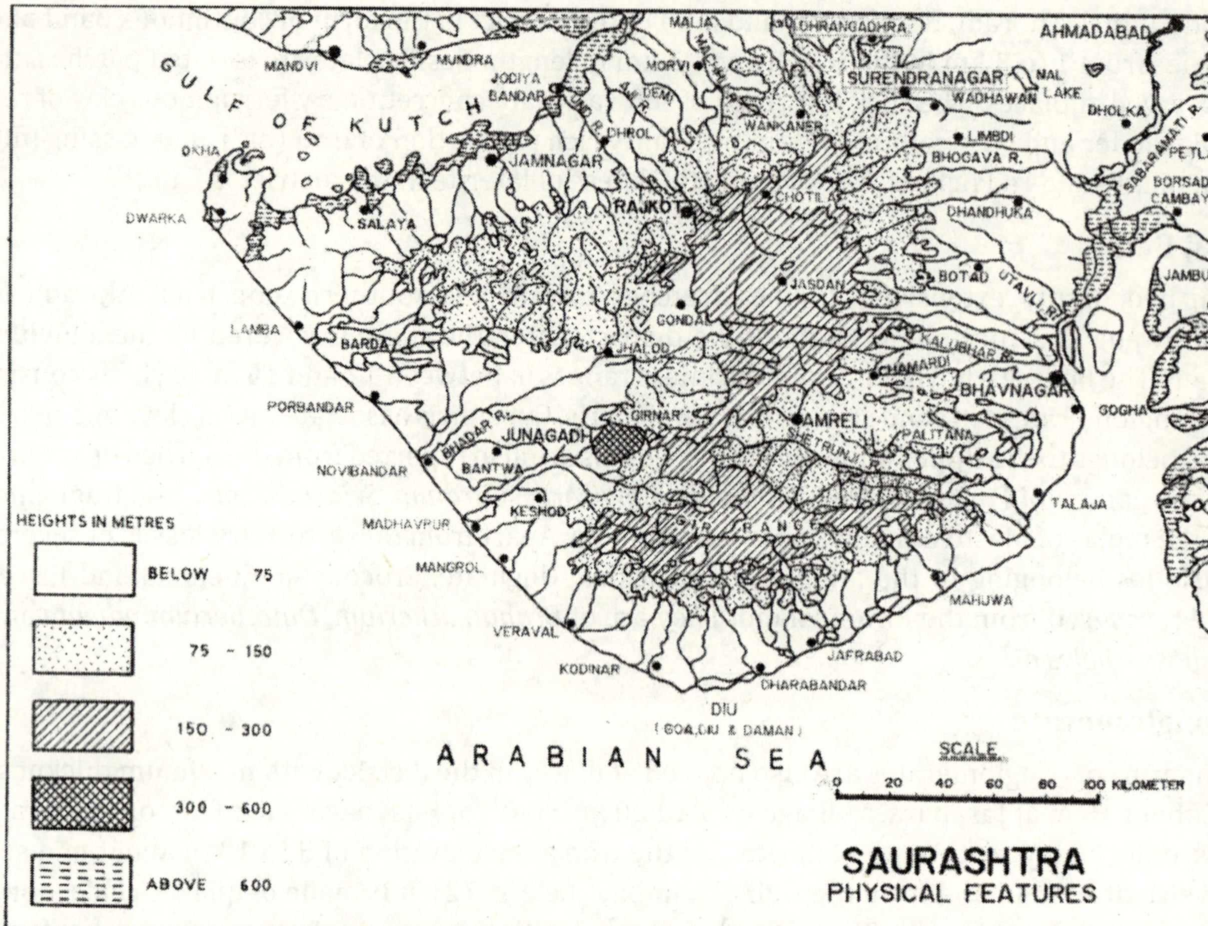

Fig. 2: Physical features of Saurashtra.

are associated with laterite near Longadi, Talgajarda, west of Gogha and near Bhavnagar. Building clays for the manufacture of bricks, are found in the river alluvium in the maximum part of the district. A greater part of the district is covered by traps, which is dense, hard and durable and yield good building material. The most important deposits in the form of veins, occur at Gadhakada in Kundla tehsil. Numerous small calcite stringers occur in traps in the Palitana *tehsil*, particularly to the east of Thadach. Various types of clays are associated with lateritic rocks and Gaj bed, at many places in the district. The variegated clays found in the Gaj beds are quarried at a number of places near Bhavnagar, Talaja and Gogha. Clays associated with lateritic rocks are quarried near Budhel, Thoradi, Tagadi, Rajpura, Morchand and Chitra. Lothomargic clay occurs both in lateritic rocks and in the Gaj beds and is quarried near Chitra, Budhel and Tagadi. Deposits of mineral pigments like yellow and red-ochres occur in a small hill west of the Lakhanka and Alapur near Tagadi and south of Thoradi. Fine yellow sand is formed due to the weathering of Gaj. Sandstone is noticed in stream beds near Malanka and Tarsamia at Bhavnagar *tehsil* and Gogha and Kuda in Gogha *Mahal*. Apart from these, some semi-precious stones like pebbles of agate, chalcedony, flint, and jasper etc., dislodged from conglomerates due to weathering are strewn along the hill slopes west of Lakhanka. An Agate-bearing conglomerate bed, about 5 m in thickness, forms the crest of the ridge running from Bedi to Chhaya, a distance of about 10 km. A conspicuous float of agate pebbles is noticed among the western flank of the ridge (Fig.3). The agate pebbles are generally small but a few selected ones can be used as semi-precious stones. Other pebbles may be suitable for ball-mills (Trivedi 1969: 22) Apart from this, salt and iron are found in the district (Thomas 1996).

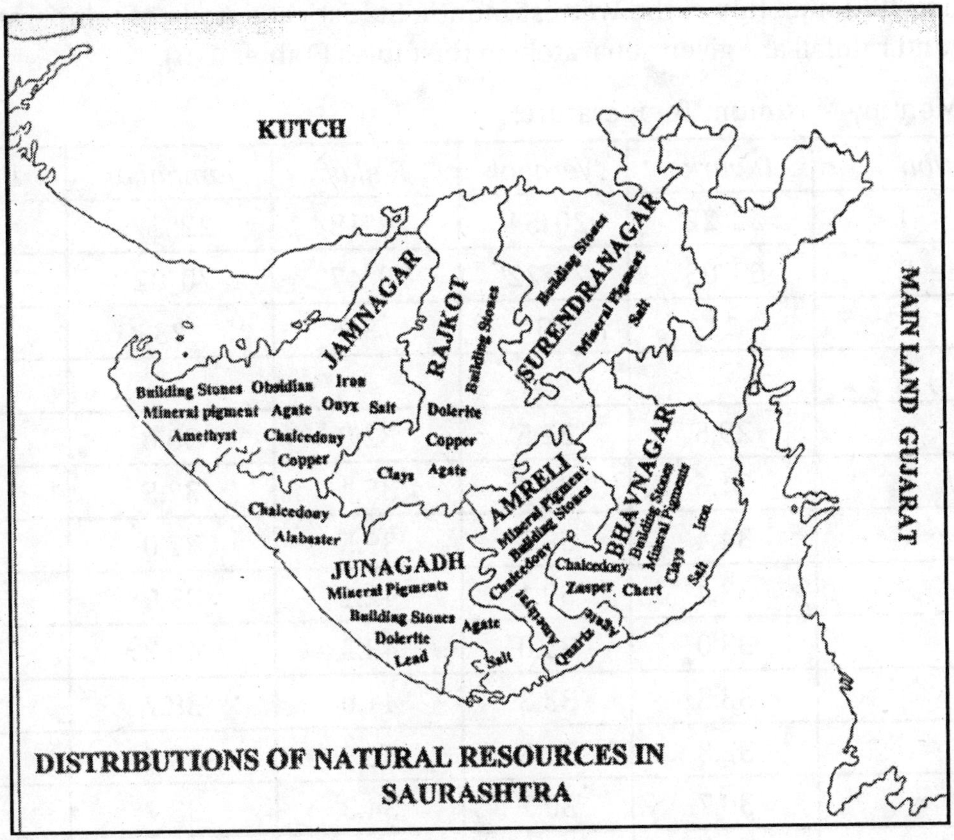

Fig. 3: Distribution of Natural resources of Saurashtra.

Climatic data

Climate is one of the important factors of a particular region as it governs, to a considerable degree, the various types of human activities including their subsistence patterns. Climate can be said to play a decisive role in the moulding of human cultures. The natural resources can play a vital role in the economy of a region (Dhavalikar 1985: 15). The district possesses a wide range of seasonal variation in a year with aridity as the prominent feature. However coastal regions are dominated by less seasonal variation. Winter occurs in the district from December to February, followed by summer which is from March to May. This district is characterized by a south-west monsoon from June to September which is followed by post monsoonal season between October and November. It records a maximum mean temperature of 33°c in January and 44.1°c in May, the mean minimum temperatures being 7.4°c in January and 23.2°c in May. The southern coastal area of the district is neither cold nor hot due to its proximity to the sea. The scorching hot wind begins blowing during the summer and is generally light but becomes strong in the latter part of the summer season and forceful during the south-west monsoon season. The monsoon wind blows from the southwest to west but it takes the direction between northwest and northeast during October and November

(Trivedi 1969: 32-33; Chakrabarti 1977). Humidity observed in the coastal region during the monsoon season is generally high, being over 60% in the northern part and over 80% in the southern part. For the rest of the year the weather becomes relatively dry in the coastal region (Trivedi 1969: 33). The average annual rainfall is 600 mm, usually varying between 300 mm and 800 mm. July is the wettest month. Statistical details of temperature, relative humidity, and rainfall are given separately in the tables (Tables 1-6).

Table 1: Monthly Maximum Temperature.

Station	*Dwarka*	*Verabal*	*Rajkot*	*Jamnagar*	*Bhavnagar*
Latitude N	22°22'	20°54'	22°18'	22°27'	21°25'
Longitude E	69°05'	70°22'	70°47'	70°02'	72°11'
Altitude AMSL (m)	11	8	13.8	23	11
January	29.5	32.5	32.8	30.0	32.8
February	31.6	34.7	35.4	32.5	35.9
March	34.4	38.3	39.5	37.0	35.9
April	33.4	39.1	42.1	39.9	42.6
May	33.0	35.0	43.3	40.3	44.4
June	33.3	33.3	41.0	38.7	41.9
July	32.3	31.5	36.8	35.8	37.5
August	30.7	30.7	34.3	33.7	35.0
September	30.9	32.4	36.3	34.9	34.5
October	35.6	37.3	37.6	37.2	37.5
November	34.7	36.2	35.6	34.6	35.1
December	31.1	33.8	33.0	33.8	32.5
Annual	37.1	40.1	43.5	40.9	44.2

After Chakrabarti 1977

Table 2: Monthly Minimum Temperature.

Station	*Dwarka*	*Veraval*	*Rajkot*	*Jamnagar*	*Bhavnagar*
Latitude N	22°22'	20°54'	22°18'	22°27'	21°45'
Longitude E	69°05'	70°22'	70°47'	70°02'	72°11'
Altitude AMSL (m)	11	8	13.8	23	11
January	12.1	9.7	5.7	7.3	7.4

February	13.3	11.1	6.6	8.2	8.5
March	17.3	14.0	11.8	13.1	13.3
April	21.6	18.0	17.0	17.8	18.9
May	25.6	22.6	21.7	22.4	23.2
June	25.8	24.8	23.7	24.4	23.9
July	24.4	24.1	22.7	23.5	23.6
August	24.2	23.8	22.3	22.2	23.3
September	23.9	22.5	20.8	21.7	21.6
October	22.6	18.8	16.8	18.1	18.8
November	17.4	15.1	12.1	12.6	12.8
December	13.7	11.5	7.7	8.8	9.1
Annual	11.6	9.0	5.2	6.3	6.6

After Chakrabarti 1977

Table 3: Relative Humidity (%)

Station	*Dwarka*	*Veraval*	*Rajkot*	*Jamnagar*	*Bhavnagar*
Latitude N	22°22'	20°54'	22°18'	22°27'	21°25'
Longitude E	69°05'	70°22'	70°47'	70°02'	72°11
Altitude	11	8	13.8	23	11
AMSL (m)					
January	65	49	51	60	44
February	72	56	57	60	44
March	78	63	63	71	39
April	81	72	66	68	44
May	82	82	72	70	54
June	81	83	76	69	65
July	84	88	85	82	77
August	85	89	86	82	77
September	84	86	85	81	74
October	79	68	70	76	60
November	68	51	50	61	50
December	63	47	49	60	45
Annual	77	69	67	70	56

After Chakrabarti 1977

Table 4: Mean Wind Speed (km/hr)

Station	*Dwarka*	*Veraval*	*Rajkot*	*Jamnagar*	*Bhavnagar*
Latitude N	22°22'	20°54'	22°18'	22°27'	21°45'
Longitude E	69°05'	70°22'	70°47'	70°02'	72°11'
Altitude	11	8	13.8	23	11
AMSL (m)					
January	15.5	12.3	13.1	8.8	8.4
February	14.8	13.2	13.6	7.8	8.6
March	16.1	14.9	16.6	8.8	9.8
April	16.7	16.6	19.7	11.1	11.3
May	2.0	17.3	26.2	15.9	13.9
June	23.5	22.5	28.1	16.2	15.3
July	27.1	28.8	28.3	15.6	14.7
August	21.9	24.1	23.2	14.2	12.5
September	15.0	15.3	17.4	9.7	10.0
October	11.8	12.1	12.1	7.0	7.7
November	12.4	10.3	10.6	6.9	6.8
December	12.3	11.1	11.3	7.5	7.0
Annual	17.1	16.5	18.3	10.8	10.5

After Chakrabarti 1977

Table 5: Monthly Total Rainfall

Station	*Dwarka*	*Veraval*	*Rajkot*	*Jamnagar*	*Bhavnagar*
Latitude N	22°22'	20°54'	22°18'	22°27'	21°45'
Longitude E	69°5'	70°22'	70°47'	70°02'	72°11'
Altitude	11	8	13.8	23	11
AMSL (m)					
January	2.1	0.7	1.1	0.6	2.5
February	2.0	1.3	0.4	0.9	0.5
March	0.9	0.2	1.0	0.1	3.4
April	0.4	4.6	2.5	0.0	12.5
May	0.4	5.3	6.6	8.4	6.2
June	48.80	130.3	99.3	63.3	13.7
July	22.0	304.8	292.8	215.8	242.8
August	75.9	145.8	143.0	125.7	152.0
September	42.1	66.9	93.3	62.1	121.9
October	4.8	29.1	25.4	9.5	37.8
November	19.2	7.3	4.8	3.1	7.3
December	2.3	1.1	3.6	0.8	0.2
Annual	218.9	702.4	673.8	490.3	600.8

After Chakarabarti 1977

Table 6: Agroclimatic Classification of Saurashtra

Station	*Potential Evaporation*	*Summer Concentration*	*Precipitation*	*Water Surplus*	*Water Deficiency*	*Humidity Index Ih*	*Aridity Index Ia*	*Moisture Index Im*	*Climatic type*
Bhuj	1897.1	37.0	348.7	00	1547.8	00	81.5	-81.5	EA' da'
Jamnagar	1714.1	35.3	490.3	0.0	1223.2	0.0	71.3	-71.3	Ea' da'
Dwarka	1773.9	31.0	418.9	4.0	1358.4	0.2	76.5	-76.3	EA' da'
Bhavnagar	1815.2	36.1	600.8	40.2	1253.8	2.2	69.0	-66.8	EA' da'
Rajkot	2144.6	36.9	673.8	0.0	1470.1	0.0	68.5	-68.5	EA' da'
Veraval	1685.6	31.6	701.4	138.1	1120.7	8.1	66.4	-58.2	EA' da'

EA': arid Megathermal; Da' Semi-arid Megathermal; EA' da' : Little or not water surplus

(After Rao *et al.* 1972)

Flora

The area under forests in the district in 1970-71 was 299.48 sq. km of which 40.62 sq. km was reserved forest, 253.38 sq. km unclassed forest and 5.48 sq. km private forest (Jairath 1986: 116). The natural vegetation of the district consists of dry deciduous scrub forest type. But due to human interference a gradual decrease of this forest has been observed in the last few decades. The remaining forest is scattered at places and concentrated mostly in the hilly areas near Sihor, Palitana, Kundla and Bhavnagar. The species included (in the deciduous forest type are *Acacia senegal* (Gorad), *Acacia arabica* (Babul), *Gymnosporia montana* (Viklo), *Balanites roxburghii* (Tingnol), *Boswellia serrata* (Salai), *Anogeissus latifolia* (Dhavdo), *Terminalia tomentosa* (Sajad), *Casuarina equiselifolia* (Saru) and *Prosopis juliflora* (Gando baval). Apart from these, *teak, deshi babul, arthi, arduso* and *semal,* etc., are also raised in various places. Moreover, mangrove species have been growing along the coast. Among the fruit trees mango, coconut, pomegranate, *chikoo,* banana, arecanut, papaya and guava are the most prominent fruit species, grown in the district.

Fauna

Due to deforestation, soil erosion has been encountered leading to ecological imbalance. As a result the wild life is declining at a steady rate. Some of the animals surviving till today are Lion (*Panthera leo*), Leopard (*Panthera pardus*), Striped hyena (*Hyaena hyaena*), Wolf (*Canis lupus*), Indian fox (*Vulpes bengalensis*), Chital (*Axis axis*), Jackal (*canis aureus*), Nilgai (*Boselaphus trago camelus*), Gazelle (*Gazelle gazella*), Black buck (*Antilope cervicapra*), Jungle cat (*Felis chaus*), Porcupine (*Hystrix indica*), Samber (*Cervus unicolor*), Longeared hedge hog (*Hamiechinus auritus*), and Ratel or ledger (*Mellivora capensis*).

Apart from this, the common birds are crows, maynas, parrots, house sparrows, pigeons, etc., (Trivedi 1969). Some of the important birds noticed in this district are Bulbul (*Pyconotus SP*), Green pigeons (*Treron phoenicoptera chlorigasler, Blyth*), Partridges (*Francolinus spp.*

liter), Baya (*Polices Philippines*), Cotton leal (*Nettapus isp*), Snipe (*Gallingo spp.*), Green bee-eater (*Meros sp.*), Cattle egret (*Babulous sp.*), etc.

Besides the birds, two varieties of snakes are found in the district -non poisonous snakes like Typhlepidae (*Typhlops sp*), Boidae (*Eryxconicus*), Colubridae (*Oligodon sp.*) and poisonous snakes like Elapidae (*Naja naja*), Viperidae (Vipera *russelli*) and Hydrophinal (*Hydrophis sp*).

Some kinds of fish are also found in the district. They include Bumla (*Horpondon neherius*), Dara (*Polynemus indicus*), Zinga (*enaeus spp*), Magra (*Charcarias spp*), Ghol (*Pseudoscioena diacanthus*), etc. (Trivedi 1969).

Soil

The geographical formation of Saurashtra is of volcanic origin. The soil of Bhavnagar district, with the exception of a few strips, is mostly derived from the trap rocks. The out-crop of granite rocks is visible at certain places, for example at Talaja it indicates that granite was the original rock formation. The basaltic topography is due to volcanic effusions and spread of lava, and denudation has resulted in the creation of low land tracts like the Shetrunji basin (Despande 1948). The soils found in the trap rocks are known as black cotton soil (Fig.4). They are not very deep and are susceptible to erosion. Near the coastal region, the black cotton soil is deeper and more plain but inundated by the entrance of the sea.

Following are the main soil types of the district (Trivedi 1969). 1) Coastal sandy alluvial soil in Mahuva *taluka*; 2) Clay lime soil in Gariadhar *mahal* and. 3) Medium black soil found in parts of Sihor, Bhavnagar, Talaja, Mahuva, Palitana and Botad *talukas* and Umrela and Gadhada *Mahals*. This is the predominant type of soil in the district and covers the major part of it. Wallace (1888: 180-81) has observed that "Black soil has wonderful power for absorbing water, and during rainy season it swells, so that the whole surface is raised. Although it continues to retain throughout abnormal amount of moisture, which is of great value to the crops grown on it, and, in short enables cultivation to be practiced without irrigation. At the same time, in the dry weather, it loses a large amount of moisture, and shrinks in consequence. The shrinking is in all directions; consequently very deep and wide tracks are formed, which make the land quite unsound and dangerous for riding. By the use of Dutch hoe-harrow, the cracks are filled and closed with the fine soil of the surface, and by this means a regular circulation of soil is established. The cracks further fulfill the functions of ploughing, by admitting air freely into the body of the soil. The objects of ploughing are attained but nature is left to do a large share of the work, and, further, she provides the means by which man can successfully carry out the remainder of it. The plentiful supply of powdery soil is useful, not only for carrying on the circulation processes, but for closing up the cracks to present excessive evaporation of moisture from the body of under-soil". Robert Bruce Foote (1916: 183-84) also expressed similar views about black cotton soil.

4) Light murram soil in elevated areas of Sihor, Bhavnagar and Palitana *talukas* and
5) Clay alluvial soil of Bhal tract.

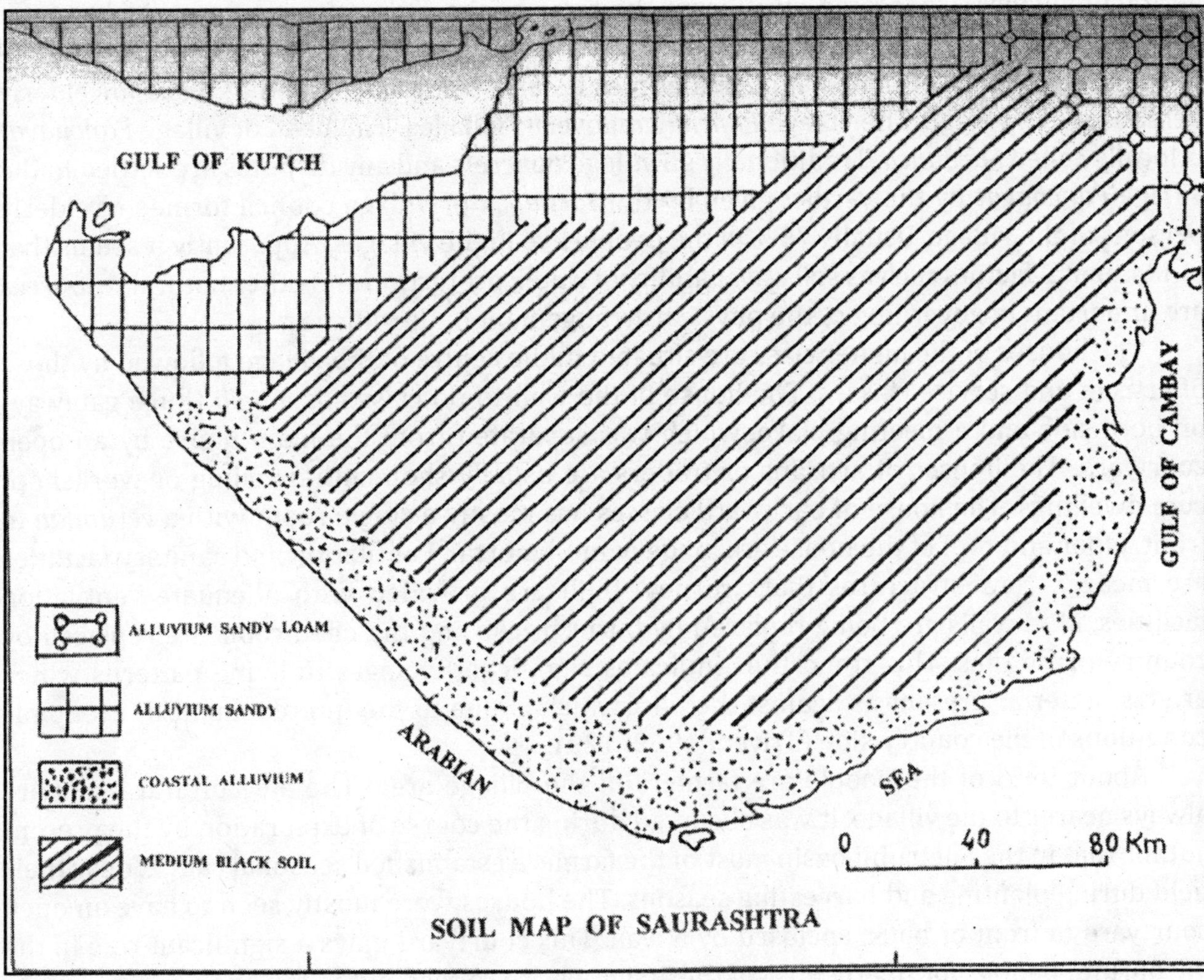

Fig.4: Soil map of Saurashtra.

Crops

The main food crops noticed in the district are *bajra*, *jowar* and wheat. Apart from this, groundnut and cotton are the principal non- food crops. The crops which are grown in the district can be divided into two classes

1. Kharip crops and 2. Rabi crops.

The Kharip crops are grown in June-July and harvested in October-November. The Rabi crops are grown in September-October and harvested in February-March. Crops grown in the district are *Bajra*, *Jowar*, Wheat, *Udid* (black gram), *Moong* (green gram), *Chana* (harsa gram), Groundnut, *Til* (sesamum) and Sugar cane (Trivedi 1969).

Present Settlement pattern

The lower Shetrunji river basin and the coastal area of this region are not densely populated. The general layout of the towns and large size villages of the district appears to be essentially same, especially with regard to the functional distribution of caste and class (Trivedi 1969: 128). Most of the *tehsil* headquarters and villages are located on the bank of some rivers.

Very few villages are located away from the river banks, along the sea coast. Most of the villages in the district have a central place known as *Chowk* with a public place called *Chora*, housing the temple of Lord Rama. Sometimes its also serve as a meeting place for elderly persons of the village. The village *Panchayat* governs villages. The head of village *Panchayat* is locally called *Sarpanch*. Traditionally all village quarrels and any disputes are settled in the village *Panchayat* by the verdict given by the *Sarpanch* or village council formed of elderly persons of the village. Usually 75% of the people live in the villages. Apparently it seems that fundamental factors such as soils, availability of water, protection and other natural resources are important in governing of the physical arrangement of the village.

The houses of the higher class are situated in the centre of the village followed by those of artisan and service classes. The house of the well-to-do class has a *delo* (huge gateway) on both side and a meeting place, which was separated from the main house by an open courtyard. The houses of artisans or traders are usually shop-cum-dwelling or workshop-cum dwellings. The house of backward classes has mostly a single room with a *verandah* in front. Floor and roof of the house are made of mud mortar. Ventilation and sanitary facilities are meager. New structures that are now built are provided with adequate ventilation facilities. Mud walls are being replaced by burnt bricks and thatched roofs are replaced by country made tiles. This trend thus indicates significant changes in living patterns which are far better at present as against the past which is due to the improvement of economic conditions in the country side (Trivedi 1969: 129).

About 99% of the people are farmers in the village area. The agricultural lands are always nearer to the village. It was observed during the course of exploration by the present author that in the Shetrunji basin most of the farmers established seasonal camps near their field during planting and harvesting seasons. The houses were mostly seen to have an open courtyard in front or back, enclosed by a wall. This courtyard plays a significant role in the life of rural people, for nearly 90% of the activities are carried out in the open.

Chapter 2

Early Historic Culture of Gujarat with Special Reference to Bhavnagar District

Introduction

Gujarat is located at the western end of the Central Indian hills. It attracted human habitations right from the Stone Age which continued to flourish in this region. Saurashtra or Kathiawar of Gujarat came into historical limelight during the Asokan period and it continued to be so in the later periods (Sharma 1987: 71; Sankalia 1987). The early history of the district of Bhavnagar is incoherent due to lack of information. To reconstruct the history of the Early Historic period, we have to depend on literary and archaeological evidence. But where direct archaeological information is not available attempts have been made to collect the same from the general history of Gujarat, in order to reconstruct the history of the district of Bhavnagar. We have some literary sources like the Buddhist records (Beal 1906: 266-68) and accounts of foreign travelers and merchants which provide useful information regarding the ancient towns, villages and rivers of the district. Besides these, a number of inscriptions found in Bhavnagar District like those of the Maitraka kings of Valabhi give us information of the then existing towns and villages of the District.

Historical outline

Political history of India based on written records begins from 6th century B.C. Inscriptional evidence is available from the Mauryan period onwards and hence continuous political history is available from this period. What the scholars call the Early Historic Period in India begins in the 6th century B.C. and continues through the 5th century A.D. In Saurashtra of Gujarat, however, the Bhavnagar district was inhabited right from the Stone Age period (Chakrabarti 1977; Sankalia 1987) and was succeeded by the Harappan culture (Possehl 1980; Sankalia 1987). The evidence of their historical antiquity comes from the legends and tradition. According to a legend Anartta, grand son of Manu and son of Saryati was reputed to have had his Capital at Kasasthali or Dwarika in Saurashtra (Virji 1952: 1). Another legend credits Yadav Krsna who is said to have ruled the whole province from his capital at Dwarka (Sankalia 1941: 7).

The Early Historic period in this region begins with the advent of the Mauryas (c.319 B.C.). Chandragupta Maurya, the king of this dynasty consolidated his power at Magadha and extended his rule both towards the east and west (Mookerji 1928: 72; Sankalia 1987). He annexed the Kathiawar region around c.304 B.C. (Kielhorn 1905-06: 8, 36-49). A later inscription of Rudradaman (150 A.D.), the Kshatrapa king makes clear mention of Vaishya Pushyagupta, as the viceroy of Chandragupta Maurya, which suggests that the latter perhaps ruled over Peninsular Gujarat (Mirashi 1981: 127-128). The fourteen rock edicts of Asoka in Girnar of Junagadh (Nikam *et al.* 1959; Lahiri 1992) and the Junagadh rock inscription of Rudradaman, wherein Tushaspa, a *Yavana* prince, is mentioned as the viceroy of Asoka provides evidence of the continuation of the rule of the Mauryas during the 3rd century B.C (Mirashi 1981: 127-28). Whether Gujarat remained under Samprati, the grandson and successor of Asoka, is a moot point. But it is certain that the Mauryan rule in Gujarat did not last after Samprati (c.200 B.C.). Soon after, the Sungas succeeded the Mauryans. But owing to the absence of positive evidence, it is not possible to say, for certain, whether the Sungas ruled over Gujarat.

The Satavahanas, established their independent Andhra kingdom in the Deccan, after the downfall of Mauryan empire. Although there is no positive evidence regarding the rule of the Early Andhras over Gujarat, nonetheless some scholars have considered its possibility (Sarma 1980: 130-31) under the kingship of Sri Satakarni who is also known from the Kharavela inscription as the "protector of the west" (Sankalia 1941: 8). The Bactrian Greeks invaded the north-west India under the leadership of Demetrius in 185 B.C. and advanced down to the Indus, after which they occupied *Patalene* (Indus delta), the kingdoms of *Saraostos* (Saurashtra), *Sigerdis* and the rest of the coastal land (Subbarao 1953; Sankalia 1987; and Tarn 1951: 147). But shortly after this success in India, Demetrius was killed (Tarn 1951: 167) and Bactria was occupied by Eucratides (Tarn 1951: 230). The Greek viceroys became independent in their respective provinces. Their independent status is evident from their coins, found in various parts of their kingdoms. Coins of Indo-Greek kings found at Hathab (Bhavnagar district) which represents ancient *Hastavapra*, or *Hastakavapra*, is rendered as *Astacampra* in Greek literature (Schoff 1912: 39-40). On the other hand, the Greek rule extended upto Broach can be justified by the evidence of coins of Eucratides, Menander and Apollodotus, found in Broach (Majumder 1960: 48-49). The Greeks were driven out by the Sakas, who entered India from *Seistan*. As there is little evidence regarding this, it is once again difficult to make a statement as to who ruled Gujarat upto c.100 A.D. Another view is that, the Sakas took Patalene, Saurashtra and coastal parts of Western India in 124 B.C. from the Greeks. This was their original kingdom in India (Sankalia 1987). They proceeded northwards from Abhira upto the Indus and conquered Northern India in about 80 B.C. According to the Indian traditional literature, the Saka rule was wiped out from Ujjain (Sankalia 1987; Tarn 1951: 320). But it is difficult to say whether they lost Gujarat or Kathiawar. Coins bearing the name of Bhumaka have been found along the coast of Gujarat and Saurashtra. As is known, he was one of the earliest kings of the *Ksharatha* dynasty (another branch of the Sakas). Evidences show that he must have ruled in Gujarat in the first quarter of the 2nd century A.D., as is also indicated by some of the inscriptions found outside

Gujarat (Mirashi 1981: 127-28). Bhumaka was succeeded by Nahapana. The latter probably raised his political power for which he called himself *Mahakshatrapa*. The above statement gets weightage from the fact that in one of his inscriptions, Nahapana is known as *Kshatrapa* and in another as *Mahakshatrapa* (Choudhary 1983: 105). It is known from the Nasik cave inscription, that Somnath, Broach, Mandasor, Nasik and Sopara were included in his empire (Sarkar 1942). The Nasik cave inscription No. III of Sri Vasisthiputra Pulumavy mentions that the *Kshatrapas* were exterminated by the Satavahana ruler Gautamiputra Satakarni (Mirashi 1981: 35; Burgess 1964 and Ray 1986) and therefore once again Gujarat including Saurashtra came under the domination of the Andhras. The death of Nahapana marked the end of the reign of the *Ksharatha* family. They were succeeded by the Scythian family of Kardamakas and also known as the Western *Kshatrapas*, who peacefully ruled over Gujarat for about two centuries. Castana, son of Ghasmotika was the first ruling member of this dynasty and he is also mentioned as Tiastenes of Ozene in Ptolemy's *Geography* (Cited from Chakrabarti 1995: 279). He proved himself a successful ruler against the Andhras as is evident from his coins (Sastri 1957: 280). The power of this dynasty reached its zenith in 50 A.D. under the leadership of Rudradaman I, the grandson of Castana. According to the Girnar inscription Rudradaman I restored the previous title and recovered the lost territories of Gujarat, Kathiawar, Sind, Rajputana and Malwa (Subbarao 1953: 108-109). After Rudradaman I, we get a continuous line of rulers, upto Visvasena. There is ample evidence to suggest that the family of Castana ruled over Gujarat without any break till Saka year 226 i.e. 304 A.D. and that Visvasena was the last ruling member of this dynasty (Sankalia 1987: 84). The *Kshatrapa* period played a very important role in the history of social and economic organization in Western India. According to Subbarao (1953: 109) "From very early times, this region including Gujarat, had cultural and commercial relations with the lands across the Arabian sea. But we have no adequate data, which can be definitely verified. For the centuries of the Christian Era, we have the definite evidence of Pliny and other classical writers including that anonymous sailor who had written a guide for his colleagues sailing from Africa and Western Asia to India (*Periplus of the Erythraean Sea*). This trade seems to have received an additional impetus with the continuous warfare between the Parthian and Roman Empires, between 50 and 200 A.D. As the Kushan Empire in the Indo-Gangetic basin with their extra-Indian possessions in Central Asia, straddled the commercial routes between Asia and Europe, the blocked trade was diverted through the Indus basin and Western India".

Afterward in 400 A.D. the Saurashtra region ruled by the Guptas. Gupta suzerainty over Gujarat was lost with the break-up of the empire, after the death of Skandagupta (c.470 A.D.). Skandagupta was defeated by the Huns and they ruled over parts of Gujarat and adjoining Madhya Pradesh (Sankalia 1987). However the Bhavnagar district gained its political prominence with the rise of the Maitrakas. The copper plate grant of Maitraka ruler suggests that Senapati Bhattarka shifted the capital from Girinagara to Valabhi around 480-490 A.D. (Sankalia 1987: 94). In the region represented by the modern Bhavnagar district, the Maitrakas were the powerful rulers in Western India from the close of the 5th century A.D. to about 8th century A.D. The early Maitraka rulers did not assume any royal title like *Chakravartin* or *Maharajadhiraja* but continued to style themselves as *Senapati* or *Maharaja*. Out of the 19 rulers of this dynasty, the 12th ruler Dharasena IV, assumed the title *Chakravartin*. Other kings to assume the title of *Maharajadhiraja* and *Paramesvara* were all Siladityas the 15th to 19th

rulers in the Maitrakas genealogical list (cited from Chakrabarti 1977). The Maitraka dynasty thus ruled over Saurashtra for about three hundred years. According to the Jaina account they were defeated by Arabs. However another view records that Maitrakas were destroyed by the Pratiharas (Majumder 1954: 151). The downfall of this dynasty took place in 788 A.D. Simultaneously, however, the Chalukyan power was reestablished by the Rashtrakutas. The Rashtrakuta rule in the region is evident from the Devalia plates (Sankalia 1987: 91). These plates record grant of land issued by the Rashtakuta king Govindaràja Prabhutavarsa to a *Brahmin* of Valabhi in the year 500 of the Valabhi Era i.e., c. A.D. 818-19. The land given in the grant, lay on the Satrunjaya (Shetrunji) river (Trivedi 1969: 57).

Valas, who trace their origin to Vrishaktu, probably returned the glory of Valabhi after an interval under the leadership of Ebhal Vala. The Vala rule continued up to the 13th century A.D. They were finally defeated by the Gohils who were overthrown by the Muslims of Delhi and in course of time, south Gujarat, the mainland and its adjunct formed into a province of the Delhi kingdom. But the Gohils during their rule emerged as a powerful Kingdom with four principal branches located at Bhavnagar, Palitana, Vala and Lathi. Bhavnagar is the largest among the states with its first capital in Umrala in 1309 A.D., second at Sihor in 1547 A.D. and finally at Bhavnagar in 1723 A.D (Cited from Chakrabarti 1977: 8).

The foundation of British rule in the 19th century is a turning point in Indian History. Gujarat ceased to be a province of the Mughals. It was, on the other hand, placed under the British rule and was included in the Bombay Presidency. After independence, Gujarat was formed into a separate state in 1950 with inclusions of princely areas like Thanas of Bhavnagar, Vala, Lathi, Palitana, Raisonkali, Jafrabad, Lakhapadar, Dedan and Songadh. The district took its present shape in 1959.

Cultural Remains

The Early Historic period is the most important phenomenon in the Indian cultural set up for state formation, imperial unity, trade activity, evolution of religions and so on as is evident from the different excavations carried out at Saurashtra in Gujarat and other adjoining states. The excavations at Devnimori (Mehta and Chowdhary 1966), Amreli (Rao 1966), Baroda (Subbarao 1953), Dwarka (Ansari and Mate 1966), Shamalaji (Mehta and Patel 1967), Valabhipur (*IAR.* 1979-80; Sharma 1987), Dhatva (*IAR.* 1967-68; Mehta *et al.* 1975; Sharma 1987), Nagara (Mehta 1968), Timbarva (Mehta 1955), Jokha (Mehta and Chowdhary 1971), Somnath (Nanavati *et al.* 1971), Girinagara inscription of Asoka (Allchin 1995: 198) and Padri (Shinde, 1992a, 1992b, 1992c 1994a, 1994b, 1996 and 1998), etc. paved the way for the study of the Early Historic materials. It has thrown sufficient light on various aspects like settlement patterns, socio-economic and religious status, etc. The history of the Early Historic period has been well documented on the basis of coins, seals and epigraphical records. Much work has been done on political, socio-economic and religious aspects, but unfortunately aspects like architecture, pottery, technology, material remains and trade and transport have received scant attention. An attempt has been made to study these in the present work.

1. Architecture

The development of cities and towns during the Early Historic period contributed immensely to the growth of town planning and house constructions and in general the architecture of this period. From about the second century B.C. to the early centuries of the Christian era a progressive trend of large settlements in habitational centres is evident from the excavations. The architecture of this period can be divided into the following classes: (1) Civil, (2) Defense and (3) Religious architecture. Apart from this, a large number of artifacts and utilities have been found in the form of building materials, which includes bricks, ring wells, tiles and door fittings, etc.

Civil architecture mainly comprises of various types of houses, roads and other structural complexes. Defense architecture includes various types of fortification, rampart, moat, bastion, etc. The presence of these indicate the danger of enemy attacks. Religious architecture comprises *temples, viharas, stupas, caves* and *chaityas.*

Houses of this period were made of both mud bricks and burnt bricks. Bricks were also used for constructing platforms and structures. A house complex with rectangular plan and central courtyard and *verandah* was exposed at Baroda (Subbarao 1953: 21-22). At Vadnagar a complete house was exposed consisting of three rooms with an opening on a narrow *verandah* to the north of it. It was made of both sundried and burnt bricks (Subbarao and Mehta 1955: 23). At Amreli the exposed houses revealed that they were made of mud with rubble footing and the floor was built with rammed *kankar* (Rao 1966: 21-22). At Prabhas Patan extensive structures of rubble with post holes were exposed (Sharma 1987). The structures found at Valabhipur were made of bricks (37.5 x 22.5 x 5/6 cm). The floors of the structures were built of ramned earth belonging to the 4th–5th centuries A.D (*IAR.* 1979-80: 24; Sharma 1987: 72). At Nagara, besides a few structures of mud bricks, an artificial embankment for water storage built of burnt bricks was also exposed (Mehta 1968: 21). Excavations at Shamalaji have revealed a fortified structure. It was built of burnt bricks during the 2nd-4th centuries A.D. The first occupants of the town of Shamalaji were the ironsmiths. Soon after this habitation, it became an important town with its fortification and moats. This suggests that it might have been a small military station overlooking a road connecting the hinterland of India to the ports on the Arabian sea (Mehta and Patel 1966: 3). Blocks of yellow sand stone (1 m × 40 × 20 cm) were used for house wall at Dwarka (Ansari and Mate 1968: 33-7). One of the most important structures of this period is a huge monastic and stupa complex at Devnimori. The excavation revealed a complete outline of the *stupa* complex. A *Maha stupa* was enclosed by four smaller *stupas* along with *Chaityas* and *Viharas*, built of bricks. *Viharas* of the *Chatuhshala* variety with the central courtyard and rooms were arranged on a raised *verandah* with drains and water channel and steps at the entrance (Mehta and Chowdhary 1966: 60-66). *Stupa* at Boria about 3 km south of the foot of Girnar in Junagadah was a very extensive establishment. The structures are generally constructed of large mud bricks. The *stupa* had solid burnt bricks. The mound has been partly exposed, in order to reach the relics. The relic-casket, and the four reliquaries enclosed (made of terracotta, copper, silver and gold), found inside the *stupa*, are now preserved in Junagadah Museum. The outermost casket that is the terracotta casket, was discovered inside a slot made into a stone slab. Apart from this, some pieces of stone railing and umbrella, forming probably a part of the crowning member of a *stupa* have also been noticed (Malik 1996). Excavations at Rudrasena *Vihara* at Int-Wa, situated on a hill hardly 3 km north of the Girnar, have unearthed a spacious quadrangular monastery measuring 19.8 × 17.4 m. This monastery shows a central brick paved courtyard, a flanking *verandah* with cells which were almost of the same dimensions (3 × 3 m). It was made of large mud bricks. In addition, side are other quadrangular brick structures-at least two on one flank and one on the other of this monastery. From a cell located on the southern side, a baked clay sealing was found. The *Brahmi* legend on the seal records that the sealing belonged to the *Bhiksu Sangha* of the *Maharaja* Rudrasena monastery. The name of the king on the sealing was identified with the Saka *Kshatrapa* Rudrasena I (199-222 A.D.) (Malik 1996).

The excavations at Padri revealed a structure, 5.20 m long. Unfortunately, its width could not be measured as the structure has not been fully exposed. The floor of this structure is well made and consists of alternative layers of gravels, hard rammed clay and plastering (Shinde 1994).

Cave architecture also developed during the period of 3rd century B.C. to 2nd A.D. Caves at Talaja in Bhavnagar district became popular during this period. According to Sankalia (Sankalia 1941: 51-52), "of the thirty caves of Talaja, only two need description and comment. The first is a large hall known as Ebhal *Mandapa*. It measures 75 feet (23 m) by 67 1/2 feet (21 m) and is 17 1/2 feet (5 m) high. Within there are no cells, nor any partition walls dividing the *verandah* and the cells within. To support the roof, there were "four octagonal pillars" whose shafts are destroyed. On the facade, there are *chaitya* windows with a broad band of *Vedika* (rail pattern) below them. The shape of the *chaitya* window is rather unusual. It is cut into a half oval, inside which is again cut a semi-circular arch; below this is a rectangle and in its smaller (vertical) side a semi-circle on the other side. The three semi-circles (minus the cross and vertical bases) thus form a trefoil. Higher up the hill, there is a ruined *Chaitya* cave having a flat roof. The *Chaitya* has lost its middle part, only the base and the "*torana*" or the capital, which is attached to the roof, remain".

Temple architecture also flourished in Saurashtra during the Early Historic Period. The earliest existing remains of the temple architecture in Saurashtra known as *Jun-Vari Gop* or Gop temple comes from Jamnagar district. This temple is situated on a lofty terrace (*Jagti*) and measures 3.62 m in height. It is square in plan with an extension on the western side. Extensive studies on this structures have been done by earlier scholars (Malik 1996). Recent excavations at Padri have also exposed a temple structure of Goddess *Lajjagauri* of the Early Historic period (Shinde 1994).

2. Pottery

In Saurashtra during the Early Historic period, a large bulk of pottery is available and the range of fabrics, technology and typology is quite immense. Therefore, it is quite difficult to classify them in any set pattern. The Early Historic pottery consists of: (1) Northern Black Polished Ware, (2) Black-and-Red Ware, (3) Burnished Black Ware, (4) Red Polished Ware, (5) Plain Red Ware, (6) Red-Slipped Ware, (7) Grey Ware, (8) Burnished Red Ware, (9) Crude Red and Black Ware, (10) Painted pottery and (11) Amphorae.

2.1 Northern Black Polished Ware

This pottery is made of well levigated clay and has been in shades of black and golden or silvery white, with a grey core and a steel-like gloss on the slip. It is well fired and therefore gives a metallic sound. This ware has been reported from a few sites in Saurashtra such as Timbarva (Mehta 1955: 6-7), Somnath (Nanavati *et. al.* 1971) and Nagara (Mehta 1968: 34). An interesting feature of this pottery in Saurashtra is its very low frequency of distribution. This gives rise to the question as to what were the reasons for its paucity in Gujarat, in general and in Saurashtra, in particular. A possible explanation is that in all probability it was not locally manufactured, but was brought from the Gangetic valley. Evidences of Mauryan influence have definitely been seen in Saurashtra which hints towards the possibility of ceramic influence (NBPW) of the former over the latter through the Buddhist monks. Excavations at Timbarva have revealed Black-and-Red Ware in association with Northern Black Polished Ware, which is crucial for dating this ware. From the stratigraphic evidence at Nagara and Timbarva, it is probable that it has come to Gujarat at least in around 400 B.C. Excavations at Timbarva have produced only six sherds of Northern Black Polished Ware, out of which one each is a slightly incurved rim of a bowl and a rimless bowl. The rest of the sherds are too fragmentary to suggest any shape. At Nagara, it occurs around 4th-3rd century B.C, but the pottery is very fragmentary and hence non-descriptive. At Somnath also, a number of these sherds have been found.

2.2 Black-and-Red Ware

Another fabric found in Saurashtra is the Black-and-Red Ware. The most characteristic feature of this ware is its method of firing in kiln. Possibly the vessels are kept inverted in the kiln making the exterior surface dull red and interior surface black. The surface of this ware is slipped and burnished. It occurs at Nagara (Mehta 1968: 34), Somnath (Nanavati *et al.* 1971: 56), Jokha (Mehta *et al.* 1971: 29) and Dhatva (Mehta and Chowdhary 1975: 37). The main forms are bowl with beveled, featureless rims either out-curved or slightly incurved with convex or concave sides and round base; dishes with beveled, nail headed or everted rim; globular pots with flared or short out-turned rim; jars with beaded rim; basins with everted rim, and lids-either solid or having well developed knobs.

2.3 Plain and Burnished Black ware

Plain and Burnished Black ware is yet another important type of the Early Historic ceramic assemblage of Saurashtra. It has been found at Dhatva (Mehta and Chowdhary 1975: 37), Nagara (Mehta 1968: 34; *IAR.* 1963-64), Shamalaji (Mehta and Patel 1967: 17), Jokha (Mehta *et al.* 1971: 31) and Devnimori (Mehta and Chowdhary 1966: 69). Its fabric is medium coarse and the surface is plain and burnished. Main forms are bowls with either beaded rim or rounded rim; globular pot with beaded or rounded rim and handi with incurved rim and a ledge having two grooves over it.

2.4 Red Polished Ware

Red Polished Ware of Saurashtra is made from fine, well levigated clay, fired in high temperature and has a smooth surface (Subbarao 1953: 32; Margabandhu 1985 and Ray 1986). It has been found at Nagara (Mehta 1968: 34), Jokha (Mehta *et al.* 1971: 31), Timbarva (Mehta 1955: 15), Shamalaji (Mehta and Patel 1967: 17), Somnath (Nanavati *et al.* 1971: 61), Dwarka (Ansari and Mate 1966: 72), Amreli (Rao 1966), Vadnagar, Variav and Vasai (Subbarao 1958: 47) and Devnimori (Mehta and Chowdhary 1966: 69). The origin of the Red Polished Ware is still a disputed problem. Sankalia and others (1958: 161) opined that it could be a local copy of Greek Samian ware produced in a region of Gujarat, particularly Saurashtra. He further added that the Red Polished Ware had been found at a number of excavated sites, which were stratigraphically datable with the *Kshatrapa* and Satavahan period in Western India and the Deccan. It is also associated with the Gupta in North India. At Rupar it occurred between the 2nd century B.C. and 6th century A.D. level. Similarly at Prakash, Red Polished Ware occurred in the 1st century B.C. level. On the basis of its wider distribution at a number of excavated sites, the chronological position of this ware could be dated from about 1st century B.C. to about 5th century A.D. On the other hand according to Rao (1966: 53-59), Early Historic site at Amreli yielded the greatest number of vessel shapes, colours of fabric ranging from pink to dark red. All the vessel forms are regional. On the basis of analysis of both of potsherds and clays which exhibited identical composition, as well as analysis of their texture and surface treatment, it was concluded that this ceramic assemblage was indigenously produced. This suggests the fact that the technology for making fine pottery existed before the appearance of Red Polished Ware and prior to Roman imports in Gujarat. Red Polished Ware occurs in Gujarat from c.1st century B.C. to the 5th century A.D. It has been found in the contexts of the Early Historic period, which maintained contact with the Mediterranean world-a period of great increase in the number of settlements in Western India (Orton 1991: 46). Orton (1991) has found about 400 sites in Gujarat associated with Red Polished Ware. The most noteworthy fact about this ware is the homogeneity of its fabric throughout western India. This ware is represented by bowls, globular pots, dishes, long necked sprinklers and spouts. The present author has also been found during the course of exploration a good number of sites in Bhavnagar district in Saurashtra revealing Red Polished Ware.

2.5 Plain Red Ware

This is the most common ware in Saurashtra in the Early Historic period, as is evident from the ceramic assemblage of Devnimori (Mehta and Chowdhary 1966: 69), Dhatva (Mehta *et al.* 1975: 42), Nagara (Mehta 1968: 34), Shamalaji (Mehta and Patel 1967: 17), Timbarva (Mehta 1955: 9), Dwarka (Ansari and Mate 1966: 65), Padri (Shinde 1992b) and Amreli (Rao 1966: 65). It is wheel-turned as well as handmade and the fabric is medium to coarse. The common shapes are globular pots, bowls, jars, cups, saucers, lids, basins, spouted vessels, etc.

2.6 Red Slipped Ware

This ware is also common in Saurashtra. It is wheel thrown as well as hand made and medium to coarse in fabric. The main forms are globular pots with out turned beaded rim and bulbous body; basins with collared rim; saucers with featureless rim; cups with convex sided body; spouted vessels and lids.

2.7 Grey Ware

This ware is wheel turned and well fired. It shows dull grey, darkish grey and black grey fabric. In Saurashtra, only a few sites like Padri (Shinde 1992b) and Amreli (Rao 1966) have yielded vessels of this ware. Common shapes are pots, spouted vessels, basins and lids.

2.8 Burnished Red Ware

Another common ceramic assemblage in Saurashtra is the Burnished Red Ware, which is present at a number of Early Historic sites such as Dhatva (Mehta *et al.* 1975: 37), Dwarka

(Ansari and Mate 1968: 66), Nagara (Mehta 1968: 34), Timbarva (Mehta 1955: 9), Jokha (Mehta *et al.* 1971: 33) and Shamalaji (Mehta and Patel 1967: 17). It is usually well fired with gritty core and burnished surface. The slip has different tones ranging from light red to deep red. The main types are pots, bowls, spouted vessels, storage jars and dishes.

2.9 Crude Red and Black Ware

Crude Red and Black Ware is another characteristic type of Early Historic pottery in Saurashtra. It occurs at Nagara (Mehta 1968: 4), Devnimori (Mehta and Chowdhary 1966: 69), Shamalaji (Mehta and Patel 1967: 17), Dhatva (Mehta *et al.* 1975: 39-40) and Jokha (Mehta *et al.* 1971: 31). It has thick, gritty core and thick fabric. The usual shapes in this ware are handi with out-curved rim; pots with out-curved rounded or featureless rim and short neck, and bowls with flared, featureless rim.

2.10 Painted pottery

Sherds of painted pottery have been reported from most of the sites in Saurashtra. The painting consists of bands of white and black colour on a red background. Most of the painted motifs occur on the upper body of the vessels. Apart from these, stamped and incised designs are also evident on pottery. The main designs are horizontal bands, embossed dots in vertical row and in oblique row, simple lines, wavy lines, etc.

2.11 Amphorae

Amphorae are imported ceramic ware from Rome. It is thick, gritty and compact in appearance and has a coarse surface. About Mediterranean amphorae, Gupta (Gupta 1997: 23-24) mention thar "The amphorae usually large double handled clay jars with elongated bodies and spike bases, were commonly used in the ancient Mediterranean as containers of liquid stock such as wine, olive oil, fish sauce and other products. Production centres of various types of amphorae proliferated in the littoral regions of the Mediterranean. During the B.C./A.D. change over, wine and other products were regularly exported in amphorae to India along the Egypt-India maritime route." An amphora whole or sherd provides a very useful datum for the chronology of a site. Brisk Roman trade with India in the early centuries of Christian Era is well documented on the basis of various literary as well as archaeological sources. According to Wheeler (1946: 22) Roman trade was known from about 1st century A.D. to 3rd century A.D. and it must have come to India during these centuries. The function of Amphorae is to preserve wine or oil. The chemical examination of the Amphora sherd has revealed on the inside a resinous asphalt-like matter possibly a coating used for reducing the porosity of the pot. The black incrustration may be the sedimented liquid contained in the pot (Mehta and Chowdhary 1966: 77). Margabandhu (1985: 133) opined about the Amphora, "Such finds in this region indicate that they were brought in from parts of Western Sea-board to the interior by land-route. Chemical examination revealed that the content was resin. *Periplus* mentions import of wine in India along with other objects from the Mediterranean". It occurs at a good number at sites of Saurashtra such as Dwarka (Ansari and Mate 1966: 72), Nagara (Mehta 1968: 78), Devnimori (Mehta and Chowdhary 1966: 9) and Shamalaji (Mehta and Patel 1967: 17). The Early Historic phase at Prabhas Patan (Pd. III to Pd.V) yielded amphorae (*IAR*. 1056-57: 16-17; Fig.28). It is also found in Central India and the Deccan (Margabandhu

1985: 133). The present author has also discovered a fragment of amphorae handle from Hathab in Bhavnagar district during his exploration in this region.

3. Technology

During the Early Historic period commendable progress was made in technology. Excavations at various sites in Saurashtra have revealed a variety of tools, weapons and other objects in copper, silver, iron, gold, lead and stone. It should be mentioned that iron was also used in the Chalcolithic period but it became widespread during the Early Historic period. In the following paragraphs, we will discuss the technological aspects of various metals:

3.1 Iron

Iron objects are found from many sites in Saurashtra like Devnimori (Mehta and Chowdhary 1966: 96-105), Dhatva (Mehta *et al.* 1975: 18), Timbarva (Mehta 1955: 25-27), Jokha (Mehta *et al.* 1971: 55), Shamalaji (Mehta and Patel 1967: 46-50), Dwarka (Ansari and Mate 1966: 50), Somnath (Nanavati *et al.* 1971: 80), Amreli (Rao 1966: 108) and Padri and they can be grouped in the following categories:

Agricultural implements and artisans' tools: They consist of sickle, chisel, pick, hoe, scissors, ploughshare, carpenter drills, axes, adzes, etc.

Domestic implements: These include door chain, rings, frying trowel (*tavetho*), fishing hook, nail, knives, ladle with large horizontal handle, pipe, shallow dish and cylindrical pounder.

Defensive and offensive weapons: They consist of arrowhead, spear head, dagger and blade, etc.

Miscellaneous objects: They comprise of handles of different kinds, folded iron sheet and iron weight, etc.

3.2 Copper

Apart from iron, copper objects are found from most of the sites in Saurashtra. They consist of ear-stud, kohl-sticks, wire, small copper box, bar, ring, nails, copper sheet, celt, bangle, bell, bowl, washer or disc, lid and a large number of inscribed, uninscribed and punch marked coins belonging to the Kshatrapa, Gupta and Maitraka dynasties. Excavations at Nagara (Mehta 1968: 113-114) have yielded a copper bell with out-curved rounded rim and a small copper lid with a perforation at the centre. The upper portion of this lid is decorated with an eight petaled flower: Each petal is pointed and has an incised line at its base. Its side has arabesque incised petals enclosed between two lines. Fragments of a badly corroded bowl, a fragmentary flat bar-like object with semi-rectangular section and three types of copper rods were also unearthed (Mehta 1968: 113-114). From Jokha a good number of copper objects such as ring, bangle with granular decoration on the outer rim, a fragment of butt end of a copper celt with some depression below the butt end and a few nails have been unearthed (Mehta *et al* 1971: 55). Excavations at Timbarva have revealed a few copper objects like a bar and a ring (Mehta 1955: 25). At Dhatva a small copper box with rounded ends resembling the shape of an ear-stud was found (Mehta *et al* 1975: 18). A decorated copper bangle and Kohl-sticks have come from Shamalaji (Mehta and Patel 1967: 48). At Devnimori a cylindrical copper box was found. Inside the box an amphora like gold bottle was found (Mehta and Chowdhary 1966: 120). At Padri a tortoise-shaped Roman copper lamp and copper bell were recovered (Shinde 1992b: 83, Fig.2). Excavations at Amreli have produced a number of copper objects such as bangle inset with semi-precious stone, rim of vessel, finger ring, fragments of blade and parts of vessel (Rao 1966: 108).

3.3 Gold

A few objects of gold were found from the different sites. At Timbarva a globular pendant (?) was found (Mehta 1955: 27). At Dhatva a copper ear-ring coated with gold was found (Mehta *et al.* 1975: 18). The gold repertoire of Devnimori consists of some foils, a triangular indented object which might have been a *triratna* symbol and one pendant like object (Mehta and Chowdhary 1966: 93).

3.4 Silver

A small number of silver objects have been noticed from the different excavated sites. At Dwarka a hair pin of folded silver strip and an unidentified silver object perhaps part of some ornament have been noticed (Ansari and Mate 1966: 47).

3.5 Lead

Lead objects also play an important role in Early Historic period. At Dhatva three fragments of ear-stud which were made of strips of lead sheets were found (Mehta *et al.* 1975: 18). This type of ear-stud is known from Nagara (Mehta 1968: 111).

4. Currency and Coinage

In Early Historic period coinage became common. We find the mention of *nishkas* as a sort of currency in the *Rigveda*. In the *Satapatha Brahmana* also we have the evidence of gold coins as *Nishkas*. The *Mahabharata* refers to two classes of wealthy people, in terms of wealth amassed, namely one hundred and one thousand *nishkas*. Kautilya mentions a coin named *kara* which is equivalent to ten *Panas*. The silver was known as *Satamana* which was mentioned in the *Satapatha Brahmana* as a gold coin. On the other hand punch marked silver coin was known as *Karshapana* or *Purana*. The copper coin however was known as *Pana* or *Karshapana* (Sastry 1983: 199-200).

The Greeks, in a sense, laid the foundation of coinage in Gujarat on which the succeeding rulers (Sankalia 1941: 184) built the superstructure. But an examination of the early coins of this part of the country also shows some indigenous coins of the pre-Greek period. These are very small silver coins weighing about 5 to 7 grams with the symbols such as *Swastika*, a *Trisula* and *Chakra* (Sankalia 1941: 184). These coins have a misshapen elephant on the obverse and unidentified symbol resembling a circle on the reverse (Virji 1955: 224). Besides these, the Bactrian Greeks issued many varieties of silver and copper coins in Gujarat, both round and square in shape. The legend on these were in the Bactro-Pali characters (Virji 1955: 224). These Bactrian coins were the proto-types for the coins of western Kshatrapas.

A large number of inscribed, uninscribed and punchmarked coins of silver, copper and lead have been found in various excavated Early Historic sites in Saurashtra. During this period coins of Satavahana and Kshatrapa dynasties were found in most of the sites in Central,

Western India and the Deccan. The rulers of the aforementioned dynasties maintained a perfect uniformity in the coin denominations issuing different types of coins with a view to meet the demands of inter-state enterprise. The Satavahana coins generally in copper potrayed the Ujjayin symbols and were perhaps suitable for commercial transactions in the Avanti region. Simultaneously Kshatrapa rulers also issued coins found in many sites up to 4th-5th century A.D. in parts of Central and Western India (Margabandhu 1985: 70-71).

In Saurashtra various excavated sites have revealed coins along with other associated objects. Excavations at Devnimori have revealed sixty nine coins of different metals. Of these fifty nine coins are made of silver, four of silver coated copper, two of copper and four of lead. Again, majority (59) belongs to the Kshatrapa (100.A.D.-400 A.D.) dynasty of Ujjain; three coins belong to the Maitrakas of Valabhi (480 A.D.-766 A.D.), two are Indo-Sasanian coins and perhaps the Abhira (Mehta and Chowdhary 1966: 104; Sankalia 1987).

Punchmarked, inscribed and uninscribed coins of silver, copper and lead have been found at Nagara (*IAR.* 1964-65: 11; Mehta 1968: 114-115). The site also reveals a coinage assemblage of the Kshatrapa dynasty from 1st to 5th century A.D. (Sharma 1987: 73). From Dhatva only four coins made of copper were found. Of these one is punch marked, two are die struck and the fourth was very fragmentary. All these coins belong to the Pre-Christian era (Mehta *et al.* 1975: 17-18). At Shamalaji eight coins made of copper and lead were obtained, of which, one is a worn-out silver Kshatrapa coin (*IAR.* 1961-62: 14; Mehta and Patel 1967: 50). From excavations at Baroda three copper coins belonging to the Kshatrapa period were discovered (Subbarao 1953: 78-79). Coins were found at Amreli. Among the Kshatrapa coin assemblage, three silver coins of Rudrasena I, one coin of Virasimha and two of Rudrasena III were recovered (Gadre 1947: 5). At Somnath 204 coins were recovered, of which 190 belong to the Gupta period, and two to the Kshatrapa period. One of these two Kshatrapa coins belongs to Bhumaka, the Kshatrapa ruler, and is very interesting from the numismatic point of view. This copper coin bears the usual *Cakra* symbol on the obverse and *Vajra* symbol on the reverse. The other coin made of silver bears the bust of the king on the obverse with the following legends:

"*Rajno mahakshatrapa-sa Damasena putra-Sa Kshatrapa Vijaysena-Sa*"

In addition, the mountain and crescent symbol on the reverse (Nanavati *et al.* 1971: 77-78).

Excavations at Padri in Early Historic level yielded two copper coins which were similar to those issued by the King Nahapana, the Kshatrapa ruler (Shinde 1992a: 81 and 1998: 173). According to Margabandhu (1985: 71) the prevalence of well established currency and means of exchange is revealed by the availability of coins. Their distribution also helps to define the physical extent of their territorial domain which is clear from the coins of Kshatrapa ruler restricted to Western India.

5. Glass

Glass objects such as the neck of a glass bottle, flat petal shaped objects and glass bowl were found at Devnimori (Mehta 1968: 103-4). Glass bottles have also been found at Padri. A green glass bottle and blue glass handle were found in the Early Historic (Pd.III) level at Nagara (Mehta 1968: 133). Besides these, Amreli yielded pieces of glass vessels and a handle fragment, which according to the excavator is an imported object (Rao 1966: 80-81).

6. Material Remains

Apart from remains of architecture, pottery, coinage and glass objects, excavations at various sites like Somnath, Devnimori, Dwarka, Padri, Jokha, Timbarva, Dhatva, Shamalaji and Nagara in Saurashtra have brought to light a variety of material remains. They can be grouped under the following headings.

6.1 Ornaments

The most popular ornaments are beads made of terracotta, glass, paste, chert, chalcedony, carnelian, agate, garnet, cystral, lapis-lazuli, quartz, steatite, jasper, chank and sand stone. They are found in a variety of shapes such as arecanut, barrel, globular, convexcone, flat bicone, cylindrical, hexagonal, toggle, spherical, disc, tubular and circular. Bangles made of shell and terracotta have also been found. Excavations at various sites in Saurashtra yielded a large number of shell bangles as well as terracotta bangles. These bangle pieces are both plain and decorated, the former being smooth with flat rectangular, pentangular or semi-triangular in section whereas the latter consisted of incised lines, floral pattern and loop pattern. Only one glass bangle has been reported from Nagara (Mehta 1968: 132). From Shamalaji a fragment of a stone bangle and a decorated copper bangle were found (Mehta 1967: 48). From Padri a thick iron bangle and a terracotta bangle have been reported.

Copper rings have been found at Jokha (Mehta *et al.* 1971: 55), Timbarva (Mehta 1955: 25) and Padri. One earring of copper coated with gold is reported from Dhatva (Mehta *et al.* 1975: 18). Ear-studs have also been found at Nagara, Jokha, Padri and Dhatva in limited number. From the latter ear-stud in glass, copper and leads were recovered (Mehta *et al.* 1975: 18). Ear-stud in black glass, crystal and lead were found at Jokha (Mehta *et al.* 1971: 50).

Pendants have also been found at a few sites. A gold pendant comes from Timbarva (Mehta 1955: 25), and a hexagonal pendant of semi-precious stone is reported from Devnimori (Mehta and Chowdhay 1966: 93). Three specimens of shell pendants have been found at Padri.

6.2 Kitchen objects

Among the kitchen objects rotary querns and pestles of stone are the most common at various sites in Saurashtra during the Early Historic period. Besides these, one piece of frying trowel (*tavetho*) of iron comes from Devnimori (Mehta and Chowdhary 1966: 101). Fragments of highly corroded copper bowl and a small dish of terracotta are reported from Nagara (Mehta 1968: 109-13). From Shamalaji a fragment of stone bowl is reported (Mehta and Patel 1967: 46) whereas Padri has revealed a terracotta spoon.

6.3 Bronze, Terracotta and Stone figurines

During the Early Historic period a number of artistic objects such as bronze, terracotta human and animal figurines and stone figurines have been found at different sites in Saurashtra. At Baroda a fragment of Roman bronze handle which represents a young nude boy identified as Cupid sitting on a bench was found. Besides a few pieces of trefoil mouth of jug have also been found (Desai 1949-50). On the other hand, a bronze statuette of Atlas were noticed from Shamalaji (Chowdhary 1961-62: 309-15). According to Chowdhary (1961-62: 309-15),

"It is a half sitting or crouching posture, almost what may be called *Virasana*. The posture is such that the legs are bent from the knees almost to an acuted angle. The heels are pressed against the respective hips. Both forefeet and right knee are resting on ground while the left knee is slightly raised. All the three points touching the ground are flattened, to produce a footing and stability." It is difficult to trace its origin, "but it is an artistic blending of perhaps of three traditions of arts- Graeco-Roman, Indian and the Indian tinge in the form and style clearly indicates that this piece is perhaps manufactured in India and belongs to the third-fourth century A.D."

Terracotta figurines of both animals and humans during this period were both handmade and moulded. Margabnadhu (1985:82) opines that, "Clay as a medium of artistic expression is easily traceable and lends itself to any shape thus satisfying the artistic urges of the common man. A variety of significant motifs and forms have been found in terracotta unlike those in other materials. Its uses were extensive and purposes varied. There were objects of domestic use, worship and household decorations as children's toys and also of popular religious and magical purposes. Apart from its aesthetic significance, the terracotta art and its varied uses and applications supply invaluable data for the study of life and culture of the people."

Both male and female human figurines are heavily decorated, and they share a family likeness in dress, ornaments and decorative motifs. About terracotta art Coomaraswamy (1927) and Gordon (1943) review that the terracotta of the Early Historic period shows an influence of Hellenistic art. Excavations at Devnimori have yielded a whole Buddhist complex with Stupa, images of Buddha, arches, capitals and medallions etc. (Mehta and Chowdhury 1966: 140-142, Pl.XXXVII-LXIV). Apart from this a *dhyani* Buddha and a few Bodhisattva figures have also been found from Amreli which indicates it to be a centre of Buddhism (Rao 1966: 99-102). Excavations at Dhatva yielded a terracotta mother goddess with a pinched face, short upper arms, breasts and fiddle type lower part (*Mehta et al.* 1975:14-15, Pl.v-b, Fig.6). Similar types of terracotta mother goddesses have also been reported from Timberva (Mehta 1955: 23, Fig.11-12), Nagara (Mehta 1968: 96) and Somnath (Nanavati *et al.* 1971). It shows that this form was widely prevalent in Gujarat. At Padri the upper half of a moulded terracotta human figurine and two boat-shaped terracotta objects have been found (Shinde 1992b: 83). Apart from this, a fragment of terracotta plaque comes from Timberva (1955: 23, Fig.13 No.9). The plaque bears floral pattern on one side whereas the other side is plain. Shamalaji has yielded one highly worn out head perhaps of a woman with three peaked hair style (Mehta and Patel 1967: 44, Fig.21.9).

Pottery handles with human figurines have been found in a good number from the sites in Saurashtra belonging to the Early Historic period. Pottery jar handles and spouts with human figures appear to have become popular among the Indian potters during the 1st century of the Christian Era, probably as a result of brisk trade with the western world. Excavations at Amreli have yielded three headless nude female figurines on jar handles of Red Polished Ware. Whereas one of the figures has prominent breasts with both hands suspended, wearing a necklace and a girdle, the second depicts a lady in *Abhanga* pose. The last figurine, however, can not be studied properly due to its bad state of preservation (Rao 1966: 101; Agrawal and Devalkar 1970: 9). Besides this, some of the terracotta spouts bearing heads almost triangular in shape with a lug comes from the village of Khakharda and Chachlona in Jamnagar district. The lug is an artistic piece of work, obtained by modeling and has a beautiful human face (Malik 1996). Excavations at Amreli have also produced a number of terracotta plaques. They are in high relief with refined forms and well regulated contours and gradations. The female figures are simple, devoid of much decoration and jewellery (Rao 1966).

Animal figurines are mainly bulls, horses, rhinoceros, nilgais, hyaenas, buffaloes, elephants, birds and goats.

Apart from these, a number of stone figurines or images of *Buddha*, *Visnu*, Goddess *Lajjagauri* and *Ganesa* have been found from different sites in Saurashtra. The excavation at Devnimori has also yielded an image of *Buddha* made of schist stone and a plaque depicting a complete stupa with two *Bodhisattvas*, perhaps one of them being *Padmapani* (Mehta and Chowdhary 1966, plate XXIII.d.e; *IAR* 1959-60: 21). A male figure and a mother and child (89X32 mms) in low relief, and the lower part of the god *Ganesa* in sand stone have been recovered from Vadnagar (Subbarao and Mehta 1955: 33-34, Fig.18). Two plaques of *Mahishamardini* and *Visnu* come from Amreli (Rao 1966). At Padri three plaques of goddess *Lajjagauri* have been found, of which two were made of terracotta and the third of slate stone (Shinde 1994). Alongside, a fragment of terracotta plaque, probably *Yoni* portion (female genitalia) of goddesses *Lajjagauri* was also recovered (Shinde 1994). A *Lajjagauri* figurine also comes from Valabhipur- made of dark green schist stone slab and measuring 11.5x5x3 cms. It depicts the human headed *Lajjagauri* in bold relief. However, the figurine is partly broken (Sonawane 1988: 30). A number of other sites in Saurashtra have also produced *Lajjagauri* figurines such as Kavi in Broach, Pavi Jetpur in Baroda, Randela in Bhavnagar, Gadhali in Gadhada, Amreli in Amreli and Dhank in Rajkot (Sonawane 1988: 34; Ray 1986). One image each of Lord *Ganesa* and *Vishnu*, made of sand stone comes from Padri in association with goddesses *Lajjagauri* (Shinde 1994: 481).

6.4 Seals and Sealings

Early Historic seals and sealings have been reported from various excavated sites in Saurashtra. They are made from a variety of materials such as terracotta, copper, stones, etc. However, the exact functions of these objects, are not known. According to some scholars, official or private letters and goods and merchandise, duly sealed were dispatched from one place to another place by the kings, private individuals or religious institutions. This is evident from the sealing bearings: on the obverse positive impressions taken from the seals, while on the reverse, impression of cords used as a document of package over which the sealing was affixed are visible (Margabandhu 1985: 66). Excavations at Nagara have yielded 28 seals and sealings. Out of these 19 sealings of black colour show a cow and calf. Another circular red sealing depicting a bull and trident was prepared by rolling strips of wet clay and then the symbol was impressed upon it. On the reverse of this sealing string impressions can be seen. Another three sealings were inscribed, one has a legend *Buddhapasya*, the second has a *Garuda* like animal and the last with *Mahasena* inscribed below it. Its reverse suggests it could be pressed on a knot. The last one was circular in shape and sub-triangular in elevation with legend *shrijayamitra* or *Vijayamitra* and shows evidence of being preserved on the reverse. Besides these, two negatives of seals were found. One of them is highly worn out, embossed with the figure perhaps of an owl whereas the other is too fragmentary to be deciphered (Mehta 1968: 106-107). At Baroda two clay seals depicting two prancing horses, in a fighting or a romantic posture with a star on the top and straight line below it were discovered (Subbarao 1953: 87). A good number of seals and sealings have been found from Amreli (Rao 1966: 89-91). One of them is an inscribed rectangular seal made of lead with the legend *Isvarasya*. Two other sealings, circular in shape and plano-convex in section with the legends *Ajitasya* and *Surasya* respectively were also unearthed. This site has also produced an interesting goldsmith's terracotta mould belonging to the 3rd-4th century A.D., and a clay die of Siladitya (Gadre 1947: 5, Pl. VIIIb). At Vadnagar two sealings were discovered, one of which has a motif of a wine glass held for drink suggest the motif is foreign while the other has impressions of string and knot with writing around a conch on the reverse. It has right turned *Swastica* with legend *Shabuta putrasya* (Subbarao and Mehta 1955: 19-44).

6.5 Votive Tanks, Votive Stupas, Tablets and Decorative pieces

A good number of votive tanks, stupas, tablets and decorative pieces made of terracotta have been reported from various sites in Saurashtra. Excavation at Devnimori has produced the evidence of votive tanks and votive stupas (Mehta and Chowdhary 1968: 90-92; Ray 1986). Two terracotta fragments of rectangular votive tanks are found from Vihara I. One terracotta die for votive stupa was also found. In addition, two solid hand-made objects, globular in shape with broken top showing a hole on the broken part and flat base could be identified as votive stupas. A fragment of rectangular votive tank has also been found at Shamalaji (Mehta and Patel 1967: 144; Ray 1986). At Padri a circular clay tablet bearing *Brahmi* script has been found in the Early Historic level (Shinde 1992b: 81 and 1998: 173).

Apart from these, a number of decorative pieces which consist of arches, capital of pilasters, medallions, pilasters, base of pilaster, dentils and decorated bricks have been unearthed at Devnimori (Mehta and Chowdhary 1968: 148).

7. Miscellaneous objects

Among the miscellaneous objects a large number of discs, stoppers, wheels, toy carts, balls, flesh rubbers and lamps, have been found. Besides, mullers of sand stone, stone balls, ivory combs, bone points, bone kohl-sticks, copper bell, etc. have been found.

8. Subsistence pattern

Apart from Nagara (*IAR*. 1964-65: 11; Mehta 1968: 153) and Somnath no other Early Historic site in Saurashtra has given evidence of cereal and other food grains. Excavations at Somnath have revealed four kinds of cereals. At Nagara some charted seeds and grains consisting of *Rice, Kodrava, Matha* were found from the deposit of periods I-II and III (*IAR*.. 1963-64: 11; Mehta 1968: 153). Therefore it can be presumed that the food habits of the Proto-historic people are continued during the Early Historic period.

9. Trade and transport

The growth and decline of towns is intimately linked with the history of trade (Sharma 1987). With the inclusion in the Mauryan empire, Gujarat played an important role in the development of India's Mediterranean trade and therefore its coast-line attained a new level of economic prosperity (Chakrabarti 1995: 226). Under the dynasties of Mauryas, Sungas, Satavahanas, Kshatrapas and Kushanas the economy of the state tends to suggest a strong industrial activity. Evidences indicate that the artisans and the other craftsmen were encouraged by the rulers to produce and manufacture goods on a large scale (Margabandhu 1985). People working in the same trades were organized into guilds. In the inscriptions and literature of this period a number of guilds are noticed such as Goldsmiths (*sauvarnikas-hairanyakas*), maker or sellers of cloaks (*pravarika-pali-pavarikas*), jewel splendeders (*maniprsatutarakas*), perfumers (*gandhikas*), oilmillers (*tailikas*), makers of pot for storing ghee (*ghrita kundikas*), makers of molasses (*golikas*), curd makers (*dadhikas*), cotton cloth makers (*karpasikas*), makers of candied sugar (*khanda-karakas*), sweet meat confectioners (*modakakarakas*), wheat-flour dealers (*samita-karakas*), grinders of barley meal (*saktu-karakas*), fruit dealers (*phalavanijas*), dealers in roots (*mulavanijas*), flour grinders (*churna kuttakas*), dealers in perfumed oil (*gandhataillakas*), provision dealers (*attavanijas*) (Puri 1965: 106). The head of the guild was called *Sreshthin* and they had their own laws to maintain their organization.

The archaeological evidence of Indo-Roman trade is one sided, much in sharp contrast to the Roman goods found in Peninsular India. The information regarding the trade activity of India with Roman Empire during the Early Historic period is obtained from the *Periplus*. Puri (1965: 117) pointed out that according to the *Periplus*, "the articles exported to Roman Empire from India were Indian pepper, ginger and articles of luxury including silk, muslin and cotton fabrics. The precious stones, pearls and minerals were also in great demand. The Indian ports at Barbaricum at the mouth of the Indus and Barygaza (Broach) were the important centers for the import and export of trade. The imported things included thin clothing, coral, frankincense, vessels of glass, silver and gold, copper, tin, lead, sweet clover, little ointment, also singing boys and beautiful maidens for the harem, fine wines, etc. The exported articles included costus, bdellium, turquoise, lapiz-lazuli, series, skins cotton cloth, silk yarn and indigo, for which there was a great demand."

The *Periplus* also informs of the trade between the Roman Empire and Barygaza, of exports of carnelian and agate extracted from the Narbada and Rajpiple to Africa and Egypt (Warmington 1974: 238-269). According to Gupta (1997:250), " one of the major reason for the prosperity of ports of Barbaricum and Barygaza was the vast hinterland that they served. The Indo-Mediterranean sea route from Egypt constituted a faster, cheaper and safer channel of trade than the overland Silk Routes connecting Central Asia and Gandhara-Bactria with the Eastern Mediterranean. Besides, the prolonged state of hostilities between the Romans and Parthians (who controlled the overland routes through Iraq-Iran) did create difficulties for the movement of trade goods across West Asia. These factors must have worked to the advantage of 'neutral' Indo-Parthian/ Kushan and Kshatrapan ports on the Lower Indus/ Gujarat which received a heavy flow of export commodities from Northern regions. Added to the long distance inland markets was the rich local/regional hinterland producing export-goods." The large scale trade always needs well defined routes and good transport. Several trade routes existed during this period connecting parts of Rajasthan, Malwa and North Gujarat-Saurasthra as the latter provided access to the western seaboard. The internal lines of communication covered not only the whole of India but also extended as far as Balkh and Khotan meeting the famous silk trade route between China and Rome. At the same time Western India especially Gujarat played an important role in Indo-Roman commerce as well as inland trade. According to Margabhandu (1985: 61), "The cultural affinity between

Gujarat and Malwa was close in the Early Historic times. Under the Mauryas both provinces were united together and Asoka is known to have been Viceroy of Ujjaini. Malwa was in fact the opening or the gateway to the rich cotton growing areas of Gujarat. Naturally whoever controlled Malwa, also controlled the route to the west. Gujarat connected itself with many ancient small settlements by caravan routes. Amreli, Baroda, Devnimori, Dwarka, Girinagara, Karvan, Somnath, Pindara, Vadnagar, Vala and Vasai were all flourishing as small industrial and administrative townships during this period. The main caravan route from Dasapura or Mandasor and Ujjayini in Malwa areas to Broach passes through Dungarpur, Bhiloda, Shamalaji, Harsapur (Harsol) to Karpatavanijya in the Khetakamandala. Harsol was perhaps a big commercial centre for traders from Khetaka and from Dasapura and Ujjayini. Shamalaji, situated in a forest valley on the outliers of the Aravalli mountains surrounding it almost on three sides, was perhaps a military outpost of which importance as an outlet to and from Dungarpur Hills was recognized from the Kshatrapa times. Its importance as a trade centre besides being a place of pilgrimage is also clear during the Kshatrapa-Gupta periods. Near at Shamalaji was situated the famous Buddhist establishment of Devnimori which flourished during the early Christian era. It seems that here existed perhaps a regular route between Nagara and Shamalaji with intermediate stations at Tarapur, Dehgam and Kathal from where ancient remains have been reported. Other places connected in the caravan route includes Vadnagar, Nagara, Vala and Baroda. Vadnagar was a strategic centre on the highway which connected Gujarat, Rajasthan and Malwa later and was an important fortified township under the Maitrakas and Solankis. Baroda was the main nodal centre on account of its location which practically linked Gujarat, Rajasthan and Malwa and was an important commercial centre connecting Broach which was an outlet for the western world. Karvan was an important religious centre associated with Lakulisa, the founder of the Pasupata sect. Nearby is Timbarva an early Iron Age town. Towards the inland of the west was situated Amreli, an important political and religious centre of Buddhism and Brahmanism under the Kshatrapas and an administrative centre later under the Guptas and Maitrakas. Many coastal towns flourished in Saurashtra. They include Dwarka, Somnath, Pindara, Mul-Dwarka, Mandhavpur, Vasai, etc."

Chapter 3

Early Historic Phase at Padri

1. The site and its location

The excavations at Padri were conducted for over five seasons under the guidance of Dr. Vasant Shinde of the Department of Archaeology, Deccan College Post Graduate and Research Institute, Pune between 1990-91 and 1995-96. The site has yielded a three-fold cultural sequence namely Early Harappan (Period I), Mature Harappan (Period II) and Early Historic (Period III).

The village *Padri-Gohil-ni* is located in *Talaja tehsil* of Bhavnagar district. The village lies hardly 2 km away from the Gulf of Cambay and is 8 km to the west of *Talaja* and 50 km south of Bhavnagar. The village is approached by the State Transport as well as private vehicle.

The ancient site at Padri is locally known as *Kerala-ni-Dhoro*. According to the inhabitants of the village it is named after the abundant growth of thorny scrubs, called "*kerala*" by the villagers. The mound is one and half kilometer south of the present village and roughly one and half kilometer away from the Gulf of Cambay. The site is spread over an area of 7.14 hectare and the total habitation deposit is 3.2 m thick. The 1.2 m of deposit belongs to the Early Historic period (1st century B.C.-A.D.). The site is located in a shallow depression on a slightly elevated ground. It was probably protected from the destructive impact of the tidal waves by the natural barrier of the basalt rock. Nearly 1/3rd of the western and north-western part of the habitational deposit has been dug up by the villagers for obtaining soil for construction purposes. A detailed survey of the mound and its surrounding area have revealed marine silt and sand around the settlement, particularly on the southern side of the ancient settlement, which suggest its close proximity to the coast during the Harappan as well as Early Historic period. On the northern side of the mound is found very good fertile black cotton soil. It was also observed that the present settlement was intended to exploit the available rich tract of fertile land (Shinde 1992b and 1998).

During the whole excavations period altogether 15 trenches namely, J2, C3, K1, K2, L1, L2, M1, M2, N1, N2, LX1, MX1, NX1, TTSA1 and TTSA2 were selected for horizontal excavation and each trench (5 m X 5 m) was divided into four quadrants and for over five seasons digging has been done in an area of about 950 sq.m.

2. Stratigraphy

The entire habitation deposit at Padri is represented by ten layers of which upper three layers belonged to the Early Historic period dated to the 1st-2nd century A.D.

Layer (1) varies from 12-30 cm in thickness and is slightly compact, relatively undisturbed and greyish in colour.

Layer (2) quite thick, slightly loose and is dark greyish in colour. This is the main occupational layer of the Early Historic period at Padri.

Layer (3) is blackish in colour, varies in thickness from 55-90 cm. It is slightly compact and homogeneous in nature. This particular layer represents a gap between the Early Historic and Harappan period. It is almost undisturbed.

3. Structures

Only two structures of the Early Historic period could be uncovered partially. Structural remains of the Early Historic period were exposed at the surface level. According to the excavator (Shinde 1994), a stone structure (No.7) was partially exposed in the southern quadrant in N1 trench. It was roughly rectangular on plan and has rounded corners. It was located in the central part of the mound. A large portion of this structure still remains unexposed. It is 5.20 m long (E-W) and the width could not be measured as the structure is not fully exposed. At least three courses of stone (basalt) have been noticed. The floor of this structure is made of alternate layers of gravel and clay rammed hard and plastered.

On the southern side of this stone structure, a well made compact floor (Structure No.3) was exposed over an area of 5.90 m (N-S) and 3.70 m (E-W). There are altogether five postholes (average diam. 13 cm) associated with this patch of floor. Two of them on the western periphery, one in the southern half of the floor and two almost in the central part of the floor. Three postholes are located in the southern periphery of the floor and are almost equidistant (1.40 m) from each other. The presence of the postholes on the periphery suggests a superstructure over this patch of the floor. In the north-west part of this floor was a hard and roughly circular (diam. 1.50 m) mud platform which was destroyed in the process of digging. To the south of this platform, at a distance of 3.80 m, was another similar mud platform, slightly smaller in size (diam. 1.10 m). This floor is connected to the stone structure (No. 7) described above and has been identified as its courtyard. The absence of evidence for cooking or storage facilities suggests that it was a non-domestic structure. Two terracotta plaques of *Lajjagauri* and one each of Lord *Ganesa* and *Visnu* made of sand stone have been recovered from the top of the floor (structure 3). The floor and the two mud platforms assume great significance in the light of these discoveries (Shinde 1994). As far as the function of the structure is concerned, it is not unlikely that the structure was associated with some religious practices. It would not be exaggeration to suggest that the structure No.7, which is well made with stone walls was a temple of *Lajjagauri.*

4. Ceramic assemblage of Padri in Early Historic Period

Trench C3, the Index trench was selected for a systematic study of the ceramic assemblage of the Early Historic period at Padri, which is dated from 2nd cent. B.C. to 2nd cent. A.D. (Shinde 1992b). With the kind permission of Dr. Vasant Shinde all potsherds from the Index Trench C3 were systematically studied in great detail. The ceramic assemblages of this period is defined on the basis of surface treatment, fabric and texture. There are three distinct wares in the Early Historic period at Padri namely, Red Ware, Red-Slipped Ware and Grey Ware. Only one specimen of Black-and-Red Ware is found in the trench. Both diagnostic and non-diagnostic sherds of each ceramic type have been examined, all potsherds counted and the percentage of the wares calculated to establish their statistical relation with each other. **(Table 7, Fig.5)**. There were in all 1775 sherds in Index Trench C-3, 1055 of Red Ware (59.43%), 474 of Red-Slipped Ware (26.70%), 245 of Grey Ware (13.80%) and 1 of Black-and-Red Ware (05%), in the total assemblage. The above statistic shows that the Red Ware was the most dominant variety followed by Red-Slipped Ware and Grey Ware respectively. The occurrence of Black-and-Red Ware in the Early Historic levels at Padri is quite significant, as it is rarely found in the Early Historic levels in Bhavnagar district of Saurashtra. It may have come here as a result of contact with other regions or due to some stratigraphic disturbance. The major wares are discussed below in their distinguishing morphological features, forms, texture (fabric), surface treatment and mode of production and firing. The specimen of each ware is discussed separately **(Plate I.a. to VIII.b.)**.

Table 7: Padri Index Trench (C3)

Frequency of Wares

Layer	Red Ware	Red-Slipped Ware	Grey Ware	Black-and-Red Ware	Total
3	253 (61.55%)	108 (26.27%)	49 (11.92%)	1 (0.24)	411
2	642 (60%)	303 (28.31%)	125 (11.68%)	0	1070
1	160 (54.42%)	63 (21.42%)	71 (24.14%)	0	294
Total	1055 (59.43%)	474 (26.70%)	245 (13.80%)	1 (0.5%)	1775

4.1. Red Ware

Red Ware is the most dominant ceramic of the Early Historic levels, recovered from the excavations at Padri, amounting to 59.43% of the total ceramic assemblage. This ware has also been reported from the Early Historic phase at Devnimori (Mehta *et al* 1966: 69), Dhatva (Mehta *et al.* 1975: 42), Dwarka (Ansari and Mate 1966: 58), Shamalaji (Mehta and Patel 1967: 18) and Nagara (Mehta 1968: 34). The specimens are both wheel turned and hand-made. The clay used for this Ware is not well levigated. The core is not very compact and dung and sand are used as tempering agents. The characteristic shapes of this ware at Padri are cups (34.05%), dishes (24.27%), globular pots (20.65%), jars (10.50%), lid (4.71%), saucers (3.26%), basins (2.27%) and spouts (0.36%) **(Fig.6)**.

Cup (34.05%) with flaring sides is the most common type in this ware. It occurs in a variety of sizes in the Early Historic levels at Padri. It has a narrow base which sometimes shows the string marks and finger impressions of the potter. The rim shows varieties: either with featureless pointed or short vertical or slightly everted or simple inverted rim **(Plate V.a. Nos.71-78 and Plate V.b. Nos. 79-86)**. The mouth of the cup ranges in diameter from 8 cm to 24 cm. This type of vessel was also found in the Early Historic level at Devnimori (Mehta *et al.* 1966: 70).

Other shapes are: Dishes (24.27%) either with simple pointed or beaded or incurved beaded or featureless and out-curved rim **(Plate. VI.b. No.102)**.

Pots (20.65%): with out-turned and externally thickened and under-cut rim, having either high or short vertical neck **(Plate. IV.b. No.63, 66)**.

Jars (10.50%) is the other dominant type in the Early Historic level at Padri. Almost all the rim fragments of the ware are either externally or internally projecting or out-turned or under-cut, thick everted with ridge, groove marks, short, high and vertical neck **(Plate IV.a. Nos.54-62, Plate IV.b. Nos.64-65, 67-69)**. The ware is also wheel turned and hand-made and the fabric ranges from coarse to medium. The diameter of the mouth ranges from 14 cm to 26 cm.

The lid (4.71%) is slightly flat with both external and internal projection and under-cut beaded rim **(Plate VI.b. Nos.93-99.1)**. The diameter of the mouth of the rim ranges from 6 cm to 22 cm.

Another type is the saucer (3.26%) either with slightly incurved and featureless or pointed or short vertical rim, having convex sided body and flat base **(Plate VI.a. Nos.87-92)**. The diameter of the mouth of the saucer ranges from 10 cm to 22 cm.

Basin (2.27%) either with under-cut or beak shaped rim **(Plate VI.b. Nos.100-101)** and channel spout (0.36%) have been found.

4.2. Red-Slipped Ware

Red-Slipped Ware, treated with a red to light grey slip on the exterior surface with coarse to medium fabric, forms the second major category of the Early Historic ceramic assemblage at Padri. This ware is made of coarse clay tempered with chopped grass and sand particles. Both hand-made and wheel turned pottery is present in this category. The black-and-light grey core in this type suggests poor firing conditions. The exterior surface, in most cases, is treated with a thick red slip (Shinde 1992). The shapes in this ware are represented by pots (37.93%), jars (27.58%), bowls (13.79%), dishes (8.96%), basins (5.51%), spouts (3.44%), lids (2.06%) and saucers (0.68%) **(Fig.7)**.

Statistics revealed that pots (37.93%) were the dominant variety in this ware with various rim forms like either flat projecting, or short out-turned, or beaded under-cut or externally projecting beaked. The neck of the pot is either short vertical or concave **(Plate II.a. No.19, 25, 28, 31.1; Plate II.b. No.32)**. The diameter of the mouth of the rim ranges from 8 cm to 12 cm.

Jars (27.58%) is the next common variety in this ware. The rims in this type are either flat projecting or inverted or everted or externally and internally projecting or beaded or under-cut and squarish with short vertical or concave or convex neck **(Plate I.a. Nos.1-6 ; Plate I.b. Nos.7-18 ; Plate II.a. Nos.20-24, 26-27, 29-31; Plate II.b. No.33)**. The diameter of the mouth ranges from 10 cm to 24 cm. Most of the sherds were undecorated but a few sherds had groove marks on the interior and exterior of the rim and horizontal incised bands on external surface.

The bowls are (13.79%) another common type in this ware. They are both shallow and convex-sided with flat, ring or disc bases (**Plate II.b. Nos.34-37 ; Plate III.a. Nos.38-42**). The diameter of the mouth of the bowl ranges from 4 cm to 26 cm. Besides these, dish is another variety found in the Red-slipped Ware with mostly internally beaked rim and a ledge on the external shoulder (**Plate III.b. No.46**).

Basins (5.51%) have vertical sides and featureless rounded rims. In some cases with identical rims, they are incurved in a triangular fashion having a convex profile with slightly externally thickened rim (**Plate III.a. Nos.43-45**).

Both tubular and channel spouts (3.44%) also occur in this ware in a large number (**Plate III.b. Nos.51-53**). In addition, other types such as lids (2.06%) with internally thickened, under-cut rim, prominent ridge and tapering base (**Plate III.b. Nos.48-49**) and Saucers (0.68%) with featureless and pointed rims are also represented in this ware.

4.3. Grey Ware

The pots of the Grey Ware were most commonly used for cooking purposes. It has been reported from other Early Historic sites such as Amreli, Baroda and Vadnagar (Subbarao *et al.* 1955). In Padri it occurs in lesser quantity. The Grey Ware is made from ordinary clay mixed with chopped grass and sand particles as tempering material. The core is greyish in colour. The pots are wheel thrown. The characteristic shapes in this wares are pots (45.20%) with everted rim having externally prominent ridge and short vertical neck with a diameter of the mouth ranging from 13 cm to 26 cm (**Plate VII.a. No.103, 110**); dishes (21.91%) either with out-turned or everted rim; jars (20.54%) either with flaring or triangular or externally thickened or short out-turned rim with deep groove marks and short vertical neck having rim diameter between 14 cm and 24 cm (**Plate VII.a Nos.104-109, 111; Plate VII.b. No.111.1**); basins (6.64%) either with vertical sides or featureless rounded or triangular rim with the rim diameter ranging from 14 cm to 26 cm; bowls (2.73%) with featureless pointed rim and groove on the exterior of the body. The diameter of mouth of the bowl ranges from 14 cm to 20 cm (**Plate VIII.a. No.113**); lids (1.36%) with rounded featureless rim (diameter of the mouth of rim ranges from 12 cm to 20 cm) (**Plate VIII.a. No.114**) and lamps (1.36%) with short out-turned sides and disc base (**Fig.8**).

4.4. Black-and-Red Ware

Black-and-Red Ware was also common in the Early Historic period. The main technique of Black-and-Red Ware, the black on the interior surface and red on the exterior surface or half black and half red colour is achieved possibly by the inverted firing technique. Black-and-Red Ware has been found at most of the sites in Gujarat such as Nagara, Shamalaji and Dhatva. At Padri only one specimen of this ware was found in the Index Trench C3. The shape is convex-sided bowl with featureless rim (**Plate VIII.b. No.115**). It is coarse in fabric. The diameter of the mouth is 10 cm.

4.5. Functional analysis

The utility of the Early Historic ceramics can be determined only tentatively, using present day parallels (Bhagat-kar *et al.* 1992c). The rural communities today use different vessels for various religious as well as household purposes. Drawing inferences from current ethnographic works and the relationship between forms and functions of rural pottery, the following broad functional categories have been identified.

I. Cooking vessels.
II. Serving vessels (Table ware)
III. Storage vessels and,
IV. Ritualistic vessels.

4.5.I. Cooking vessels

The function of a vessel, used for the purpose of cooking, can be determined from its shape and fabric. They are, in most cases, wheel made and of thin fabric. All the sites of Early Historic phase in the study area, yielded cooking vessels like globular or carinated pots in grey ware. From close observation it was seen that cooking pots were rarely made in Red Ware. The types of vessels used for cooking purposes were large-mouthed globular pot without neck, and lids.

4.5.II. Serving vessels (Table ware)

From their shapes, it may be suggested that vessels such as cups, bowls, dishes, saucer, plates and small pots probably were meant for serving food and water. While certain shapes like the cup may have mainly been used for the intake of liquids, others such as the bowl may have been a multipurpose-drinking water or for the consumption of liquid vegetables while eating. Similarly, dishes too may have served more than one function.

4.5.III. Storage vessels

Globular pots of different sizes could have been used to store food grain, cereals, water and other domestic objects. Small vessels may also have served as storage. They are thick and the pot, which were used to store water, were treated with thick slip.

4.5.IV. Ritualistic vessels

In the Early Historic period of Padri a number vessels were found which, by their size and form, do not seem to have been used for an ordinary purposes. They may have been used for performing some religious ceremonies. These include spouted pots, miniature bowls and pots.

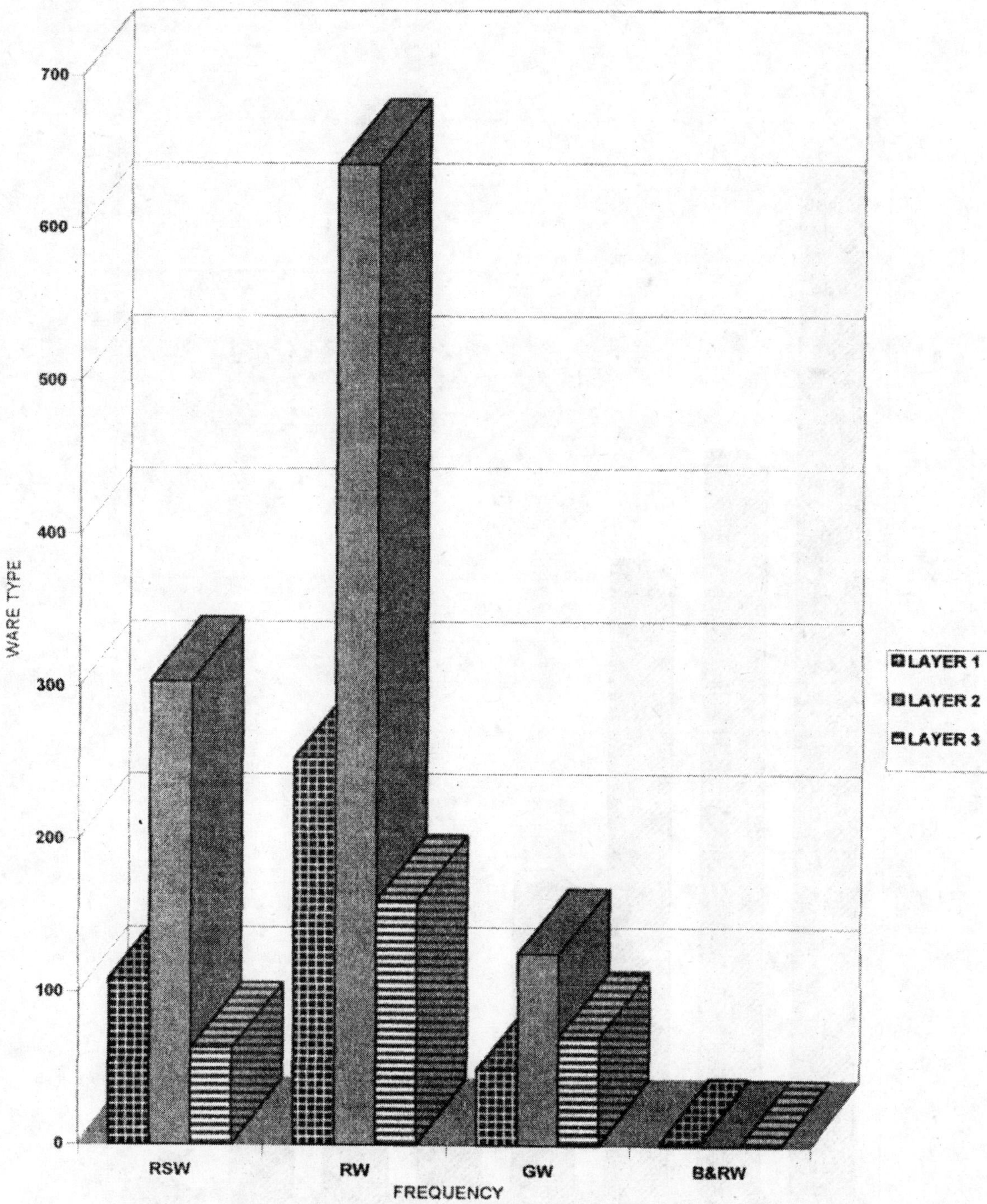

Fig.5: Frequency of different Wares.

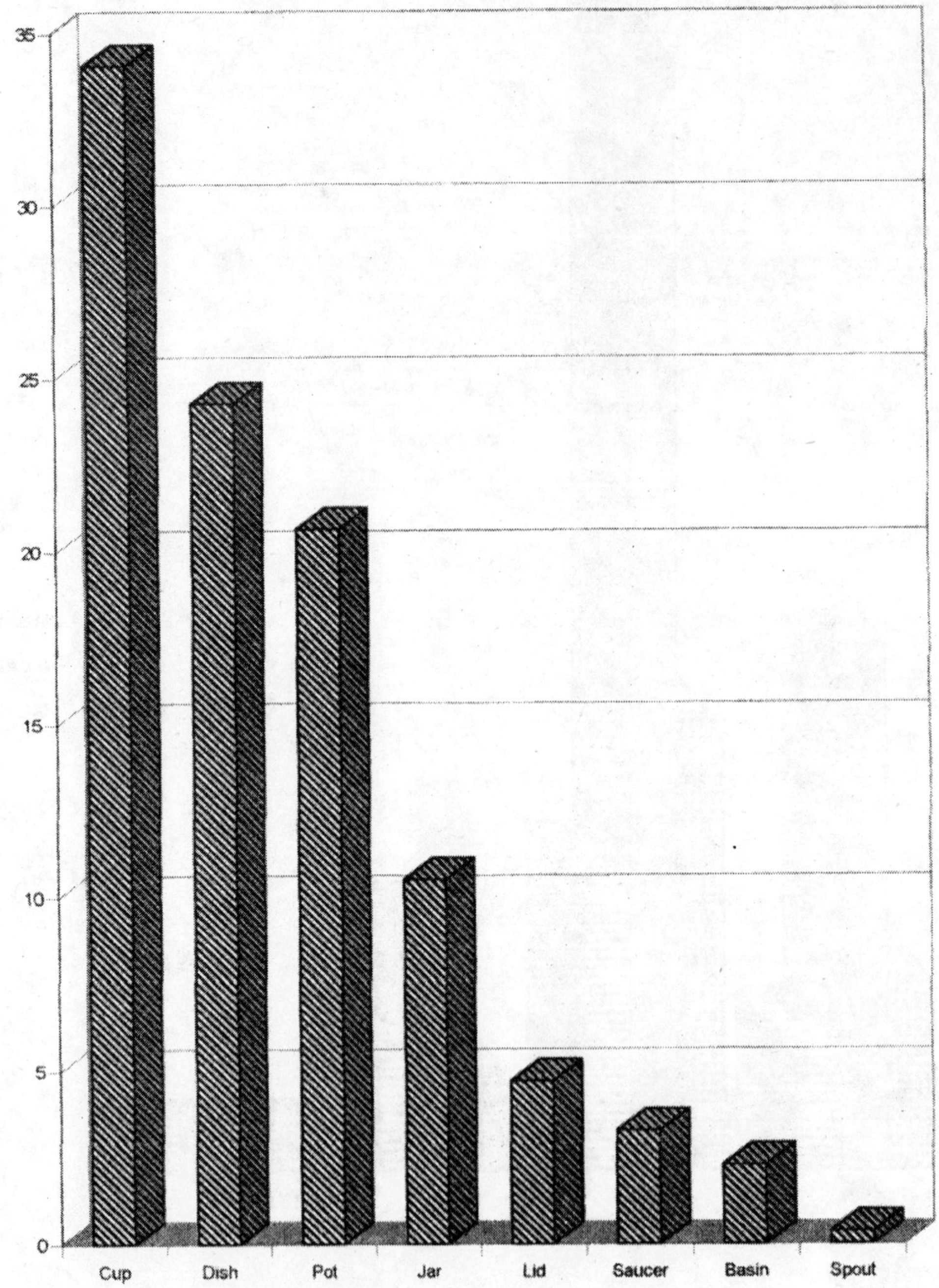

Fig.6: Percentage of various shapes of Red Ware.

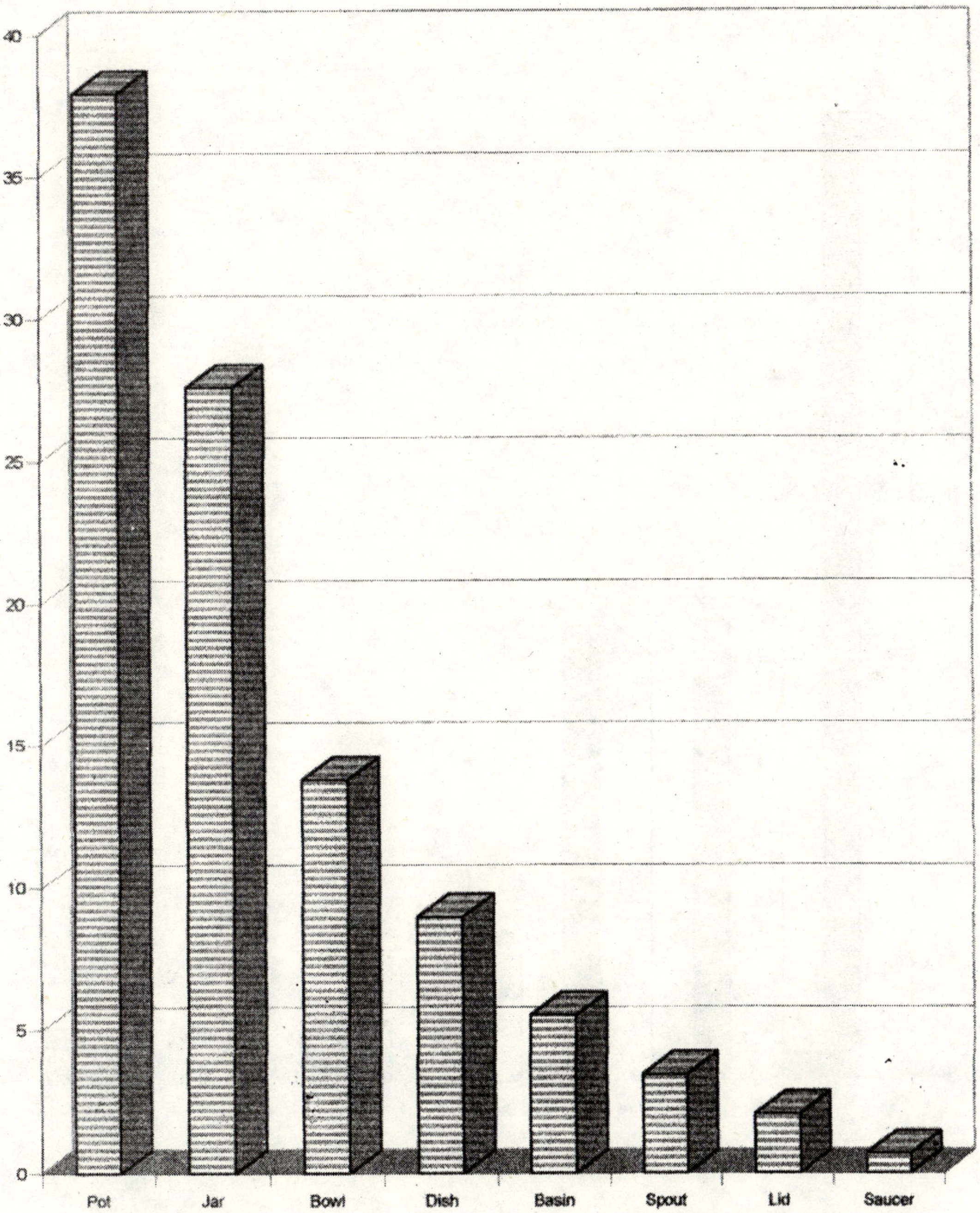

Fig.7: Percentage of various shapes of Red-Slipped Ware.

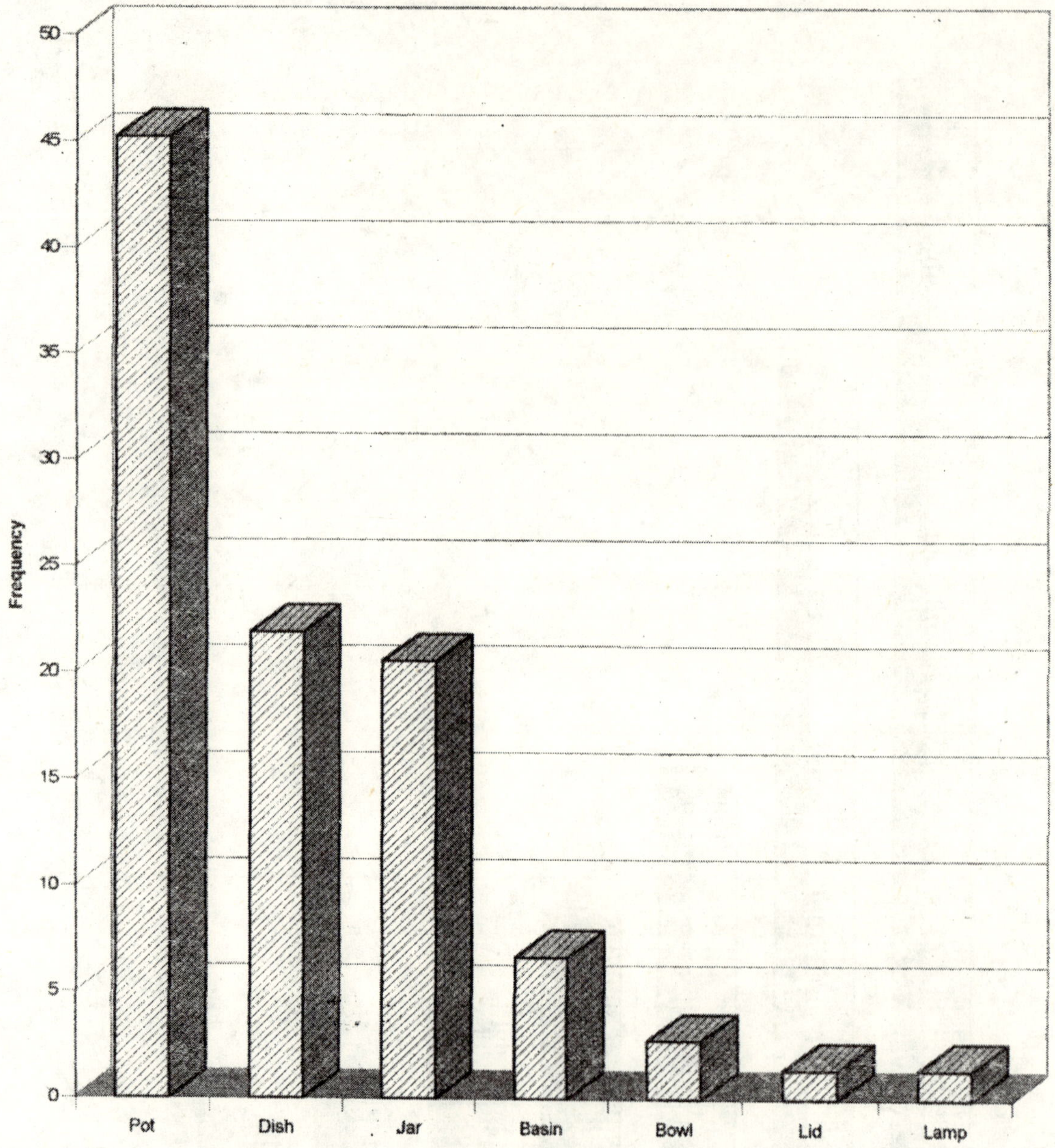

Fig.8: Percentage of various shapes of Grey Ware.

4.5.V Selected specimen of each Wares is as follows

*Diam=Diameter ; Sr. No.=Serial Number.

Plate I.a., Nos. 1-6 Red-Slipped Ware jars.

Sr. No. 1
Location: C3 NW Lot 1037 depth 0.71m (2).
Fragment: Rim, neck and body. Diam. 10cm.
Form: Jar-everted rim, narrow neck, globular body and thick wall.
Fabric: Coarse.
Surfaces: Red slipped, rough.

Sr. No. 2
Location: C3 NW Lot 1018 depth 0.55m (2).
Fragment: Rim, neck and upper body. Diam. 22cm.
Form: Storage Jar-flat projecting short rim but with a very prominent projection, almost no neck, thick wall, narrow mouth.
Fabric: Coarse.
Surfaces: Red slipped, weathered.

Sr. No. 3
Location: C3 NW Lot 1018 depth 0.55m (2).
Fragment: Rim, neck and upper body. Diam. 14cm.
Forms: Jar-flat projecting short rim, almost no neck, thick wall and narrow mouth.
Fabric: Coarse.
Surfaces: Red slipped, rough.

Sr. No. 4
Location: C3 NE Lot 1008 depth 0.40m (1).
Fragment: Rim and upper body. Diam. 26cm.
Form: Jar-externally thickened and rounded rim, groove on the interior, complete form unknown.
Fabric: Coarse.
Surfaces: Red slipped, rough.

Sr. No. 5
Location: C3 NW Lot 1006 depth 0.25m (1).
Fragment: Ring base.
Form: Jar-ring base of a jar, short slightly flared base with flat projecting end.
Fabric: Medium.
Surfaces: Red slipped, smooth.

Sr. No. 6
Location: C3 NE Lot 1008 depth 0.40m (1).

Fragment: Rim and upper body. Diam. 20cm.
Form: Jar-slightly out turned and externally thickened rim.
Fabric: Medium.
Surfaces: Red slipped.

Plate I.b., Nos.7-18 Red-Slipped Ware jars.

Sr. No. 7
Location: C3 SW Lot 1028 depth 0.38m (2).
Fragment: Rim and neck. Diam. 20cm.
Form: Jar-out turned externally thickened rounded rim, short neck.
Fabric: Medium.
Surfaces: Red slipped on exterior, weathered.

Sr. No. 8
Location: C3 SE Lot 1025 depth 0.30m (2).
Fragment: Rim, neck and upper body. Diam. 24cm.
Forms: Jar-triangular rim, slightly vertical neck.
Fabrics: Coarse.
Surfaces: Red slipped on both sides, weathered.

Sr. No. 9
Location: C3 SE Lot 1045 depth 0.90m (3).
Fragment: Rim, neck and upper body. Diam. 12cm.
Form: Jar-flat projecting rim , vertical neck.
Fabric: Coarse.
Surfaces: Red slipped on both sides, weathered.

Sr. No. 10
Location: C3 NW Lot 1006 depth 0.25m (1)
Fragment: Rim and upper body. Diam. 24cm.
Form: Jar-short out turned rim, externally thickened and globular body.
Fabric: Medium.
Surfaces: Red slipped, rough.

Sr. No. 11
Location: C3 NW Lot 1037 depth 0.71m (2).
Fragment: Rim and shoulder. Diam. 20cm.
Form: Jar-out turned and internally thicken rim, short concave neck, groove on the top of the rim.
Fabric: Coarse.
Surfaces: Red slipped, Weathered.

Sr. No. 12
Location: C3 NE Lot 1016 depth 0.50m (2).

Fragment: Rim and neck. Diam. 16cm.
Form: Jar-internally flat, slightly projecting rim, and externally thicken, groove on interior of rim.
Fabric: Coarse.
Surfaces:, Red slipped, Weathered.

Sr. No. 13
Location: C3 NE Lot 1018 depth 0.60m (2).
Fragment: Rim and neck. Diam. 24cm.
Form: Jar-squarish rim, vertical neck, complete form unascertained.
Fabric: Medium.
Surfaces: Red slipped, rough.

Sr. No. 14
Location: C3 NW Lot 1015 depth 0.48m (3).
Fragment: Rim and neck. Diam. 16cm.
Form: Jar-externally projecting beak rim, vertical neck and wide groove on the rim.
Fabric: Medium.
Surfaces: Red slipped on both sides, weathered.

Sr. No. 15
Location: C3 SW Lot 1044 depth 0.80m (3).
Fragment: Rim, neck and upper body. Diam. 20cm.
Form: Jar-flared out rim with a groove on the rim, internally bevelled, a small ridge on the shoulder and grafitti in the form of vertical lines on the internal rim.
Fabric: Coarse
Surfaces: Red slipped, smooth.

Sr. No. 16
Location: C3 SW Lot 1044 depth 0.80m (3).
Fragment: Rim. Diam. 16cm.
Form: Jar-flat projecting rim with the prominent ridge on the external of the rim and slightly vertical neck, narrow mouth.
Fabric: Medium.
Surfaces: Red slipped on both sides, weathered.

Sr. No. 17
Location: C3 NW Lot 1010 depth 0.40m (2).
Fragment: Rim and neck. Diam. 24cm.
Form: Jar-externally projecting squarish rim, short vertical neck, groove on interior of the rim.
Fabric: Medium.
Surfaces: Red slipped on both sides, weathered.

Sr. No. 18
Location: C3 NW Lot 1013 depth 0.43m (2)
Fragment: Rim. Diam. 12cm.
Form: Jar-flat projecting rim with a groove and narrow mouth.
Fabric: Fine.
Surfaces: Red slipped on both sides, weathered.

Plate II.a., No.19 Red-Slipped Ware pots, Nos.20-24 Red-Slipped Ware jars, No. 25, 28, Red-Slipped Ware pot, Nos. 26-27, 29-31 Red-Slipped Ware jars, Nos. 31.1 Red-Slipped Ware pot.

Sr. No 19
Location: C3 SE Lot 1045 depth 0.90m (3).
Fragment: Rim, neck and upper body. Diam. 22cm.
Form: Small pot-short out turned rim, convex neck, possibly globular body.
Fabric: Coarse.
Surfaces: Red slipped on the exterior, weathered.

Sr. No 20
Location: C3 NW Lot 1018 depth 0.55m (2).
Fragment: Rim and neck. Diam. 18cm.
Form: Jar-beaked shape rim and vertical neck, complete vessel form unknown.
Fabric: Coarse.
Surfaces: Red slipped on exterior, weathered.

Sr. No. 21
Location: C3 NW Lot 1013 depth 0.43m (2)
Fragment: Rim and neck. Diam. 14cm.
Form: Jar-beaded under-cutting rim and vertical neck.
Fabric: Coarse.
Surfaces: Red slipped on both sides, weathered.

Sr. No. 22
Location: C3 NE Lot 1118 depth 0.50m (2).
Fragment: Rim, neck and body. Diam. 10cm.
Form: Jar-everted rim, short vertical neck.
Fabric: Medium.
Surfaces: Red slipped, weathered.

Sr. No. 23
Location: C3 NW Lot 1013 depth 0.43m (2).
Fragment: Rim and neck. Diam. 14cm.
Form: Jar-slightly out turned with flat projecting rim, narrow mouth and long neck.
Fabric: Medium.
Surfaces: Red slipped, rough.

Sr. No 24
Location: C3 NW Lot 1037 depth 0.71m (2).
Fragment: Rim and neck. Diam. 16cm.
Form: Jar-out turned rim, globular body, short neck, and thick wall.
Fabric: Coarse.
Surfaces: Red slipped on both sides, smooth.

Sr. No. 25
Location: C3 SW Lot 1044 depth 0.80m (3).
Fragment: Rim and neck. Diam. 8cm.
Form: Miniature pot-beaded under-cutting rim, probably vertical neck.
Fabric: Medium.
Surfaces: Red slipped on both sides, weathered.

Sr. No. 26
Location: C3 NW Lot 1014 depth 0.46m (2).
Fragment: Rim, neck and upper body. Diam. 18cm.
Form: Jar-out turned and externally thickened rim, concave neck, and groove on the interior below the rim portion.
Fabric: Coarse.
Surfaces: Red slipped, weathered.

Sr. No. 27
Location: C3 SW Lot 1026 depth 0.35m (2).
Fragment: Rim, neck and upper body. Diam. 20cm.
Form: Jar-externally out turned rim, rounded on the top, concave neck, globular body.
Fabric: Coarse.
Surfaces: Red slipped, weathered.

Sr. No. 28
Location: C3 SW Lot 1026 depth 0.35 (2).
Fragment: Rim and neck. Diam. 10cm.
Form: Miniature pot-externally projecting beaked rim.
Fabric: Fine.
Surfaces: Red slipped, weathered.

Sr. No. 29
Location: C3 SE Lot 1025 depth 0.30m (2).
Fragment: Rim, neck and upper body. Diam. 18cm.
Form: Jar-externally projecting rounded rim, short vertical neck.
Fabric: Medium.
Surfaces: Red slipped on exterior side, weathered.

Sr. No. 30
Location: C3 NE Lot 1041 depth 0.82m (3).
Fragment: Rim and neck. Diam. 12cm.
Form: Small jar-short out turned rim and concave neck.
Fabric: Medium.
Surfaces: Red slipped, weathered.

Sr. No. 31
Location: C3 NE Lot 1818 depth 0.60m (2).
Fragment: Rim, neck and shoulder. Diam. 14cm.
Form: Jar-out turned and slightly pointed rim , concave neck, possibly globular body.
Fabric: Medium.
Surfaces: Thin red slipped on both sides, exterior rough.

Sr. No. 31.1
Location: C3 NW Lot 1018 depth 0.55m (2).
Fragment: Base and lower body.
Form: Pot-flat base, thin wall, possibly globular body.
Fabric: Coarse.
Surfaces: Red slipped on exterior, weathered.

Plate II.b. No.32 Red-Slipped Ware pot, No.33 Red-Slipped Ware jar, Nos. 34-37 Red-Slipped Ware bowls

Sr. No. 32
Location: C3 NW Lot 1006 depth 0.25m (1).
Fragment: Rim and upper body. Diam. 8cm.
Form: Small pot-everted rim, concave neck, possibly globular body.
Fabric: Medium.
Surfaces: Red slipped, smooth.

Sr. No. 33
Location: C3 SE Lot 1045 depth 0.45m (3).
Fragment: Rim and neck. Diam. 22cm.
Form: Uncertain or Unascertained, probably jar-out turned externally thickened rim.
Fabric: Medium.
Surfaces: Red slipped, weathered.

Sr. No. 34
Location: C3 NE Lot 1008 depth 0.40m (1).
Fragment: Rim and upper body. Diam. 24cm.
Form: Bowl-featureless rim with flat top, slightly side tapers towards the base, thin wall.
Fabric: Coarse.
Surfaces: Red slipped on both sides, smooth.

Sr. No. 35
Location: C3 NE Lot 1005 Depth 0.25m (1)
Fragment: Rim and body. Dia 22cm.
Form: Shallow bowl-featureless rim but thin on the top and tapering towards the base, sagging body.
Fabric: Coarse.
Surfaces: Red slipped on both sides, rough.

Sr. No. 36
Location: C3 NW Lot 1013 depth 0.43m (2).
Fragment: Rim and body. Diam. 12cm.
Form: Bowl-convex body with groove.
Fabric: Medium.
Surfaces: Red slipped on both sides, weathered.

Sr. No. 37
Location: C3 NE Lot 1017 0.55 (2).
Fragment: Rim and lower body. Diam. 4cm.
Form: Small bowl/Lid-short vertical rim, prominent ridge on the outer side and convex profile.
Fabric: Coarse.
Surfaces: Red slipped, rough.

Plate III.a. Nos. 38-42 Red-Slipped Ware bowls, Nos. 43-45 Red-Slipped Ware basins.

Sr. No. 38
Location: C3 NW Lot 1014 depth 0.46m (2).
Fragment: Rim and body. Diam. 10cm.
Form: Convex sided bowl-featureless rim, shallow groove on the exterior of rim.
Fabric: Medium.
Surfaces: Red slipped, smooth.

Sr. No. 39
Location: C3 NW Lot 1037 depth 0.71m (2).
Fragment: Rim and body. Diam. 16cm.
Form: Bowl-featureless rim, convex sided body.
Fabric: Medium.
Surfaces: Red slipped on both sides, smooth.

Sr. No. 40
Location: C3 NW Lot 1006 depth 0.25m (1).
Fragment: Rim and body. Diam. 26cm.
Form: Convex side bowl-featureless rim but rounded, groove on the body of the bowl.
Fabric: Coarse.
Surfaces: Thin red slipped, rough on exterior and smooth on interior,.

Sr. No 40.1
Location: C3 NE Lot 1018 depth 0.60m (1).
Fragment: Base and lower part
Form: Shallow bowl-disc base.
Fabric: Coarse.
Surfaces: Red slipped on both sides, smooth.

Sr. No. 41
Location: C3 NW Lot 1006 depth 0.25m (1).
Fragment: Rim. Diam.6cm.
Form: Unascertained-possibly a bowl with beaded rim.
Fabric: Coarse.
Surfaces: Red slipped, weathered.

Sr. No. 42
Location: C3 NW Lot 1006 depth 0.25m (1).
Fragment: Base and lower body.
Form: Convex sided bowl-flat base.
Fabric: Medium.
Surfaces: Thin red slipped, weathered on exterior.

Sr. No. 43
Location: C3 SE Lot 1045 depth 0.90m (3)
Fragment: Rim and body. Diam. 28cm.
Form: Small basin-flat slightly externally thickened rim.
Fabric: Coarse.
Surfaces: Red slipped on both sides, rough.

Sr. No. 44
Location: C3 SW Lot 1033 depth 0.48m (2).
Fragment: Rim and neck. Diam. 24cm.
Form: Basin-vertical sides featureless rounded rim with a prominent ridge on the external below the rim portion.
Fabric: Coarse.
Surfaces: Red slipped on both sides, weathered.

Sr. No. 45
Location: C3 SW Lot 1044 depth 0.80m (3)
Fragment: Rim and neck. Diam. 28cm.
Form: Basin-incurved in a triangular fashion, convex profile.
Fabric: Coarse.
Surfaces: Red slipped on both sides, weathered.

Plate III.b. No.46 Red-Slipped Ware dish, No.47 Red-Slipped Ware cylindrical jar, Nos. 48-49 Red-Slipped Ware Lids, No. 50 Red-Slipped Ware flare stand, Nos. 51-53 Red-Slipped Ware spouts.

Sr. No. 46
Location: C3 NW Lot 1014 depth 0.46m (2).
Fragment: Rim and body. Diam. 24cm.
Form: Dish-internally beaked rim and ledge on exterior shoulder.
Fabric: Coarse.
Surfaces: Red slipped on both sides, smooth.

Sr. No. 47
Location: C3 SE Lot 1032 depth 0.45m (2).
Fragment: Base and lower body.
Form: Cylindrical jar-convex base, roughly cylindrical side.
Fabric: Coarse.
Surfaces: Red slipped, weathered.

Sr. No. 48
Location: C3 NE Lot 1017 depth 0.55m (2).
Fragment: Rim and body. Diam. 4cm.
Form: Lid-closing-inside, prominent ridge, carination on the waist end and tapering base.
Fabric: Coarse.
Surfaces: Red slipped, rough.

Sr. No. 49
Location: C3 SW Lot 1026 depth 0.35m (2).
Fragment: Rim and body. Diam. 26cm.
Form: Possibly lid-internally thickened under-cut rim, thick wall.
Fabric: Coarse.
Surfaces: Red slipped, weathered.

Sr. No. 50
Location: C3 NW Lot 1018 depth 0.55m (2).
Fragment: Rim and neck. Diam. 6cm.
Form: Miniature hollow flare stand.
Fabric: Medium.
Surfaces: Red slipped on exterior, smooth.

Sr. No. 51
Location: C3 SE 1027 depth 0.35m (2).
Fragment: Spout.
Form: Spout-knobbed spout.
Fabric: Coarse.
Surfaces: Red slipped, weathered.

Sr. No. 52
Location: C3 NE Lot 1041 depth 0.82m (3)
Fragment: Spout.
Form: Spout with a knob at its base.
Fabric: Medium.
Surfaces: Red slipped, rough.

Sr. No. 53
Location: C3 NE Lot 1018 depth 0.60m (1).
Fragment: Spout.
Form: Spout-almost tubular.
Fabric: Coarse.
Surfaces: Red slipped on the both sides, rough.

Plate IV.a. Nos.54-62 Red Ware jars.

Sr. No. 54
Location: C3 NW Lot 1018 depth 0.55m (2).
Fragment: Rim, neck and body. Diam. 20cm.
Form: Jar-vertical externally thickened rim.
Fabric: Coarse.
Surfaces: Unslipped weathered.

Sr. No. 55
Location: C3 NW Lot 1006 depth 0.25m (1)
Fragment: Body portion.
Form: Storage jar-decorated with two appliquéd horizontal bands in the lower portion, one being wavy, hand made.
Fabric: Coarse.
Surfaces: Unslipped, weathered.

Sr. No. 56
Location: C3 NW Lot 1037 depth 0.71m (2).
Fragment: Rim and neck. Diam. 18cm.
Form: Jar-externally projecting rim with slightly convex top and vertical neck.
Fabric: Coarse.
Surfaces: Unslipped, weathered.

Sr. No. 57
Location: C3 NW Lot 1009 depth 0.30m (2).
Fragment: Rim and neck. Diam. 26cm.
Form: Jar-slightly out-turned externally thickened under cut rim.
Fabric: Coarse.
Surfaces: Unslipped, weathered.

Sr. No. 58
Location: C3 NW Lot 1014 depth 0.46m (2).
Fragment: Rim and neck. Diam. 26cm.
Form: Jar-out turned thickened rim, short concave neck.
Fabric: Coarse.
Surfaces: Unslipped, weathered.

Sr. No. 59
Location: C3 NW Lot 1006 depth 0.25m (1).
Fragment: Rim. Diam. 20cm.
Form: Jar-out turned rim, pointed on the top and thick lower portion.
Fabric: Coarse.
Surfaces: Unslipped, weathered.

Sr. No. 60
Location: C3 NW Lot 1037 depth 0.71m (2).
Fragment: Rim and neck. Diam. 24cm.
Form: Jar-prominent externally projecting rim, almost straight side.
Fabric: Medium.
Surfaces: Unslipped, weathered.

Sr. No. 61
Location: C3 SE Lot 1045 depth 0.90m (3).
Fragment: Rim and neck. Diam. 14cm.
Form: Jar-slightly out turned thickened rim, narrow orifices.
Fabric: Coarse.
Surfaces: Unslipped, rough.

Sr. No. 62
Location: C3 NE Lot 1018 depth 0.60m (2).
Fragment: Rim, neck and shoulder. Diam.16cm.
Form: Jar-externally thickened rim, short neck.
Fabric: Coarse.
Surfaces: Unslipped, weathered.

Plate IV-b: Red Ware: No. 63-Pot, Nos. 64-65-Jars, No.66-Pot, Nos. 67-69-Jars, No.70-Unascertained vessel.

Sr. No. 63
Location: C3 SE Lot 1045 depth 0.90m (3).
Fragment: Rim, neck and upper body. Diam. 14cm.
Form: Small pot-slightly out-turned and externally thickened rim, high neck.
Fabric: Coarse.
Surfaces: Unslipped, weathered.

Sr. No. 64
Location: C3 NE Lot 1008 depth 0.40m (1).
Fragment: Rim, neck and upper body. Diam. 16cm.
Form: Jar-vertical pointed rim with a prominent ridge on the outer side of the rim which is under cut .
Fabric: Medium.
Surfaces: Unslipped.

Sr. No. 65
Location: C3 NE Lot 1003 depth 0.16m (1).
Fragment: Rim. Dia 20cm.
Form: Jar-out curved beak rim with a deep groove on the top and internally bevelled rim.
Fabric: Coarse.
Surfaces: Unslipped, rough.

Sr. No. 66
Location: C3 SW Lot 1044 depth 0.80m (3).
Fragment: Rim neck and upper body. Diam. 16cm.
Form: Pot-out turned externally thickened under-cut rim, grove on the top of the rim, thin wall.
Fabric: Coarse.
Surfaces: Unslipped, weathered.

Sr. No. 67
Location: C3 NW Lot 1006 depth 0.25m (1).
Fragment: Rim, neck and upper body. Diam. 24cm.
Form: Jar-externally thickened rim, short vertical neck, globular body.
Fabric: Coarse.
Surfaces: Unslipped, weathered.

Sr. No. 68
Location: C3 NE Lot 1003 depth 0.16m (1).
Fragment: Rim and neck. Diam. 14cm.
Form: Jar-simple everted rim with ridge, short neck, probably rounded body.
Fabric: Coarse
Surfaces: Unslipped, rough on both sides.

Sr. No. 69
Location: C3 NE Lot 1017 depth 0.55m (2).
Fragment: Rim, neck and upper body. Diam. 14cm.
Form: Jar-perpendicular rim with a groove in the centre, thickened externally.
Fabric: Coarse.
Surfaces: Unslipped.

Sr. No. 70
Location: C3 NW Lot 1037 depth 0.71m (2).
Fragment: Body and neck.
Form: Complete form Unascertained, two horizontal band on the lower neck.
Fabric: Coarse.
Surfaces: Unslipped.

Plate V.a. Red Ware: Nos. 71-78-Cups.

Sr. No. 71
Location: C3 SE Lot 1025 depth 0.30m (2).
Fragment: Rim and body. Diam. 18cm.
Form: Cup-featureless pointed rim, tapering body, thin wall.
Fabric: Coarse.
Surfaces: Unslipped, rough.

Sr. No. 72
Location: C3 SW Lot 1028 depth 0.38m (2)
Fragment: Rim and body. Diam. 24cm.
Form: Pointed cup-short featureless vertical rim.
Fabric: Coarse.
Surfaces: Unslipped, rough.

Sr. No. 73
Location: C3 NE Lot 1018 depth 0.60m (2).
Fragment: Rim and body. Diam.26cm.
Form: Cup-slightly pointed rim, thick upper body wall.
Fabric: Coarse.
Surfaces: Unslipped, rough.

Sr. No. 74
Location: C3 SW Lot 1028 depth 0.38m (2).
Fragment: Rim and body. Diam. 24cm.
Form: Cup-short featureless pointed rim.
Fabric: Coarse.
Surfaces: Unslipped, rough.

Sr. No. 75
Location: C3 NW Lot 1009 depth 0.30m (2)
Fragment: Rim and body. Diam. 16cm.
Form: Cup-short vertical featureless rim, pointed on the top and tapering side.
Fabric: Medium.
Surfaces: Unslipped, rough.

Sr. No. 76
Location: C3 NE Lot 1018 depth 0.60m (2).
Fragment: Rim and body. Diam. 28cm.
Form: Cup-inverted rim, tapering body.
Fabric: Coarse
Surfaces: Unslipped, rough.

Sr. No. 77
Location: C3 NE Lot 1008 depth 0.40m (1).
Fragment: Rim and body. Diam. 8cm.
Form: Small cup-featureless pointed rim, probably rounded body.
Fabric: Coarse.
Surfaces: Unslipped, rough.

Sr. No. 78
Location: C3 NE Lot 1018 depth 0.60m (2).
Fragment: Rim and body. Diam. 22cm.
Form: Small cup-slightly everted rim, thin wall, tapering body.
Fabric: Coarse.
Surfaces: Unslipped, rough.

Plate V.b. Red Ware: Nos. 79-86-Cups.

Sr. No. 79
Location: C3 SW Lot 1024 depth 0.30m (2).
Fragment: Rim and upper body. Diam. 36cm.
Form: Thick walled cup-vertical sides, featureless but flat rim.
Fabric: Coarse.
Surfaces: Unslipped, rough.

Sr. No. 80
Location: C3 NE Lot 1016 depth 0.50m (2).
Fragment: Rim and body. Diam. 24cm.
Form: Cup-simple inverted pointed and internally bevelled rim, slightly convex base, thick wall.
Fabric: Coarse.
Surfaces: Unslipped, rough.

Sr. No. 81
Location: C3 NE Lot 1008 depth 0.40m (1).
Fragment: Rim and body. Diam. 24cm.
Form: Cup-featureless rim, slightly incurved.
Fabric: Coarse.
Surfaces: Unslipped, rough.

Sr. No. 82
Location: C3 NE Lot 1041 depth 0.82m (3)
Fragment: Rim and body. Diam. 6cm.
Form: Cup-inverted side, convex body.
Fabric: Coarse.
Surfaces: Unslipped, rough.

Sr. No. 83
Location: C3 NE Lot 1041 depth 0.82m (3).
Fragment: Rim and body. Diam. 20cm.
Form: Cup-slightly inverted rim and blunt carination on the shoulder, rounded body.
Fabric: Coarse.
Surfaces: Unslipped, rough.

Sr. No. 84
Location: C3 SE Lot 1045 depth 0.90m (3).
Fragment: Base and lower body.
Form: Probably cup, disc base, flaring sides.
Fabric: Coarse.
Surfaces: Unslipped, rough.

Sr. No. 85
Location: C3 NE Lot 1008 depth 0.40m (1).
Fragment: Lower body and base.
Form: Cup-disc base of a shallow bowl, grooves on the interior part.
Fabric: Coarse.
Surfaces: Unslipped, rough.

Sr. No. 86
Location: C3 NE Lot 1008 depth 0.40m (1).
Fragment: Base and lower body.
Form: Cup-disc base of a cup, string cutting mark on the bottom.
Fabric: Coarse.
Surfaces: Unslipped, rough.

Plate VI.a. Red Ware: Nos.87-92: Saucers.

Sr. No. 87
Location: C3 NE Lot 1012 depth 0.45m (2).
Fragment: Fragment of saucer. Diam. 10cm.
Form: Small saucer-short slightly out turned sides and flat base, almost complete vessel.
Fabric: Coarse.
Surfaces: Unslipped, rough.

Sr. No. 88
Location: C3 NW Lot 1037 depth 0.71m (2)
Fragment: Rim and body. Diam. 24cm.
Form: Saucer-short slightly incurved and featureless rim, flat base.
Fabric: Coarse.
Surfaces: Unslipped, rough.

Sr. No. 89
Location: C3 NW Lot 1013 depth 0.43m (2).
Fragment: Rim and body. Diam. 14cm.
Form: Saucer-short inverted and pointed rim.
Fabric: Medium.
Surfaces: Unslipped, rough.

Sr. No. 90
Location: C3 NW Lot 1009 depth 0.30m (2).
Fragment: Rim and body. Diam. 22cm.
Form: Small saucer-slightly pointed rim and flat base.
Fabric: Medium.
Surfaces: Unslipped, rough.

Sr. No. 91
Location: C3 SE Lot 1027 depth 0.35m (2).
Fragment: Rim and upper body. Diam. 30cm.
Form: Saucer-convex sided body.
Fabric: Coarse.
Surfaces: Unslipped, rough.

Sr. No. 92
Location: C3 SE Lot 1045 depth 0.90m (3).
Fragment: Rim and neck. Diam. 14cm.
Form: Saucer-featureless pointed rim.
Fabric: Coarse.
Surfaces: Unslipped, rough.

Plate VI.b.: Red Ware: Nos.93-99.1-Lids, Nos. 100-101-Basins, No. 102-Dish/barin.

Sr. No. 93
Location: C3 NE Lot 1018 depth 0.60m (2).
Fragment: Rim and upper body. Diam. 18cm.
Form: Lid-externally projecting rim and having a groove on the rim.
Fabric: Coarse.
Surfaces: Unslipped, rough.

Sr. No. 94

Location: C3 NW Lot 1006 depth 0.25m (1).
Fragment: Rim, body and base. Diam. 8cm.
Form: Lamp/Lid-slightly flat out side, disc base.
Fabric: Coarse.
Surfaces: Unslipped, rough.

Sr. No. 95
Location: C3 SW Lot 1044 depth 0.80m (3).
Fragment: Rim and neck. Diam. 16cm.
Form: Lid-conical with a flat internally projecting rim.
Fabric: Coarse.
Surfaces: Unslipped, rough.

Sr. No. 96
Location: C3 NE Lot 1012 depth 0.45m (2).
Fragment: Rim and body. Diam. 18cm.
Form: Lid-internally thickened and under cut rim.
Fabric: Coarse.
Surfaces: Unslipped.

Sr. No. 97
Location: C3 NW Lot 1006 depth 0.25m (1).
Fragment: Rim. Diam. 22cm.
Form: Lid-flat rim, projection on exterior and interior.
Fabric: Medium.
Surfaces: Unslipped, rough.

Sr. No . 98
Location: C3 NW Lot 1018 Depth 0.55m (2).
Fragment: Rim and body. Diam. 22cm.
Form: Lid/Small bowl-simple perpendicular rim, ledge shoulder, sharp curve from shoulder to rim.
Fabric: Coarse
Surfaces: Unslipped, rough.

Sr. No. 99
Location: C3 NE Lot 1017 depth 0.55m (2).
Fragment: Rim, neck and body. Diam. 6cm.
Form: Miniature lid-closing-inside, prominent ridge, carination on the waist end and tapering base.
Fabric: Coarse.
Surfaces: Unslipped, rough.

Sr. No. 99.1

Location: C3 NW Lot 1006 depth 0.25m (1)
Fragment: Rim and body. Diam. 16cm.
Form: Lid-closing-inside, prominent ridge, carination on the waist end, tapering base.
Fabric: Coarse.
Surfaces: Unslipped, rough.

Sr. No. 100
Location: C3 SE Lot 1027 depth 0.35m (2).
Fragment: Rim and upper body. Diam. 24cm.
Form: Basin-incurved externally thickened under-cut rim, tapering side.
Fabric: Medium.
Surfaces: Unslipped, rough.

Sr. No. 101
Location: C3 NE Lot 1018 depth 0.60m (2).
Fragment: Rim and upper body. Diam. 26cm.
Form: Basin-beaked rim.
Fabric: Coarse.
Surfaces: Unslipped, weathered.

Sr. No. 102
Location: C3 NE Lot 1003 depth 0.16m (1).
Fragment: Rim and neck. Diam. 12cm.
Form: Dish/barin-simple pointed rim, thickened on the exterior.
Fabric: Medium.
Surfaces: Unslipped, rough.

Plate VII.a.: Grey Ware: No.103-Pot, Nos.104-109-Jars, No.110-Globular pot, No.111-Jar.

Sr. No. 103
Location: C3 SE Lot 1032 depth 0.45m (2).
Fragment: Rim, neck and upper body. Diam. 12cm.
Form: Small pot-everted rim with a externally prominent ridge, short vertical neck.
Fabric: Medium.
Surfaces: Grey slipped, smooth.

Sr. No. 104
Location: C3 NW Lot 1006 depth 0.25m (1).
Fragment: Rim, shoulder and upper body. Diam. 22cm.
Form: Jar-out curved rim with deep groove on the top and internally bevelled rim.
Fabric: Medium.
Surfaces: Grey slipped, smooth.

Sr. No. 105
Location: C3 NW Lot 1018 depth 0.55m (2).
Fragment: Rim and neck. Diam. 18cm.
Form: Jar-out curved rim with deep groove on the top and internally bevelled rim.
Fabric: Coarse.
Surfaces: Grey slipped, smooth.

Sr. No. 106
Location: C3 NW Lot 1010 depth 0.40m (2).
Fragment: Rim and neck. Diam. 24cm.
Form: Jar-drooping rim, two horizontal band on the internal side of the rim.
Fabric: Medium.
Surfaces: Grey slipped on both sides, smooth.

Sr. No. 107
Location: C3 NE Lot 1003 depth 0.16m (1).
Fragment: Rim, neck and upper body. Diam. 20cm.
Form: Medium size jar-flared out rim, short neck, globular body.
Fabric: Coarse.
Surfaces Grey slipped on both sides, exterior rough but interior is smooth.

Sr. No. 108
Location: C3 NE Lot 1003 depth 0.16m (1)
Fragment: Rim. Diam. 14cm.
Form: Jar-out turned pointed rim, pronounced groove at the lower side.
Fabric: Coarse.
Surfaces: Grey slipped, smooth.

Sr. No. 109
Location: C3 NW Lot 1009 depth 0.30m (2).
Fragment: Rim, neck and upper body. Diam. 22cm.
Form: Jar-long out-turned and externally thickened rim, possibly globular body.
Fabric: Coarse.
Surfaces: Grey slipped on both sides, rough.

Sr. No. 110
Location: C3 NW Lot 1018 depth 0.55m (2)
Fragment: Rim, neck and body. Diam. 18cm.
Form: Globular pot-flared out and externally thickened rim, short neck.
Fabric: Coarse.
Surfaces: Grey slipped, rough.

Sr. No. 111
Location: C3 NW Lot 1013 depth 0.43m (2).

Fragment: Rim. Diam. 18cm.
Form: Jar-out curved rim, probably globular body.
Fabric: Coarse
Surfaces: Grey slipped on both sides, rough.

Plate VII.b: Grey Ware: No.111.1-Jar.

Sr. No. 111.1
Location: C3 NE Lot 1003 depth 0.16m (1)
Fragment: Rim, neck and body. Diam. 18cm.
Form: Jar-triangular rim, short vertical neck, probably rounded base.
Fabric: Coarse.
Surfaces: Grey slipped on both sides, exterior surface is smooth.

Plate VIII.a: Grey Ware: No. 112-Lamp. No.113-Bowl, No.114-Lid, No.114.1-Unascertained vessel.

Sr. No. 112
Location: C3 NE Lot 1017 depth 0.55m (2)
Fragment: Rim, body and base. Diam. 6cm.
Form: Lamp-short out turned rim, disc base.
Fabric: Coarse.
Surfaces: Grey slipped.

Sr. No. 113
Location: C3 NE Lot 1041 Depth 0.82m (3).
Fragment: Rim and body. Diam. 20cm.
Form: Shallow bowl-featureless pointed rim, grooves on exterior of body, complete form unknown.
Fabric: Coarse.
Surfaces: Unslipped.

Sr. No. 114
Location: C3 SW Lot 1028 depth 0.38m (2).
Fragment: Rim and body. Diam. 18cm.
Form: Probably lid-rounded featureless rim.
Fabric: Coarse.
Surfaces: Unslipped, weathered.

Sr. No. 114.1
Location: C3 NE Lot 1005 depth 0.25m (1).
Fragment: Rim and neck. Diam. 18cm.
Form: Uncertain-slightly out turned rim, probably globular body.
Fabric: Coarse.
Surfaces: Grey slipped on the outer and internal surface.

Plate VIII.b. No.115 Black-and -Red Ware bowl.

Sr. No. 115
Location: C3 NE Lot 1041 depth 0.82m (3).
Fragment: Rim and body. Diam. 10cm.
Form: Deep bowl-inverted side, convex body.
Fabric: Coarse.
Surfaces: Smooth, slipped, black and red.

5. Minor objects from Padri

5.1. Introduction

The Early Historic level at Padri yielded a large number of antiquities made of terracotta, stones, semi-precious stones, glass, shell, bones and metal. Antiquities of stone are different household objects, human figurines, discs and beads. The terracotta objects include beads, human and animal figurines, boat-shaped motifs, discs, wheels, balls, ear-studs and clay tablet bearing *Brahmi* letters. Besides terracotta, beads of glass and semi-precious stones were recovered from the excavation. On the other hand metal objects consist of iron and copper. There are various objects like points, pendants and arrowheads made of bone. A detailed description of the antiquities is given below.

5.2. Bangles

Bangle is a familiar ornament which is used by people for the purpose of adornment right from the ancient times. During the Early Historic period it has been used as one of the most popular ornaments. Plain and decorated bangles have been found at Ahar (Sankalia *et al.* 1969: 204-205), Kaundinyapur (Dikshit 1968: 123-24), Maheshwar (Sankalia *et al.* 1958: 229-230), Nagara (Mehta 1968: 127-30, Fig.51, 60), Somnath (Nanavati *et al.* 1971: 72-73, Fig.33.3, 15, 16, 18), Amreli (Rao 1966: 109, Plate XLIV, LVA) and Shamalaji (Mehta and Patel 1967: 44-45, Fig.23.1-3). During the period of 100-300 A.D. the shell industry became a common craft. In this period almost all the designs have been found consistently from many places. The five-season excavations at Padri yielded 191 fragments of shell bangle and one fragment of copper bangle. They are found in different shapes and sizes. This crafting of shell bangle is of considerable antiquity and it continued for a long time. The shell working industry expanded here for the production of bangles and various types of beads. Padri, located near the Gulf of Cambay in Saurashtra, produces the evidence of finished bangles and by-products such as debitage, flakes and chips. This suggests that Padri was a shell bangle manufacturing centre as the raw material was easily accessible to the craftsmen. Waste products have been recovered from other sites in Gujarat like Baroda, Vadnagar and Amreli (Mehta and Shah 1968: 129). At Padri shell bangles are mainly of two types- plain and decorated. The plain bangles are very smooth and show flat surface and area either triangular or rectangular or squarish or oval in section. The decorated bangles show incised lines on the outer surface and with occasional perforations. The layer-wise distribution has been given in **Table 8.**

Table 8: Distribution of bangles

Object	Surface	Layer (1)	Layer (2)	Layer (3)
Bangles	23	29	103	36

The following descriptions will give an idea of different shapes of shell bangles which were obtained from Padri. The important shapes are given below.

Plate IX. Nos.1-19-Shell bangles, No.20-copper bangle.

* T.=Thickness, W.=Width

No. 1

A fragment of plain bangle, squarish in section. Measurement 4.98/3.86 mm (L1 NE, Lot 7302, depth 0.30 m., (2)).

No.2

A thick variant of No. 1, rectangular in section. Measurement T.3.85 mm, W.9.13 mm (M1 NW, Lot 9303, depth 0.35 m, (2)).

No.3

A fragment of bangle with a ridge in the central part, rectangular in section. Measurement. T. 3.82 mm, W. 13.23 mm (Surface collection.91-92)

No.4.

A fragment of bangle, rectangular in section. Measurement T.5.66 mm, W.11.00 mm (M2 SW, Lot 11006, depth 0.43 m., (2)).

No.5

A thick variant of No.4, squarish in section. Measurement T.3.82 mm W.20.10 mm (TTN A2, NW, Lot 120002, depth 0.35 m, (2)).

No.6

A thin variant of No.4, squarish in section. Measurement T. 4.87 mm, W.7.35 mm (L1 SE, Lot 7102, depth 0.35 m, (2)).

No.7

A fragment of bangle, rectangular in section. Outer surface having circular panel in relief and incised floral pattern. Measurement T. 4.94 mm W. 7.42 mm (TTN A2 NW, Lot 20103, depth 0.37 m, (2)).

No.8

A fragment of bangle, irregularly circular, outer surface having segments, squarish in section. Measurements T. 4.86 mm, W. 4.91 mm (M2 SE, Lot 11105, depth 1.67 m, (1)).

No.9

A fragment of bangle, outer surface having leaf like decorations, squarish in section. Measurements T. 6.71 mm, W. 5.77 mm (MX1 SW, Lot 8002, depth 0.23 m, (2)).

No.10

A fragment of a bangle with one vertical line on the upper surface, rectangular in section. Measurements T. 3.26 mm, W. 5.64 mm (A1 SW, Lot 10011, depth o.63 m (2)).

No.11

A fragment of bangle, squarish in section. Measurement T. 5.34 mm, W. 3.60 mm (TTE A1 SW, Lot 110011, depth 0.63 m, (3)).

No.12

A fragment of bangle, broad and thick, outer surface having group of incised vertical lines and leaf like decoration, rectangular in section. Measurements T. 5.86 mm, W. 17.06 mm (TTE A1 SW, Lot 110014, depth 0.74 m, (3)).

No.13

Same as No.12, rectangular in section. Measurements T. 7.11 mm, W.16.48 mm (LX1 NW, Lot 10102, depth 0.21 m, (1)).

No.14

Same as No.13, rectangular in section. (A1 SW, Lot 110008, depth 0.47 m, (2)).

No.15

A fragment of bangle with two incised lines on the top, rectangular in section. Measurements T. 4.66 mm, W.7.30 mm (A1 SW, Lot 110008, depth 0.47 m, (2)).

No.16

Same as No.12, squarish in section . Measurements T. 13.40 mm, W.14.18 mm (K1 NE, Lot 12010, depth 0.80 m, (3)).

No.17

A fragment of plain bangle with three incised lines on the top and flat oval in section. Measurements T. 1.57 mm, W. 1.03 mm (TTE A1 SW, Lot 110001, depth 0.15 m, (2)).

No.18

A variant of No.7, squarish in section. Measurements T. 2.80 mm, W. 2.93 mm (O2 SE, Lot 15006, depth 0.54 m, (3)).

No. 19

A fragment of plain bangle with perforated design, oval in section. Measurement T. 7.27 mm, W.23.03 mm (M1 NW Lot 9306, depth 0.50 m (2)).

No. 20

A fragment of copper bangle, badly corroded, round in section. Measurements T. 0.22 mm, W. 1.27 mm (N2 NE, Lot 14307, depth 0.60 m, (3)).

5.3. Beads

The Early Historic level at Padri yielded a total number of one hundred and twenty seven beads (**Table 9 and Fig.9**) of different raw materials. Numerically, the maximum number of (61) beads are of terracotta, followed by the shell (38), carnelian (8), glass (8), steatite (4), sand stone (2), agate (2), quartz (1), lapis lazuli (1), crystal (1) and chert (1). They are of different shapes. The common shapes are arecanut, truncated, convex, bicone, barrel, globular, convex cone, flat bicone, short cylindrical, hexagonal and disc. Beads have been worn as necklaces. It is a common mode of ornamentation which was known right from the ancient period. As C. Margabandhu (1985: 195) aptly puts, "Beads found from various places not only enable one to judge their aesthetic and technological standards through the successive period in the history of arts and manufacture of beads but also suggest an accurate estimate of cultural contacts with the different region and other parts of India as also perhaps the outside world". Right from the Harappan to the Early Historic period in Indian sub-continent, many lapidaries flourished like Cambay and Broach (Sankalia and Deo 1955: 92-93), Nevasa (Sankalia *et al.* 1960: 367-368). According to Dhavalikar, (Dhavalikar *et al.* 1996:191) Saurashtra is an important bead making centre. It was Yan Chwang (c 629-41 A.D.), a Chinese traveler, who mentioned in the Chinese testimony that beads were exported from Cambay to Egypt and Far eastern countries during the Historical period.

Table 9: Distribution of Beads

Objects	Layer (1)	Layer (2)	Layer (3)	Total
Carnelian	2	4	2	8
Agate	0	0	2	2
Quartz	0	0	1	1
Glass	1	6	1	8
Steatite	3	0	1	4
Lapis-lazuli	0	0	1	1
Terracotta	12	38	11	61
Crystal	1	0	0	1
Chert	0	0	1	1
Sand Stone	1	1	0	2
Shell	12	15	11	38
Total	32	64	31	127

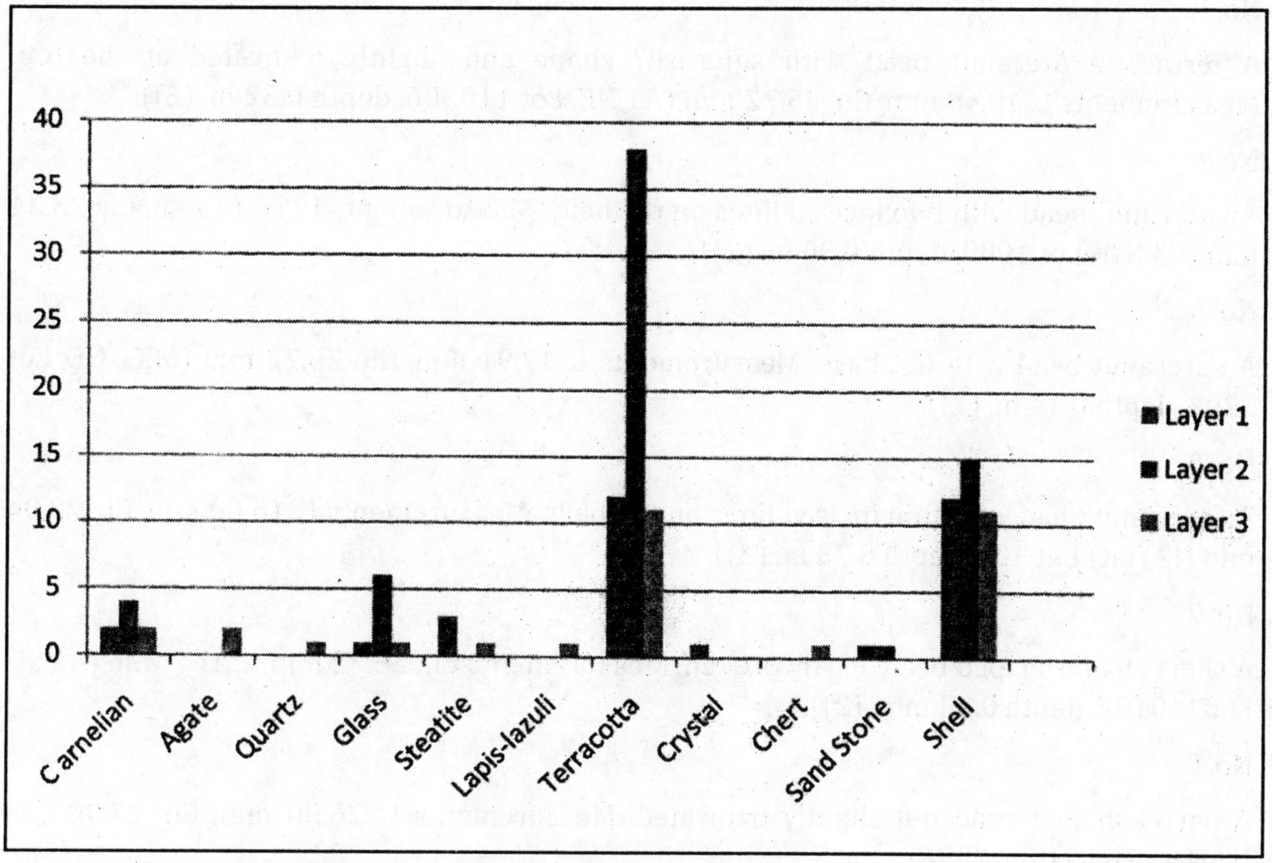

Fig.9: Frequency of beads.

5.3.I. Terracotta beads

Terracotta beads were very popular during the Early Historic period. It is cheaper and easier to make than that of other semi-precious stone beads. Most of the rural poorer section of the society could afford these beads. excavations at Padri yielded sixty one beads of terracotta. The common shapes are arecanut, globular, barrel and toggle. This type of terracotta beads have been found from other sites in western India like Eran, Karad, Chandravali, Karvan, Kaundinyapura, Kayatha, Kondapur, Maheshwar, Maski, Nagar, Nagara, Prabhas Patan, Shamalaji and Timbarva (Margabandhu 1985: 200). The important shapes of terracotta beads are given below.

Plate X.a. Nos.1-11

No.1

A terracotta arecanut bead slightly truncated at the top. Measurements L. 11.79 mm, Cir. 17.78 mm (C3 Lot 1018, NW, depth 0.55 m, (2)).

No.2

A terracotta arecanut bead slightly truncated at the top and rather elongated. Measurements L. 23.14 mm, Cir. 23.81 mm (C3 SE, Lot 1039, depth 0.73 m, (2)).

No.3

A terracotta arecanut bead with squarish? shape and slightly truncated at the top. Measurements L. 18.48 mm, Cir. 25.72 mm (A1 NE, Lot 110306, depth 0.32 m, (2)).

No.4

An arecanut bead with two incised lines on the belly. Measurements L. 17.11 mm, Cir. 23.34 mm (C3 NW, Lot 1009, depth 0.30 m, (2)).

No. 5

An arecanut bead with flat base. Measurements L. 17.91 mm, Cir. 26.22 mm (MX1 NE, Lot 1202, depth 0.14 m, (1)).

No. 6

An arecanut bead with thin incised lines on the belly. Measurements L. 16.60 mm, Cir. 23.94 mm (J2 (pit) Lot 121, depth 0.75 m, (2)).

No. 7

A short bicone shaped bead. Partly broken. Measurements Cir. 26.22 mm, T. 16.9 mm (A1 SE, Lot 110107, depth 0.53 mm, (2)).

No. 8

A barrel-shaped bead but slightly truncated. Measurements L. 26.80 mm, Cir. 27.90 mm (surface collection, 1996)

No.9

A globular bead. Measurements L. 16.44 mm, Cir. 17.62 mm, (NX1 SE, Lot 15006, depth 0.40 m, (2)).

No.10

An arecanut bead. Measurements L. 24.90 mm, Cir. 25.75 mm (C3 NE, Lot 1051, (3)).

No. 11

A arecanut bead with one incised line on the belly. Measurements L. 20.78 mm, Cir. 23.76 mm (LX1 NW, Lot 10109, depth 0.60 m, (2)).

5.3.II. Carnelian

During the Early Historic period, carnelian was the most popular semi-precious stone all over India. The excavation at Padri yielded eight carnelian beads. The lack of evidence for the manufacture of carnelian beads and their small number indicate that these beads were not made at Padri but were imported from elsewhere. During this period Broach and Cambay were well known for bead industries which continued since very early time (Arkell 1936: 292-305). It was Daurte Borbosa, the Portuguese traveler who mentioned in his account that in early 16th century carnelian and other semi-precious stones were exported to the other countries from Cambay. This trade reached its zenith between 13th and 18th century A.D. (Arkell 1936). At present, Cambay is known to other countries as an important bead making centre (Dhavalikar *et al.* 1996: 193). Common shapes in carnelian at Padri include bicone, globular, and barrel.

The important shapes are given below:

Plate X.b. Nos.12-17

No. 12

A bead with short bicone shape. Measurements T.1.87 mm, Cir.5.76 mm (TTN A2 NW, Lot 120104, depth 0.50 m, (2)).

No.13

A globular bead. Measurements Cir. 6.97 mm. (from dugout, 91-92).

No. 14

A short, cylindrical and hexagonal bead. Measurements L. 2.65 mm, Cir. 3.27 mm (K2 NE/SE, Lot 5311, depth 0.90 m, (2)).

No. 15

A standard, circular, barrel-shaped bead. Measurements L. 5.99 mm, T. 4.86 mm (LX1 NW, Lot 10117, depth 0.93 m, (3)).

No. 16

A truncated barrel-shaped bead. Measurements L. 5.99 mm, T. 4.86 mm (LX1 NW, Lot 10117, depth 0.93 m, (3)).

No. 17

A truncated biconvex-shaped bead. Measurements L. 8.18 mm, T. 7.29 mm (TTE A1 SW, Lot 110012, depth 0.68 m, (2)).

5.3.III. Shell beads

The excavation at Padri yielded 38 shell beads. Shell was a popular material for bead in the Early Historic period in this region. The common shapes are disc, cylinder, circular etc. Sometime a few complete shells have also been utilized as beads with hole pierced through them. This type of shell beads have also been reported from other sites in Gujarat like Amreli (Rao 1966: 109, Plate XI.17-19) and Dhatva (Mehta *et al.* 1975: 20).
The important shapes are given below.

Plate X.b. Nos.18-26

No. 18

A short cylindrical-shaped bead. Measurements L. 5.30 mm, Cir. 6.00 mm (NX1 SE, Lot 15002, depth 0.22 m, (1)).

No. 19

A toggle-shaped bead. Measurements L. 12.00 mm, T. 3.16 mm (LX1 NW, Lot 10103, depth 0.30 m, (2)).

No. 20

A convex-shaped bead. Measurements L. 16.44 mm, T. 7.08 mm (O2 SE Lot 15006, depth 0.54 m, (3)).

No. 21

A circular, bicone bead. Measurements L. 10.50 mm, T. 6.91 mm (MX1 SW, Lot 8111, depth 0.92 m, (3)).

No. 22

A short cylindrical bead. Measurements L. 2.94 mm, T. 3.32 mm (L2 NE/SE, Lot 6314, depth 1.05 m, (3)).

No. 23

An oblate-shaped bead. Measurements T. 5.43 mm, Cir.13.43 mm (surface collection, 25/02/96).

No. 24

It is a perforated shell which might have been used as a bead. Measurements L. 21.27 mm, T. 9.17 mm (N1 SW, Lot 13007, depth 0.55 m, (2)).

No. 25

A spherical-shaped bead. Measurements Cir. 10.16 mm (A1 NW, Lot 110202, depth 0.25 m, (2)).

No. 26

A disc-shaped bead. Measurements T.2.89 mm, Cir. 13.10 mm (M1 NE, Lot 9208, depth 0.55 m, (2)).

5.3.IV. Glass beads

The excavation yielded eight glass beads from different layers of habitational deposit at Padri. Glass beads occur from other sites of western India like Ahar, Devnimori, Dwarka, Maheshwar, Nagara, and Vadnagar (Margabandhu 1985). The Early Historic levels at Balathal in Rajasthan have also yielded a large number of glass beads (Misra *et al.* 1995). The important shapes are given below:

Plate X.b. Nos.27-30

No. 27

A spherical-shaped bead. Measurements Cir. 4.57 mm (TTE A1 NW, Lot 110211, depth 0.42 m, (2)).

No.28

A tubular-shaped bead. Color is opaque, orange. Measurements L. 2.78 mm, T. 3.50 mm (L2 NE Lot 6206, depth 0.50 m, (2)).

No. 29

A disc bead. Measurements Cir. 3.31 mm (N2 NE, Lot 14307, depth 0.60 m, (3)).

No.30

A tubular-shaped bead. Color is opaque, red. Measurements L. 12.31 mm, T.3.90 mm (L2 NE, Lot 6209, depth 0.70 m, (2)).

5.3.V. Crystal bead

Plate X.b. No.31

A crystal bead of spherical-shape, slightly truncated. Measurements Cir. 6.91 mm (surface collection 95-96).

5.3.VI. Lapis lazuli beads

Plate X.b. No.32

A lapis lazuli bead of tubular-shape, partly broken. Measurements L. 6.68 mm, T. 4.42 mm (TTN A2 NE, Lot 120006, depth 0.67 m, (3)). This discovery suggests contact with the Afghanistan region, where Lapis lazuli of fine quality is available.

5.3.VII. Chert bead

Plate X.b. No.33

A chert bead of barrel-shape, but slightly truncated at the end. Measurements L. 5.75 mm, T. 4.54 mm. (MX1 NE, Lot 8210, depth 0.72 m, (3)).

5.3.VIII. Agate bead

The excavation yielded two beads of agate which are of barrel shape. Out of these, one is unfinished which indicates the bead making activity at the site. The specimen is made of banded stone. Banded stone is available in Saurashtra, specially in Rajapipla region (Dhavalikar *et al.* 1996: 196).

Plate X.b. No.34

An unfinished agate bead, long, barrel-shaped, circular section without perforation. Measurements L. 10.05 mm, T. 7.46 mm (N2 SE, Lot 14112, depth 0.75 m, (3)).

6. Copper Objects

Few copper objects were found in the excavation at Padri in the Early Historic levels. These objects include a rod, ring, pendant, chisel, knife blade, bangle, couple of coins, tortoise-shaped lamp, bell and a few unidentified fragments.

Plate XI.a. Nos.1-10

No.1

Copper bell, partly broken and corroded. Measurement L. 31.52 mm (MX1 NE, Lot 8201, depth 0.10 m, (1)).

No. 2

A small copper coin. The symbols and the script are not clear. Round shape. Measurements Cir. 12.09 mm, T. 02.87 mm (LX1 NW, Lot 10107, depth 0.50 m, (2))

No. 3

Same as No. 2 but square shaped. Measurements T. 3.75 mm, Cir.12.27 mm (C3 NE, Lot 1003, depth 0.30 m, (1))

No.4

It may be a copper finger ring, round in section. broken and badly corroded. Measurement Cir. 16.4 mm (M2 SW, Lot 11303, Depth 0.53 m, (2))

No. 5

A copper rod, probably kohl-sticks, round in section and rounded at the end. Measurement L.77.25 mm (LX1 NE, Lot 10002, depth 0.32 m, (1)).

No. 6

Copper fragment, it may be a piece of blade. Measurements T.4.44 mm, W.9.12 mm, (L1 SE, Lot 7102, depth 0.35 m, (2)).

No.7

A fragment of antimony rod, round in section. Measurement T.3.79 mm (LX1 NE, Lot 10002, depth 0.32 m, (1)).

No. 8

Copper fragment, it may be a rod. (TTNA4 SE, Lot 18302, depth 1.40 m, (2)).

No. 9

It may be a part of copper knife blade. (TTNA4 SE, Lot 18302, depth 1.40 m, (2))

No. 10

A fragment of plain copper bangle, rectangular in section. Measurements T 0.22 mm, W. 1.47 mm (N2 NE, Lot 14307, depth 0.60 m, (3)).

Plate XI.b.

No. 11

A tortoise-shaped copper lamp : "The copper lamp has a channel to accommodate a wick and four projections on four sides, possibly for tying it with a thread to suspend it." (Shinde 1992: 79-86) Very fragile condition. Measurements L. 9.12 cm, W. 6.32 cm, T. 3.18 cm (C3 SE, Lot 1060 depth 1.45 m, (4)). Similar tortoise-shaped copper objects have been made in India for a variety of purposes like lamp, ash-tray etc. (**Plate XI.c.**).

7. Iron Objects

The five season excavations at Padri yielded a total of thirty three iron objects, out of which sixteen are nails, two knives, a chisel, a pick, a fish hook, a dagger, a bob (or pendulum of bell?) of pendulum, an arrow head, a door chain, a bangle piece, a clamp (?), a hoe, a sickle and four unidentified fragments.

7.1. Nail

Nails are very commonly found in the Early Historic periods. They were used for a number of purposes. But predominantly they were found to have been used for fixing the tiles to the rafters of roof of house (Sankalia *et al.* 1960: 435-36). Nail is the most predominant iron object. But most of them are very fragmentary with their heads and shanks broken. The classification of nail found at Padri is based on the section and form. They can be divided into the following types.

(1) Nail without head and with rectangular cross section,
(2) Nail with knobbed head,
(3) Nail with featureless head and in oval cross section and
(4) Nail with flat square head.

These types of nails have been reported from Somnath (Nanavati *et al.* 1971: 81-83, Fig.37.6-7), Dhatva (Mehta *et al.* 1975: 18-19, Fig.7.3), Nagara (Mehta 1968: 117-118, Fig.55.1-8), Shamalaji (Mehta and Patel 1967: 49-50, Fig.25.4-7), Timbarva (Mehta 1955: 27) and Devnimori (Mehta and Chowdhary 1966: 101-103, Fig.44.21, 44.27).

The important shapes are given below.

Plate XII.a. Nos.1-4

No. 1

Nail with rectangular cross section and featureless head, having tapering end; badly corroded and broken. Measurements L.45.67 mm (L2 NE, Lot 6203, depth 0.35 m, (2)).

No. 2

Similar as No. 1 but with oval cross section. Measurements L.51.27 mm, T. 5.75 mm (MX1 SW, Lot 8106, depth 0.94 m, (2)).

No. 3

Nail with knobbed head, badly corroded. Measurement L.47.40 mm (C3 SE, Lot 1027, depth 0.35 m, (2)).

No. 4

Nail with a flat square head. Partly broken. Measurements L.40.54 mm, T. 13.54 mm (C3 NE, Lot 1007, depth 0.35 m, (1)).

7.2. Chisel

Plate XII.a. No.5

No.5

Only one chisel has been recovered from the excavations. Chisel is usually used by the carpenters. But a blacksmith uses chisel of a very thick, solid metal which can bear the direct blows on its shanks (Coughlan 1956: 113-4, 129). Chisels have been reported from Devnimori (Mehta and Chowdhary 1966: 98-100, Fig.43.12), Paunar (Deo and Dhavalikar 1968, Fig.29.12, 24) and Shamalaji (Mehta and Patel 1967: 48, Fig.25.10) in Western India.

No. 5

Chisel of cylindrical shaped. Measurement L.87.56 mm (J2 NW, Lot 117, depth 0.60 m, (2)).

7.3. Knife

Plate XII.a. No.6

Only two specimens of knives (broken blades) with concave back have been recovered from the excavations at Padri. These types of knives occur at a number of Early Historic sites such as Maheshwar (No.830), Nevasa (Nos. 8 and 9), Nasik (Fig. 54, No. 4), Sisupalgarh (No.42), Devnimori (Mehta and Chowdhary 1966: 98-99, Fig.42.4) and Amreli (Rao 1966: 108, Fig.29.7).

No. 6

Possibly a knife blade with concave back and bent tip. Measurements L.65.84 mm, T.10.27 mm, (M2 SW, Lot 11006, depth 0.43 m, (2)).

7.4. Hoe

Plate XII.a. No.7

Hoe is used for ploughing and digging the earth. The excavations yielded only one specimen of hoe. This type of hoe has been reported from Kaundinyapura (Dikshit 1968: 120, Fig.36.30), Sisupalgarh (Lal 1948: 95, Fig. 11.36), Dhatva (Mehta *et al.* 1975: 18-19, Fig.7.1) and Balathal (Shinde pers. comm.).

No. 7

Butt end of a hoe, badly corroded and broken. Measurement T.17.33 mm. (MX1 SW, Lot 8104, depth 0.40 m, (2)).

7.5. Pick

Plate XII.a. No.8

Only one specimen of iron pick has been recovered from the excavation. Similar types of pick have been reported from Devnimori (Mehta and Chowdhary 1966: 98, Fig.43.13).

No. 8

Pick with a flattened heel which is slightly curved. Four sided blade tapering towards the point. Measurements L.85.39 mm, T.9.16 mm (C3 SE, Lot 1029, depth 0.42 m, (2)).

6. Fish hook

Plate XII.a. No.9

The excavations unearthed one specimen of iron fish-hook. It reveals the food habit of the people. From the specimen we can deduce that fishing activity was quite common in the Early Historic period at this site. Similar type of fish-hooks have been reported from Nevasa (Sankalia *et al.* 1960: 416-29, Fig.188.18-21), Amreli (Rao 1966, Fig.29.20), Maheshwar (Sankalia *et al.* 1958, Fig.108.17), Nagara (Mehta 1968: 122-123, Fig.58.2), Devnimori (Mehta and Chowdhary 1966: 101, Fig.43.16) and Somnath (Nanavati *et al.* 1971: 81-83, Fig.37.10).

No. 9

Complete specimen of a fish hook, unbarbed. Measurement L.51.86 mm (MX1 SW, Lot 8106 (pit hole), depth 0.94 m, (2)).

Plate XII.b. Nos.10-17

No. 10

Unidentified Iron object, it may have been part of a knife/dagger. Badly corroded. Measurements L. 61.18 mm, T. 12.24 mm (TTE A1 NW, Lot 110213, depth 0.35 m, (2)).

No. 11

Pendulum of a bell. Badly corroded. Measurement L.40.87 m. (TTN A2 NW, Lot 120002, depth 0.35 m, (2)).

No. 12

It may have been an arrowhead. Measurement L.49.72 mm (LX1 SE, Lot 10203, depth 0.26 m, (2)).

No. 13

Unidentified Iron object, probably part of a door chain. Partly broken. (MX1 SW, Lot 8105, depth 0.50 m, (2)).

No. 14

Unidentified iron object. It may have been part of a knife, with concave back. Measurement L.80.82 mm (J2 NW, Lot 116, depth 0.50 m, (2)).

No. 15

Thick iron bangle with round section, partly broken. Measurement Cir. 75.48 mm (TTE A1 SE, Lot 110108, depth 0.50 m, (2)).

No. 16

Unidentified iron object. Clamp (?), broken. (M2 NW, Lot 11310, depth 0.73 m, (2)).

No.17

Unidentified iron object It may have been used as a dagger. Broken. Measurements L.81.86 mm, T.27.68 mm (MX1 SW, Lot 8105, depth 0.76 m, (2)).

8. Bone Objects (Point and arrowhead)

The excavations unearthed a small quantity of bone objects including five points and two arrowheads. It is difficult to define exactly the purpose of these bone points; they were perhaps multipurpose implements. They can be used as arrowheads, modeling tools, inscribing styluses, weaving needles, etc. It will be interesting to see how these bone tools were made. According to Narian (1974) who has made a special study of Neolithic bone industry, animal bones are first boiled in a solution of soda water to a boiling point to extract fat and marrow which are organic materials. After this, bone becomes porous, light in weight and immune to decay. It is then immersed for about two weeks in a solution of silicate of soda (one part) and water (three parts and again in calcium chloride solution (two parts) and water (three parts) for a week or two. These solution fill the porous surface and lend strength to the bone and can then be worked upon by stone or copper blades and the working point can be hardened by burning. During the Early Historic period, bone industry flourished on a wider scale. But it is difficult to determine as why it did not occur in large scale at Padri. A small number of artefacts indicates its unpopularity at the sites. These types of bone points and arrowheads occur at various places in India like, Nagara (Mehta 1968: 148-49, Fig. Nos. 64.5,14), Amreli (Rao 1966: 109, Plate XLVB.10), etc.

Plate XIII. Nos.1-5

No. 1

Bone arrowhead with a sharp point. Measurements L.37.07 mm, T.3.62 mm (K2 NE/SE, Lot 5312, depth 0.95 m, (1)).

No. 2

Bone point with pronged side-edges, pointed at the end, partly broken. Measurement L.68.83 mm (C3 SW, Lot 1022, depth 0.20 m, (1)).

No. 3

Bone point with a socket for the shaft tenon, broken. Measurement L.58.36 mm (J2 NE, Lot 110, depth 0.60 m, (2)).

No. 4

Bone point, long and having broad base. Point is missing. Measurement L.185.23 mm (LX1 NW, Lot 10118, depth 0.95 m, (3)).

No. 5

Tanged bone arrowhead; tang partly broken. Measurement L.85.18 mm (C3 SW, Lot 1022, depth 0.20 m, (1)).

9. Terracotta objects

The excavation yielded a large number of terracotta objects such as discs, lamps, female figurines, ear studs, sling balls, wheels, incense burners, pellets, spindle whorls, goblet, cylindrical objects, toy pots, boat-shaped motifs, sharpners, animal figurines, pendants, conical objects, circular tablet, and eight unidentified objects, etc. The total number is one hundred and ninety three (**Table 10**). A few of them are made of pot sherds but most of them were made from clay and usually hand made but well fired.

9.1. Female figurine

The excavation yielded two figurines each of *Lajjagauri* and female figurines, which are made of terracotta. But both are in broken condition. Though the collection of these female figurines is small in number but it is interesting from the various point of view. We could understand the cultural significance of the inhabitants of the sites. *Lajjagauri* figurines have also been reported from various sites in Gujarat, such as Kanad and Variav in Surat, Kavi in Broach, Pavti Jetpur in Baroda, Tarsang and Bavaka in Panchmahal, Valabhipur and Gagdhali in Bhavnagar, Amreli in Amreli district, Dhanak in Rajkot and Sathal in Ahmedabad (Shinde 1994: 81-85; Sonawane 1988: 27-35).

Plate XIV.a. No.1

Lajjagauri: The figure is in bas relief and all the details are not clearly visible. The figure is shown seated as usual in her characteristic form, legs stretched apart and bent at the knees and hand raised upward at the elbow. The figurine are shown without any ornamentation. On the left side of the sculpture there appears to be a seated Nandi in north-south direction with its head towards the south, whereas the figure on its right, which is partially damaged, appear to be a devotee. The image is roughly rectangular in shape and it measurements are 8 cm X 6.5 cm X 1. 8 cm (Shinde 1994) (L1 SW, Lot 7003, depth 0.30 m, (2)).

Plate XIV.b. No.3

A terracotta broken piece of Lajjagauri. This specimen belongs to a *Yoni* portion (female genitalia) of the goddess Lajjagauri is made of terracotta plaque. This fragment displays the pudenda prominently, often exaggerated in size. A central portion of this organ bears incised decorations consisting of a group of five horizontal lines and an upside-down latticed triangular pattern suspended from the lower most horizontal line. The image is characteristic with bold relief and detailed visibility (Shinde 1994). (L1 SW, Lot 7004, depth 0.42 m, (2)).

Plate XIV.a. No.7

Torso of a nude standing female figurine, left arm akimbo and right one suspended by the side. It is made of terracotta (surface collection, 12/01/93).

Plate XIV.c. No.10

A fragment of a human figurine. Only right hand is visible. It could be a female figurine. It is shown seated with the hand placed on folded legs. (C3Q SW, Lot 1033, depth 0.48 m, (2))

9.2. Animal figurine

The excavations yielded 14 bulls, most of which are humped. The nose of bulls are either perforated or unperforated. At present on the basis of current ethnographic study it revealed that bull with perforated nose is an oxen. The bull with unperforated nose is usually called a stud-bull. Bulls in Saurashtra locally known as *kankrej,* have prominent humps. This breed may have been present in Saurashtra from the very early period. These types of bulls are reported from other sites in Gujarat in the Early Historic period such as Amreli (Rao 1966: 103, Plate XXXVII.1-2,4,10-12), Shamalaji (Mehta and Patel 1967: 41, Fig.22.1), Dhatva (Mehta *et al.* 1975: 15, Fig.6.12), Devnimori (Mehta and Chowdhary 1966: 91, Fig.39.11, 13) and Nagara (Mehta 1968: 92, Fig.2,6,8-9).

The selected shapes are given below.

9.2.I. Bull

Plate XIV.b. No.1, 4-7, 9, 11

No.1

A stylized bull. Three legs and horns are broken, tail is visible, well fired to red colour. (LX1 NW, Lot 10105, depth 0.38 m, (2)).

No. 4

A stumpy bull figurine, one leg and head portion are broken and the tail is also partly broken. (LX1 NE, Lot 10003, depth 0.36 m , (2)).

No. 5

Only the trunk portion of the bull figurine has survived. (LX1 SE, Lot 10201, depth 0.12 m, (1)).

No. 6

A bull with partly broken legs and head. It has a prominent hump. (C3Q NE, Lot 1008, depth 0.40 m, (2)).

No. 7

A humped bull; head portion is missing. (LX1 SW, Lot 201, depth 0.12 m, (2)).

No. 9

Body portion of a bull. (L2 SE, Lot 6306, depth 0.44 m, (2)).

No. 11

Body portion of a bull. (LX1 NW, Lot 10112, depth 0.70 m, (3)).

Plate XIV.c. No.3, 8-9

No. 3

Body portion of a bull. Legs, tail and head are missing. (LX1 NE, Lot 10004, depth 0.48 m, (2)).

No. 8

A fragment of a bull. Body and two legs are broken. Prominent hump and horns.

No. 9

A miniature figurine of a bull with a pinched mouth. Three legs are partly broken. (L1 NW, Lot 7306, depth 0.80 m, (3)).

9.2.II. Birds

The excavation yielded only three specimens of the head portion of birds. However, the identification is difficult as it is survived in the form of bits. These are given below

Plate XIV.b. No.10

No. 10

A head portion of a bird. Only eyes are clear. (LX1 NW, Lot 10116, depth 0.90 m, (3)).

Plate XIV.c. No.1

No. 1

Head portion of a bird. Only eyes and nose are clear. (MX1 SW, Lot 8101, depth 0.20 m, (1)).

9.2.III. Elephant

Only one fragment of elephant head could be recovered from the excavations. It represents trunk and ears.

Plate XIV.b. No.12

No. 12

Head portion of a terracotta elephant, half portion of trunk is broken, eyes are clear. (N1 SW, Lot 6006 depth. 0.38 cm. (2)).

9.2.IV. Dog

Only three specimens of terracotta dogs have been found in the excavations.

Plate XIV.c. No.4-5

No.4

A stumpy figure of a dog. One leg and some portion of mouth are broken. (L2 SW, Lot 6004, depth 0.40 m, (2)).

No. 5

A stumpy figure of a dog. Two hind legs are broken. (L1 SE, Lot 7101, depth 0.32 m, (1)).

9.2.V. Boat-shaped motifs

Plate XIV.d. Nos.1&2

The excavation yielded two boat-shaped objects. The objects are made of fine clay and treated with red slip. According to Shinde (1992a: 81), "Both bear two perforation on the projected central portion, resembling a mast and have three grooves on the underside of one end and two on the other. The exact function of these grooves is hard to imagine, but since they are aligned parallel to the perforations it would not be far-fetched to surmised that they were associated with weaving activities." Measurements No.1 L.6.5 cm, W.2.1 cm, T. 2.70 cm, No.2. L.8.40 cm, W.3.40 cm, T.3.60 cm (C3 NE, Lot 1003, depth 0.16 m & 0.35 m, (7))

9.2.VI. Miscellaneous objects

Plate XIV.c. Nos.6-7

No.6

A fragment of a terracotta ring. (LX1 NW, Lot 10105, depth 0.38 m, (2)).

No. 7

A fragment of a horn. (TTC A1 SW, Lot 110016, depth 0.85 m, (3)).

Plate XIV.b. No. 8

No.8

A figurine-shaped spout. (Surface 1991-92).

Plate XIV.c. No. 2

No.2

A hand-made torso-like object. (C3 SE, Lot 1021, depth 0.12 m, (1)).

Plate XV.a. No.1, 4, 5

No.1

A small clay toy pot. (TTN A4 NE, Lot 10204, depth 1.24 m, (3)).

No. 4

A fragment of pottery lamp, oval-shaped and having a channel for a wick. (Surface collection 1991).

No. 5

A fragment of pottery lamp, bowl-shaped, with a pinched projection for a wick. (K2 SW, Lot 5006, depth 0.95 m, (3)).

Plate XV.b. No.1-9

No.1

Incense burner, designed on the shaft portion, nicely decorated. (TTN A2 SW, Lot 120202, depth 0.35 m, (2)).

No. 2

Lid finial with decoration of a star at the top, broken. (C3 NW, Lot 1014, depth 0.46 m, (2)).

No. 3

Crucible: Lower part of a small crucible, grey in colour. (L1 SW, Lot 7004, depth 0.42 m, (2)).

No. 4

Fragment of an incense burner with rectangular section. (C3 SE, Lot 1025, depth 0.30 m, (2)).

No. 5

A fragment of a gamesman. (M2 SW, Lot 11008, depth 0.65 m, (2)).

No. 6

Circular base of a small goblet? (MX1 SE, Lot 8006, depth 0.54 m, (3)).

No. 7

A wheel: Almost complete specimen, hubbed on both sides. (A1 SE, Lot 110109, depth 0.60 m, (2)).

No. 8

A wheel, complete specimen with a small perforation. (C3 SE, Lot 1057, depth 1.25 m, (3)).

No. 9

A terracotta fragment of an incense burner? (C3 SE, Lot 1025, depth 0.30 m, (2)).

Plate XV.c. No.3, 6

No.3

Complete specimen of a plain terracotta ball. (L2 SW, Lot 6003, depth 0.30 m, (1)).

No. 6

Same as No. 3. but smaller in size. (TTN A4 NE, Lot 18201, depth 0.96 m, (1)).

Plate XVI. Nos.2, 5

Stopper: A cone with truncated top. There is a perforation at the top. Measurement L. 38.03 mm (MX1 SE. Lot 8002, depth 0.23 m, (2)).

No.5

Stopper: A cone with depression on the truncated part made of terracotta. Measurement L.31.86 mm. (LX1 NE, Lot 10003, depth 0.36 m, (2)).

Plate XV.c. No.2

No.2

Stopper : A terracotta cone with blind hole on the truncated part. (LX1 NE, Lot 10002, depth 0.32 m, (1)).

Plate XV.d.

A circular clay tablet bearing a Brahmi inscription on the reverse side. The letters are not clear. Measurement Cir. 48.76 mm, T.13.52 mm. (C3 NE, Lot 1012, depth 0.40 m, (2)).

9.3. Discs

Ninety one terracotta discs have been reported from the excavations. They are of two types: 1. perforated and 2. unperforated. According to Singh (1994: 182), disc is a flat circular object which is made of levigated clay and fired under oxidizing condition. They have been identified as discs. On the other hand according to Rhyd (1959: 163) the terracotta discs may have been used to cover the tobacco in Hukkas, a smoking device which is Central Asian in origin and still in use in Kashmir. Such discs are also reported from various sites in Gujarat like Nagara (Mehta 1968: 97-100), Dhatva (Mehta *et al.* 1975: 6), Shamalaji (Mehta and Patel 1967: 44, Fig.22.5) and Devnimori (Mehta and Chowdhary 1966: 92, Fig.39,4-6).

The selected specimens are given below

Plate XVII.a. Nos.1-5

No. 1

A circular terracotta disc, grey in colour, unperforated. Measurement Cir.91.99 mm, T.22.57 mm. (surface collection 18/03/91).

No. 2

Same as No. 1 but broken and perforated. Measurement T.18.79 mm. (MX1 SE, Lot 8007, depth 0.70 m, (3)).

No. 3

Circular disc of potsherd, grey in colour. It is slightly convex-shaped. There is a small perforation at the centre. Measurements Cir.91.99 mm, T.22.57 mm (LX1 NE, Lot 10017, depth 1.50 m, (3)).

No.4

A roughly rectangular piece of disc, perforated. Measurements Cir.52.69 mm, T.12.89 mm (L1 NW, Lot 7305, depth 0.70 m, (2)).

No.5

A circular disc, grey in colour, broken and perforated. Measurement T.4.70 mm (M1 NW, Lot 9304, depth 0.40 m, (2)).

Plate XVII.b. Nos.1-7

No.1

A circular terracotta disc, red in colour. Unperforated. Measurements Cir.48.37 mm, T.3.16 mm (J2 NW, Lot 121, depth 0.90 m, (3)).

No. 2

A circular terracotta disc, red in colour. It is slightly convex-concave shaped. Unperforated. Measurements Cir.43.58 mm, T.2.75 mm. (L2 NE, Lot 6210, depth 0.75 m, (3)).

No.3

Same as No. 2 but smaller in size. Measurements Cir.51.27 mm, T.12.43 mm (MX1 SW, Lot 8103, depth 0.35 m, (2)).

No. 4

Same as No.3 but smaller in size. Measurements Cir.41.55 mm, T.11.29 mm (M1 SE, Lot 9001, depth 0.10 m, (1)).

No.5

A circular disc. Unperforated. Measurements Cir.37.54 mm, T.4.58 mm (L2 SE, Lot 6305, depth 0.40 m, (2)).

No.6

A circular disc, smaller in size, red in colour. Unperforated. Measurements Cir.29.71 mm, T.6.50 mm (L2 SE, Lot 6305, depth 0.40 m, (2)).

No. 7

Same as No. 6, smaller in size. Measurements Cir.23.17 mm, T.6.65 mm (L1 SW, Lot 7010, depth 0.90 m, (3)).

9.4. Ear Studs

Only seven ear studs of terracotta have been recovered from the excavation. Out of seven only one is standard vase shape and the rest of the cylindrical in shapes. These are given below.

Plate XVIII. Nos.1-7

No. 1

Ear stud of terracotta, standard vase-shaped. Measurement L.38.26 mm (surface collection 1995-96).

No. 2

Ear stud of terracotta. Cylindrical, circular with a very little depressed profile, grey in colour. Measurements Cir.32.16 mm, T.18.59 mm (surface collection 1995-96).

No. 3

Damru-shaped ear stud, black in colour. Measurements Cir.26.00 mm, T.19.33 mm (MX1 SW, Lot 3104, depth 0.40 m, (2)).

No. 4

Ear stud of terracotta, same as No. 3 but grey in colour. Measurements Cir. 26.64 mm, T.15.75 mm (MX1 SW, Lot 8103, depth 0.35 m, (2)).

No. 5

Ear stud of terracotta same as No. 2 but smaller in size. Measurements Cir.24.69mm, T.19.41 mm (C3 SE, Lot 1045, depth 0.90 m, (3)).

No. 6

Ear stud of terracotta, same as No. 5 but smaller in size. Measurements Cir.22.27 mm, T.13.81 mm (C3 SW, Lot 1044, depth 0.80 m, (3)).

No. 7

Ear stud of terracotta, same as No.6 but bigger in size. Measurements Cir. 31.27 mm, T.19.83 mm (LX1 NW, Lot 10105, depth 0.38 m, (2)).

Table 10: Distribution of Terracotta objects

Objects	Surface	Layer (1)	Layer (2)	Layer (3)	
Disc (unperforated)	8	7	32	16	63
Disc (perforated)	7	6	8	7	28
Lamp	1	0	2	1	4
Bull	0	3	11	0	14
Ear-stud	2	0	3	2	7
Tablet	0	0	1	0	1
Sling ball	3	0	14	7	24
Wheel	0	0	1	1	2
Incense burner	0	0	1	1	2
Pellet	0	1	2	0	3
Pendant	0	0	1	1	2
Horn	0	1	1	1	3
Bird	0	1	1	1	3
Dog	0	1	1	1	3
Lajjagauri	0	0	2	0	2
Spout (Fig. shaped)	1	0	0	0	1
Conical object	0	1	3	1	5
Goblet	0	0	0	1	1
Cylindrical object	0	2	2	1	5
Toy pot	0	1	1	0	2
Sharpner	0	0	1	0	1
Female Figurine	1	1	0	0	2
Boat motif	Layer (7) 2	0	0	0	2
Figurine (unidentified)	1	1	2	3	7
Stopper	0	1	2	0	3
Crucible	0	0	2	0	2
Lid	0	1	0	0	1
Total	25 2	29	92	45	193

10. Pendants

Only three pendants have been found in the Early Historic levels at Padri. They are made of shell. The following description will give an idea about the shapes of pendants found at Padri.

Plate XVI. Nos.1, 3-4

A drop shaped (?) shell pendant with two horizontal lines in the middle of the body. At the top of the body there are two perforations. Measurements L.26.03 mm, T.6.54 mm (N1 SE, Lot 13104, depth 0.25 m, (2)).

No. 3

It is a disc like pendant with a hole in the centre made of shell. Measurement Cir.29.41 mm (Surface collection 26/12/96).

No. 4

Similar to No.1 with three horizontal lines in the middle of the body and one perforation at the top. Measurements L.25.11 mm, T.7.18 mm (surface collection 02/01/92).

11. Stone objects

A small number of stone objects have been recovered from the excavation. Their layer-wise distribution has been given in **Table 11**. They comprise eleven discs both perforated and unperforated, one Lajjagauri figurine, four rubber stone, four sling balls, one nodule, one pellet, one pebble, one net sinker, two hammer stones, two mullers, one sharpener, one figurine each of Lord *Vishnu* and *Ganesa*, two potter's dabbers, two unidentified figurines, and two unidentified objects. Their distribution and details are as follows.

Table 11: Distribution of Stone objects

Objects	Surface	Layer (1)	Layer (2)	Layer (3)	Total
Disc (perforated)	0	0	2	0	2
Disc (unperforated)	0	1	7	1	9
Sling ball	0	4	5	2	11
Nadulas	1	0	0	0	1
Rubber stone	2	0	1	1	4
Pellet	0	1	0	0	1
Pebble	0	1	0	0	1
Net sinker	0	0	0	1	1
Hammer stone	0	0	2	0	2
Muller	0	0	2	0	2
Sharpner	0	1	0	0	1
Lajjagauri	1	0	0	0	1
Unidentified objects	2	0	0	0	0
Total	6	8	19	5	38

From the distribution it appears that layer (2) was the most important as there is more evidence of human habitation.

Plate XIV.a. No.2, 3-6

No. 2

A slate stone of Lajjagauri: The Lajjagauri goddess is engraved in black slate stone. According to Shinde (1994: 483) the plaque, the upper part of which partly broken, appears to be squarish in shape, measuring 8.5 cm X 8.5 cm X 1 cm. The head and right hand of the figurine are missing as the plaque is partially broken. The figure is shown in deep relief with all the parts of the body shown in perfect portion and is highly polished. The nude deity is shown seated on a roughly circular *asana* (seat), which is decorated by radiating incised lines. in her characteristic form. What is interesting about this figure is that the pudenda and breasts are not exaggerated as is the case of most of the *Lajjagauri* figures found elsewhere, but are in perfect proportion. The deity is shown wearing a necklace and a double-waist girdle, both decorated with vertical short strokes, and had eight bangles in her left hand. In her left hand, which is raised at the elbow, is a Lotus-bud. Near the elbow on the eastern side is a human head between double incised horizontal bands whereas on the right-hand side, slightly below the knee portion, there appears to be the head of some animal, probably a Nandi. (Surface collection near J5 in 1992-93.)

No. 3

A fragment of figurine, most probably *Vishnu* made of sand stone. Only legs are visible. (surface collection near J5, from section in 1992-93.)

No. 4

Lower portion of a deity made of basalt. (L2 SW, Lot 6003, depth 0.30 m, (1)).

No. 5

A head of Lord Ganesa, only eyes, trunk and halo are visible. It is made of fine-grained sand stone showing very fine workmanship, broken. (Shinde 1994: 483). (L2 SW, Lot 6003, depth 0.30 m, (1).

No. 6

An unidentified fragment of a figurine made of sand stone. Only belly and right leg are visible. (TTS A3 SE, Lot 17101, depth 3.39 m, (2)).

Plate XIV.b. No.2

No.2

An unidentified stone figurine. (surface find, eastern side of the mound, 21/12/96)

Plate XVII.a. No. 6

A circular disc of sand stone, unperforated. Measurements Cir.68.68 mm, T.9.68 mm (M2 SW, Lot 11003, depth 0.25 m, (2)).

Plate XV.a. No.6, 8-9

Potter's dabber: It is circular with constricted middle part, half broken, made of basalt. (L1 SE, Lot 7106, depth 0.65 m, (2)).

No. 8

Muller: Fragment of a muller made of basalt, with squarish in section. (K2 NW/SW, Lot 5004, depth 0.40 m, (2)).

No 9

Rubber stone: Solid oval shaped, made of basalt. (Surface collection, 17/12/91)

Plate XV.c. Nos.4-5

No.4

Complete specimen of sling ball, it is made of stone and bigger in size. (J2 NE, Lot 110, depth 0.60 m, (2)).

No. 5

Fragment of a hammer stone, slightly conical in shape which is made of basalt. Section is triangular. (N2 SW, Lot 14007, depth 0.40 m, (2)).

15.1. Miscellaneous Objects

Plate XV.a. Nos.2-3, 7

No. 2

Weight: cylindrical shape, made of black jasper. Approximate weight is 60 gm. Measurements Cir. 40 mm, T. 23.16 mm (surface find near JS 1992-93).

No. 3

Weight: Rectangular shape, made of dolorite. (TTN A2 NE, Lot 12006, depth 0.67 m, (3)).

No. 7

Columellar: Ventral view of a naked columellar piece of *Xancus pyrum pyrum* (Linnaeus). (J2 NE, Lot 110, depth 0.60 m, (2)).

Plate XV.b. No.10

Ground shell: A small disc. (K2 NE/SE, Lot 5307, depth 0.40 m, (2)).

Plate XV.c. No.1, 7-8

No.1

Complete specimen of a used shell with ground edge. (C3 SE, Lot 1057, depth 1.25 m, (3)).

No. 7

Two fragments of chert flake. (O2 SE, Lot 1001, depth 0.15 m, (1)).

No. 8

Two fragments of white glass. (LX1 SE, Lot 10202, depth 0.21 m, (2)).

Chapter 4

Explorations along the coast and Lower part of Shetrunji River Basin of Bhavnagar District.

The collection and interpretation of data form the main theme of this chapter. The objective was to study the regional variations in settlement patterns through time and space. The author has employed a methodology that suggested by Trigger (1968) which is the third level of settlement pattern studies, that is the regional level. To understand the trend of regional distribution of settlements during the course of exploration, greatest emphasis was laid on locating sites. Keeping in mind the objective and methodology I conducted intensive and extensive field surveys along the coast and in the lower basin of Shetrunji river of Bhavnagar district.

It is important to state the reasons for selecting the area for the present study. There are two well studied sites in this region namely, Padri (Shinde 1992a; 1992b; 1992c; 1994a; 1994b; 1996 and 1998) and Hathab (*IAR.* 1979-80, 1980-81) in this region. The site of Padri, was extensively and systematically excavated for over five seasons by Deccan Collage, Pune (Shinde 1992a; 1992b; 1996 and 1998). The site yielded an Early Historic phase confined to the first three layers. On the basis of a couple of coins and clay tablet bearing *Brahmi* letters, it has been dated to the 1st century B.C.-A.D. On the other hand the discovery of tortoise-shaped copper lamp at the same site in the Early Historic levels suggests Roman contact with the region in the first century B.C.-A.D. The site of Hathab, mentioned in the *Periplus of the Erythraean Sea* (Schoff 1912: 39-40), lies 23 km east of Bhavnagar town near the Gulf of Cambay. It may have played very important role in the socio-economic organization of the Early Historic period. The systematic study of these sites inspired the author to select the region around Padri and Hathab for detailed investigation. In fact, the discovery of these sites revealed the archaeological potential of this region. Efforts are made to study factors like surrounding ecological conditions, location of the sites, thickness and extent of each settlement and its role in the international and hinterland trade. The total explored area is about 1000 sq. km. The antiquity of the sites and the chronology of the cultural remains have been decided on the basis of comparative study with the well known ceramic assemblages at

Padri. The extent of the habitational area is measured on the basis of the spread of habitational deposit. In the case of multiculture site, the extent of each culture was measured on the basis of area represented by the distribution of the respective ceramic assemblage. For locating sites I had given emphasis on the following three methods:

1. Village to village survey on foot and relying on the local information's.
2. Survey along the coast and both the banks of lower Shetrunji river and its tributaries.
3. The survey maps of India (1886, 1 inch = 1 miles).

An extensive survey was carried out during the field seasons of 1996-97, 1997-98 and 1998-99. During the course of exploration, the sites were examined from visible surface remains and exposed sections to obtained information about the thickness of the deposit, stratigraphy and cultural sequence. It should be mentioned that the ancient sites in Gujarat are known as *Timbo.* While conducting village to village survey, the information about the sites was supplied by the villagers. Besides, information about local agricultural practices, sources of water, land forms, the condition of the sites and other pertinent facts were also recorded. In all, 22 Early Historic sites have been studied along the coast and the lower part

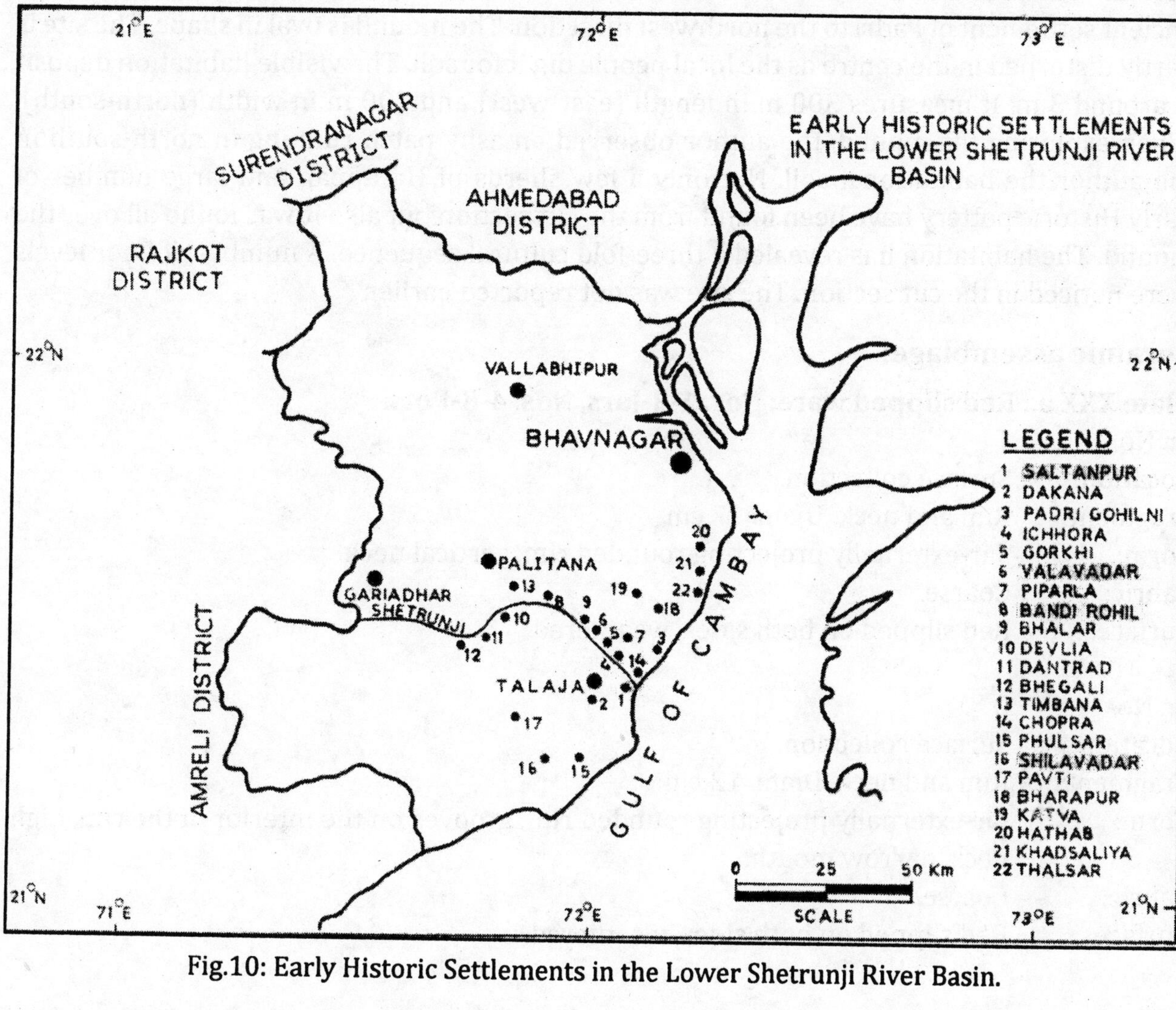

Fig.10: Early Historic Settlements in the Lower Shetrunji River Basin.

of Shetrunji river of which eight were already reported by earlier scholars. I collected pottery and other artifacts from the sites. Mostly representative pottery samples were collected randomly.

The sites have been plotted by location on **Fig.10.** Apart from this, in the following pages a detailed descriptions of these sites and ceramic assemblage and minor objects recovered from them are given below along with the site. Most of the sites studied fall in Talaja Tehsil of Bhavnagar District of Saurashtra.

1. **Site name:** *Bandi Rohil* **(Plate XIX.a).**
   Co-ordinate: Lat. 21°24' N; Long. 72°4' E.
   Period of occupation: Early and Mature Harappan and Early Historic.
   Reference: New discovery.

Location: Village Bandi Rohil is located around 5 km away towards the north of Talaja town and 2 km west of Bhalar village. The village is well connected to Taluka head-quarter by metalled road.

The site: The ancient site is located around 2 km from the present settlement on the left bank of the Shetrunji river and is roughly 200 m away from the present metaled road running between Talaja and Bhavnagar town. The ancient settlement is roughly 9 km away from the ancient settlement of Padri to the northwest direction. The mound is oval in shape. The site is partly disturbed in the centre as the local people dig it for soil. The visible habitation deposit is around 3 m. It measures 300 m in length (east-west) and 100 m in width (north-south). When exploring the mound, the author observed an ashy patch running in north-south in the author the habitational soil. Not only a few sherds of Harappan and large number of Early Historic pottery have been found from the cut section but also it was found all over the mound. The habitation has revealed a three-fold cultural sequence. A number of floor levels were noticed in the cut section. The site was not reported earlier.

Ceramic assemblage:

Plate XXX.a.: Red slipped ware: Nos. 1-3-Jars, Nos. 4-5-Pots.

Sr. No.	1
Location:	Surface collection.
Fragment:	Rim and neck. Diam. 17 cm
Form:	Jar-externally projecting rounded rim, vertical neck.
Fabric:	Coarse.
Surfaces:	Red slipped on both sides, weathered.

Sr. No.	2
Location:	Surface collection.
Fragment:	Rim and neck. Diam. 12 cm
Form:	Jar-externally projecting rounded rim, grooves on the interior of the rim, high neck, narrow mouth.
Fabric:	Coarse.
Surfaces:	Red slipped on both sides, weathered.

Sr. No. 3
Location: Surface collection.
Fragment: Rim and neck. Diam. 12 cm
Form: Jar-squarish rim, vertical neck.
Fabric: Coarse.
Surfaces: Red slipped on both sides, weathered.

Sr. No. 4
Location: Surface collection.
Fragment: Rim and neck. Diam. 15 cm
Form: Pot-externally projecting and under-cut rim, groove on the interior of the rim, thick cross section.
Fabric: Coarse.
Surfaces: Red slipped on both sides, weathered.

Sr. No. 5
Location: Surface collection.
Fragment: Rim and upper body. Diam. 16 cm
Form: Globular pot-externally projecting flat rim, wide mouth, almost no neck.
Fabric: Coarse.
Surfaces: Red slipped on both sides, weathered.

Sr. No. 6
Location: Surface collection.
Fragment: Rim and upper body. Diam. 14 cm
Form: Globular pot-externally projecting flat rim, wide mouth, almost no neck.
Fabric: Coarse.
Surfaces: Unslipped, rough.

Plate XXX.b. Nos.7-12

Sr. No. 7
Location: Surface collection.
Fragment: Rim and upper body. Diam. 21 cm
Form: Jar-featureless rim.
Fabric: Coarse.
Surfaces: Unslipped, rough.

Sr. No. 8
Location: Surface collection.
Fragment: Rim and upper body. Diam. 18 cm
Form: Jar-flared out rim, short vertical neck, narrow mouth.
Fabric: Coarse.
Surfaces: Grey slipped externally, weathered.

Sr. No. 9
Location: Surface collection.
Fragment: Rim and upper body. Diam. 24 cm
Form: Pot-triangular rim, slightly under-cut, groove on the top of the rim, wide mouth.
Fabric: Coarse.
Surfaces: Grey slipped, rough.

Sr. No. 10
Location: Surface collection.
Fragment: Base and lower body.
Form: Cup-disc base, flaring sides.
Fabric: Coarse.
Surfaces: Unslipped, rough.

Sr. No. 11
Location: Surface collection.
Fragment: Base and lower body.
Form: Cup-disc base.
Fabric: Coarse.
Surfaces: Unslipped, rough.

Sr. No. 12
Location: Surface collection.
Fragment: Base and lower body.
Form: Conical lid with pinnacle.
Fabric: Coarse.
Surfaces: Unslipped, weathered.

2. **Site name**: Bhegali (**Plate XIX.b**).
Co-ordinate: Lat. 21°25' N ; Long. 72°1' E
Period of occupation: Early Historic.
Reference: Ghosh 1989: 69; *IAR.* 1960-61.

Location: Bhegali is located 2 km away from the Dantrad village to the north west direction. It is roughly 12 km upstream of Talaja taluka head quarter and situated on the right bank of river Shetrunji about one km away from the present river course.

The site: The ancient mound is located 1 km away from the village. The site is about 17 km away from the ancient site of Padri to the northwest direction. This site was reported by earlier explorers as belonging to the Early Historic period (*IAR.* 1960-61). The site is completely disturbed as the habitational soil was dug out to construct a road. The site spreads over an area of 200 m (north-south) X 100 m (east-west). The maximum habitational deposit is around one meter. Most probably the site was either occupied seasonally or for a short duration. It was occupied during the Early Historic phase only. Along with the ceramics other objects like a terracotta animal figurine probably the head of a dog, a muller made of sand stone and pottery discs have been recovered from the surface of the mound. The mound is rectangular in shape.

Ceramic assemblage:

Plate XXXI. a. Nos.1-12

Sr. No. 1
Location: Surface collection.
Fragment: Rim, neck and upper body. Diam. 24 cm
Form: Jar-short out-turned and externally thickened rim.
Fabric: Coarse
Surfaces: Red slipped, rough.

Sr. No. 2
Location: Surface collection.
Fragment: Rim. Diam. 12 cm
Form: Small globular pot (lota)-flat and featureless rim, groove at the neck in the interior of the rim.
Fabric: Coarse
Surfaces: Unslipped on both sides, weathered.

Sr. No. 3
Location: Surface collection.
Fragment: Rim and neck. Diam. 13 cm
Form: Jar-flat projecting short rim.
Fabric: Coarse to medium.
Surfaces: Red slipped on both sides, weathered.

Sr. No. 4
Location: Surface collection.
Fragment: Rim and neck. Diam. 21 cm
Form: Pot-flared out and thickened rim.
Fabric: Coarse.
Surfaces: Grey slipped, weathered.

Sr. No. 5
Location: Surface collection.
Fragment: Rim and neck. Diam. 22 cm
Form: Dish-triangular rim.
Fabric: Coarse.
Surfaces: Grey slipped, weathered.

Sr. No. 6
Location: Surface collection.
Fragment: Spout.

Form: Spout-pointed.
Fabric: Coarse.
Surfaces: Red slipped, weathered.

Sr. No. 7
Location: Surface collection.
Fragment: Base and lower part.
Form: Lamp-on-stand.
Fabric: Coarse.
Surfaces: Unslipped, weathered.

Sr. No. 8
Location: Surface collection.
Fragment: Rim and neck. Diam. 25 cm
Form: Jar-external projecting flat rim, high neck.
Fabric: Fine.
Surfaces: Slipped on both sides, Red Polished Ware, weathered.

Sr. No. 9
Location: Surface collection.
Fragment: Rim and neck. Diam. 18 cm
Form: Small size jar-beaked rim, short vertical neck.
Fabric: Fine.
Surfaces: Slipped on both sides, Red Polished Ware, weathered.

Sr. No. 10
Location: Surface collection.
Fragment: Rim and upper body. Diam. 16 cm
Form: Bowl-featureless pointed rim.
Fabric: Fine.
Surfaces: Slipped on both sides, Red Polished Ware, weathered.

Sr. No. 11
Location: Surface collection.
Fragment: Rim. Diam. 20 cm
Form: Bowl-featureless rim, blunt carinated shoulder.
Fabric: Fine.
Surfaces: Slipped on both sides, Red Polished Ware, weathered.

Sr. No. 12
Location: Surface collection.
Fragment: Rim and upper body. Diam. 22 cm
Form: Bowl-inturned knife edge rim.
Fabric: Fine.

Surfaces: Slipped on both sides, Red Polished Ware, weathered.

Minor objects

1. A fragment of terracotta animal figurine, probably head of a dog, red in color. **(Plate XLIX.a.)**.
2. A fragment of muller, sand stone. Measurement: Cir.68.92 mm. **(Plate XLVII.a)**.
3. A circular terracotta disc, red in color. Measurement: T.16.41 mm, Cir.47.64 mm. **(Plate XLVI.b.No.19)**

3. **Site name**: Bhalar **(Plate XX.a)**.
Co-ordinate: Lat. 21°24' N; Long. 72°6' E
Period of occupation: Early Harappan, Mature Harappan and Early Historic.
Reference: New discovery.

Location: The village Bhalar is located 4 km away to the north of Talaja town, 2 km east of Rohil village and 5 km west of Bapada village. The village is well connected with Talaja town by jeepable road.

The site: The ancient site is located one and half km from the road running between Talaja and Bhavnagar and on the left bank of river Shetrunji. The ancient settlement is roughly 10 km towards the north-east direction of Padri. The habitational deposit could not be ascertained as the mound is under cultivation. It measures about 200 m (east-west) and 100 m (north-south). The surface is littered with pottery, bones and other objects. The site presents a three-fold cultural sequence namely Early Harappan, Mature Harappan and Early Historic. The most noteworthy discovery is a fragment of dish with green-glaze on the inner side. This shows contact of this region with the Persian Gulf in the beginning of the Christian Era. Besides, few pieces of shell bangles have also been recovered. The site has been discovered by the author during the course of exploration in the river basin of Shetrunji.

Ceramic assemblage:

Plate XXXI.b. Nos.1-9

Sr. No. 1
Location: Surfaces collection.
Fragment: Rim and neck. Diam. 14 cm
Form: Globular pot-flaring rim, groove on the interior of the rim.
Fabric: Coarse.
Surfaces: Red slipped on both sides, rough.

Sr. No. 2
Location: Surface collection.
Fragment: Rim and neck. Diam. 22 cm
Form: Jar-internally flat, slightly projecting rim and externally thickened.
Fabric: Coarse.
Surfaces: Red slipped on both sides, smooth.

Sr. No. 3
Location: Surface collection.
Fragment: Rim. Diam. 18 cm
Form: Pot-flaring rim.
Fabric: Coarse.
Surfaces: Red slipped on both sides, rough.

Sr. No. 4
Location: Surface collection.
Fragment: Rim and neck. Diam. 17 cm
Form: Globular pot-externally thickened under-cut rim, wide mouth.
Fabric: Coarse.
Surfaces: Red slipped on both sides, weathered.

Sr. No. 5
Location: Surface collection.
Fragment: Rim, neck and upper body. Diam. 20 cm
Form: Pot-externally projecting rim, high neck, ridge on the interior.
Fabric: Coarse.
Surfaces: Red slipped on both sides, smooth.

Sr. No. 6
Location: Surface collection.
Fragment: Rim and neck. Diam. 19 cm
Form: Jar-triangular rim, short vertical neck, probably globular body.
Fabric: Coarse.
Surfaces: Grey slipped on both sides, rough.

Sr. No. 7
Location: Surface collection.
Fragment: Rim and neck. Diam. 19 cm
Form: Pot-out turned and externally thickened rim, short neck.
Fabric: Coarse.
Surfaces: Grey slipped externally, smooth.

Sr. No. 8
Location: Surface collection.
Fragment: Base and lower body.
Form: Cup-disc base, flaring sides.
Fabric: Coarse.
Surfaces: Unslipped, rough.

Sr. No. 9
Location: Surface collection.

Fragment: Base and lower body.
Form: Cup-disc base.
Fabric: Coarse.
Surfaces: Unslipped, rough.

Plate XXXI.c. Nos.10-18

Sr. No. 10
Location: Surface collection.
Fragment: Base and lower body.
Form: Cup-disc base.
Fabric: Coarse.
Surfaces: Unslipped, rough.

Sr. No. 11
Location: Surface collection.
Fragment: Rim and upper body. Diam. 15 cm
Form: Globular pot-externally projecting rounded rim, narrow mouth.
Fabric: Coarse.
Surfaces: Red slipped on both sides, weathered.

Sr. No. 12
Location: Surface collection.
Fragment: Rim and neck. Diam. 15 cm
Form: Small globular pot-externally projecting rim, narrow mouth.
Fabric: Coarse.
Surfaces: Red slipped on both sides, smooth.

Sr. No. 13
Fragment: Rim. Diam.13 cm
Form: Small globular pot-beaded rim, groove on the interior of the rim, narrow mouth.
Fabric: Coarse.
Surfaces: Red slipped on both sides, weathered.

Sr. No. 14
Location: Surface collection.
Fragment: Rim and upper body. Diam.12 cm
Form: Saucer-flaring rim, deep groove on interior of rim.
Fabric: Coarse.
Surfaces: Red slipped on both sides, weathered.

Sr. No. 15
Location: Surface collection.
Fragment: Rim and upper body. Diam. 16 cm

Form: Pot-externally projecting flat rim, groove on the interior, almost no neck.
Fabric: Coarse.
Surfaces: Grey slipped on both sides, weathered.

Sr. No. 16
Location: Surface collection.
Fragment: Rim. Diam. 20 cm
Form: Pot-externally projecting rim, groove on the interior of the rim, narrow mouth.
Fabric: Coarse.
Surfaces: Grey slipped on the both sides, weathered.

Sr. No. 17
Location: Surfaces collection.
Fragment: Rim and neck. Diam. 10 cm
Form: Miniature globular pot-externally projecting flat rim, groove on the interior.
Fabric: Coarse.
Surfaces: Unslipped, weathered.

Sr. No. 18
Location: Surface collection.
Fragment: Rim and upper body.
Form: Dish-externally projecting rim.
Fabric: Medium to fine.
Surfaces: Rough on the exterior but green glazed on the interior surface.

Minor objects.

1. A fragment of plain shell bangle and triangular in cross section. Measurement: .4.34mm, W.7.03 mm. **(Plate XLVII.b. No. 8)**

4. **Site name**: *Bharapur Juno Timba* **(Plate XX.b)**.
Co-ordinate: Lat. 21°24' N; Long. 72°12' E.
Period of occupation: Early Historic.
Reference: New discovery

Location: The village Bharapur is located 10 km to the east of Talaja Tehsil head-quarter, 5 km to the north of village Padri Gohel-ni and roughly 1 km east of the Gulf of Cambay.

The site: The ancient habitational settlement is close to the village and is known as *Bharapur Juno Timba*. The mound is quite extensive and intact. Its spreads over an area 300 m (east-west) and 400 m (north-south) and the habitational deposit is clear from the cut section and measures 2 m. From the surface occasionally brick structures are noticed and a large number of hero stones have been noticed on the southern side of the mound. From the ceramic assemblage it is deduced that the site was either occupied seasonally or a short time during the Early Historic period.

Ceramic assemblage

Plate XXXII.a. Nos.1-9

Sr. No. 1
Location: Surface collection.
Fragment: Rim and neck. Diam. 22 cm
Form: Jar-vertical and externally thickened rim.
Fabric: Coarse.
Surfaces: Unslipped, weathered.

Sr. No. 2
Location: Surface collection.
Fragment: Rim and neck. Diam. 23 cm
Form: Pot-beaded under-cut rim, almost no neck.
Fabric: Coarse.
Surfaces: Unslipped, rough.

Sr. No. 3
Location: Surface collection.
Fragment: Rim, neck and shoulder. Diam. 19 cm
Form: Globular pot-outcurved beaded rim, grooved on the interior of the rim, short vertical neck.
Fabric: Coarse.
Surfaces: Unslipped, weathered.

Sr. No. 4
Location: Surface collection.
Fragment: Rim and shoulder. Diam. 10 cm
Form: Miniature jar-out turned and thickened rim.
Fabric: Coarse.
Surfaces: Unslipped, weathered.

Sr. No. 5
Location: Surface collection.
Fragment: Base and lower body.
Form: Cup-disc base, flaring sides.
Fabric: Coarse.
Surfaces: Unslipped, rough.

Sr. No. 6
Location: Surface collection.
Fragment: Rim and neck. Diam. 22 cm
Form: Jar-beaded rim, short vertical neck.
Fabric: Coarse.

Surfaces: Unslipped, weathered.

Sr. No. 7
Location: Surface collection.
Fragment: Rim and neck. Diam. 22 cm
Form: Jar-flared rim, short neck.
Fabric: Coarse.
Surfaces: Unslipped, weathered.

Sr. No. 8
Location: Surface collection.
Fragment: Rim and neck. Diam. 26 cm
Form: Small jar-out turned beaded rim.
Fabric: Coarse.
Surfaces: Red slipped on both sides, weathered.

Sr. No. 9
Location: Surface collection.
Fragment: Rim and neck. Diam. 17 cm
Form: Jar-beaked shape rim, vertical neck.
Fabric: Coarse.
Surfaces: Red slipped on both sides, smooth.

Plate XXXII.b. Nos.10-17

Sr. No. 10
Location: Surface collection.
Fragment: Rim and neck. Diam. 22 cm
Form: Pot-flared rim, grooved on the interior of the rim.
Fabric: Coarse.
Surfaces: Red slipped on both sides, weathered.

Sr. No. 11
Location: Surface collection.
Fragment: Rim and neck. Diam. 19 cm
Form: Jar-out turned and slightly pointed rim, concave neck.
Fabric: Coarse.
Surfaces: Red slipped on both sides, weathered.

Sr. No. 12
Location: Surface collection.
Fragment: Rim. Diam. 22 cm
Form: Pot-externally projecting flat rim, vertical neck.
Fabric: Coarse.
Surfaces: Red slipped on both sides, weathered.

Sr. No. 13
Location: Surface collection.
Fragment: Rim and neck. Diam. 15 cm
Form: Jar-beaked rim, grooved on the exterior of the rim, short vertical neck.
Fabric: Coarse.
Surfaces: Red slipped on both sides, weathered.

Sr. No. 14
Location: Surface collection.
Fragment: Rim and neck. Diam. 27 cm
Form: Pot-externally projecting beaked rim, short neck.
Fabric: Coarse.
Surfaces: Red slipped on both sides, weathered.

Sr. No. 15
Location: Surface collection.
Fragment: Rim and neck. Diam. 17 cm
Form: Pot-flat projecting rim, vertical neck.
Fabric: Coarse.
Surfaces: Red slipped on the exterior of the rim, weathered.

Sr. No. 16
Location: Surface collection.
Fragment: Rim and neck. Diam. 21 cm
Form: Jar-externally out turned rim, concave neck.
Fabric: Coarse.
Surfaces: Red slipped on both sides, weathered.

Sr. No. 17
Location: Surface collection.
Fragment: Rim and body. Diam. 42 cm
Form: A large shallow bowl-broad beaded rim, two deep grooved on the interior side and one deep grooved on the outer side of the rim.
Fabric: Coarse.
Surfaces: Red slipped on both sides, weathered.

Plate XXXII.c. Nos.18-26

Sr. No. 18
Location: Surface collection.
Fragment: Rim and body. Diam. 35 cm
Form: Basin-broad flaring mouth, rounded rim, applique wavy line on the shoulder, decorated with single row of incised short slant lines.
Fabric: Coarse.
Surfaces: Red slipped on both sides, weathered.

Sr. No. 19
Location: Surface collection.
Fragment: Rim and body. Diam. 16 cm
Form: Small bowl/lid-short vertical rim, prominent ridge on the outer side.
Fabric: Coarse.
Surfaces: Red slipped on both sides, weathered.

Sr. No. 20
Location: Surface collection.
Fragment: Body sherd.
Form: Undetermined-decorated with white bands and loops attached to the bands on exterior surface.
Fabric: Coarse.
Surfaces: Red slipped on exterior of the body, weathered.

Sr. No. 21
Location: Surface collection.
Fragment: Rim and neck. Diam. 21 cm
Form: Pot-beaked rim, squat neck.
Fabric: Coarse.
Surfaces: Grey slipped on both sides, smooth.

Sr. No. 22
Location: Surface collection.
Fragment: Rim and shoulder. Diam. 20 cm
Form: Pot-out-curved beaded rim, grooved on the interior of the rim.
Fabric: Coarse.
Surfaces: Grey slipped on both sides, weathered.

Sr. No. 23
Location: Surface collection.
Fragment: Rim and body. Diam. 38 cm
Form: Shallow dish-externally projecting beaded rim, deep grooved on the interior of the rim.
Fabric: Coarse.
Surfaces: Grey slipped on interior of the rim, exterior rough and interior smooth.

Sr. No. 24
Location: Surface collection.
Fragment: Rim and body. Diam. 39 cm
Form: Shallow dish-beaded rim.
Fabric: Coarse.
Surfaces: Grey slipped on the interior of the rim, exterior rough and interior smooth.

Sr. No. 25
Location: Surface collection.
Fragment: Rim and body. Diam. 38 cm
Form: Deep dish-externally projecting beaked rim, grooved on the exterior of the rim.
Fabric: Coarse.
Surfaces: Grey slipped on the interior of the rim, exterior rough and interior smooth.

Sr. No. 26
Location: Surface collection.
Fragment: Rim and body. Diam. 38 cm
Form: Dish-featureless rim.
Fabric: Coarse.
Surfaces: Grey slipped, weathered.

Plate XXXII.d. Nos.27-29

Sr. No. 27
Location: Surface collection.
Fragment: Rim and neck. Diam. 23 cm
Form: Medium size jar- flaring grooved rim, flanged shoulder and bulbous body.
Fabric: Fine.
Surfaces: Both surfaces of the rim polished, Red Polished Ware.

Sr. No. 28
Location: Surface collection.
Fragment: Rim. Diam. 26 cm
Form: Bowl-inturned flattened beaked rim.
Fabric: Fine.
Surfaces: Weathered, slipped on both sides, Red Polished ware.

Sr. No. 29
Location: Surface collection.
Fragment: Rim. Diam. 21 cm
Form: Bowl-flaring rim, bulbous body.
Fabric: Fine.
Surfaces: Slightly weathered, slipped on both sides, Red polished Ware.

Minor objects.

1. A fragment of iron object probably part of a bowl. **(Plate L. No.6)**.

5. **Site name**: Chopra **(Plate XXI.a)**.
Co-ordinate: Lat. 21°21' N; Long. 72°10' E.
Period of occupation: Early Historic.
Reference: New discovery.

Location: The locality called Chopra, 2 km to the northeast of Padri, Talaja tehil, falls in the jurisdiction of the same village. It is close to the village called Takhatgarh.

The site: The ancient site is known as Chopra, which is roughly 2 km away from the Gulf of Cambay and on the left bank of river Shetrunji. The site, which is almost intact, measures 300 m (north-south) in length and 200 m (east-west) in width. The habitation deposit is 3 m. Only few fragments of pottery and bones are exposed on the surface as the site is covered with grass and other natural vegetation. From the ceramic assemblage it is clear that the site was under occupation only during the Early Historic period. The site is discovered by the author.

Ceramic assemblage:

Plate XXXIII.a. Nos.1-6

Sr. No. 1
Location: Surface collection.
Fragment: Rim. Diam. 25 cm
Form: Jar-externally projecting triangular rim.
Fabric: Coarse to medium.
Surfaces: Red slipped on both sides, weathered.

Sr. No. 2
Location: Surface collection.
Fragment: Rim and neck. Diam. 24 cm
Form: Jar-externally projecting squarish rim, groove on the interior of the rim.
Fabric: Coarse.
Surfaces: Red slipped on both sides, weathered.

Sr. No. 3
Location: Surface collection.
Fragment: Rim and upper body. Diam. 22 cm
Form: Jar-clubbed rim.
Fabric: Coarse.
Surfaces: Red slipped on both sides, weathered.

Sr. No. 4
Location: Surface collection.
Fragment: Rim. Diam. 23 cm
Form: Jar-externally projecting flat rim.
Fabric: Coarse.
Surfaces: Unslipped, rough.

Sr. No. 5
Location: Surface collection.
Fragment: Rim and neck. Diam. 24 cm

Form: Jar-externally thicken rounded rim, groove on the top of the rim, ridge on the waist.
Fabric: Coarse to medium.
Surfaces: Red slipped, weathered.

Sr. No. 6
Location: Surface collection.
Fragment: Rim. Diam. 22
Form: Jar-triangular under-cut rim.
Fabric: Coarse.
Surfaces: Unslipped, rough.

Plate XXXIII.b. Nos.7-12
Sr. No. 7
Location: Surface collection.
Fragment: Base and lower body.
Form: Cup-disc base, flaring sides.
Fabric: Coarse.
Surfaces: Unslipped, rough.

Sr. No. 8
Location: Surface collection.
Fragment: Base and lower body.
Form: Deep bowl-disc base.
Fabric: Coarse.
Surfaces: Grey slipped on internally, externally rough but internally smooth.

Sr. No. 9
Location: Surface collection.
Fragment: Rim. Diam. 28 cm
Form: Vessel form unascertained-rounded rim with applique design.
Fabric: Coarse.
Surfaces: Grey slipped on interior of the rim, weathered.

Sr. No. 10
Location: Surface collection.
Fragment: Rim. Diam. 16 cm
Form: Basin-pointed rim, ledge on the exterior of rim.
Fabric: Coarse.
Surfaces: Grey slipped, weathered.

Sr. No. 11
Location: Surface collection.
Fragment: Rim. Diam. 18 cm

Form: Dish-flat rim, grooves mark on the interior of the rim.
Fabric: Coarse.
Surfaces: Grey slipped, weathered.

Sr. No. 12
Location: Surface collection.
Fragment: Spout.
Form: Conical spout.
Fabric: Coarse.
Surfaces: Grey slipped, weathered.

Minor objects.

1. Specimens of used shell. (**Plate XLVIII.b. Nos.2-3**).

6. **Site name**: *Dard* (**Plate XXI.b**).
Co-ordinate: Lat. 21°19' N; Long. 72°7' E.
Period of occupation: Mature Harappan and Early Historic.
Reference: New discovery.
Location: The village Dakana is located around 6 km south of Talaja town close to the road going towards Gopnath and 7 km north of Saltanpur which is near the Gulf of Cambay.

The site: The ancient habitational mound is roughly 2 km away from the present village and on the right bank of Shetrunji river. The mound is locally known as *Dard*. The site is 7 km west of ancient settlement of Padri. The site was not earlier reported. It site is quite extensive but the modern road running through the mound has divided the site into two parts. The habitation mound measures 300 m (east-west) X 400 m (north-south) with a maximum deposit of 1.50 m. A few shell pieces have been recovered from the surface. The site was under occupation during the Mature Harappan and Early Historic periods.

Ceramic assemblage:

Plate XXXIV.a. Nos.1-10

Sr. No. 1
Location: Surface collection.
Fragment: Rim and neck. Diam. 29 cm
Form: Jar-internally flat, slightly projecting rim and externally thickened.
Fabric: Coarse to medium.
Surfaces: Red slipped on both sides, smooth.

Sr. No. 2
Location: Surface collection.
Fragment: Rim and neck. Diam. 23 cm
Form: Jar-short out turned rim, externally thickened and globular body.
Fabric: Coarse.
Surfaces: Red slipped, smooth.

Sr. No. 3
Location: Surface collection.
Fragment: Rim and neck. Diam. 20 cm
Form: Jar-beaked rim, short vertical neck.
Surfaces: Red slipped, smooth.

Sr. No. 4
Location: Surface collection.
Fragment: Rim. Diam. 23 cm
Form: Small globular pot-flat projecting rim, vertical neck.
Fabric: Coarse.
Surfaces: Red slipped on both sides, smooth.

Sr. No. 5
Location: Surface collection.
Fragment: Rim and neck. Diam. 18 cm
Form: Jar-out turned and externally thickened rounded rim, short neck.
Fabric: Coarse.
Surfaces: Red slipped on both sides, smooth.

Sr. No. 6
Location: Surface collection.
Fragment: Rim and neck. Diam. 17 cm
Form: Jar-slightly out turned and externally thickened rim.
Fabric: Coarse.
Surfaces: Red slipped on both sides, weathered.

Sr. No. 7
Location: Surface collection.
Fragment: Rim. Diam. 18 cm
Form: Pot-short beaked rim, ridge at the neck, short vertical neck.
Fabric: Coarse.
Surfaces: Red slipped on both sides, weathered.

Sr. No. 8
Location: Surface collection.
Fragment: Rim and body. Diam. 12 cm
Form: Pot-externally thickened rim.
Fabric: Coarse.
Surfaces: red slipped on both side, weathered.

Sr. No. 9
Location: Surface collection.
Fragment: Rim and body. Diam. 13 cm

Form: Cup-short featureless rim.
Fabric: Coarse.
Surfaces: Red slipped on both sides.

Sr. No. 10
Location: Surface collection.
Fragment: Base and lower body.
Form: Cup-disc base, flaring sides.
Fabric: Coarse.
Surfaces: Red slipped on both sides.

7. **Site name**: *Khodiyar* **(Plate XXII.a)**.
Co-ordinate: Lat. 21°24' N Long. 72°2' E
Period of occupation: Early and Harappan and Early Historic.
Reference: Ghosh 1989: 227; *IAR*. 1960-61.

Location: The modern village Dantrad is located on the right bank of the river Shetrunji and roughly 10 km upstream of the town of Talaja.

The site: The ancient mound locally known as *Khodiyar*, is located one and half km away from the village. The site is roughly 15 km away from the ancient site of Padri towards the north east. This site was discovered in the early sixties (*IAR*. 1960-61). The site is quite extensive measuring 300 m (east-west) and 150 m (north-south). The upper level of the mound is highly disturbed due to the agricultural activities. The habitational deposit of the site is around one and half meter thick, which is visible in the cut section. From the ceramic assemblage it is clear that the site has a three-fold cultural sequence namely, the Early Harappan, Mature Harappan and Early Historic. Besides, few objects like a muller made of sand stone and terracotta spindle whorls have been found.

Ceramic assemblage:

Plate XXXIV.b. Nos.1-13

Sr. No. 1
Location: Surface collection.
Fragment: Rim. Diam. 9 cm
Form: Small globular pot (lota)-everted rim.
Fabric: Medium to fine.
Surfaces: Red slipped on both sides, weathered.

Sr. No. 2
Location: Surface collection.
Fragment: Rim. Diam. 36 cm
Form: Dish-everted rim.
Fabric: Coarse.
Surfaces: Red slipped on both sides, smooth.

Sr. No. 3
Location: Surface collection.
Fragment: Rim. Diam. 26 cm
Form: Basin-inverted rim, slightly under-cut on exterior, groove on the top of the rim.
Fabric: Coarse.
Surfaces: Grey slipped on both sides, weathered.

Sr. No. 4
Location: Surface collection.
Fragment: Rim. Diam. 18 cm
Form: Unascertained-flat rim, groove on the top of the rim.
Fabric: Coarse.
Surfaces: Grey slipped on both sides, weathered.

Sr. No. 5
Location: Surface collection.
Fragment: Rim and neck. Diam. 22 cm
Form: Jar-flared out rim, short neck, globular body.
Fabric: Coarse.
Surfaces: Grey slipped on both sides, weathered.

Sr. No. 6
Location: Surface collection.
Fragment: Rim and upper body. Diam. 17 cm
Form: Jar-out curved rim with deep grooved on the top and internally beveled rim.
Fabric: Coarse.
Surfaces: Grey slipped on exterior, smooth.

Sr. No. 7
Location: Surface collection.
Fragment: Rim and upper body. Diam. 26 cm
Form: Pot-externally projecting beaked rim, slight carination at the shoulder, short vertical neck.
Fabric: Coarse.
Surfaces: Grey slipped on exterior of the rim, weathered.

Sr. No. 8
Location: Surface collection.
Fragment: Rim and upper body. Diam. 20 cm
Form: Jar-flaring rim, short neck, globular body.
Fabric: Coarse.
Surfaces: Grey slipped on both sides, smooth.

Sr. No. 9
Location: Surface collection.
Fragment: Base and lower body.
Form: Small saucer-short slightly out-curved and featureless rim, flat base.
Fabric: Coarse.
Surfaces: Unslipped on both sides, rough.

Sr. No. 10
Location: Surface collection.
Fragment: Rim and upper body. Diam. 20 cm
Form: Jar-beaded rim, low flaring neck, bulbous body.
Fabric: Fine.
Surfaces: Smooth, slipped on both sides, Red Polished Ware.

Sr. No. 11
Location: Surface collection.
Fragment: Rim. Diam. 15 cm
Form: Jar-rectangular rim.
Fabric: Fine.
Surfaces: Smooth, slipped on both sides, Red Polished Ware.

Sr. No 12
Location: Surface collection.
Fragment: Rim. Diam. 30 cm
Form: Bowl-beaded rim.
Fabric: Fine.
Surfaces: Weathered, slipped on both sides, Red Polished Ware.

Sr. No. 13
Location: Surface collection.
Fragment: Rim and Body. Diam. 22 cm
Form: Bowl-inturned nail shaped rim.
Fabric: Fine.
Surfaces: Weathered, slipped on both sides, Red Polished Ware.

8. **Site name**: *Vikra Dhoro* **(Plate XXII.b)**.
Co-ordinate: Lat. 21°21' N; Long. 72°7' E.
Period of occupation: Early Historic.
Reference: New discovery.

Location: The village Devalia is located 5 km to the west of Talaja town and one and half km south of Dantrad village. It is on the right bank of Shetrunji river. There is no direct communication to the village from the taluka head-quarter.

The site: The ancient mound is located roughly one and half km to the south of present village and locally known as *Vikra Dhoro* and 7 km away from the ancient settlement of Padri. It is spread over an area of 75 m (north-south) by 150 m (east-west). The habitation mound is divided into two parts by the modern road. The thickness of the habitation deposit is not certain as it is covered by grass and vegetation. The mound is quite intact and oval in shape. The site was not reported earlier. Few pieces of iron slag have been noticed on the surface. The site was occupied only during the Early Historic period.

Ceramic assemblage:

Plate XXXV.a. Nos.1-12

Sr. No. 1
Location: Surface collection.
Fragment: Rim and neck. Diam. 14 cm
Form: Small globular pot-externally projecting under-cut rim and projection on the interior of the rim.
Fabric: Coarse.
Surfaces: Red slipped on both sides, weathered.

Sr. No. 2
Location: Surface collection.
Fragment: Rim, neck and upper body. Diam.16 cm
Form: Small jar-externally projecting beaked rim, vertical neck.
Fabric: Coarse.
Surfaces: Unslipped, weathered.

Sr. No. 3
Location: Surface collection.
Fragment: Rim and neck. Diam. 16 cm
Form: Jar-externally thicken rim.
Fabric: Coarse.
Surfaces: Unslipped, rough.

Sr. No. 4
Location: Surface collection.
Fragment: Rim, neck and upper body. Diam. 16 cm
Form: Jar-flared out rim, short neck.
Fabric: Coarse.
Surfaces: Red slipped on exterior of the rim, weathered.

Sr. No. 5
Location: Surface collection.
Fragment: Rim and neck. Diam. 30 cm
Form: Dish-flaring rim, carination at the shoulder.
Fabric: Coarse.
Surfaces: Grey slipped on the interior of the rim, exterior rough and interior smooth.

Sr. No. 6
Location: Surface collection.
Fragment: Rim and neck. Diam. 21 cm
Form: Jar-out curved rim, grooved on the top.
Fabric: Coarse.
Surfaces: Grey slipped on the interior side.

Sr. No. 7
Location: Surface collection.
Fragment: Rim and body. Diam. 27 cm
Form: Dish-externally thickened rim, slightly internally projection.
Fabric: Coarse.
Surfaces: Grey slipped on both sides, rough.

Sr. No. 8
Location: Surface collection.
Fragment: Rim and body. Diam. 28 cm
Form: Dish-slightly internally projecting and externally rounded rim.
Fabric: Coarse.
Surfaces: Grey slipped on both sides, rough.

Sr. No. 9
Location: Surface collection.
Fragment: Rim and neck. Diam. 26 cm
Form: Jar-out curved rim
Fabric: Coarse.
Surfaces: Grey slipped on the both sides, weathered.

Sr. No. 10
Location: Surface collection.
Fragment: Rim and neck.
Form: Jar-flaring rim, almost no neck.
Fabric: Coarse.
Surfaces: Grey slipped, weathered.

Sr. No. 11
Location: Surface collection.
Fragment: Base and lower body.
Form: Shallow bowl-flat base.
Fabric: Coarse.
Surfaces: Unslipped, rough.

Sr. No. 12
Location: Surface collection.

Fragment: Lower part.
Form: Dish-on-stand ?, hollow at the bottom.
Fabric: Coarse.
Surfaces: Unslipped, rough.

Minor objects.

1. A fragment of vitrified clay. **(Plate L. No.1)**

9. **Site name**: *Alidhar* **(Plate XXIII. a)**.
Co-ordinate: Lat. 20°21' N; Long. 72°6' E
Period of occupation: Early Harappan, Mature Harappan and Early Historic.
Reference: Ghosh 1989: 14; *IAR.* 1960-61.

Location: The present village Gorkhi in Talaja Tehsil of Bhavnagar district is located around 200 m from the metal road running between Padri Gohel-ni and Talaja, taluka head-quarter.

The site: The ancient site is located on the left bank of Shetrunji river. It is roughly 6 km to the west of Padri. The ancient site locally known as *Alidhar*, was already reported as an Early Historic site (*IAR.* 1960-61; Ghosh 1984: 14). The settlement is rectangular in shape. It is quite extensive and measures 300 m in length (north-south) and 150 m in width (east-west). The upper deposit of the site is disturbed due to agricultural activities. The ceramic assemblage recovered from 1.50 m thick habitational deposit, however, revealed a three-fold cultural sequence namely, Early Harappan, Mature Harappan and Early Historic. A part of the ancient site is under the modern occupation. All over the mound sherds of Red-slipped ware and Red ware are found. A good number of Red Polished Ware sherd has also been found from the site.

Ceramic assemblage:

Plate XXXV.b. No.1-13

Sr. No. 1
Location: Surface collection.
Fragment: Rim and neck. Diam.18 cm
Form: Pot-externally out-turned rim, rounded on the top, concave neck.
Fabric: Coarse.
Surfaces: Red slipped on both sides, rough.

Sr. No. 2
Location: Surface collection.
Fragment: Rim and neck. Diam. 20 cm
Form: Jar-internally flat and slightly projecting rim.
Fabric: Coarse.
Surfaces: Red slipped on both sides, rough.

Sr. No. 3
Location: Surface collection.

Fragment: Rim and neck. Diam. 18 cm
Form: Small jar-slightly out turned and externally thickened rim.
Fabric: Coarse.
Surfaces: Red slipped on both sides, weathered.

Sr. No. 4
Location: Surface collection.
Fragment: Rim and shoulder. Diam. 19 cm
Form: Pot-flaring rim, short neck.
Fabric: Coarse.
Surfaces: Red slipped on both sides, weathered.

Sr. No. 5
Location: Surface collection.
Fragment: Rim and neck. Diam. 18 cm
Form: Jar-slightly out turned and externally thickened rim.
Fabric: Coarse.
Surfaces: Red slipped on both sides, weathered.

Sr. No. 6
Location: Surface collection.
Fragment: Rim and neck. Diam. 20 cm
Form: Pot-external projecting beaded under cut rim.
Fabric: Coarse.
Surfaces: Red slipped on both sides, weathered.

Sr. No. 7
Location: Surface collection.
Fragment: Rim and Body. Diam. 25 cm
Form: Shallow dish-out curved beaded rim.
Fabric: Coarse.
Surfaces: Red slipped on both sides, weathered.

Sr. No. 8
Location: Surface collection.
Fragment: Rim and body. Diam. 11 cm
Form: Dish-externally flat projecting rim, projection on interior of the rim.
Fabric: Coarse.
Surfaces: Red slipped on both sides, weathered.

Sr. No. 9
Location: Surface collection.
Fragment: Rim and upper body. Diam. 36 cm
Form: Jar-projecting beaded rim, flaring neck.

Fabric: Fine.
Surfaces: Smooth, slipped on both sides, Red Polished Ware.

Sr. No. 10
Location: Surface collection.
Fragment: Rim. Diam. 22 cm
Form: Bowl-out turned rim.
Fabric: Fine.
Surfaces: Smooth, slipped on both sides, Red Polished Ware.

Sr. No. 11
Location: Surface collection.
Fragment: Rim. Diam. 18 cm
Form: Bowl-beaded rim.
Fabric: Fine.
Surfaces: Weathered, slipped on both sides, Red Polished Ware.

Sr. No. 12
Location: Surface collection.
Fragment: Rim and neck. Diam. 20 cm
Form: Jar-beaked rim, flaring neck.
Fabric: Fine.
Surfaces: Weathered, slipped on both sides, Red Polished Ware.

Sr. No. 13
Location: Surface Collection.
Fragment: Neck.
Form: Sprinkler-concavo-convex profile.
Fabric: Fine.
Surfaces: Weathered, slipped on exterior surface, Red Polished Ware.

Minor objects.

1. A circular terracotta disc, unperforated. Measurement: T. 23.57 mm, Cir. 66.13 mm. **(Plate XLVI.b. No. 13)**

10. **Site name**: *Hastinapur Timba* **(Plate XXIII.b)**.
Co-ordinate: Lat. 21°36′ N; Long. 72°21′ E.
Period of occupation: Late Harappan and Early Historic.
Reference: *IAR* 1979-80, as Early Historic site and *IAR*. 1980-81 as Harappan and Early Historic site.

Location: Village Hathab is located about 15 km to the west of Bhavnagar town and 1.5 km west of Gulf of Cambay.

The site: The ancient site is located 1 km to the north of the present village of Hathab and is known as *Hastinapur Timba*. Hathab represents ancient Hastavapra or Hastakavapra, which is rendered as Astacampra in Greek literature (Schoff 1912: 39-40; Trivedi 1969: 47;

Jairath 1986: 151 and Bharucha 1997). Jairath further says (Jairath 1986: 151) " Hathab in the past was the port of Gundi-Koliyak, the ancient Gundigarh and has been identified by colonel Yale with Astakampra of the earlier Greek navigators. Dr. Buhler carried this identification a step further and recognised it as the Hasta-Kavapra; of the copper plate grant of Dhruvasena, found at Kukad, which has been alluded to in the same grant as Kukata". The habitational mound is quite extensive but one modern road running through the mound has divided it into two parts. The habitational settlement measures about 800 m (east-west) and 500 m (north-south) with a 5 m thick habitational deposit. One modern temple is constructed on the eastern side of the mound. The surface of the mound is littered with pottery, bones and other objects. Besides pottery, a large number of unperforated terracotta discs, vitrified clay, shell bangles, a fragment of amphorae handle and shell debitage have been collected. Apart from this four pieces of rectangular punch marked copper coins are collected from the land owner of the site.

Ceramic assemblage:

Plate XXXVI.a. Nos.1-9

Sr. No. 1
Location: Surface collection.
Fragment: Rim and neck. Diam. 19 cm
Form: Globular pot-external projecting beaked rim, short vertical neck.
Fabric: Coarse.
Surfaces: Unslipped, weathered.

Sr. No. 2
Location: Surface collection.
Fragment: Rim and neck. Diam. 21 cm
Form: Jar-prominently externally projecting rim.
Fabric: Coarse.
Surfaces: Unslipped, weathered.

Sr. No. 3
Location: Surface collection.
Fragment: Rim and neck. Diam. 18 cm
Form: Pot-externally projecting flat rim, short neck.
Fabric: Coarse.
Surfaces: Unslipped, weathered.

Sr. No. 4
Location: Surface collection.
Fragment: Base and lower body.
Form: Shallow bowl-flat base.
Fabric: Coarse.
Surfaces: Unslipped, rough.

Sr. No. 5
Location: Surface collection.
Fragment: Base and lower body.
Form: Cup-disc base.
Fabric: Coarse.
Surfaces: Unslipped, rough.

Sr. No. 6
Location: Surface collection.
Fragment: Base and lower body.
Form: Cup-disc base.
Fabric: Coarse.
Surfaces: Unslipped, rough.

Sr. No. 7
Location: Surface collection.
Fragment: Base and lower body.
Form: Bowl-ring foot base.
Fabric: Coarse.
Surfaces: Unslipped, rough.

Sr. No. 8
Location: Surface collection.
Fragment: Body sherd.
Form: Undetermined. Probably pot, stamped and two bands of oblique incision on the exterior of the body.
Fabric: Coarse.
Surfaces: Unslipped, rough.

Sr. No. 9
Location: Surface collection.
Fragment: Stem.
Form: Unknown, Stem or part of a finial of a vessel, irregular wall, fluted ? ledges.
Fabric: Coarse.
Surfaces: Unslipped, rough.

Plate XXXVI.b. Nos.10-15

Sr. No. 10
Location: Surface collection.
Fragment: Stem.
Form: Unknown. Same as No.9 but small in size.
Fabric: Coarse.
Surfaces: Unslipped, rough.

Sr. No.	11
Location:	Surface collection.
Fragment:	Rim and neck. Diam. 21 cm
Form:	Jar-rounded thickened rim, projecting internally and externally, short neck.
Fabric:	Coarse.
Surfaces:	Red slipped on both sides, weathered.

Sr. No.	12
Location:	Surface collection.
Fragment:	Rim. Diam.16 cm
Form:	Jar-out turned and slightly projecting rim, concave neck.
Fabric:	Coarse.
Surfaces:	Red slipped on both sides, weathered.

Sr. No.	13
Location:	Surface collection.
Fragment:	Rim neck and shoulder. Diam. 25 cm
Form:	Jar-out turned and externally thickened rim, concave neck.
Fabric:	Coarse.
Surfaces:	Red slipped on exterior of the rim, weathered.

Sr. No.	14
Location:	Surface collection.
Fragment:	Rim and neck. Diam. 24 cm
Form:	Pot-beaked rim, almost no neck, globular body, grooved on the exterior of the rim.
Fabric:	Coarse.
Surfaces:	Red slipped on both sides, weathered.

Sr. No.	15
Location:	Surface collection.
Fragment:	Rim, neck and shoulder. Diam. 17 cm
Form:	Small jar-concave neck and beaded rim, globular body.
Fabric:	Coarse.
Surfaces:	Red slipped on the exterior of the rim, weathered.

Plate XXXXVI.c. Nos.16-21

Sr. No.	16
Location:	Surface collection.
Fragment:	Rim. Diam. 19 cm
Form:	Bowl-slightly out curved and internally thickened rim.
Fabric:	Coarse.
Surfaces:	Red slipped on both sides, weathered.

Sr. No. 17
Location: Surface collection.
Fragment: Rim and neck. Diam. 23 cm
Form: Jar-beaded and slightly under cut rim, high neck.
Fabric: Coarse.
Surfaces: Red slipped on the exterior of the rim, weathered.

Sr. No. 18
Location: Surface collection.
Fragment: Base and lower body.
Form: Unascertained-ring foot base.
Fabric: Coarse.
Surfaces: Red slipped on the exterior of the ring base, weathered.

Sr. No. 19
Location: Surface collection.
Fragment: Base and lower body.
Form: Undetermined-small ring foot base.
Fabric: Coarse.
Surfaces: Red slipped on both sides, weathered.

Sr. No. 20
Location: Surface collection.
Fragment: Body sherd.
Form: Unknown, probably lid, grooves on the exterior of the body.
Fabric: Coarse.
Surfaces: Red slipped on the exterior of the body, weathered.

Sr. No. 21
Location: Surface collection.
Fragment: Rim and neck. Diam. 39 cm
Form: Big jar-thickened and rounded rim, ledge on the exterior of the neck.
Fabric: Coarse.
Surfaces: Red slipped on both sides, weathered.

Plate XXXVI.d. Nos.22-27

Sr. No. 22
Location: Surface collection.
Fragment: Body sherd.
Form: Unascertained. Some wavy lines on the body.
Fabric: Coarse.
Surfaces: Red slipped on both sides, weathered.

Sr. No. 23
Location: Surface collection.
Fragment: Rim and neck. Diam. 22 cm
Form: Jar-beaded and under cut rim, long neck.
Fabric: Coarse.
Surfaces: Grey slipped on both sides, rough.

Sr. No. 24
Location: Surface collection.
Fragment: Rim and neck. Diam. 22 cm
Form: Medium size jar-flared out and externally thickened rim.
Fabric: Coarse.
Surfaces: Grey slipped on both sides, smooth.

Sr. No. 25
Location: Surface collection.
Fragment: Rim and neck. Diam. 25 cm
Form: Pot-outcurved beaded rim, short vertical neck.
Fabric: Coarse.
Surfaces: Grey slipped on both sides, weathered.

Sr. No. 26
Location: Surface collection.
Fragment: Rim and neck. Diam. 22 cm
Form: Handi-out-curved beaded rim, no neck.
Fabric: Coarse.
Surfaces: Grey slipped on both sides, weathered.

Sr. No. 27
Location: Surface collection.
Fragment: Rim and neck. Diam. 26 cm
Form: Pot-out-curved rim, high neck.
Fabric: Coarse.
Surfaces: Grey slipped on both sides, weathered.

Plate XXXVI.e. No.28

Sr. No. 28
Location: Surface collection.
Fragment: Handle.
Form: Handle of a Roman amphorae.
Fabric: Medium to fine.
Surfaces: Thin slipped on both sides.

Plate XXXVI.f. Nos. 29-33

Sr. No. 29
Location: Surface collection.
Fragment: Rim and neck. Diam. 10 cm
From: Jar-grooved rim, flaring neck and bulbous body.
Fabric: Fine.
Surfaces: Smooth, slipped on both sides, Red polished Ware.

Sr. No. 30
Location: Surface collection.
Fragment: Rim and neck. Diam. 14 cm
Form: Jar-out turned beaded rim.
Fabric: Fine.
Surfaces: Smooth, slipped on both sides, Red Polished Ware.

Sr. No. 31
Location: Surface collection.
Fragment: Spout.
Form: Basin-beaded mouth.
Fabric: Fine.
Surfaces: Smooth, slipped on exterior surface, Red Polished ware.

Sr. No. 32
Location: Surface collection.
Fragment: Spout.
Form: Basin-spout at its base.
Fabric: Fine.
Surfaces: Smooth, slipped on exterior surface, Red Polished Ware.

Sr. No. 33
Location: Surface collection.
Fragment: Spout.
Form: Spouted basin- decorations on the exterior surface.
Fabric: Fine.
Surfaces: Smooth, slipped on exterior surface Red Polished Ware.

Minor objects.

1. A unperforated terracotta disc. Measurements: T. 17.94 mm, Cir. 66.41 mm **(Plate XLVI.a. No. 4)**.
2. A fragment terracotta disc, unperforated. Measurements: T. 18.4 mm, Cir. 94.59 mm. **(Plate XLVI.a. No. 5)**
3. A unperforated terracotta disc. Measurements: T. 17.57 mm, Cir. 54.85 mm **(Plate XLVI.a. No. 6)**.

4. A unperforated terracotta disc, red in color. Measurements: T. 16.65 mm, Cir.61.44 mm. **(Plate XLVI.a. No.7)**
5. A unperforated terracotta disc. Measurements: T. 15.59 mm, Cir. 53.02 mm **(Plate XLVI.a. No.8)**.
6. A fragment of terracotta disc, unperforated. Measurement: T. 11.84 mm , Cir. 57.1 mm. **(Plate XLVI.a. No. 9)**.
7. A terracotta disc. Measurement: T. 15.18 mm, Cir. 39.08 mm **(Plate XLVI.a No. 10)**
8. A circular terracotta disc, unperforated and small in size. Measurement: T. 8.03 mm, Cir.27.56 mm. **(Plate XLVI.a. No.11)**
9. A fragment of plain shell bangle, thin cross section. Measurements: T. 5.30 mm, W. 9.56 mm **(Plate XLVII.b. No.1)**.
10. A fragment of plain shell bangle, thin cross section. Measurements: T. 5.05 mm, W. 7.62 mm. **(Plate XLVII.b. No. 2)**.
11. A fragment of plain shell bangle, thick cross section. Measurements: T. 7.36 mm, W. 17.54 mm **(Plate XLVII.b. No. 6)**.
12. Same as No. 9 but smaller in size. Measurements: T. 2.70 mm, W. 6.02 mm **(Plate XLVII.b. No.4)**.
13. Same as No.12 but thick cross section. Measurements: T. 4.25 mm, W. 8.37 mm **(Plate XLVII.a. No. 5)**.
14. Shell dibatage **(Plate. XLVIII.a)**.
15. A complete specimen of used shell. **(Plate XLVIII.b. No. 1)**.
16. A fragment of vitrified clay **(Plate L. Nos.2)**.
17. A fragment of vitrified clay **(Plate L. No. 3)**.
18. A small punchmarked copper coin. It is imbossed with six armed (*Sadara-Chakra*) and victory banner surmounted by Taurine symbol on one side and on the other side is a *Swastika* symbol at its four orbs indistinct objects. On the left side of this symbol there is a galloping horse and on the horse some unidentified symbol is visible, it may be a horse rider. Rectangular-shaped. Measurements Cir. 19.43 mm, T. 2.09 mm. **(Plate LII.a and b.)**.
19. A small punchmarked copper coin. The symbol and script are not clear, corroded rectangular-shaped. Measurements. Cir. 21.83 mm, T. 2.70 mm. **(Plate LII: No.1.)**
20. Same as No. 19. Measurements. Cir. 18.95 mm, T. 1.37 mm. **(Plate LII. No.2.)**.
21. Same as 20 but small in size. Measurements. Cir. 14.62 mm. T. 1.41 mm **(Plate LII. No.3.)**.

11. **Site name**: Ichhora **(Plate XXIV.a)**.
Co-ordinate: Lat. 21°21' N; Long. 72°8' E
Period of occupation: Early Historic.
Reference: New discovery.
Location: The village Ichhora located roughly 6 km away from Talaja to the east and 3 km to the west of Padri Gohil-ni village.

The site: The ancient site is close to the present village and is located on the left bank of river Shetrunji. The site has been discovered by the author for the first time. The mound measures 300 m in length (north-south) and 100 m in width (east-west). The habitational deposit is one and half meter thick. One hero-stone was noticed on the outskirts of the mound which is kept by the villagers. It was occupied only during the Early Historic period. Only representative pot sherd have been collected from the surface.

Ceramic assemblage:

Plate XXXVII.a. Nos.1-9

Sr. No. 1
Location: Surface collection.
Fragment: Rim, neck and upper body. Diam. 14 cm
Form: Jar-out turned and externally thickened rim.
Fabric: Coarse.
Surfaces: Red slipped on both sides, weathered.

Sr. No. 2
Location: Surface collection.
Fragment: Rim and neck. Diam. 19 cm
Form: Jar-out-turned and externally thickened rim, groove on the interior of the rim, concave neck.
Fabric: Coarse.
Surfaces: Red slipped on both sides, weathered.

Sr. No. 3
Location: Surface collection.
Fragment: Rim. Diam. 21 cm
Form: Dish-flat and slightly projecting rim, appliqué design on the interior and globular stamped design on the interior and ledge on the exterior.
Fabric: Coarse.
Surfaces: Red slipped on both sides, weathered.

Sr. No. 4
Location: Surface collection.
Fragment: Rim and upper body. Diam. 22 cm
Form: Globular pot with middle mouth-externally projecting moulded rim, grove on the top of the rim, short vertical neck.
Fabric: Coarse.
Surfaces: Red slipped on both sides, weathered.

Sr. No. 5
Location: Surface collection.
Fragment: Rim. Diam. 8 cm
Form: Cup-convex sided body.
Fabric: Coarse.
Surfaces: Red slipped on both sides, weathered.

Sr. No. 6
Location: Surface collection.
Fragment: Rim neck and upper body. Diam. 20 cm
Form: Jar-externally projecting beaked rim, groove and ledge on the exterior of the rim.
Fabric: Coarse.
Surfaces: Red slipped on exterior, weathered.

Sr. No. 7
Location: Surface collection.
Fragment: Rim and neck. Diam. 18 cm
Form: Jar-externally projecting rim, short vertical neck.
Fabric: Coarse.
Surfaces: Red slipped on exterior, weathered.

Sr. No. 8
Location: Surface collection.
Fragment: Rim, neck and upper body. Diam. 20 cm
Form: Globular pot-externally thickened rounded rim, groove on the top of the rim, short vertical neck.
Fabric: Coarse.
Surfaces: Red slipped on externally, weathered.

Sr. No. 9
Location: Surface collection.
Fragment: Rim and neck. Diam. 16 cm
Form: Jar-squarish rim.
Fabric: Coarse.
Surfaces: Unslipped, rough.

Plate XXXVII.b. Nos.10-18

Sr. No. 10
Location: Surface collection.
Fragment: Spout.
Form: Spout-conical channel.
Fabric: Coarse.
Surfaces: Red slipped on exterior, weathered.

Sr. No. 11
Location: Surface collection.
Fragment: Base and lower body.
Form: Shallow bowl-disc base.
Fabric: Coarse.
Surfaces: Red slipped on the interior of the body, rough.

Sr. No. 12
Location: Surface collection.
Fragment: Base and lower body.
Form: Shallow bowl-stand like base, hand made.
Fabric: Coarse.
Surfaces: Red slipped on the interior of the body, rough.

Sr. No. 13
Location: Surface collection.
Fragment: Spout.
Form: Spout-circular.
Fabric: Coarse.
Surfaces: Red slipped, weathered.

Sr. No. 14
Location: Surface collection.
Fragment: Rim, neck and upper body. Diam. 20 cm
Form: Jar-out turned rim with deep grooved on the top and internally beveled rim.
Fabric: Coarse.
Surfaces: Grey slipped on both sides, rough.

Sr. No. 15
Location: Surface collection.
Fragment: Rim and neck. Diam. 22 cm
Form: Globular pot-externally projecting rounded rim, grooves on the interior of the rim, vertical neck.
Fabric: Coarse.
Surfaces: Grey slipped on both sides, weathered.

Sr. No 16
Location: Surface collection.
Fragment: Rim and neck. Diam. 15 cm
Form: Jar-out curved rim, globular body.
Fabric: Coarse
Surfaces: Grey slipped on exterior, weathered.

Sr. No. 17
Location: Surface collection.
Fragment: Rim. Diam. 17 cm
Form: Pot-ledge pointed rim.
Fabric: Coarse
Surfaces: Grey slipped, weathered.

Sr. No. 18
Location: Surface collection.
Fragment: Rim and neck. Diam. 12 cm
Form: Pot-externally projecting pointed rim. slight projection on the interior, groove and circular design at the top.
Fabric: Coarse
Surfaces: Grey slipped, rough.

Plate XXXVII.c. Nos.19-23

Sr. No. 19
Location: Surface collection.
Fragment: Rim and neck. Diam. 15 cm
Form: Small globular pot-externally flaring rim, ridge at the neck on the exterior.
Fabric: Coarse
Surfaces: Grey slipped, weathered.

Sr. No. 20
Location: Surface collection.
Fragment: Rim, neck and body. Diam. 24 cm
Form: Dish-out curved flaring rim, grooves on the interior.
Fabric: Coarse
Surfaces: Grey slipped, exterior rough and interior smooth.

Sr. No. 21
Location: Surface collection.
Fragment: Lower part.
Form: Dish-on-stand(?) flat base.
Fabric: Coarse
Surfaces: Grey slipped, rough.

Sr. No. 22
Location: Surface collection.
Fragment: Part of the lid .
Form: Lid, knobbed is decorated with groove, circular.
Fabric: Coarse
Surfaces: Grey slipped, weathered.

Sr. No. 23
Location: Surface collection.
Fragment: Spout.
Form: Spout-channel.
Fabric: Coarse
Surfaces: Grey slipped, weathered.

Minor objects:

1. A circular pot sherd disc, red in color. Measurement: T.20.70 mm, Cir.77.93 mm. **(Plate XLVI.b. No. 14)**

12. **Site name**: Katva (**Plate XXIV.b**).
Co-ordinate: Lat. 21°26' N; Long. 72°12' E.
Period of occupation: Early Historic.
Reference: New discovery.

Location: The modern village Katva is located 8 km to the north-east of Talaja town and 3 km to the west of Alang village, where the biggest ship-wreck industry in Asia is located.

The site: The ancient habitational settlement is located roughly 1 km away from the present village to the southern direction and on the left side of the mound is the metal road running between Alang and the district head-quarter, Bhavnagar. The shaped of the mound is squarish. The site is quite extensive and spreads over an area 150 m (east-west) X 90 m (north-south). The thickness of the habitational deposit is roughly 1.5 m which was visible from the cut section. The mound is highly disturbed because it is under cultivation. The surface of the mound is littered with pottery. Besides pottery, few pieces of shell bangle, unperforated terracotta disc and unidentified fragment of animal figurines have been collected from the site.

Ceramic assemblage:

Plate XXXVIII.a. Nos.1-9

Sr. No. 1
Location: Surface collection.
Fragment: Rim and neck. Diam. 14 cm
Form: Jar-prominent externally projecting rim.
Fabric: Coarse to medium.
Surfaces: Unslipped, weathered.

Sr. No. 2
Location: Surface collection.
Fragment: Rim and upper shoulder. Diam. 18 cm
Form: Jar-out turned under cut rim, grooved on the exterior of the rim, short vertical neck.
Fabric: Coarse.
Surfaces: Unslipped, weathered.

Sr. No. 3
Location: Surface collection.
Fragment: Rim. Diam. 22 cm
Form: Jar-externally projecting thick rim, grooved on the interior of the rim, short neck.
Fabric: Coarse.

Surfaces: Unslipped, weathered.

Sr. No. 4
Location: Surface collection.
Fragment: Rim and neck. Diam. 19 cm
Form: Same as No. 3 but deep groove on the interior of the rim.
Fabric: Coarse.
Surfaces: Unslipped, weathered.

Sr. No. 5
Location: Surface collection.
Fragment: Rim and shoulder. Diam. 16 cm
Form: Jar-vertical pointed rim, high neck.
Fabric: Coarse.
Surfaces: Unslipped, weathered.

Sr. No. 6
Location: Surface collection.
Fragment: Rim and neck. Diam. 14 cm
Form: Jar-externally projecting rounded rim, groove on the interior of the rim.
Fabric: Coarse.
Surfaces: Unslipped, weathered.

Sr. No 7
Location: Surface collection.
Fragment: Rim and neck. Diam. 13 cm
Form: Globular pot-outcurved lightly beaded rim, short vertical neck.
Fabric: Coarse to medium.
Surfaces: Red slipped on both sides, weathered.

Sr. No. 8
Location: Surface collection.
Fragment: Rim and neck. Diam. 16 cm
Form: Pot-flared and slightly beaded rim, deep grooved on the top of the rim, short vertical neck, thin cross section.
Fabric: Coarse to medium.
Surfaces: Red slipped on both sides, weathered.

Sr. No. 9
Location: Surface collection.
Fragment: Base and lower body.
Form: Cup-disc base, flaring sides.
Fabric: Coarse.
Surfaces: Unslipped, weathered.

Plate XXXVIII.b. Nos.10-21

Sr. No. 10
Location: Surface collection.
Fragment: Rim and neck. Diam. 22 cm
Form: Jar-internally flat and slightly projecting rim.
Fabric: Medium to fine.
Surfaces: Red slipped on the exterior of the rim, weathered.

Sr. No. 11
Location: Surface collection.
Fragment: Rim and neck. Diam. 22 cm
Form: Jar-out turned and internally thickened rim, concave neck.
Fabric: Coarse.
Surfaces: Red slipped on exterior of the rim, weathered.

Sr. No. 12
Location: Surface collection.
Fragment: Rim and neck. Diam. 17 cm
Form: Pot-flat projecting rim, vertical neck.
Fabric: Coarse.
Surfaces: Red slipped on both sides, weathered.

Sr. No. 13
Location: Surface collection.
Fragment: Rim and neck. Diam. 14 cm
Form: Small pot-rounded rim, short neck.
Fabric: Coarse.
Surfaces: Red slipped on both sides, smooth.

Sr. No. 14
Location: Surface collection.
Fragment: Rim and body.
Form: Basin-flat slightly externally thickened rim.
Fabric: Coarse.
Surfaces: Red slipped on both sides, weathered.

Sr. No. 15
Location: Surface collection.
Fragment: Rim neck and shoulder. Diam. 16 cm
Form: Globular pot-out turned beaked rim.
Fabric: Coarse.
Surfaces: Grey slipped on both sides, smooth.

Sr. No. 16
Location: Surface collection.
Fragment: Rim. Diam. 24 cm
Form: Jar/pot-long out turned and external thickened rim, globular body.
Fabric: Coarse.
Surfaces: Grey slipped on both sides, weathered.

Sr. No. 17
Location: Surface collection.
Fragment: Rim and neck. Diam. 19 cm
Form: Globular pot-out turned beaded rim.
Fabric: Coarse.
Surfaces: Grey slipped, weathered.

Sr. No. 18
Location: Surface collection.
Fragment: Rim. Diam. 21 cm
Form: Pot-out turned beaded rim, sharp projection on the interior of the rim and grooved on the interior.
Fabric: Coarse.
Surfaces: Grey slipped, weathered.

Sr. No. 19
Location: Surface collection.
Fragment: Rim and body. Diam. 24 cm
Form: Shallow dish-featureless rim.
Fabric: Coarse.
Surfaces: Grey slipped, weathered.

Sr. No. 20
Location: Surface collection.
Fragment: Rim. Diam. 28 cm
Form: Shallow dish/bowl-beaded rim.
Fabric: Coarse.
Surfaces: Grey slipped on the interior of the rim, weathered.

Sr. No. 21
Location: Surface collection.
Fragment: Rim and body. Diam. 22 cm
Form: Deep bowl-incurved beaded rim having ledge below the rim.
Fabric: Coarse.
Surfaces: Grey slipped on the interior of the body, weathered.

Plate XXXVIII.c. Nos.22-27

Sr. No. 22
Location: Surface collection.
Fragment: Rim and neck. Diam. 10 cm
Form: Small size jar-knife edged rim and short flaring neck.
Fabric: Fine.
Surfaces: Smooth, slipped. Red Polished Ware.

Sr. No. 23
Location: Surface collection.
Fragment: Rim. Diam. 15 cm
Form: Small size jar-beaked rim.
Fabric: Fine.
Surfaces: Smooth, polished, Red Polished Ware.

Sr. No. 24
Location: Surface collection.
Fragment: Rim. Diam. 12 cm
Form: Jar-beaded rim.
Fabric: Fine.
Surfaces: Smooth, polished, Red Polished Ware.

Sr. No. 25
Location: Surface collection.
Fragment: Rim and neck. Diam. 8 cm
Form: Jar-beaked rim, flaring neck.
Fabric: Fine.
Surfaces: Smooth, polished, Red Polished Ware.

Sr. No. 26
Location: Surface collection.
Fragment: Rim and neck. Diam. 7 cm
Form: Jar-beaked rim, flaring neck and bulbous body.
Fabric: Fine.
Surfaces: Smooth, polished, Red Polished Ware.

Sr. No. 27
Location: Surface collection.
Fragment: Rim. Diam. 17 cm
Form: Bowl-knife-edged rim and receding sides.
Fabric: Fine.
Surfaces: Weathered, Red Polished Ware.

Minor objects.

1. A fragment of unidentified terracotta figurine. **(Plate XLIX.b. No.7)**

13. **Site name**: Khadsaliya **(Plate XXV.a)**.
Co-ordinates: Lat. 21°34' N; Long. 72°17' E.
Period of occupation: Early Historic period.
Reference: *IAR.* 1980-81: 12

Location: The village Khadsaliya is located about 23 km to the present Bhavnagar town and one and half km to the north of Thalsar village and the village is well connected with the State Transport bus which operates from the Bhavnagar city.

The site: The ancient mound is located around 100 m to the west of the present village and one and half km to the west of Gulf of Cambay. The site spreads over an area of 500X500 m and is under cultivation. The height of the mound is 5 m. The site was occupied only during the Early Historic period. The site yielded sherds of Red Ware and Red-slipped Ware, but when earlier scholar explored the site he found some sherd of Burnished Red Ware also.

Ceramic assemblage

Plate XXXIX.a. Nos.1-11

Sr. No. 1
Location: Surface collection.
Fragment: Rim and body. Diam. 6 cm
Form: Lamp/lid-slightly flat out sides, disc base.
Fabric: Coarse.
Surfaces: Unslipped, rough.

Sr. No. 2
Location: Surface collection.
Fragment: Upper body. Diam 17 cm
Form: Cup-short pointed featureless rim.
Fabric: Coarse.
Surfaces: Unslipped, rough.

Sr. No. 3
Location: Surface collection.
Fragment: Base.
Form: Probably cup-disc base.
Fabric: Coarse.
Surfaces: Unslipped, rough.

Sr. No. 4
Location: Surface collection.
Fragment: Rim and body. Diam.22 cm
Form: Dish-featureless pointed rim.
Fabric : Coarse.
Surfaces: Unslipped, rough.

Sr. No. 5
Location: Surface collection.
Fragment: Rim. Diam 13 cm
Form: Pot-external projecting beaded rim.
Fabric: Coarse.
Surfaces: Unslipped, rough.

Sr. No. 6
Location: Surface collection.
Fragment: Rim. Diam. 20 cm
Form: Jar-externally thickened rim, short vertical neck.
Fabric: Coarse.
Surfaces: Unslipped, rough.

Sr. No. 7
Location: Surface collection.
Fragment: Rim and neck. Diam. 17 cm
Form: Jar-beaked shape rim, vertical neck.
Fabric: Coarse.
Surfaces: Red slipped on exterior, weathered.

Sr. No. 8
Location: Surface collection.
Fragment: Rim and neck. Diam. 17 cm
Form: Jar-externally projecting under-cut rim.
Fabric: Coarse.
Surfaces: Red slipped on exterior, weathered.

Sr. No. 9
Location: Surface collection.
Fragment: Rim and neck. Diam. 24 cm
Form: Jar-externally out turned rim, concave neck, globular body.
Fabric: Coarse.
Surfaces: Red slipped on both sides, smooth.

Sr. No. 10
Location: Surface collection.
Fragment: Rim. Diam. 20 cm
Form: Dish-internally beaked rim, ledge on exterior shoulder.
Fabric: Coarse.
Surfaces: Red slipped on both sides, smooth.

Sr. No. 11
Location: Surface collection.

Fragment: Rim and upper body. Diam. 21 cm
Form: Storage jar-flat projecting short rim, but with a very prominent projection.
Fabric: Coarse.
Surfaces: Red slipped on exterior, weathered.

14. **Site name**: *Kerala ni dhoro* **(Plate XXV.b)**.
Co-ordinates: Lat. 21°22' N; Long. 72°95' E.
Period of occupation: Early and Mature Harappan and Early Historic.
Reference: *IAR.* 1972-73.Ghosh 1989: 206; Shinde 1992a; 1992b; 1992c; 1994a; 1994b and 1996;

Location: Village Padri is situated in the Talaja tehsil of Bhavnagar district. It is lies 2 km from the Gulf of Cambay and 8 km to the west of present tehsil head quarter and 50 km to the south of Bhavnagar district.

The site: The ancient settlement is located about 2.5 km south of the present village and locally known as *Kerala ni dhoro*. The site is roughly 2 km away from the Gulf of Cambay, but its southern edge is affected by tidal fluctuations. The site is located in a shallow depression on a slightly elevated sand dune. The ancient settlement was probably protected from the destructive impact of tidal waves by a natural barrier of basalt rock, roughly 6 m high and running parallel to the sea coast. There is no source of potable water within a radius of 1.5 km of the site. On the northern side of the site there is vast tract of fertile land (Shinde 1992a). The site is quite extensive and spreads over an area of 340 m (E-W) X 210 m (N-S) with a 3.2 m thick habitational deposit. When the present author visited the site has saw the villagers taking away the habitational soil from the site and destroying the northern part of the mound. Dr.Vasant Shinde conducted excavations at the site for over five seasons on behalf of Deccan College, have revealed three fold cultural sequence namely, Early Harappan (3000-2600 B.C.), Mature Harappan (2500-1900 B.C.). and Early Historic (1st century B.C.-A.D.) The excavation at Padri have thrown light not only on the various aspects of Early Historic and Harappan culture in Saurashtra but also produced a stratified phase of the Early Harappan period (Shinde 1992a; 1992b; 1995 and 1998). The Early Historic period is represented by the Red-slipped Ware, Red Ware and Grey Ware. Besides these, an array of antiquities such as a couple of copper coins similar to that of the Kshatrapa king Nahapan, a clay tablet bearing *Brahmi* script, a tortoise shaped copper lamp, two boat shaped terracotta objects, goddess *Lajjagauri* figurines made of terracotta and slate stone, a few bones objects, beads of terracotta, glass and semi-precious stones, terracotta human and animal figurines, stone and terracotta discs, copper and iron objects, etc.

15. **Site name**: *Nariya Timbo* **(Plate XXVI.a)**.
Co-ordinate: Lat. 21°20' N ; Long. 72°5' E
Period of occupation: Early Historic.
Reference: New discovery

Location: The present village of Pavti is located about 3 km south of Talaja Tehsil and about 55 km away from the Bhavnagar town. The ancient mound is located roughly 1 km from the village on the north-western side.

The site: The site, locally called *Nariya Timbo*, is little away from the right bank of Shetrunji river but there is no dearth of drinking water. The site is considerably small which spreads over an area of 38 m east-west and 75 m north-south with a habitational deposit of 1 m visible from the surrounding area. The mound is shallow and highly disturbed due to modern agricultural activity. From the ceramic assemblage it can be said that the site was occupied during the Early Historic period. Besides pottery, other objects like terracotta discs, fragments of shell bangle have been collected from the site.

Ceramic assemblage:

Plate XXXIX.b. Nos.1-9

Sr. No. 1
Location: Surface collection.
Fragment: Rim. Diam. 22 cm
Form: Jar-externally projecting rim with slightly concave top.
Fabric: Coarse.
Surfaces: Unslipped, weathered.

Sr. No. 2
Location: Surface collection.
Fragment: Rim and neck. Diam. 17 cm
Form: Jar-slightly out turned and thickened rim.
Fabric: Coarse.
Surfaces: Unslipped, weathered.

Sr. No. 3
Location: Surface collection.
Fragment: Rim and body. Diam. 22 cm
Form: Cup-short featureless pointed rim.
Fabric: Coarse.
Surfaces: Unslipped, rough.

Sr. No. 4
Location: Surface collection.
Fragment: Base and lower body.
Form: Cup-disc base, flaring sides.
Fabric: Coarse.
Surfaces: Unslipped, rough.

Sr. No. 5
Location: Surface collection.
Fragment Rim and body.
Form: Dish-internally beaked rim, ledge on the exterior shoulder.
Fabric: Medium.
Surfaces: Red slipped on both sides, smooth.

Sr. No. 6
Location: Surface collection.
Fragment: Rim and neck. Diam. 14 cm
Form: Globular pot-externally projecting under cut rim, short neck.
Fabric: Coarse.
Surfaces: Red slipped on both sides, weathered.

Sr. No. 7
Location: Surface collection.
Fragment: Rim. Diam. 17 cm
Form: Jar-flat projecting short rim.
Fabric: Coarse.
Surfaces: Red slipped on both sides, weathered.

Sr. No. 8
Location: Surface collection.
Fragment: Rim and body. Diam. 24 cm
Form: Deep bowl-incurved rim and a pronounced ledge below the rim.
Fabric: Coarse.
Surfaces: Red slipped on the interior of the rim, weathered.

Sr. No. 9
Location: Surface collection.
Fragment: Body sherd.
Form: Undetermined-painted dots on the exterior of the body.
Fabric: Coarse.
Surfaces: Red slipped on the exterior of the body, smooth.

Plate XXXIX.c. Nos.10-12

Sr. No. 10
Location: Surface collection.
Fragment: Rim and neck. Diam. 35 cm
Form: Jar-triangular rim.
Fabric: Coarse.
Surfaces: Grey slipped on both sides, smooth.

Sr. No. 11
Location: Surface collection.
Fragment: Rim and neck. Diam. 24 cm
Form: Jar-drooping rim.
Fabric: Coarse.
Surfaces: Grey slipped on both sides, weathered.

Sr. No. 12
Location: Surface collection.
Fragment: Rim and neck. Diam. 21 cm
Form: Jar-out curved rim.
Fabric: Coarse.
Surfaces: Grey slipped on the exterior of the rim, weathered.

Plate XXXIX.d. Nos.13-19

Sr. No. 13
Location: Surface collection.
Fragment: Rim, neck and upper body. Diam. 20 cm
Form: Pot-thickened rounded rim, grooves on the interior of the rim.
Fabric: Coarse.
Surfaces: Grey slipped on both sides, weathered.

Sr. No. 14
Location: Surface collection.
Fragment: Rim and neck. Diam. 19 cm
Form: Pot-outcurved beaded rim.
Fabric: Coarse.
Surfaces: Grey slipped, weathered.

Sr. No. 15
Location: Surface collection.
Fragment: Rim. Diam. 26 cm
Form: Jar-out curved rim, deep grooved on the top.
Fabric: Coarse.
Surfaces: Grey slipped on both sides, weathered.

Sr. No. 16
Location: Surface collection.
Fragment: Rim. Diam. 17 cm
Form: Pot-outcurved beaded rim.
Fabric: Coarse.
Surfaces: Grey slipped, rough.

Sr. No. 17
Location: Surface collection.
Fragment: Rim and body. Diam. 17 cm
Form: Deep dish-beaded rim, small ledge below the neck.
Fabric: Coarse.
Surfaces: Grey slipped on the exterior of the rim, smooth.

Sr. No. 18
Location: Surface collection.
Fragment: Base and lower body.
Form: Shallow bowl-disc base.
Fabric: Coarse.
Surfaces: Grey slipped, rough.

Sr. No. 19
Location: Surface collection.
Fragment: Body.
Form: Undetermined. Probably conical spout.
Fabric: Coarse.
Surfaces: Grey slipped on the exterior of the body, smooth.

Plate XXXIX.e. Nos. 20-23

Sr. No. 20
Location: Surface collection.
Fragment: Rim and body. Diam. 12 cm
Form: Bowl-blunt rim, incurved sides.
Fabric: Very fine
Surfaces: Smooth, red, slipped on both sides, Red Polished Ware.

Sr. No. 21
Location: Surface collection.
Fragment: Base and lower body.
Form: Bowl-disc base, convex sides.
Fabric: Fine.
Surfaces: Smooth, slipped on both sides, Red Polished Ware.

Sr. No. 22
Location: Surface collection.
Fragment: Bottle neck.
Form: Unascertained, probably part of a sprinkler with long bottle neck.
Fabric: Fine.
Surfaces: Smooth on exterior surface and slipped. Red Polished Ware.

Sr. No. 23
Location: Surface collection.
Fragment: Ring foot base.
Form: Jar-thick ring footed base.
Fabric: Fine.
Surfaces: Smooth, slipped on both sides, Red Polished Ware.

Minor objects.

1. A circular terracotta disc, unperforated. Measurements: T. 18.30 mm, Cir. 58.47 mm **(Plate XLVI.a. No. 2)**
2. A fragment of shell bangle with dot like design on the top. Measurements: T. 3.14 mm, W.11.28 mm. **(Plate XLVII.b. No. 7)**.
3. A fragment of terracotta bell. **(Plate XLIX.b No. 2)**.

16. **Site name**: *Nehada* **(Plate XXVI.b)**.
Co-ordinate: Lat. 21°20' N; Long. 72°5' E
Period of occupation: Mature Harappan and Early Historic.
Reference: New discovery.

Location: Village Phulsar is located around 10 km away from the Talaja Tehsil head-quarters towards southern direction and 5 km to the west of Saltanpur, the mouth of Shetrunji river.

The site: The ancient settlement is locally known as *Nehada* and 2 km away from the village of Phulsar to the western direction and right bank of Shetrunji river. The site is close to the metalled road running from the Phulsar village towards Shilavadar village. It is also very close to the Gulf of Cambay. One modern temple is constructed on the southern side of the mound. The shape of the ancient habitational mound is rectangular in shape and is quite extensive. Its spreads over an area of 200 m (east-west) X 100 m (north-south). The habitational deposit is under cultivation. The maximum habitational deposit is 1.5 m. Ceramic assemblage yielded a two-fold cultural sequence namely, Mature Harappan and Early Historic. Apart from pottery, few objects like perforated discs, perforated potsherds, bones and horn like stone object were collected from the site.

Ceramic assemblage:

Plate XL.a. Nos.1-12

Sr. No.	1
Location:	Surface collection.
Fragment:	Rim, neck and upper body. Diam. 12 cm
Form:	Globular pot-beaded rim, shallow grooved on the interior of the rim, long neck.
Fabric:	Coarse.
Surfaces:	Red slipped on both sides, weathered.

Sr. No.	2
Location:	Surface collection.
Fragment:	Rim and neck. Diam. 26 cm
Form:	Jar-externally projecting beaked rim.
Fabric:	Coarse.
Surfaces:	Unslipped, rough.

Sr. No. 3
Location: Surface collection.
Fragment: Rim, neck and upper body. Diam. 12 cm
Form: Jar-flat projecting short rim.
Fabric: Coarse.
Surfaces: Unslipped, rough on both sides.

Sr. No. 4
Location: Surface collection.
Fragment: Rim and neck. Diam. 14 cm
Form: Jar-everted rim.
Fabric: Coarse.
Surfaces: Red slipped on both sides, smooth.

Sr. No. 5
Location: Surface collection.
Fragment: Rim and body. Diam. 24 cm
Form: Cup-short vertical featureless rim.
Fabric: Coarse.
Surfaces: Unslipped, rough.

Sr. No. 6
Location: Surface collection.
Fragment: Base and lower body.
Form: Cup-disc base, flaring sides.
Fabric: Coarse.
Surfaces: Unslipped, weathered.

Sr. No. 7
Location: Surface collection.
Fragment: Rim and neck. Diam. 23 cm
Form: Jar-beaded under cut rim, grooved on the interior of the rim.
Fabric: Coarse.
Surfaces: Red slipped on both sides, weathered.

Sr. No. 8
Location: Surface collection.
Fragment: Rim and neck. Diam. 22 cm
Form: Same type as Ichhora No.19
Fabric: Coarse.
Surfaces: Red slipped on both sides, weathered.

Sr. No. 9
Location: Surface collection.

Fragment: Rim and body. Diam. 30 cm
Form: Shallow basin-flat rim, grooves on the interior of the rim.
Fabric: Coarse.
Surfaces: Red slipped on both sides, weathered.

Sr. No. 10
Location: Surface collection.
Fragment: Rim and upper body.
Form: Lid / bowl-short vertical rim.
Fabric: Coarse.
Surfaces: Red slipped on exterior of the body, rough.

Sr. No 11
Location: Surface collection.
Fragment: Rim neck and upper body. Diam. 22 cm
Form: Pot-externally projecting rounded rim, ridge at the neck, deep grooved on the interior of the rim, short vertical neck.
Fabric: Coarse.
Surfaces: Grey slipped on both sides, weathered.

Sr. No. 12
Location: Surface collection.
Fragment: Rim and neck. Diam. 20 cm
Form: Pot-externally projecting slightly under cut rim, high neck.
Fabric: Coarse.
Surfaces: Grey slipped on both sides, weathered.

Plate XL.b. Nos.13-21

Sr. No. 13
Location: Surface collection.
Fragment: Rim and neck. Diam. 22 cm
Form: Globular pot-externally projecting rounded rim, short vertical neck.
Fabric: Coarse.
Surfaces: Grey slipped on both sides, weathered.

Sr. No. 14
Location: Surface collection.
Fragment: Rim and body. Diam. 17 cm
Form: Jar-flared out rim, globular body.
Fabric: Coarse.
Surfaces: Grey slipped on the exterior of the rim, rough.

Sr. No. 15
Location: Surface collection.
Fragment: Rim and neck. Diam. 23 cm
Form: Globular pot-externally projecting perpendicular rim, short vertical neck.
Fabric: Coarse.
Surfaces: Grey slipped on the interior of the rim, rough.

Sr. No. 16
Location: Surface collection.
Fragment: Rim and neck. Diam. 22 cm
Form: Jar-out curved rim, grooved on the top.
Fabric: Coarse.
Surfaces: Grey slipped on both sides, weathered.

Sr. No. 17
Location: Surface collection.
Fragment: Rim, neck and body. Diam. 12 cm
Form: Pot-externally projecting rim, carinated body, wide orifice.
Fabric: Coarse.
Surfaces: Grey slipped on the exterior of the body, weathered.

Sr. No. 18
Location: Surface collection.
Fragment: Rim and neck.
Form: Unknown-flat rim, ridge on the exterior of the rim and deep groove on the interior of the rim.
Fabric: Coarse.
Surfaces: Grey slipped, rough.

Sr. No. 19
Location: Surface collection.
Fragment: Rim and body. Diam. 19 cm
Form: Dish. Same as Devalia No.8
Fabric: Coarse.
Surfaces: Unslipped, rough.

Sr. No. 20
Location: Surface collection.
Fragment: Rim and most of the body. Diam. 13 cm
Form: Bowl-simple featureless rim, hemispherical body.
Fabric: Coarse.
Surfaces: Grey slipped, weathered.

Sr. No. 21
Location: Surface collection.
Fragment: Base and lower body.
Form: Deep bowl-disc base.
Fabric: Coarse.
Surfaces: Grey slipped, weathered.

Minor objects.

1. A circular terracotta disc, perforated. Measurements: T. 17.96 mm, Cir. 93.36 mm. **(Plate XLVI.b. No.12)**
2. A fragment of terracotta object possibly bell **(Plate XLIX.b. No. 4)**.
3. A fragment of iron slag **(Plate L. No. 7)**.

17. **Site name**: *Timbo* **(Plate XXVII.a)**.
Co-ordinate: Lat.21°23'N ; Long. 72°8' E.
Period of occupation: Early Harappan, Mature Harappan and Early Historic.
Reference: New discovery.

Location: Village Piparla is located around 6 km away from Talaja towards its northwest direction and 2 km to the southeast of ancient site of Padri. On the east of the Piparla, the village of Shatara is situated. From the Talaja taluka headquarters jeepable road is available up to the village. The ancient site is roughly 5 km away from the river bank of Shetrunji, but there is no dearth of sweet water around it as there are ample wells.

The site: The ancient mound, locally known as *Timbo* is roughly one and half km away to the west of the Piparla village. It is quite extensive and has remained intact. Only some peripheral area on the southern side is disturbed due to agricultural activities. The site spreads over an area of 130 m (east-west) by 125 m (north-south) with a habitational deposit of two and half meters. According to the villagers erosion on the mound had exposed a hoard of copper coins a few years ago. But unfortunately not a single coin is traceable now. The site, as is clear from the ceramic assemblage, has a three-fold cultural sequence, namely Early Harappan, Mature Harappan and Early Historic. Besides pottery, few objects like a stopper, a perforated disc made of terracotta, a bangle fragment and a core of agate were collected from the surface of the mound. The site was brought to light by the author for the first time.

Ceramic assemblage:

Plate XLI.a. Nos.1-9

Sr. No. 1
Location: Surface collection.
Fragment: Rim and body. Diam. 37 cm
Form: Dish-externally projecting triangular rim, wide mouth.
Fabric: Coarse.
Surfaces: Red slipped on both sides, smooth.

Sr. No. 2
Location: Surface collection.

Fragment: Rim and neck. Diam. 11 cm
Form: Pot-externally projecting beaked rim, high neck, groove on the interior of the rim, narrow mouth.
Fabric: Coarse.
Surfaces: Red slipped on both sides, smooth.

Sr. No. 3
Location: Surface collection.
Fragment: Rim, neck and upper body. Diam. 20 cm
Form: Jar-out turned rim, globular body.
Fabric: Coarse.
Surfaces: Red slipped on both sides, weathered.

Sr. No. 4
Location: Surface collection.
Fragment: Rim and neck. Diam. 24 cm
Form: Jar-triangular rim, slightly vertical neck.
Fabric: Coarse.
Surfaces: Red slipped on both sides, weathered.

Sr. No. 5
Location: Surface collection.
Fragment: Rim and neck. Diam. 22 cm
Form: Pot-flat projecting rim, vertical neck.
Fabric: Coarse.
Surfaces: Red slipped on both sides, weathered.

Sr. No. 6
Location: Surface collection.
Fragment: Rim and neck. Diam. 19 cm
Form: Pot-flat projecting rim.
Fabric: Coarse.
Surfaces: Red slipped on both sides, weathered.

Sr. No. 7
Location: Surface collection.
Fragment: Rim and neck. Diam. 20 cm
Form: Globular pot-externally projecting rounded and slightly under-cut rim, narrow mouth.
Fabric: Coarse.
Surfaces: Red slipped on both sides, weathered.

Sr. No. 8
Location: Surface collection.

Fragment: Rim and neck. Diam. 20 cm
Form: Same as above but slightly under-cut in the interior.
Fabric: Coarse.
Surfaces: Red slipped on both sides, weathered.

Sr. No. 9
Location: Surface collection.
Fragment: Rim. Diam. 23 cm
Form: Unascertained-featureless pointed rim.
Fabric: Coarse.
Surfaces: Red slipped on both sides, weathered.

Plate XLI.b. Nos.10-18

Sr. No. 10
Location: Surface collection.
Fragment: Rim and upper body. Diam. 23 cm
Form: Jar-beaked shape rim, wide mouth.
Fabric: Coarse.
Surfaces: Unslipped, weathered.

Sr. No. 11
Location: Surface collection.
Fragment: Rim and upper body. Diam. 24 cm
Form: Pot-externally thickened under-cut and pointed rim ,wide mouth.
Fabric: Coarse.
Surfaces: Red slipped on both sides, weathered.

Sr. No. 12
Location: Surface collection.
Fragment: Rim and body. Diam. 33 cm
Form: Storage jar-externally thickened and pointed rim, groove on the interior of the rim, thick cross section.
Fabric: Coarse.
Surfaces: Red slipped on both sides, weathered.

Sr. No. 13
Location: Surface collection.
Fragment: Rim and upper body. Diam. 24 cm
Form: Jar-externally out turned rim and rounded on the top, globular body.
Fabric: Coarse.
Surfaces: Red slipped on both sides, weathered.

Sr. No. 14
Location: Surface collection.

Fragment: Rim and upper body. Diam. 20 cm
Form: Jar-everted rim, globular body, hand made.
Fabric: Coarse.
Surfaces: Red slipped on both sides, weathered.

Sr. No. 15
Location: Surface collection.
Fragment: Rim and neck. Diam. 18 cm
Form: Pot-flat projecting rim, slight projection on the interior, high neck.
Fabric: Coarse.
Surfaces: Red slipped on both sides, weathered.

Sr. No. 16
Location: Surface collection.
Fragment: Rim and neck. Diam. 14 cm
Form: Small globular pot (lota)-externally projecting beaked rim, short vertical neck, narrow mouth.
Fabric: Coarse.
Surfaces: Unnslipped on both side, weathered.

Sr. No. 17
Location: Surface collection.
Fragment: Rim and neck. Diam. 17 cm
Form: Small globular pot-rounded rim, narrow mouth.
Fabric: Coarse.
Surfaces: Red slipped on both sides, weathered.

Sr. No. 18
Location: Surface collection.
Fragment: Rim. Diam. 19 cm
Form: Jar-externally projecting rim with slightly convex top.
Fabric: Coarse.
Surfaces: Grey slipped on both sides, weathered.

Plate XLI.c. Nos.19-22

Sr. No. 19
Location: Surface collection.
Fragment: Rim and body. Diam. 26 cm
Form: Dish-internally beaked rim, ledge on the exterior shoulder, thick cross section.
Fabric: Coarse.
Surfaces: Red slipped on both sides, weathered.

Sr. No. 20
Location: Surface collection.
Fragment: Lower body.
Form: Lid-small knobbed at the centre.
Fabric: Coarse to medium.
Surfaces: Unslipped on both sides, weathered.

Sr. No. 21
Location: Surface collection.
Fragment: Spout.
Form: Spout-knob at its base.
Fabric: Coarse.
Surfaces: Red slipped on exterior side, weathered.

Sr. No. 22
Location: Surface collection.
Fragment: Base and lower body.
Form: Bowl-short slightly out-turned sides.
Fabric: Coarse.
Surfaces: Unslipped on both sides, weathered.

Plate XLI.d. No.23

Sr. No. 23
Location: Surface collection.
Fragment: Rim and neck. Diam. 23 cm
Form: Jar-triangular rim, almost no neck, wide mouth.
Fabric: Coarse to medium.
Surfaces: Grey slipped on both sides, smooth.

Minor objects

1. A fragment of plain bangle, squerish in section. Measurement: T.5.06 mm, W.10.43 mm. **(Plate XLVII.b No.3)**
2. A circular terracotta disc, unperforated, red in color. Measurement: T.26.66 mm, Cir. 69.28 mm. **(Plate XLVI.b. No.15)**
3. A cylindrical shape terracotta stopper, grey in color. Measurement: L.37.24 mm, T.24.19 mm. **(Plate XLIX.b. No.6)**
4. A fragment of shell. **(Plate XLVIII.b. No. 4)**
5. Agate, flake or core(?) **(Plate XLIX.b. No.8)**

18. **Site name**: *Shilavadar Timbo* **(Plate XXVII.b)**.
Co-ordinate: Lat. 21°3' N; Long. 72°3' E
Period of occupation: Mature Harappan and Early Historic.
Reference: New discovery.

Location: Shilavadar village is located in Bhavnagar district about 9 km to the south of the Talaja town and 2 km west of Phulsar village. The ancient mound is about 2 km to the east of present village and locally called as *Shilavadar Timbo.*

The site: The ancient settlement is roughly 6 km away from Talaja town and on the right bank of Shetrunji river. The site is quite extensive and measures about 150m (east-west) by 200 m (north-south) with a habitational deposit of 2 m visible from the cut section. The surface is littered with pottery, terracotta discs, bones, perforated pots, flakes and iron slags. The mound is badly disturbed as it is under cultivation. The site presents a two-fold cultural sequence namely Mature Harappan and Early Historic.

Ceramic assemblage:

Plate. XLII.a. Nos.1-10

Sr. No. 1
Location: Surface collection.
Fragment: Base and lower body.
Form: Cup-disc base.
Fabric: Coarse.
Surfaces: Unslipped, rough.

Sr. No. 2
Location: Surface collection.
Fragment: Lower body.
Form: Conical lid-pinnacle and same as Rohil No.12
Fabric: Coarse.
Surfaces: Unslipped, weathered.

Sr. No. 3
Location: Surface collection.
Fragment: Rim, neck and shoulder. Diam. 17 cm
Form: Jar-beaded rim, grooved on the interior of the rim, concave neck, globular body.
Fabric: Coarse.
Surfaces: Red slipped on both sides, weathered.

Sr. No. 4
Location: Surface collection.
Fragment: Rim and neck. Diam. 22 cm
Form: Jar-triangular rim, slightly vertical neck.
Fabric: Coarse.
Surfaces: Red slipped on both sides, weathered.

Sr. No. 5
Location: Surface collection.
Fragment: Rim. Diam. 17 cm

Form: Bowl-flaring rim.
Fabric: Coarse.
Surfaces: Red slipped on both sides, weathered.

Sr. No. 6
Location: Surface collection.
Fragment: Rim and neck. Diam. 24 cm
Form: Pot-beaded rim, short neck.
Fabric: Coarse.
Surfaces: Red slipped on both sides, weathered.

Sr. No. 7
Location: Surface collection.
Fragment: Rim and neck. Diam. 22 cm
Form: Jar-out turned and internally thickened rim, short concave neck.
Fabric: Coarse.
Surfaces: Red slipped on exterior of the rim, weathered.

Sr. No. 8
Location: Surface collection.
Fragment: Rim. Diam. 23 cm
Form: Jar-externally thickened and rounded rim.
Fabric: Coarse.
Surfaces: Red slipped on both sides, weathered.

Sr. No. 9
Location: Surface collection.
Fragment: Rim. Diam. 17 cm
Form: Large shallow bowl-beaded rim, rounded body.
Fabric: Coarse.
Surfaces: Red slipped on both sides, weathered.

Sr. No. 10
Location: Surface collection.
Fragment: Rim and body. Diam. 20 cm
Form: Jar-externally projecting beaked rim.
Fabric: Coarse.
Surfaces: Red slipped on both sides, weathered.

Plate XLII.b. Nos.11-18

Sr. No. 11
Location: Surface collection.
Fragment: Rim and neck. Diam. 16 cm
Form: Pot-beaded rim, short vertical neck.
Fabric: Coarse to medium.
Surfaces: Red slipped on the exterior of the rim, weathered.

Sr. No. 12
Location: Surface collection.
Fragment: Rim. Diam. 10 cm
Form: Pot-flared rim, short neck.
Fabric: Coarse.
Surfaces: Grey slipped on both sides, weathered.

Sr. No. 13
Location: Surface collection.
Fragment: Rim and neck. Diam. 22 cm
Form: Jar-squarish rim.
Fabric: Coarse.
Surfaces: Grey slipped on the interior of the rim, rough.

Sr. No. 14
Location: Surface collection.
Fragment: Rim and body. Diam. 29 cm
Form: Bowl-flattened top.
Fabric: Coarse.
Surfaces: Grey slipped on both sides, rough.

Sr. No. 15
Location: Surface collection.
Fragment: Rim. Diam. 20 cm
Form: Shallow dish-Outcurved beaded rim.
Fabric: Coarse.
Surfaces: Unslipped, rough.

Sr. No. 16
Location: Surface collection.
Fragment: Base and lower body.
Form: Shallow bowl-disc base.
Fabric: Coarse.
Surfaces: Unslipped, rough.

Sr. No. 17
Location: Surface collection.
Fragment: Rim. Diam. 33 cm
Form: Handi like bowl-beaded rim.
Fabric: Coarse.
Surfaces: Red slipped on both sides, weathered.

Sr. No. 18
Location: Surface collection
Fragment: Rim and body. Diam. 24 cm
Form: Handi like bowl-incurved beaded rim.
Fabric: Coarse.
Surfaces: Red slipped on both sides, smooth.

Plate XLIIc. Nos.19-20

Sr. No. 19
Location: Surface collection.
Fragment: Rim and upper body. Diam. 29 cm
Form: Dish-nail headed rim.
Fabric: Fine.
Surfaces: Weathered, slipped on both sides, Red Polished Ware.

Sr. No. 20
Location: Surface collection.
Fragment: Rim and body. Diam. 18 cm
Form: Bowl-everted rim, internally notched wall.
Fabric: Fine.
Surfaces: Weathered, slipped on both sides, Red Polished Ware.

Minor objects.

1. A circular terracotta disc, unperforated. Measurements: T. 33.29 mm, Cir. 66.54 mm. **(Plate. XLVI.b. No. 16)**
2. Unidentified stone object (**Plate L. No.5**).

19. **Site name**: *Timba* **(Plate XXVIII.a)**.
 Co-ordinate: Lat. 21°18' N; Long. 72°8' E
 Period of occupation: Early Harappan, Mature Harappan and Early Historic.
 Reference: New discovery.
 Location: Saltanpur is located on the Gulf of Cambay near the mouth of Shetrunji river and is an important small natural port. It is 8 km away and located towards the west of Talaja town.

The site: The ancient mound, locally known as *Timba* is located around 2 km to the east of the present village. The site is discovered by the author for the first time. The site is badly disturbed as it is under cultivation. The mound is quite extensive and covers roughly 200 X 100 m area. The maximum habitational deposit is about 2 m. Few objects like terracotta discs (both perforated and unperforated), one terracotta stopper and lamp, few used shells and sling balls made of stone have been recovered from the surface of the mound. Along with this, few pieces of vitrified clay have been noticed which indicate the local manufacture of the pottery. The cultural sequence of the site is same as that of Padri.

Ceramic assemblage:

Plate XLIII.a. Nos. 1-9

Sr. No. 1
Location: Surface collection.
Fragment: Rim and upper body. Diam.12 cm
Form: Globular pot-externally projecting rim, short vertical neck, narrow mouth.
Fabric: Coarse.
Surfaces: Red slipped on both sides, weathered.

Sr. No. 2
Location: Surface collection.
Fragment: Rim. Diam. 12 cm
Form: Globular pot-beaded rim, short vertical neck.
Fabric: Coarse.
Surfaces: Red slipped on both sides, weathered.

Sr. No. 3
Location: Surface collection.
Fragment: Rim. Diam.13 cm
Form: Pot-flaring and pointed rim, groove on the outer surfaces of the rim.
Fabric: Coarse.
Surfaces: Red slipped on both sides, weathered.

Sr. No. 4
Locations: Surface collection.
Fragment: Rim, neck and upper body. Diam.14 cm
Form: Pot-externally projecting beaked rim, short vertical neck, narrow mouth.
Fabric: Coarse.
Surfaces: Red slipped on both sides, weathered.

Sr. No. 5
Location: Surface collection.
Fragment: Rim and upper body. Diam. 14 cm
Form: Pot-short beaked rim.
Fabric: Coarse.
Surfaces: Red slipped on exterior, rough.

Sr. No. 6
Location: Surface collection.
Fragment: Rim and neck. Diam.17 cm
Form: Pot-externally thicken under-cut rim, short vertical neck.
Fabric: Coarse.
Surfaces: Red slipped on both sides, weathered.

Sr. No. 7
Location: Surface collection.
Fragment: Rim and upper body. Diam. 21 cm
Form: Jar-triangular rim.
Fabric: Medium to fine.
Surfaces: Unslipped, weathered.

Sr. No. 8
Location: Surface collection.
Fragment: Rim, neck and upper body. Diam. 25 cm
Form: Deep bowl-externally projecting rim, short vertical neck, ridge on the waist.
Fabric: Coarse to medium.
Surfaces: Grey slipped on the exterior, smooth.

Sr. No. 9
Location: Surface collection.
Fragment: Rim and upper body. Diam. 20 cm
Form: Pot-externally projecting under-cut rim, vertical neck, ridge on the exterior of the neck and groove on the top of the rim.
Fabric: Coarse.
Surfaces: Grey slipped, weathered.

Plate XLIII.b. Nos.10-18

Sr. No. 10
Location: Surface collection.
Fragment: Rim and upper body. Diam. 29 cm
Form: Pot-externally projecting beaked rim, ridge on the neck, short vertical neck.
Fabric: Coarse.
Surfaces: Grey slipped, weathered.

Sr. No. 11
Location: Surface collection.
Fragment: Rim and upper body. Diam. 23 cm
Form: Pot-externally projecting beaked rim, grooves on the interior of the rim, almost no neck.
Fabric: Coarse.
Surfaces: Grey slipped on both sides, smooth.

Sr. No. 12
Location: Surface collection.
Fragment: Rim, neck and upper body. Diam. 21 cm
Form: Jar-out curved rim with deep groove on the top and internally beveled rim.
Fabric: Coarse.
Surfaces: Grey slipped on both sides, smooth.

Sr. No. 13
Location: Surface collection.
Fragment: Rim, neck and upper body. Diam. 24 cm
Form: Pot-externally projecting flat rim, ridge at the neck, short vertical neck.
Fabric: Coarse.
Surfaces: Grey slipped, weathered.

Sr. No. 14
Location: Surface collection.
Fragment: Rim and neck. Diam. 19 cm
Form: Pot-slightly flaring rim, short vertical neck.
Fabric: Coarse.
Surfaces: Grey slipped on both sides, weathered.

Sr. No. 15
Location: Surface collection.
Fragment: Body portion.
Form: Body portion of deep bowl-stamped circular design placed horizontally.
Fabric: Coarse.
Surfaces: Grey slipped, smooth.

Sr. No. 16
Location: Surface collection.
Fragment: Body portion.
Form: Vessel form uncertain. Design like vertical grooves made on the exterior surface of the body.
Fabric: Coarse.
Surfaces: Grey slipped on the exterior of the rim, weathered.

Sr. No. 17
Location: Surface collection.
Fragment: Rim and upper body. Diam. 22 cm
Form: Pot-rounded rim, short vertical neck, groove on the interior of the rim.
Fabric: Coarse.
Surfaces: Grey slipped on both sides, weathered.

Sr. No. 18
Location: Surface collection.
Fragment: Rim and upper body. Diam.18 cm
Form: Small jar-externally projecting short beaked rim, almost no neck.
Fabric: Coarse.
Surfaces: Grey slipped on the exterior of the rim, weathered.

Plate XLIII.c. Nos.19-27

Sr. No. 19
Location: Surface collection.
Fragment: Rim and upper body. Diam. 21 cm
Form: Pot-externally projecting beaked rim, almost no neck, groove on the interior top of the rim.
Fabric: Coarse.
Surfaces: Grey slipped, weathered.

Sr. No. 20
Location: Surface collection.
Fragment: Rim and upper body. Diam. 20 cm
Form: Pot-rounded and under-cut rim, short vertical neck.
Fabric: Coarse.
Surfaces: Grey slipped, weathered.

Sr. No. 21
Location: Surface collection.
Fragment: Rim, neck and upper body. Diam. 23 cm
Form: Pot-externally projecting rounded rim, grooves on the both side of the rim, short vertical neck.
Fabric: Coarse.
Surfaces: Grey slipped on both sides, weathered.

Sr. No. 22
Location: Surface collection.
Fragment: Rim. Diam. 21 cm
Form: Jar/pot-drooping rim, two horizontal band on the interior of the rim.
Fabric: Coarse.
Surfaces: Grey slipped on both sides, smooth.

Sr. No. 23
Location: Surface collection.
Fragment: Rim and body. Diam. 14 cm
Form: Deep dish-internally projecting rim, ridge on the waist.
Fabric: Coarse.
Surfaces: Grey slipped, weathered.

Sr. No. 24
Location: Surface collection.
Fragment: Rim and body. Diam. 18 cm
Form: Deep dish-internally projecting knife face rim, ridge on the waist.
Fabric: Coarse.
Surfaces: Grey slipped, weathered.

Sr. No. 25
Location: Surface collection.
Fragment: Rim and body. Diam. 27 cm
Form: Dish-internally projecting triangular rim, thick cross section.
Fabric: Fine.
Surfaces: Red slipped on the both sides, weathered.

Sr. No. 26
Location: Surface collection.
Fragment: Rim and body. Diam. 28 cm
Form: Dish-featureless pointed rim with slightly internal projection.
Fabric: Coarse.
Surfaces: Red slipped on both sides, weathered.

Sr. No. 27
Location: Surface collection.
Fragment: Rim and body. Diam. 18 cm
Form: Deep dish-internally projecting knife face rim, ridge on the waist.
Fabric: Coarse.
Surfaces: Red slipped on the both sides, weathered.

Plate. XLIII.d. Nos.28-35

Sr. No. 28
Location: Surface collection.
Fragment: Spout.
Form: Small spout-pointed.
Fabric: Coarse to medium.
Surfaces: Red slipped, smooth.

Sr. No. 29
Location: Surface collection.
Fragment: Spout.
Form: Spout-pointed.
Fabric: Coarse.
Surfaces: Red slipped, weathered.

Sr. No. 30
Location: Surface collection.
Fragment: Base and lower body.
Form: Shallow bowl-stand like base.
Fabric: Coarse.
Surfaces: Grey slipped, rough.

Sr. No. 31
Location: Surface collection.
Fragment: Upper body.
Form: Lid-hollow in shape, moulded at the top.
Fabric: Coarse.
Surfaces: Grey slipped, weathered.

Sr. No. 32
Location: Surface collection.
Fragment: Base and lower body.
Form: Saucer-short slightly out turned side and flat base.
Fabric: Coarse.
Surfaces: Unslipped, weathered.

Sr. No. 33
Location: Surface collection.
Fragment: Body portion.
Form: Unascertained-comb like design on the exterior of the body.
Fabric: Coarse.
Surfaces: Unslipped, rough.

Sr. No. 34
Location: Surface collection.
Fragment: Body portion.
Form: Unascertained-horizontally painted design.
Fabric: Coarse.
Surfaces: Red slipped on exterior.

Sr. No. 35
Location: Surface collection.
Fragment: Base and lower body.
Form: Vessel form undetermined-disc base, perforation in the middle of the base.
Fabric: Coarse to medium.
Surfaces: Unslipped, weathered.

Minor objects.

1. Fragment of terracotta stopper. Measurement: L.37.10 mm. (**Plate XLIX.b. No. 5**)
2. Almost complete specimen of terracotta lamp with featureless and slightly internal projecting rim and disc base. Measurement: Cir. 60.37 mm. (**Plate XLIX.b. No.1**)
3. Complete specimen of used shell. (**Plate XLVIII.b. No.5**)
4. Complete specimen of stone ball. Measurement: T.24.41 mm. (**Plate XLIX.b. No.3**)
5. A circular pot sherd disc of red ware, unperforated. Measurement: T.13.93 mm, Cir.54.10 mm. (**Plate XLVI.b. No.17**).

6. A circular pot sherd disc and red in color, unperforated, a blind hole at the centre. Measurement: T.13.16 mm, Cir.55.89 mm. **(Plate XLVI.b. No. 18)**
7. A circular pot sherd disc and grey in color. Unperforated. Measurement: T.6.54 mm, Cir.49.27 mm. **(Plate XLVI.a. No. 3)**
8. Fragment of iron slag. **(Plate L. No.4)**

20. **Site name:** *Butona-ni-Dhar* **(Plate XXVIII.b).**
Co-ordinates: Lat. 21°32' N; Long. 72°17.6' E.
Period of occupation: Early Historic period.
Reference: *IAR.* 1980-81:1
Location: Thalsar village is located 20 km to the south of Bhavnagar city and 7 km west of Hathab village. The village is approachable with the help of State Transport Bus.

The site: The ancient mound is located about half km to the east of the present village and very closed to the sea and locally called as *Butona-ni-Dhar*. It measures 500 m (east-west) X 500 m (north-south) and is nearly 5 m high. Some brick structures in the section and partly buried on the surface of the mound can be seen. The site has produced sherd of plain Red Ware, Red-slipped Ware and Grey Ware.

Ceramic assemblage:

Plate XLIV.a. Nos.1-10

Sr. No. 1
Location: Surface collection.
Fragment: Base and lower body.
Form: Probably lid-round base.
Fabric: Coarse.
Surfaces: Unslipped, weathered.

Sr. No. 2
Location: Surface collection.
Fragment: Base.
Form: Probably bowl-ring foot base.
Fabric: Coarse.
Surfaces: Red slipped on exterior, weathered.

Sr. No. 3
Location: Surface collection.
Fragment: Rim and upper body. Diam. 23 cm
Form: Dish-internally beaked rim, ledge on exterior shoulder.
Fabric: Coarse.
Surfaces: Red slipped on both sides, smooth.

Sr. No. 4
Location: Surface collection.
Fragment: Rim and upper body. Diam 16 cm

Form: Cup-short featureless pointed rim.
Fabric: Coarse.
Surfaces: Unslipped, rough.

Sr. No. 5
Location. Surface collection.
Fragment: Rim and upper body. Diam. 13 cm
Form: Cup-featureless pointed rim, tapering body, thin wall.
Fabric: Coarse.
Surfaces: Unslipped, rough.

Sr. No. 6
Location: Surface collection.
Fragment: Rim and body. Diam.19 cm
Form: Jar-externally projecting beaked rim.
Fabric: Coarse.
Surfaces: Red slipped on exterior, weathered.

Sr. No. 7
Location: Surface Collection.
Fragment: Rim. Diam. 14 cm
Form: Pot-flat projecting under-cut rim.
Fabric: Coarse.
Surfaces: Red slipped on both sides, weathered.

Sr. No. 8
Location: Surface collection.
Fragment: Rim and neck. Diam. 23 cm
Form: Globular pot-flared out and externally thickened rim, short neck.
Fabric: Coarse.
Surfaces: Grey slipped on exterior, rough.

Sr. No. 9
Location: Surface collection.
Fragment: Coarse.
Form: Jar-out turned rim.
Fabric: Coarse.
Surfaces: Grey slipped on both sides, smooth.

Sr. No. 10
Location: Surface collection.
Fragment: Rim and upper body. Diam. 25 cm
Form: Jar-triangular rim, short vertical neck, probably rounded body.
Fabric: Coarse.
Surfaces: Grey slipped on both sides, smooth.

21. **Site name:** *Uparkot* **(Plate XXIX.a).**
Co-ordinate: Lat. 21°26' N ; Long. 72°3' E
Period of occupation: Early Historic.
Reference: *IAR* 1967-68
Location: Present village Timbana in Talaja tehsil is located roughly 20 km to the north west direction of the town. On the south west of this another village called Bhegali is situated.
The site: The ancient site is located on the left bank of river Shetrunji. The habitation mound is roughly 2 km away from the present village. The site is roughly 18 km away from the ancient site of Padri to the northeast direction. The mound locally known as *Uparkot* is partially covered with a Medieval fort. A few modern houses have been constructed inside the fort. The mound is quite extensive and measures 150 m (north-south) in length and 75 m (east-west) in breadth. The periphery of the mound is quite disturbed due to the modern settlement, but the central part of the mound has remained intact. A large number of hero stones were noticed near the site, which were taken away from the site by the villagers. The maximum habitational deposit which is visible at the site is around 8 to 10 m. The site is littered with pottery belonging to the Early Historic period and vitrified clay lumps indicating manufacture of pottery at the site. The site was reported by the earlier scholar.

Ceramic assemblages:

Plate XLIV.b. Nos.1-9

Sr. No. 1
Location: Surface collection.
Fragment: Base and lower body.
Form: Cup-disc base, thick cross section.
Fabric: Coarse.
Surfaces: Unslipped, rough.

Sr. No. 2
Location: Surface collection.
Fragment: Rim and neck. Diam. 14 cm
Form: Globular pot (lota)-out turned rim, ridge on the waist.
Fabric: Coarse.
Surfaces: Unslipped, rough.

Sr. No. 3
Location: Surface collection.
Fragment: Rim and body. Diam. 26 cm
Form: Dish-out-turned beaded rim.
Fabric: Coarse.
Surfaces: Unslipped, rough.

Sr. No. 4
Location: Surface collection.

Fragment: Rim and body. Diam. 25 cm
Form: Dish-internally projecting rounded rim.
Fabric: Coarse.
Surfaces: Unslipped, rough.

Sr. No. 5
Location: Surface collection.
Fragment: Rim and neck. Diam. 14 cm
Form: Pot-out-turned rim, ledge at the neck, narrow mouth.
Fabric: Coarse.
Surfaces: Red slipped on both sides, weathered.

Sr. No. 6
Location: Surface collection.
Fragment: Rim and upper body. Diam. 23 cm
Form: Jar-flat projecting short rim.
Fabric: Coarse.
Surfaces: Red slipped on both sides, weathered.

Sr. No. 7
Location: Surface collection.
Fragment: Rim, neck and upper body. Diam. 17 cm
Form: Jar-triangular rim, short vertical neck.
Fabric: Coarse.
Surfaces: Grey slipped on both sides, smooth.

Sr. No. 8
Location: Surface collection.
Fragment: Rim and neck. Diam. 18 cm
Form: Jar-long out turned and externally thickened rim.
Fabric: Coarse.
Surfaces: Rough, unslipped, grey.

Sr. No. 9
Location: Surface collection.
Fragment: Body sherd.
Form: Unascertained.
Fabric: Coarse.
Surfaces: Red slipped, smooth, painted horizontal loop between two horizontal band.

22. **Site name**: *Daya Bhai-No-Dhoro* **(Plate XXIX.b)**.
Co-ordinate: Lat. 21°23' N; Long. 72°6' E
Period of occupation: Early Harappan, Mature Harappan and Early Historic.
Reference: New discovery.

Location: The modern village of Valavadar is located 4 km to the north of Talaja town and roughly one and half km to the west of the river Shetrunji and 6 km north west of ancient settlement of Padri. The village is connected to the taluka head-quarter by a good motorable road.

The site: The ancient settlement, located close to the village, is locally known as *Daya Bhai-No-Dhoro*. It is spread over an area of 200 m (east-west) by 75 m (north-south). The habitational deposit of the mound is shallow and is under cultivation. Therefore, the site is badly disturbed. The site presents a three-fold cultural sequence, e.g. Early Harappan, Mature Harappan and Early Historic. Besides pottery, a terracotta stopper and possibly a head of an animal figurine have been found on the surface of the mound. The site was discovered by the author.

Ceramic assemblage

Plate XLV.a. Nos.1-9

Sr. No. 1
Location: Surface collection.
Fragment: Rim and body. Diam. 22 cm
Form: Deep dish-internally projecting triangular rim.
Fabric: Medium.
Surfaces: Red slipped, weathered.

Sr. No. 2
Location: Surface collection.
Fragment: Rim and neck. Diam. 14 cm
Form: Pot-externally thickened rim, concave shape and under-cut on the exterior.
Fabric: Coarse to medium.
Surfaces: Red slipped on both sides, weathered.

Sr. No. 3
Location: Surface collection.
Fragment: Rim and neck. Diam. 11 cm
Form: Same as No.2 but flat rim and narrow mouth.
Fabric: Coarse to medium.
Surfaces: Red slipped on both sides, weathered.

Sr. No. 4
Location: Surface collection.
Fragment: Rim. Diam. 32 cm
Form: Jar-internally flat, slightly projecting rim and externally thickened, shallow grooves on the interior of the rim.
Fabric: Medium to fine.
Surfaces: Red slipped on both sides, weathered.

Sr. No. 5
Location: Surface collection.
Fragment: Rim and body. Diam. 17 cm
Form: Jar-out turned and externally thickened rim.
Fabric: Coarse to medium.
Surfaces: Red slipped on both sides, weathered.

Sr. No. 6
Location: Surface collection.
Fragment: Rim and upper body. Diam. 12 cm
Form: Small pot-short out turned rim.
Fabric: Medium to fine.
Surfaces: Red slipped on both sides, weathered.

Sr. No. 7
Location: Surface collection.
Fragment: Rim and neck. Diam. 19 cm
Form: Jar-out curved rim with deep groove on the top and internally beveled rim.
Fabric: Coarse to medium.
Surfaces: Grey slipped on the both sides, rough.

Sr. No. 8
Location: Surface collection.
Fragment: Rim and upper body. Diam. 23 cm
Form: Same as No.7
Fabric: Coarse.
Surfaces: Thin grey slipped, weathered.

Sr. No. 9
Location: Surface collection.
Fragment: Rim and neck. Diam. 25 cm
Form: Pot-flat rim, deep groove on the top of the rim, short vertical neck.
Fabric: Coarse.
Surfaces: Grey slipped on both sides, weathered.

Plate XLV.b. Nos.10-16

Sr. No. 10
Location: Surface collection.
Fragment: Rim. Diam. 22 cm
Form: Jar-long out-turned and externally thickened rim
Fabric: Coarse.
Surfaces: Grey slipped on both sides, smooth.

Sr. No. 11
Location: Surface collection.

Fragment: Rim and upper body. Diam. 22 cm
Form: Pot-externally projecting rounded rim, grooves on the exterior of the rim, almost no neck.
Fabric: Coarse.
Surfaces: Grey slipped, weathered.

Sr. No. 12
Location: Surface collection.
Fragment: Rim. Diam. 23 cm
Form: Vessel form unascertained, Probably-basin-flat rim with little internal projection, ridge on the exterior of the rim.
Fabric: Coarse.
Surfaces: Grey slipped, weathered.

Sr. No. 13
Location: Surface collection.
Fragment: Base and lower body.
Form: Bowl-flat base.
Fabric: Coarse.
Surfaces: Unslipped, weathered.

Sr. No. 14
Location: Surface collection.
Fragment: Base and lower body.
Form: Shallow bowl-disc base.
Fabric: Coarse.
Surfaces: Grey slipped, rough.

Sr. No. 15
Location: Surface collection.
Fragment: Base and lower body.
Form: Shallow bowl-stand like disc base.
Fabric: Coarse.
Surfaces: Grey slipped, weathered.

Sr. No. 16
Location: Surface collection.
Fragment: Handle.
Form: Vessel form unascertained. Circular in shape.
Fabric: Coarse to medium.
Surfaces: Unslipped, weathered.

Minor objects.

1. A fragment of circular pot sherd disc, perforated. Measurement: T.8.29 mm, Cir.67.16 mm. **(Plate XLVI.a. No. 1)**

Chapter 5

Settlement Pattern

Introduction

The present chapter deals with the settlement pattern in Bhavnagar district, especially in the lower part of Shetrunji river basin, during the Early Historic period. The data gathered in the field has been utilized to draw inferences about the way in which the Early Historic people disposed their settlements in this region. The chapter consists of three sections. The first section gives a brief summary of the origin and development of the concepts of settlement pattern in archaeology. Section two deals with the size and distribution of the settlements and in the last section analysis of demographic pattern has been made.

Development of settlement pattern studies

The study of settlement pattern in archaeology occupies an important place in the western world. The concept of settlement pattern is derived from geography. In archaeology its application is relatively recent. It was Gordon R. Willey who was inspired to undertake the study of distribution of sites by Julian Steward, an ethnographer (Willey 1953). An excellent definition of the term has been given by Willey. According to him settlement pattern is "the way in which man disposed himself over the landscape on which he lived. It refers to dwellings, to their arrangement and to the nature and disposition of other buildings pertaining to community life. These settlements reflect the natural environment, the level of technology on which the builders operated and various institutions of social interaction and control, which the culture maintained. Because settlement pattern is, to a large extent, directly shaped by widely held culture needs, they offer a strategic starting point for functional interpretation of archaeological cultures" (Willey 1953: 1). The study deals with the settlement pattern along the coast and in the lower part of Shetrunji river basin in Bhavnagar district of Saurashtra during the Early Historic period and is concerned with the working relationship between people and their technology and the landscape. As determinant of settlement patterns Butzer (1987: 43) has stated that "The most detailed is the site microenvironment, defined in terms of local physical and biotic parameters that influenced the original site selection, that were effective during the period of site use, and that were responsible for its burial and subsequent preservation." He also says that (1987: 278) "reasonable frameworks for systematic regional analysis exist, and they call for the development and testing the spatial models tailored to the nature of the available information. These models should seek to elucidate the patterns of site location, the utilization and the modification of resource spaces, and interactions within and between site networks. Such comprehensive explanatory models of the human landscape should transcend the classic goal of abstract spatial behavior by identifying resource patterns as well as those interactions between societies and their environments that are reflected in cultural configurations and other imprints on the biophysical landscape. This will require new multidimensional criteria that can be applied to the component data that can be generated by an explicitly contextual approach. It is, therefore, vital that new archaeological projects incorporate strategies that will allow more comprehensive analysis of such human landscape." Therefore, settlement pattern, in very simple words, can be described as the study of the logic behind the location of a particular site.

Bruce Trigger (1963) says by a settlement pattern is meant the manner in which people's cultural activities and social institutions are distributed over the landscape.

K. C. Chang (1958) defined the settlement pattern as "the manner in which human settlements are arranged over the landscape in relation to the physiograpic, geographic environments and community pattern as the manner in which the inhabitants arrange their various structures with the community and their communities within the aggregate". By the term "aggregate" he means a gathering of certain number of communities which are bound by close social, political, commercial or religious ties.

Ruth Trigham's (1972) analysis of settlement pattern comprises of:

"a. the location of settlements and their relationship to the ecology, the available natural resources, the relative ease of communication;

b. the overall density and the distribution of settlements;
c. the exploitation area and the subsistence economy of the settlements;
d. the distribution of specialized activity loci- burial sites, butchering sites etc.;
e. the population movement among the various loci, the degree of seasonal and non-seasonal mobility;
f. the exchange of commodities between settlements by short- and long- range trade;
g. the social relationships between the settlements (communities ties, kingship ties etc.);
h. the political relationships between the settlements including the political domination and hierarchy, and centralization of political, religious and military activities; warfare, defense;
i. the differential exploitation of the same gross ecological zones."

In 1962 K. C. Chang classified settlements on the basis of time -space relationship into two types (1) year round settlement and (2) seasonal settlement.

Year round settlement, is that within which the annual cycle of main subsistence activities of occupants can be completed. It can be divided again into two sub phases:

(a) Permanent settlement : occupied permanently.
(b) Semi-permanent settlement: abandoned after the occupancy of one year or several years because (among other factors) the ecological potential of the locale is exhausted and occupants are unable to restore it.

(2) Seasonal settlement complex: a network of seasonal settlements occupied by a group of people in turn of different seasons of year, distributed within confines of an annual subsistence region. He further divided this seasonal settlement into two-sub section.

A. Sedentary seasonal settlements: annual subsistence region of a group of occupants remaining permanently unchanged.

1. With permanent basis: locales of main seasonal settlement remain permanently unchanged.
2. With transient basis: locale of the various seasonal settlement (particularly main sites of occupation) keep changing after one year's or several years' occupancy because (among other factors) the ecological potential of a particular locale is exhausted and the occupants are unable to restore it, though the whole annual subsistence region of the group remains unchanged.

B. Temporary seasonal settlements: a group of people has to change its habitation from one annual subsistence region to another after one year's or several years' occupancy because (among other factors) ecological potential of the whole region is exhausted and occupants are unable to restore it.

E. Z. Vogt (1956) pointed out the scope of settlement pattern study as a description of:

1. "the nature of the individual domestic house type or types;
2. the spatial arrangement of these domestic houses types with respect to one another within the village or community unit;
3. the relationship of domestic house types to other spatial architectural features, such as temples, places, ball courts, kivas;
4. the overall village and community plan and
5. the spatial relationships of the villages or communities to one another over as large an area as is feasible."

He again stresses and urges that it will be very useful for the study of settlement pattern investigation if archaeologists, ethnologists and geographers work together.

Sanders (1956: 16) has developed a new concept of symbiotic regions into the archaeological context. He distinguished between community settlement patterns and zonal settlement patterns. According to him community patterns will constitute:
1. the individual units of population, 2. types of communities, 3. Organization of public buildings, 4. population distribution and form, 5. density of community population and house types.

Zonal pattern will be concerned with the distribution of community sizes, distance between communities, density of population and the symbiotic interrelationship between communities.

Paddayya (1982: 61) distinguished between settlement pattern and settlement system. According to him, settlement pattern is narrower in scope and refers only to the number, nature, size and distribution of archaeological sites. Whereas settlement system is concerned with the functional interrelationships among various classes of sites within a given region and their articulation with the environment in order to ensure the survival of the human group. Thus there are two fundamental assumptions underlying the concept of settlement system of functionally interrelated elements. A settlement system is peculiar to a given social group and the regional environment it exploits. Although the neighboring groups may share similar genetic, linguistic and historical traditions, they will have their own settlement system because of the differences in both natural and social environments.

According to Trigger (1963) settlement pattern studies not only help us to interpret the distribution pattern but also reconstruct the social or religious aspect of the ancient cultures (Sears 1961). To understand the settlement pattern studies three different terms viz. settlement pattern, settlement archaeology and settlement system are in use. The settlement pattern is a study of the distribution of sites over a given area (Trigger 1968), on the other hand settlement system is the study of rules governing the physical arrangement of sites across a landscape (Flannery 1967) and the settlement archaeology includes the study of reconstruction of cultural lifeways and processing of change (Rouse 1972).

A number of well documented studies have been carried out all over the world in this field (Sander 1956, Chang 1958, Binford 1964) after the publication G. R. Willey's work entitled "*Prehistoric Settlement Patterns in Veru Valley, Peru*" (Willey 1953).

Bruce Trigger (1967 and 1968) has developed new approaches and level of studies in the field of settlement archaeology in his two classic papers:

1. Ecological interaction of two variables, environment and technology,
2. Sociological-reconstructing social, political and religious organization of cultures.

Trigger (1968) has suggested that settlement pattern study can be more profitably done if studied on:

1. Individual buildings and structures

In this level, Trigger has given a number of factors, which affect the individual structures and their layouts. The nature of building determines a settlement pattern. For example, migratory people always prefer to have round huts that are easy to build and easy to transport from place to place. On the other hand, the sedentary communities prefer to stay in permanent rectangular houses (Flannery 1972). There is specific correlation between house types and their availability of raw material. For example, due to scarcity of raw material in desert, people live in tents. The size and layout of a structure not only reflect the position of a family but also in the wealth and rank.

2. Community layout

The arrangement of building in a particular locality reflects social stratification and economic activities. Environment and subsistence technology, family and kingship organization, class, religious and ethnic groups play a very important role in determining the size and stability of a community. The studies at this level are numerous like the works of Adams (1961, 1965), Flannery (1971, 1976), Chang (1962), Clark (1972), Fletcher (1977), Hill (1966, 1970), Dhavalikar (1977, 1978) etc. are very important.

3. Zonal pattern

The zonal pattern is largely determined by the availability of natural resources. Farming communities tend to settle near good arable land and perennial supply of water whereas pastoral groups settle near the pasture land. Various factors like trade, political organization, warfare, religion and their subsistence technology determine the location of a particular settlement. The works of Adams (1961, 1965), Flannery (1971), Renfrew (1972), Sanders (1965), Willey *et al.* (1965), Parson (1971), Dhavalikar (1977, 1978, 1984), Shinde (1984, 1990, 1995), Chitalwala (1979), Possehl (1980), Dhavalikar and Possehl (1974), David Raju (1985, 1990), Paddayya (1982), Bhan (1979), M. Lal (1984), Joshi *et al.* (1982) Haque (1992), Erdoshi (1988), Flemming (1971) are important at this level.

Size and Distribution of the Early Historic Settlements along the Coast and in the Lower part of Shetrunji River Basin

The ecological zones and many other factors like trade, political organization, warfare, religion and subsistence technology have affected the settlement pattern, distribution and their size in different ways (Trigger 1968). Out of the twenty two sites, seven are located along the coast, eleven are located on the lower Shetrunji river basin and the rest of the settlements are away from the river. The main concentrations of settlements are found on the Shetrunji river basin and most of them are multi-cultural sites. The extent and thickness of the habitational deposit varies from site to site (Table 12). Maximum sites are under cultivation and few sites have preserved some amount of habitation deposits in the form of mounds. Lithostratigraphically, the region was confined to basalt formation with some intrusive veins of chert, chalcedony, agate and calcite. The soil is black cotton and very fertile, which overlaps the lateritic deposit of about 5 m. Of the twenty two settlements one falls in the category of below 1 ha (hectare) in size, nine sites fall in the category of 1-2 ha. There are three settlements, which fall in the category of 3 ha. In the category between 4-5 ha, there are two sites. One settlement each in the category of 6 ha and between 7-8 ha, whereas other two settlements fall in the category of 12 ha. In the category of 25 ha, there are two settlements. There is only one settlement which is more than 39 ha in extent (Table 13; Fig.11 and 12).

Table 12: Sites: Their extent and thickness of the habitation.

Site dimension (Extent of occupation deposit)

S.No.	*Site name*	*Length (M)*	*Breadth (M)*	*Thickness (M)*	*Area in Ha.*
1	Bandi Rohil	300	100	3.00	3.0
2	Bhegali	200	100	1.00	2.00
3	Bhalar	200	100	--	2.0
4	Bharapur	300	400	2.00	12.0
5	Chopra	300	200	3.00	6.00
6	Dakana	300	400	1.50	12.0
7	Dantrad	300	150	1.50	4.5
8	Devalia	75	150	--	1.125
9	Gorkhi	300	150	1.50	4.5

10	Hathab	800	500	5.00	40.0
11	Ichhora	300	100	1.50	3.00
12	Katva	150	90	1.50	1.35
13	Khadsaliya	500	500	5.0	25.0
14	Padri	340	210	3.2	7.14
15	Pavti	38	75	1.00	0.285
16	Phulsar	200	100	1.50	2.0
17	Piparla	130	125	2.50	1.165
18	Shilavadar	150	200	2.00	3.0
19	Saltanpur	200	100	2.0	2.0
20	Thalsar	500	500	5.0	25.0
21	Timbana	150	75	10.0	1.125
22	Valavadar	200	75	--	1.5

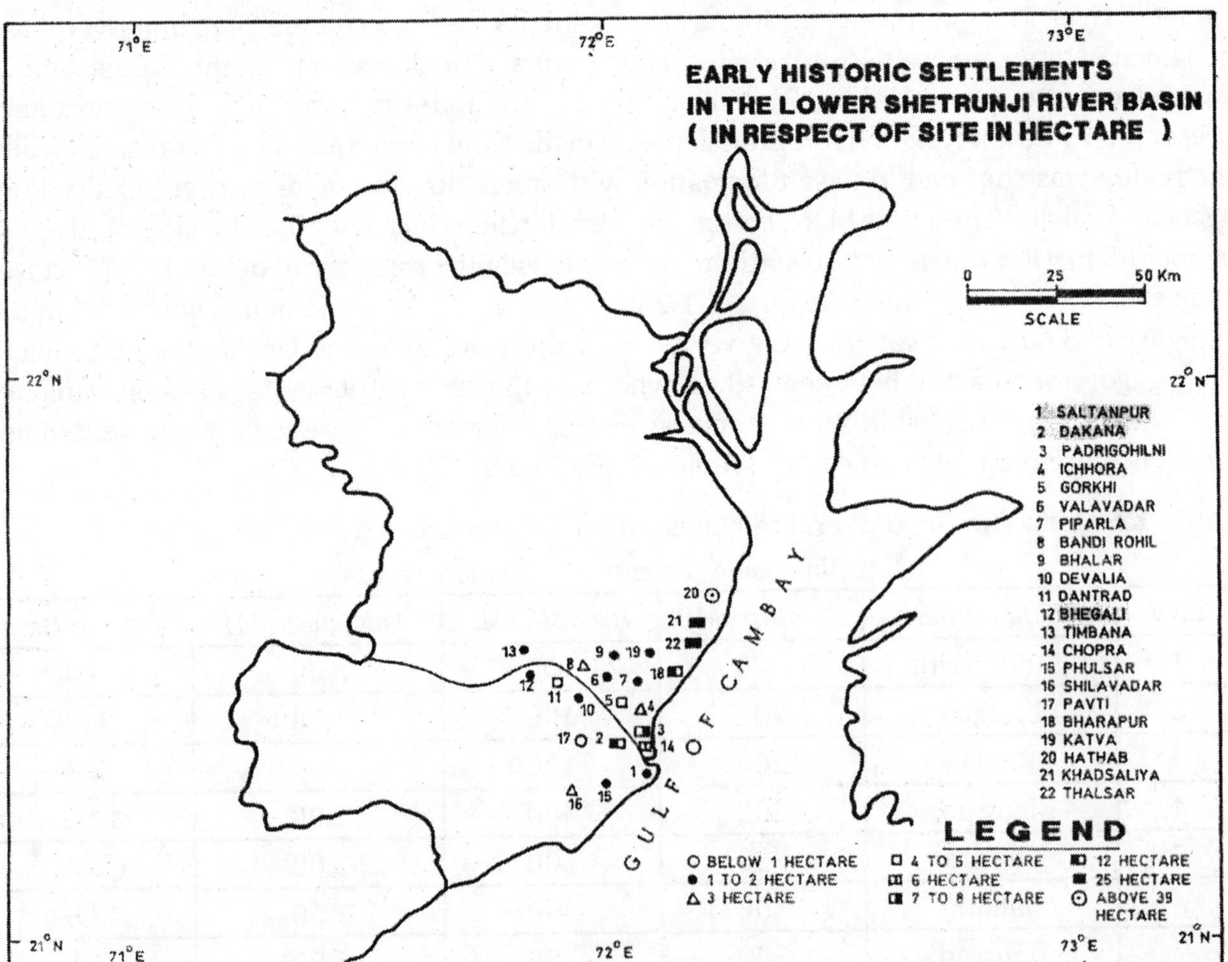

Fig. 11: Early Historic Settlements in the Lower Shetrunji River Basin (in respect of size in hectare).

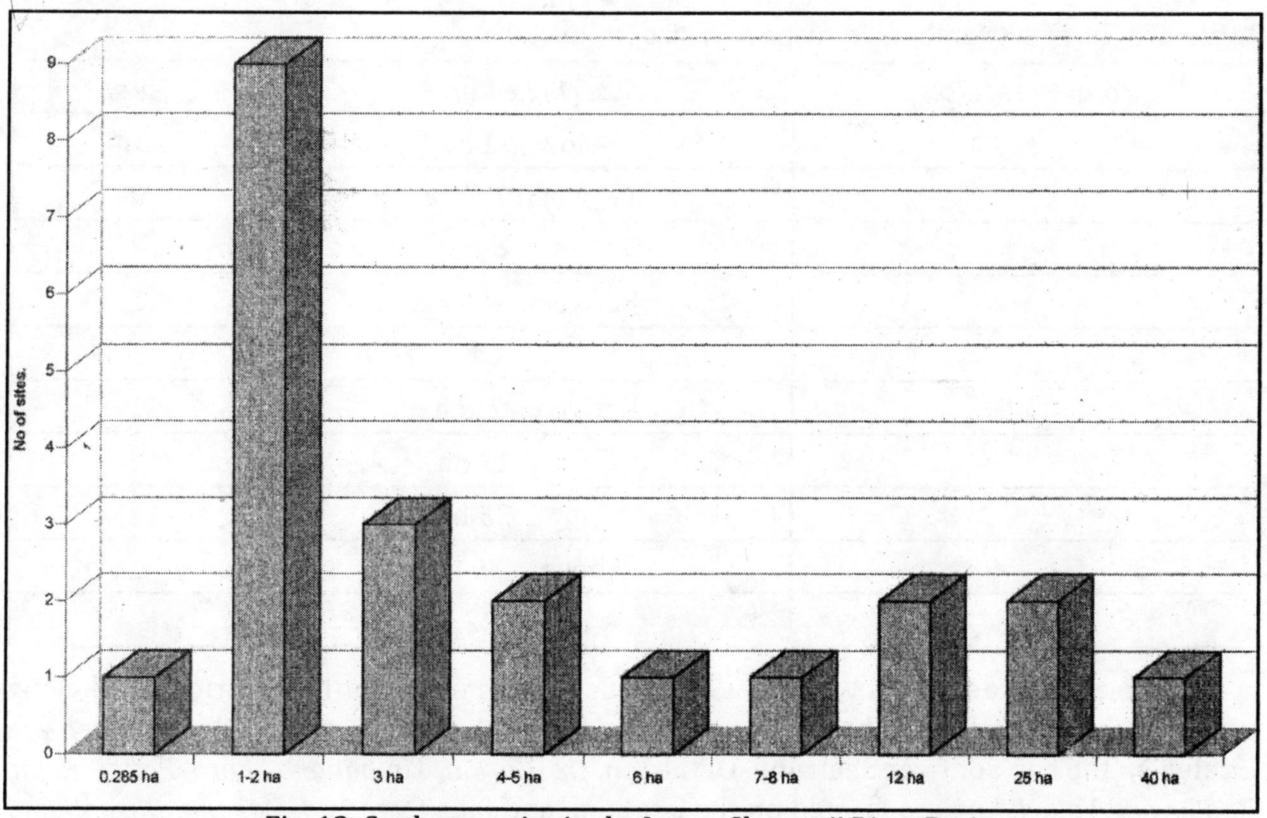

Fig. 12: Settlement size in the Lower Shetrunji River Basin.

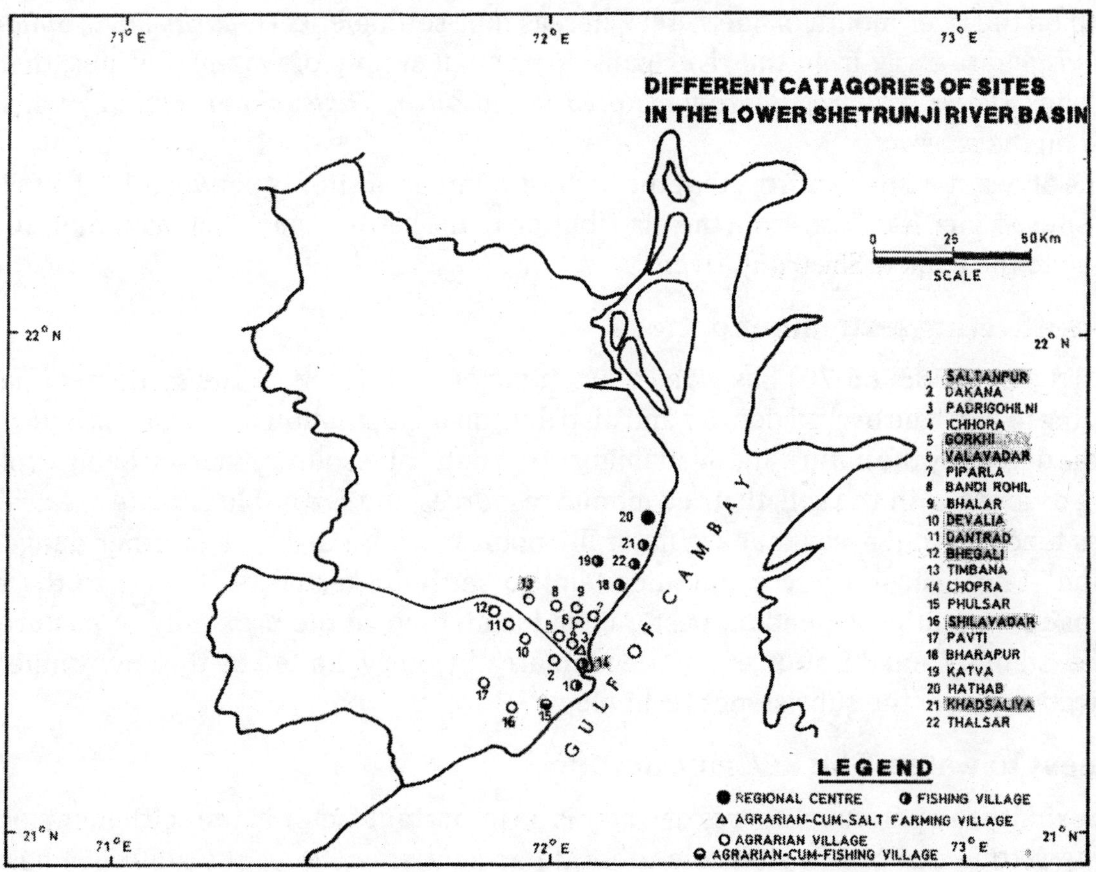

Fig. 13: Different categories of sites in the Lower Shetrunji River Basin.

Table 13: No. of settlements in respect of size (in hectare)

Total No. of sites	*Size (in hectare)*	*Total*
22	Below 1 ha	1
	Between 1-2 ha	9
	3 ha	3
	Between 4-5 ha	2
	6 ha	1
	Between 7-8 ha	1
	12 ha	2
	25 ha	2
	Above 39 ha	1
	22	

The present study deals with the settlement pattern in the Early Historic period along the coast and in the lower Shetrunji river basin. Out of the twenty two settlements ten are located on the bank of river Shetrunji. Of the ten, *six (Gorkhi, Timbana, Ichhora, Bandi- Rohil, Bhalar and Valavadar*) are located on the left bank and four (*Dantrad, Dakana, Bhegali and Devalia*) are located on the right bank. There is only one settlement (*Saltanpur*) which is situated on the river mouth of Shetrunji whereas four settlements (*Piparla, Pavti, Shilavadar and Phulsar*) are away from the river bank (perennial supply of water). Besides, there are seven sites *(Padri, Chopra, Bharapur, Katva, Khadsaliya, Thalsar and Hathab*) which are located on the coast.

The above statistic confirms that the highest number of sites is between 1-2 ha followed by the sites of 3 ha. It is clear from the distribution of the settlements, that maximum sites are confined to the bank of Shetrunji river.

Factors affecting settlement pattern

Bruce Trigger (1968: 66-70) has given a list of factors, which affect the settlement pattern. According to him "the overall density and distribution of population of a region is determined to a large degree by the nature and availability of the natural resources that are being exploited. As long as areas with the soil, their economic resources and favorable climate are available, settlers tend to avoid areas that are naturally poor or where diseases or other dangers are common." The agricultural communities tend to settle on fertile land close to the rivers, whereas communities depend on pastoralism locate their in the proximity of pasture land. The size, stability and duration of a settlement are obviously limited by the environment and the effectiveness of the subsistence technology.

Nearness to water: The Riverine Setting

The proximity to a perennial source of water is an important factor in the settlement location. Riverine setting can play a vital role to locate ancient sites. Possehl (1980: 85) has given more importance to the riverine setting in a particular region to locate ancient settlements.

According to him, "An obvious advantage to a riverine location is reliable supply of water for human and animal consumption as well as for general domestic use. It would seem unlikely, however, that this alone could so unflexibly mould a settlement pattern in the environment. Ground water in Gujarat is readily available, even during the dry season (April and May), with fairly shallow wells." He also says (1980: 85) that "another possibility is that the riverine location was selected because it afforded a potential for irrigation. Substantial increase over dry farming be expected from irrigated land in Gujarat. As a rule of thumb the local farmers in Bhavnagar district expect irrigation to double yields which would materialize from the dry farming." The riverine setting of the Bhavnagar district has been described in the chapter on environmental background.

The author has made careful observations during the course of exploration concerning the nearness of water sources to the Early Historic sites. The major sources of water in the study region is the Shetrunji river and its tributary -the Shel. Of the twenty two sites, eleven are in the vicinity of the perennial source of water, seven are near the coast and rest of the sites are away from the perennial source of water. The Shetrunji river is sluggish in character and dries during the summer. Panini also mentions that villages depended for their water supply on wells (*Kupas*) to which were attached *Nipanas* or water trough from which the cattle would drink (Agrawala 1953: 141). At present it is observed that villagers or local people obtain drinking water during the summer by digging temporary wells in the river bed. On the whole Bhavnagar is well watered. Along the coast, however, the water is brackish and charged with salt except where sweet water springs occur (Trivedi 1969). Such an opportunity could have been exploited by the Early Historic people too.

Soil and settlement

"Soil conditions are recognized to be one of the most important factors in the distribution of settlements" (Houston 1953: 99). On the other hand fertility of the soil is another important factor determining the location of human settlement especially in the case of agricultural-cum- industrial communities. The study region is occupied by the black cotton soil and maximum settlements are covered by this soil. Possehl (1980: 53) says that the early farming communities in the western India are closely associated with the black cotton soils. A British agriculturist, who traveled in India in the latter part of the nineteenth century, was very impressed by the characteristics of black cotton soil. He made remarks about the soil in these words: "Black soil has wonderful power for absorbing water, and during rainy season it swells, so that the whole surface is raised. Although it continues to retain throughout abnormal amount of moisture, which is of great value to the crops grown on it, and, in short, enables cultivation to be practiced without irrigation, at the same time, in the dry weather, it loses a large amount of moisture, and shrinks in consequence. The shrinking is in all directions; consequently very deep and wide tracks are formed, which make the land quite unsound and dangerous for riding. By the use of Dutch hoe-harrow, the cracks are filled and closed with the fine soil of the surface and by this means a regular circulation of soil is established. The cracks further fulfill the functions of ploughing, by admitting air freely into the body of the soil. The objects of ploughing are attained but nature is left to do a large share of the work, and, further, she provides the means by which man can successfully carry out the remainder of it. The plentiful supply of powdery soil is useful, not only for carrying on the circulation processes, but for closing up the cracks to present excessive evaporation of moisture from the body of under-soil." (Wallace 1888: 180-181).

From the above statement it is observed that black cotton soil played a very important role in determining the settlement pattern of the Early Historic peoples who mostly practiced dry farming. Of the twenty two settlements, thirteen sites such as *Bandi Rohil, Bhalar, Bhegali, Dakana, Dantrad, Devalia, Gorkhi, Ichhora, Pavti, Piparla, Shilavadar, Timbana* and *Valavadar* are located in the black cotton soil zone. The above mentioned sites could be agrarian settlements. From the available artifacts it can be said that the inhabitants of the above mentioned sites established their settlements to exploit the rich fertile land for producing food and might have supplied to the other settlement in exchange of other commodities. Apart from this, the site of *Phulsar* is very close to the sea, it could be identified agrarian-cum-fishing settlement. About the dry farming cultivation Leshnik has pointed out in the absence of artificial irrigation intensive farming is not possible but in turn extensive farming can be practiced in the dry farming areas (Leshnik 1967). Of the fourteen settlements, one settlement called *Bhalar* played very important roles during the Early Historic period. When the present author explored the site, he found a fragment of pottery dish with green glaze on the inner side. It shows the contacts between the Persian Gulf and this study region in the beginning of the Christian Era. Similar dish fragments of BI Ware vessels have been found at the excavated Early Historic sites in the Persian Gulf (Paul *et al.*, 1997: 58, Fig.28; Bernard *et al.* 1990, Fig.4 and Gupta 1997, Plate No. XXV.b, c and d). Therefore, on the basis of there artifacts it can be said that these settlements could be identified as trade-cum-agrarian settlements whereas another six settlements such *as Bharapur, Chopra, Katva, Khadsaliya, Saltanpur* and *Thalsar* are very close to the sea shore, but do not seem to have played an important role in the overseas trade because the sites were not situated directly on the coast. Secondly the Gulf of Cambay does not have natural ports because of silting problem. On the basis of ethnographic parallel and surrounding ecological conditions it can be deduced that these settlements were established for the fishing purpose and inhabitants of these sites obtained food grain and other commodities from the other settlements in exchange of fish.

Another ancient site, Padri is located in a shallow depression on a slightly elevated dune. In spite of the site being close to the coast, it doesn't appear to have played an important role in the external trade. Because the settlement was not located directly on the coast. The site could have been situated at least 3-4 km inland had the main intention of the occupants been cultivation. Therefore, the settlement appears to be have been a processing centre where the salt was made and then supplied to the other settlements (Shinde 1992a: 79-86). Even today many families from the Padri and nearby villages are engaged in the manufacture of salt. The Early Historic levels at Padri have produced the evidence of Goddess *Lajjagauri* temple and figurines of goddesses *Lajjagauri* (Shinde 1994). Besides, the site also yielded a good number of cultural materials of the Early Historic phase. Among the materials mention should be made of two copper coins, similar to those is issued by the *Kshatrapa* king Nahapan, two boat-shaped terracotta motifs and one tortoise-shaped copper lamp. They indicate the overseas trading activity. Besides, an array of antiquities such as pottery, iron, copper, terracotta objects and beads of glass and semi-precious stones and shell bangles etc, have been found. Another settlement is called Hathab which is located very close to the sea and covers an area of 40 hectare. Of the twenty two settlements, Hathab is the largest settlement in the study region. From the close observation of the location of the site and surrounding ecology it can be said the site could have been a regional centre. This site is also mentioned in the *Periplus of the Erythraean Sea* as a port (Schoff 1912: 390-40) during the Early Historic period (Fig.13).

The Early Historic settlements distributed in the Shetrunji basin are in a linear pattern. They form what Flannery (1979) describes as long strings of villages in "ribbon band fashion." Possehl (1980) has stated that the resources, especially fertile land and grass belts, are evenly spread all along rivers. With growing population, acquisition of new land for agriculture is inevitable and people spread their activities to the other rivers. Flannery (1976: 177) has suggested that villages will be located on a particular river bank which affords the best catchment area with respect to mountains, hunting lands, piedmont wild plant collection area and special resources like pottery clay, raw material so on. The formula for determining the spacing of settlements is based on the density of rural settlements. The average spacing between the two settlements is determined by dividing the total area surveyed by total number of settlements. In the study region there were altogether twenty two settlements. The average spacing between two settlements is 3.78 km. It is true that the factors other than size affected the spacing of settlements. King (1961) has carried out spacing in Washington state and observed that the spacing of settlements was governed not only by the size of population but also by the economic potentialities of the area.

Demographic Study

During the last two decades, there has been growing emphasis on the estimation of population size, density and growth rate and more importantly the role of demographic features in cultural change. Several methods have been adopted to estimate population size of the past in different areas. According to Hassan (1978: 51), the important source of demographic information are 1. human skeletal remains; 2. artifacts used by the people; 3. food remains; 4. the ecological potentials of human habitat and 5. the settlement pattern. Peterson criticizes the archaeologists for over analyzing their data and the use of methods that are crude. But he (1975: 227) again admits that even in the modern estimates "no nation has ever made a complete and accurate data of its inhabitants. The demographic data of most of the world are quite unreliable". The present author has made an attempt to estimate the population of the Early Historic period on the basis of settlement size. It is based on the principle that there is some relationship between the number of people and the area they occupy. The formula is as follows.

Number of inhabitants = Constant X site area (Hassan 1978), where the number of persons per unit of site are determined from the modern village in the area, which is compared with the archaeological settlements under consideration (Shinde 1984). There are many shortcomings in this method. The length of occupation and the thickness of habitation deposit seriously affect the estimate of population (Tolstoy and Fish 1973). In fact what we want is to estimate of a population at a fixed point of time and not over long period. Leshnik (1967) has conducted ethnographic survey in Nimad district of Central India. According to him 200 persons dwell in one hectare of area in this area (Leshnik 1967). The present author has applied the same method to estimate the Early Historic population along the coast and in the lower Shetrunji river basin (Table 14). There is only one settlement with a population of around 57 persons. There are nine settlements in the category between 200-400 persons, whereas in the category between 600-900 persons there are five settlements. In the category between 1200-2400 there are only four settlements. There are two settlements in the category of 5000 persons and in the category of 8000 persons there is one settlement (Table 15, Fig.14 and Fig.15). Settlements wise population estimate is given in Table 16.

Table 14: Population size (in ha).

No. of sites	*Size in hectare*	*Occupational area (ha)*	*Population*
1	Below 1 ha	0.285	57
9	Between 1-2 ha	14.725	2945
3	Between 3 ha	9.0	1800
2	Between 4-5 ha	9.0	1800
1	Between 6 ha	6.0	1200
1	Between 7-8 ha	7.14	1428
2	Between 12 ha	24	4800
2	Between 25 ha	50	10,000
1	Between 40 ha	40	8000
Total 22		160.150 ha	32030

Table 15: Population of each category.

Population size	*Total settlements*
Below 100 persons	1
Between 200-400 persons	9
Between 600-900 persons	5
Between 1200-2400 persons	4
5000 persons	2
8000 persons	1
	22

Table 16: Settlement-wise population estimate along the coast and in the lower Shetrunji river basin.

No.	*Site name*	*Area of occupation in ha.*	*Population*
1	Bandi Rohil	3.0	600
2	Bhegali	2.0	400
3	Bhalar	2.0	400
4	Bharapur	12.0	2400
5	Chopra	6.0	1200
6	Dakana	12.0	2400
7	Dantrad	4.5	900
8	Devalia	1.125	225
9	Gorkhi	4.5	900
10	Hathab	40	8000
11	Ichhora	3.0	600
12	Katva	1.35	270
13	Khadsaliya	25.0	5000
14	Padri	7.14	1428
15	Pavti	0.285	57
16	Phulsar	2.0	400
17	Piparla	1.625	325
18	Shilavadar	3.0	600
19	Saltanpur	2.0	400
20	Thalsar	25.0	5000
21	Timbana	1.125	225
22	Valavadar	1.5	300
Total		160.15	32,030

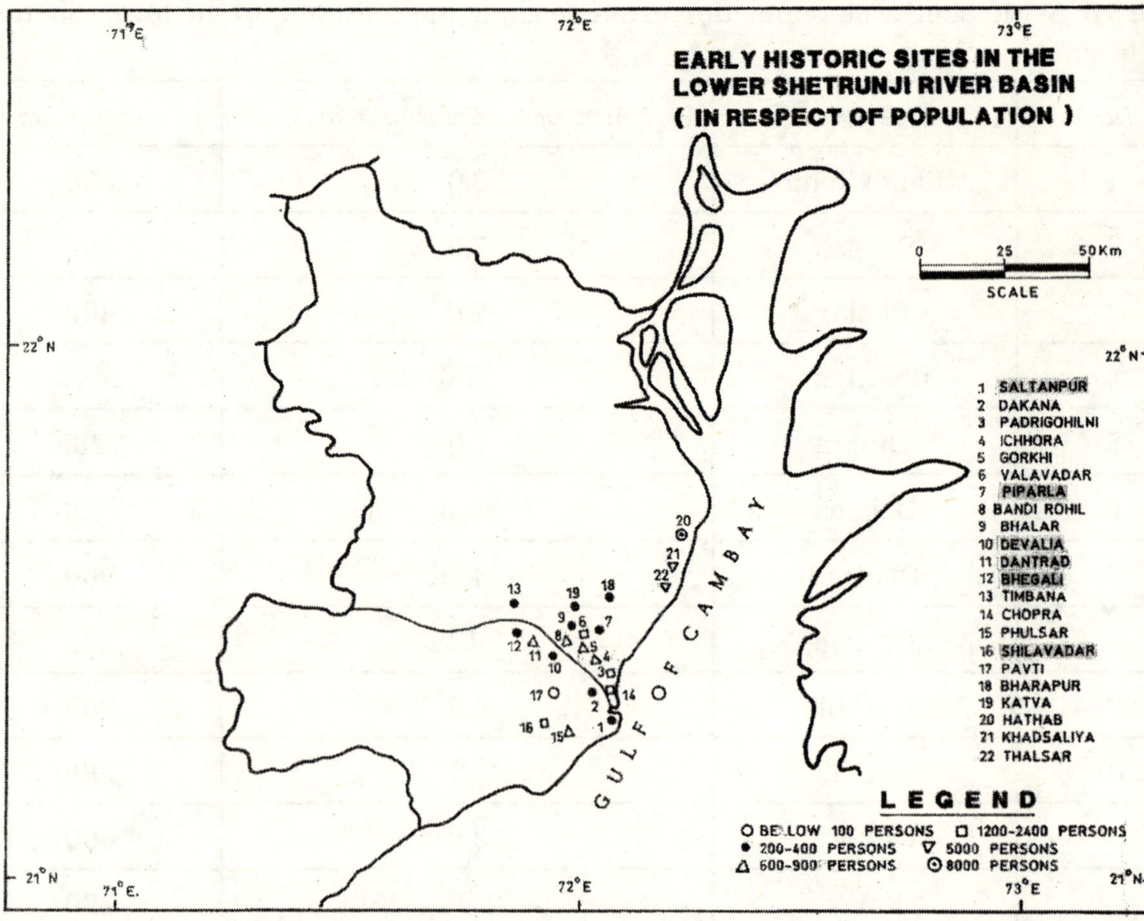

Fig. 14: Early Historic sites in the Lower Shetrunji River Basin (in respect of population).

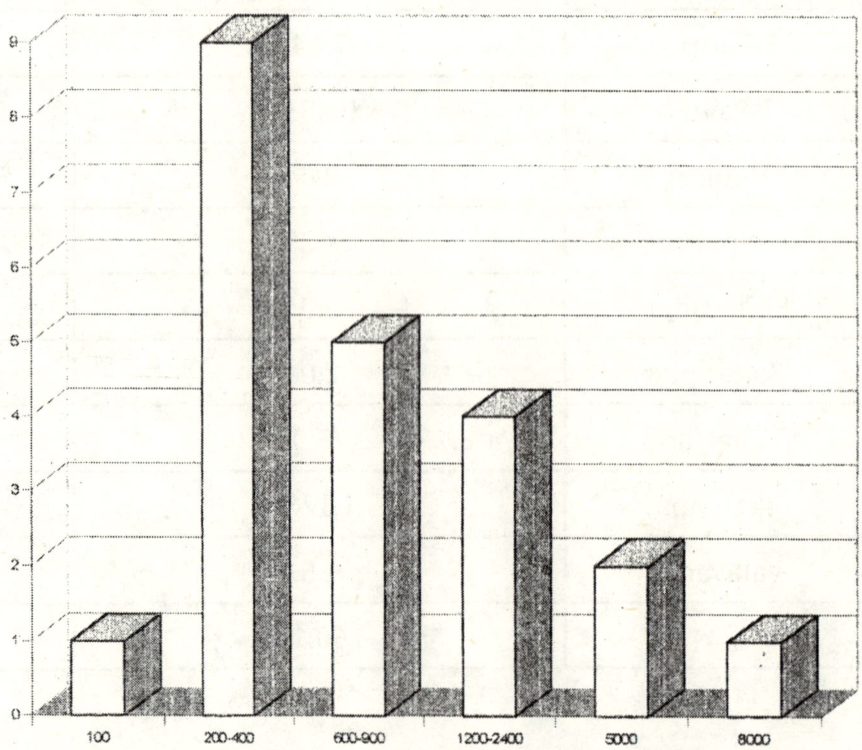

Fig. 15: Population size in the Lower Shetrunji River Basin.

Chapter 6

Chronology of the Early Historic Settlements in Relation to the Excavated site at Padri

Introduction

The main purpose of this chapter is to compare the ceramic assemblage of the explored sites with the systematic excavated site of Padri. The intensive and extensive explorations carried out by the present author in the lower part of Shetrunji river basin, Bhavnagar district, resulted in the discovery of 22 Early Historic as well as Harappan affiliated sites. The material remains particularly the ceramic assemblages from these explored sites have been compared with Padri material, which are obtained from proper stratigraphy and have been precisely dated. The Early Historic period at Padri is represented by the Red-Slipped Ware, Red Ware and Grey Ware. The shapes include cups with tapering sides; globular jar/pot with out-curved rim; deep dish and lid, etc. This period can be dated to the beginning of 1st century B.C. -A.D. on the basis of evidences like the circular clay tablet bearing *Brahmi* script, a couple of copper coins similar to those issued by the *Kshatrapa* king Nahapana, a tortoise-shaped Roman copper lamp, two boat-shaped terracotta motifs, figurines of goddesses *Lajjagauri* and structure of goddesses *Lajjagauri's* temple (Shinde 1992a; 1994 and 1998). This period can be chronologically correlated with Valabhipur period III phase I (Jairath 1986: 344-46), Devnimori (Mehta and Chowdhary 1966: 27), Shamalaji periods I and II (Mehta and Patel 1967: 8) and with Nagara period III (Mehta 1968: 19). As far as present study is concerned in the Early Historic period, the stratified ceramic assemblage of Padri provides a chronological index to the pottery obtained as a result of exploration from the Early Historic settlements in the lower part of Shetrunji river basin. On the basis of forms, fabric and decorations the Early Historic ceramic assemblage from the explored sites have been divided into the following categories:

1.1. Red Ware,
1.2. Red-Slipped Ware,
1.3. Grey Ware,

1.4. Red Polished Ware and
1.5. Roman amphorae.

The first three categories are the same as Padri and have already been dealt in great details in chapter 3. In order to avoid repetition these will not be discussed in this chapter, only their shapes will be compared. It has been displayed in the tabular form **(Table.17)**. Only those wares and shapes from this explored sites, which are new, have been discussed here.

Red Polished Ware

Red Polished Ware is an interesting Early Historic ceramic assemblage which is used for the dating of Early Historic sites (1st century A.D. to the 5th century A.D.). The characteristic feature of this ware have already been discussed in detailed in chapter 2. From a good number of sites such as Alidhar (*IAR.* 1960-61: 7-8; Ghosh 1989: 12), Bhegali (*IAR.* 1960-61: 7-8; Ghosh 1989: 69) and Dantrad (*IAR.* 1960-61: 7-8; Ghosh 1989: 227) in the lower part of Shetrunji river basin, Red Polished Ware have been found. It should be mentioned that when the present author explored the same river basin for locating archaeological settlements he brought to light for the first time 5 sites namely *Bharapur, Hathab, Katva, Pavti* and *Shilavadar* which yielded Red Polished Ware with other associated ceramic assemblage. The author has also found a number of Red Polished Ware sherds from the sites at *Alidhar, Bhegali* and *Dantrad.* The shapes include bowl with nail headed or featureless pointed or flared out or blunt or inturned nail shaped or beaded or inturned knife edge rim and with flat or disc base; jar either with beaked or rectangular or beaded or external projecting or beaked or knife edge or grooved or flaring grooved rim; basin with internally beveled rim having spout with knob and decorated on the exterior surface; deep dish either with nail headed or out-turned rim, and fragments of sprinkler with concavo-convex profile, etc. Red Polished Ware also occurs with other associated wares from the excavations at Baroda (Subbarao 1953: 35-36), Timbarva (Mehta 1955: 15), Vadnagar (Subbarao and Mehta 1955: 25), Amreli (Rao 1966: 51), Jokha (Mehta *et al.* 1971: 29-31), Nagara (Mehta 1968: 78), Devnimori (Mehta and Chowdhary 1966: 82), Shamalaji (Mehta and Patel 1967: 34-35), Dwarka (Ansari and Mate 1966: 72), Somnath (Nanavati *et al.* 1971: 61-67) and Maheshwar and Navdatoli (Sankalia *et al.* 1958: 159). It has been found in association with other wares in the layers which are dated to the early centuries of Christian Era. Therefore, on the basis of these stratified datum, the above mentioned explored sites can be taken as contemporary with the sites of Baroda, Amreli, Vadnagar, Timbarva, Jokha, Padri, Nagara, Devnimori, Shamalaji, Dwarka, Somnath and Maheshwar and Navdatoli.

Roman Amphorae

Roman amphorae are definitely an imported ware. The main features of this ware have also been dealt in great detail in chapter 2. The present author has also found only one piece of amphorae handle sherd along with other ceramic assemblage from the site at Hathab. In Gujarat Mediterranean amphorae sherds have also been found from the excavations at Amreli (Rao 1966: 80-81), Dhatva (*IAR.* 1967-68: 19-20; Mehta and Chowdhary 1975: 9), Devnimori (Mehta and Chowdhary 1966: 77), Nagara (*IAR.*.1963-64: 9-10; Mehta 1968: 78),

Dwarka (*IAR.* 1962-63: 7; Ansari and Mate 1966: 72-73), Vadnagar (Subbarao and Mehta 1955: 19-44), Valabhipur (phase I and II) (*IAR.* 1979-80: 24; Mehta 1983), Somnath (Nanavati *et al.* 1971) and Shamalaji (*IAR.* 1961-62: 13-14; Mehta and Patel 1967: 17). On the basis of this particular sherd found at *Hathab* with other associated pottery, the site appears to be contemporary with the above mentioned sites.

Table 17: Comparative study for Early Historic sites in relation to Padri.

* RW=Red Ware; RSW=Red-Slipped Ware and GW=Grey Ware. Corres.=Correspondent. Pl.=Plate.

Index site	*Ware*	*Shapes (in brief)*	*Pl. No.*	*Corres. site*	*Ware*	*Pl. No.*	*Shapes*	*Remarks*
Padri	RW	Cup-disc base, flaring sides.	Pl.V.b. No.84	**Bhalar**	RW	Pl. XXXI.b. No.8	Same as Padri Pl.V.b. No.84	New shapes are globular pot with flaring, externally thickened, under-cut, rounded or beaded rim; saucer with flaring rim in RSW. Dish with internally projecting rim having green glaze on the interior of the surface in RW. Pot with flat projecting rim in GW.
Do	Do	Cup-disc base.	Pl.V.b. No.85	Do	Do	Pl. XXXI. b. No.9	Same as Padri Pl.V.b. No.85	
Do	Do	Cup-disc base, string cutting marks on the bottom.	Pl.V.b. No.86	Do	Do	Pl. XXXI. b. No.10	Same as Padri Pl.V.b. No.86	
Do	RSW	Jar-internally flat and slightly proj-ecting rim.	Pl.I.b. No.12	Do	RSW	Pl. XXXI. b. No.2	Same as Padri Pl.I.b. No.12	
Do	GW	Globular pot-flared out and externally thickened rim.	Pl.VII.a. No.110	Do	GW	Pl. XXXI. b. No.7	Same as Padri Pl.VII.a. No.110	
Do	Do	Jar-triangular rim, short vertical rim.	Pl. VII.b. No.111.1	Do	Do	Pl. XXXI. b. No.6	Same as Padri Pl.VII.b No.111.1	
Padri	RW	Small saucer-short slightly out-turned sides and flat base.	Pl.VI.a No.87	**Saltanpur**	RW	Pl. XLIII. d. No.32	Same as Padri Pl.VI.a. No.87	New shapes are globular pot with externally projecting, beaked, thickened under-cut rim; dish with featureless pointed rim; deep dish with internally projecting rim

contd...

Index site	*Ware*	*Shapes (in brief)*	*Pl. No.*	*Corres. site*	*Ware*	*Pl. No.*	*Shapes*	*Remarks*
								and conical spout in RSW. Jar with triangular rim; pot with externally projecting beaked rim in RW. Deep bowl with projecting rim; dish with internally projecting knife face, internally projecting triangular, featureless pointed rim and lid in GW.
Do	RSW	Spout-pointed.	Pl.III.b. No.53	Do	RSW	Pl. XLIII. d. No.53	Same as Padri Pl.III.b. No.53	
Do	RSW	Jar-externally projecting beaked rim.	Pl.I.b. No.14	Do	Do	Pl. XLIII. a. No.4	Same as Padri Pl.I.b. No.14	
Do	GW	Jar-out curved rim.	Pl.VII.a. No.105	Do	GW	Pl. XLIII.b. No.12	Same as Padri Pl.VII.a. No.105	
Do	Do	Jar-dropping rim.	Pl.VII.a. No.106	Do	Do	Pl. XLIII.c. No.22	Same as Padri Pl.VII.a. No.106	
Padri	RSW	Jar-internally flat and slightly projecting rim.	Pl.I.b. No.12	**Valavadar**	RSW	Pl. XLV.a. No.4	Same as Padri Pl.I.b. No.12	New shapes are deep dish with internally projecting triangular rim; pot with externally thickened rim in RSW. Pot with flat, externally projecting rim; bowl with flat, disc base in GW.
Do	Do	Jar-out turned and externally thickened rim.	Pl.II.a. No.26	Do	Do	Pl. XLV.a. No.5	Same as Padri Pl.II.a. No.26	
Do	Do	Small pot-short out turned rim and concave neck.	Pl.II.a. No.19	Do	Do	Pl. XLV.a. No.6	Same as Padri Pl.II.a. No.19	
Do	GW	Jar-out -curved rim with deep groove(s) on the top.	Pl.VII.a. No.105	Do	GW	Pl. XLV.a. No.7	Same as Padri Pl.VII.a. No.105	
Do	Do	Jar-out-curved rim with deep groove(s) on the top.	Pl. VII.a. No.105	Do	Do	Pl. XLV.a. No.8	Same as Padri Pl.VII.a. No.105	

contd...

Index site	*Ware*	*Shapes (in brief)*	*Pl. No.*	*Corres. site*	*Ware*	*Pl. No.*	*Shapes*	*Remarks*
Do	Do	Jar-long out-turned and externally thickened rim.	Pl.VII.a. No.109	Do	Do	Pl. XLV.b. No.10	Same as Padri Pl.VII.a. No.109	
Padri	RW	Cup-short vertical featureless rim.	Pl. V.a. No.74	**Dakana**	RW	Pl. XXXIV.a. No.9	Same as Padri Pl.V.a. No.74	New shape is pot with beaked rim in GW.
Do	Do	Cup-disc base, flaring sides.	Pl.V.a. No.84	Do	Do	Pl. XXXIV.a. No.10	Same as Padri Pl.V.a. No.84	
Do	RSW	Jar-internally flat and slightly projecting rim.	Pl.I.b. No.12	Do	RSW	Pl. XXXIV.a. No.1	Same as Padri Pl.I.b. No.12	
Do	Do	Jar-short out turned rim.	Pl.I.b. No.10	Do	Do	Pl. XXXIV.a. No.2	Same as Padri Pl.I.b. No.10	
Do	Do	Jar-beaked shaped rim	Pl.II.a. No.20	Do	Do	Pl. XXXIV.a. No.3	Same as Padri Pl.II.a. No.20	
Do	Do	Pot-flat projecting rim.	Pl.I.b. No.9	Do	Do	Pl. XXXIV.a. No.4	Same as Padri Pl.I.b. No.9	
Do	Do	Jar-out turned and thickened rim.	Pl.I.b. No.7	Do	Do	Pl. XXXIV.a. No.5	Same as Padri Pl.I.b. No.7	
Do	Do	Jar-slightly out turned and externally thickened rim.	Pl.I.a. No.6	Do	Do	Pl. XXXIV.a. No.6	Same as Padri Pl.I.a. No.6	
Padri	RW	Jar-externally thickened rim.	Pl.IV.b. No.67	**Devalia**	RW	Pl. XXXV.a. No.3	Same as Padri Pl.IV.b. No.67	New shapes are globular pot with externally projecting, under-cut rim in RSW. Dish-on-stand ? in RW. Dish with flaring, externally thickened and internally projecting rim in GW.

contd...

Index site	*Ware*	*Shapes (in brief)*	*Pl. No.*	*Corres. site*	*Ware*	*Pl. No.*	*Shapes*	*Remarks*
Do	RSW	Jar-externally projecting beaked rim.	Pl.I.b. No.14	Do	RSW	Pl. XXXV.a. No.2	Same as Padri Pl.I.b. No.14	
Do	GW	Jar-out-curved rim with deep grooved on the top.	Pl.VII.a. No.105	Do	GW	Pl. XXXV.a. No.6	Same as Padri Pl.VII.a. No.105	
Do	Do	Jar-out-curved rim..	Pl.VII.a. No.111	Do	Do	Pl. XXXV.a. No.9	Same as Padri Pl.VII.a. No.111	
Padri	RW	Cup-disc base, flaring sides	Pl.V.b. No.84	**Chopra**	RW	Pl. XXXIII.b. No.7	Same as Padri Pl.V.b. No. 84	New shapes are jar with externally projecting flat rim in RW. Jar with externally thickened rounded, triangular under-cut rim; deep bowl with disc base; basin with pointed rim; dish with flat base and conical spout in GW.
Do	RSW	Jar-triangular rim.	Pl.I.b. No.8	Do	RSW	Pl. XXXIII.a. No.1	Same as Padri Pl.I.b. No.8	
Do	Do	Jar-externally projecting squarish rim	Pl.I.b. No.17	Do	Do	Pl. XXXIII.a. No.2	Same as Padri Pl.I.b. No.17	
Padri	RW	Cup-disc base, flaring sides.	Pl.V.b. No.84	**Bandi Rohil**	RW	Pl.XXX.b. No.10	Same as Padri Pl.V.b. No.84	New shapes are pot with externally projecting under-cut, flat rim in RSW. Jar with featureless rim and conical lid with pinnacle in RW.
Do	Do	Cup-disc base.	Pl.V.b. No.85	Do	RW	Pl.XXX.b. No.11	Same as Padri Pl.V.b. No.85	
Do	RSW	Jar-external projecting rounded rim.	Pl.II.a. No.29	Do	RSW	Pl.XXX.a. No.1	Same as Padri Pl.II.a. No.29	

contd...

Index site	*Ware*	*Shapes (in brief)*	*Pl. No.*	*Corres. site*	*Ware*	*Pl. No.*	*Shapes*	*Remarks*
Do	Do	Jar-externally projecting rounded rim.	Pl.II.a. No.29	Do	Do	Pl.XXX.a. No.2	Same as Padri Pl.II.a. No. 29	
Do	Do	Jar-squrish rim.	Pl.I.b. No.13	Do	Do	Pl.XXX.a. No.3	Same as Padri Pl.I.b. No.13	
Padri	RSW	Jar-Out turned rim.	Pl.II.a. No.24	**Piparla**	RSW	Pl.XLI.a. No.3	Same as Padri Pl.II.a. No.24	New shapes are dish with externally projecting, triangular rim; globular pot with projecting rounded, thickened under-cut, flat projecting rounded rim in RSW. Lid with knob at the centre in RW.
Do	Do	Jar-triangular rim.	Pl.I.b. No.8	Do	Do	Pl.XLI.a. No.4	Same as Padri Pl.I.b. No.8	
Do	Do	Pot-flat projecting rim.	Pl.I.b. No.9	Do	Do	Pl.XLI.a. No.6	Same as Padri Pl.I.b. No.9	
Do	Do	Jar-beaked shaped rim.	Pl.II.a. No.20	Do	Do	Pl.XLI.b. No.10	Same as Padri Pl.II.a. No.20	
Do	Do	Jar-externally thickened and rounded rim.	Pl.I.a. No.4	Do	Do	Pl.XLI.b. No.12	Same as Padri Pl.I.a. No.4	
Do	Do	Jar-externally out-turned rim.	Pl.II.a. No.27	Do	Do	Pl.XLI.b. No.13	Same as Padri Pl.II.a. No.27	
Do	Do	Jar-everted rim.	Pl.I.a. No.1	Do	Do	Pl.XLI.b. No.14	Same as Padri Pl.I.a. No.1	
Do	Do	Jar-externally projecting rim.	Pl.IV.a. No.56	Do	Do	Pl.XLI.b. No.18	Same as Padri Pl.IV.a. No.56	

contd...

Index site	*Ware*	*Shapes (in brief)*	*Pl. No.*	*Corres. site*	*Ware*	*Pl. No.*	*Shapes*	*Remarks*
Do	Do	Dish-internally beaked rim.	Pl.III.b. No.46	Do	Do	Pl.XLI.c. No.19	Same as Padri Pl.III.b. No. 46	
Do	Do	Spout with a knob at its base.	Pl.III.b. No.52	Do	Do	Pl.XLI.c. No.21	Same as Padri Pl.III.b. No.52	
Do	Do	Small saucer-short slightly out-turned sides.	Pl.VI.a. No.87	Do	Do	Pl.XLI.c. No.22	Same as Padri Pl.VI.a. No. 87	
Do	GW	Jar-triangular rim.	Pl.VII.a. No.111.1	Do	GW	Pl.XLI.d. No.23	Same as Padri Pl.VII.a. No.111.1	
Padri	RW	Small saucer-short slightly out-curved and featureless rim.	Pl.VI.a. No.87	**Dantrad**	RW	Pl. XXXIV.b. No.9	Same as Padri Pl.VI.a. No.87	New shapes are small globular pot with everted rim; Pot with everted rim and dish with everted rim in RSW. Basin with everted rim in GW.
Do	GW	Medium size jar-flared out rim.	Pl.VII.a. No.107	Do	Do	Pl. XXXIV.b. No.5	Same as Padri Pl.VII.a. No.107	
Do	Do	Jar-out-curved rim with deep on the top.	Pl.VII.a. No.104	Do	Do	Pl. XXXIV.b. No.6	Same as Padri Pl.VII.a. No.104	
Do	Do	Medium size jar-flared out rim.	Pl.VII.a. No.107	Do	Do	Pl. XXXIV.b. No.8	Same as Padri Pl.VII.a. No.107	
Padri	RW	Shallow bowl with disc base.	Pl.V.b. No.85	**Ichhora**	RW	Pl. XXXVII.b. No.11	Same as Padri Pl.V.b. No.85	New shapes are dish with flat projecting; globular pot with externally projecting, thickened rim; spout with conical channel in RSW. Globular pot with projecting rounded rim; dish with out turned rim; spout with conical channel and lid with knob in GW.
Do	RSW	Jar-out-curved and externally thickened rim.	Pl.II.a. No.26	Do	RSW	Pl. XXXVII.a No.2	Same as Padri Pl.II.a. No.26	

contd...

Index site	*Ware*	*Shapes (in brief)*	*Pl. No.*	*Corres. site*	*Ware*	*Pl. No.*	*Shapes*	*Remarks*
Do	Do	Jar-externally projecting rounded rim.	Pl.II.a No.29	Do	Do	Pl. XXXVII.a. No.7	Same as Padri Pl.II.a. No.29	
Do	Do	Jar-externally projecting beaked rim.	Pl.I.b. No.14	Do	Do	Pl. XXXVIl.a. No.6	Same as Padri Pl.I.b. No.14	
Do	GW	Jar-out-curved rim with deep grooved on the top.	Pl.VII.a. No.104	Do	GW	Pl. XXXVII.b. No.14	Same as Padri Pl.VII.a. No.104	
Do	Do	Jar-out-curved rim.	Pl.VII.a. No.111	Do	Do	Pl. XXXVII.b. No16	Same as Padri Pl.VII.a. No.111	
Padri	RSW	Jar-short out-turned rim.	Pl.I.b. No.10	**Bhegali**	RSW	Pl. XXXI. a. No.1	Same as Padri Pl.I.b. No.10	New shapes are globular pot with flat rim in RW. Dish with triangular rim in GW.
Do	Do	Storage jar-flat projecting rim.	Pl.I.a. No.2	Do	Do	Pl. XXXI. a. No.3	Same as Padri Pl.I.a. No.2	
Do	Do	Spout-pointed	Pl.III.b. No.53	Do	Do	Pl. XXXI. a. No.7	Same as Padri Pl.III.b. No.53	
Do	GW	Globular pot-flared out and externally thickened rim.	Pl.VII.a. No.110	Do	GW	Pl. XXXI. a.No.4	Same as Padri Pl.VII.a. No.110	
Padri	RW	Cup-disc base, flaring sides.	Pl.V.b. No.84	Timbana	RW	Pl. XLIV. b. No.1	Same as Padri Pl.V.b. No.84	New shapes are dish with out-turned beaded rim in RW. Pot with out turned rim in RSW. Body sherd with painted horizontal loop between two horizontal band.
Do	Do	Small pot-out-turned and thickened rim.	Pl.IV.b. No.63	Do	Do	Pl. XLIV. b. No.2	Same as Padri Pl.IV.b. No.63	
Do	RSW	Jar-flat projecting short rim.	Pl.I.a. No.3	Do	RSW	Pl. XLIV. b. No.6	Same as Padri Pl.I.a. No.3	

contd...

Index site	Ware	Shapes (in brief)	Pl. No.	Corres. site	Ware	Pl. No.	Shapes	Remarks
Do	GW	Jar-triangular rim.	Pl.VII.a. No.111.1	Do	GW	Pl. XLIV. b. No.7	Same as Padri Pl.VII.a. No.111.1	
Do	Do	Jar-long out-turned and externally thickened rim.	Pl.VII.a. No.109	Do	Do	Pl. XLIV. b. No.8	Same as Padri Pl.VII.a. No.109	
Padri	RSW	Jar-internally flat and slightly projecting rim.	Pl.I.b. No.12	**Gorkhi**	RSW	Pl. XXXV.b. No.2	Same as Padri Pl.I.b. No.12	New shapes are pot with out-turned, flaring, beaded under-cut rim in RSW. Dish with out-curved, flat projecting rim in GW.
Do	Do	Jar-slightly out-turned and externally thickened rim.	Pl.I.a. No.6	Do	Do	Pl. XXXV.b. No.3	Same as Padri Pl.I.a. No.6	
Do	Do	Jar-externally out-turned rim.	Pl.IIa. No.27	Do	Do	Pl. XXXV.b. No.1	Same as Padri Pl.II.a. No.27	
Padri	RW	Cup-short vertical featureless rim.	Pl.V.a. No.74	**Phulsar**	RW	Pl.XL.a No.5	Same as Padri Pl.V.a. No.74	New shapes are globular pot with beaded rim; jar with beaded under-cut rim and basin with flat rim in RSW. Pot with externally rounded, projecting , under-cut, perpendicular rim; bowl with disc base in GW.
Do	Do	Cup-disc base, flaring sides,	Pl.V.b. No.84	Do	Do	Pl.XL.a No.6	Same as Padri Pl.V.b. No.84	
Do	RSW	Jar-externally projecting beaked rim.	Pl.I.b. No.14	Do	RSW	Pl.XL.a. No.2	Same as Padri Pl.I.b. No.14	
Do	Do	Jar-flat projecting short rim.	Pl.I.a. No.2	Do	Do	Pl.XL.a. No.3	Same as Padri I.a. No.2	
Do	Do	Lid/bowl-short vertical rim.	Pl.II.b. No.37	Do	Do	Pl.XL.a. No.10	Same as Padri Pl.II.b. No.37	

contd...

Index site	*Ware*	*Shapes (in brief)*	*Pl. No.*	*Corres. site*	*Ware*	*Pl. No.*	*Shapes*	*Remarks*
Do	Do	Jar-everted rim.	Pl.I.a. No.1	Do	Do	Pl.XL.a. No.4	Same as Padri Pl.I.a. No.1	
Do	GW	Jar-out curved rim.	Pl.VII.a. No.105	Do	GW	Pl.XL.b. No.16	Same as Padri Pl.VII.a. No.105	
Do	Do	Jar-flared out rim.	Pl.VII.a. No.107	Do	Do	Pl.XL.b. No.14	Same as Padri Pl.VII.a. No.107	
Do	Do	Shallow bowl-featureless pointed rim.	Pl.VIII.a. No.113	Do	Do	Pl.XL.b. No.20	Same as Padri Pl.VIII.a. No.113	
Padri	RW	Cup-disc base, flaring sides.	Pl.V.b. No.84	**Shilavad-ar**	RW	Pl.XLII.a. No.1	Same as Padri Pl.V.b. No.84	New shapes conical lid with pinnacle in RW. Jar with beaded rim; pot with beaded rim and bowl with flaring, beaded rim in RSW. Bowl with flattened top and handi like bowl with beaded rim in GW.
Do	RSW	Jar-triangular rim.	Pl.I.b. No.8	Do	RSW	Pl.XLII.a. No.4	Same as Padri Pl.I.b. No.8	
Do	Do	Jar-out turned and internally thickened rim.	Pl.I.b. No.11	Do	Do	Pl.XLII.a. No.7	Same as Padri Pl.I.b. No.11	
Do	Do	Jar-externally projecting beaked rim.	Pl.I.b. No.13	Do	Do	Pl.XLII.b. No.10	Same as Padri Pl.I.b. No.13	
Padri	RW	Jar-external projecting rim.	Pl.IV.a. No.56	**Pavti**	RW	Pl. XXXIX.b. No.1	Same as Padri Pl.IV.a. No.56	New shapes are globular pot with externally projecting under-cut rim; deep bowl with incurved rim and body sherd with painted dots on the exterior surface in RSW. Pot with thickened rounded, out-curved beaded rim; dish with beaded rim; shallow bowl with disc base and conical spout in GW.

contd...

Index site	*Ware*	*Shapes (in brief)*	*Pl. No.*	*Corres. site*	*Ware*	*Pl. No.*	*Shapes*	*Remarks*
Do	Do	Jar-slightly out turned thickened rim	Pl.IV.a. No.61	Do	Do	Pl. XXXIX.b. No.2	Same as Padri Pl.IV.a. No.61	
Do	Do	Cup-short featureless pointed rim.	Pl.V.a. No.74	Do	Do	Pl. XXXIX.b. No.3	Same as Padri Pl.V.a. No.74	
Do	Do	Cup-disc base, flaring sides.	Pl.V.b. No.84	Do	Do	Pl. XXXIX.b. No.4	Same as Padri Pl.V.b. No.84	
Do	RSW	Dish-internally beaked rim.	Pl.III.a. No.46	Do	RSW	Pl. XXXIX.b. No.5	Same as Padri Pl.III.a. No.46	
Do	Do	Storage jar-flat projecting short rim.	Pl.I.a. No.2	Do	Do	Pl. XXXIX.b. No.7	Same as Padri Pl.I.a. No.2	
Do	GW	Jar-out-curved rim.	Pl.VII.a. No.105	Do	GW	Pl. XXXIX.d. No.15	Same as Padri Pl.VII.a. No.105	
Do	Do	Jar-dropping rim.	Pl.VII.a. No.106	Do	Do	Pl. XXXIX.c. No.11	Same as Padri Pl.VII.a. No.106	
Do	Do	Jar-out-curved rim.	Pl.VII.a. No.111	Do	Do	Pl. XXXIX.c. No.12	Same as Padri Pl.VII.a. No.111	
Do	Do	Jar-triangular rim.	Pl.VII.b. No.111.1	Do	Do	Pl. XXXIX.c. No.10	Same as Padri Pl.VII.b. No.111.1	
Padri	RW	Jar-prominent externally projecting rim.	Pl.IV.a. No.60	**Katva**	RW	Pl. XXXVIII. a No.1	Same as Padri Pl.IV.a. No.60	New shapes: jar with out turned, externally projecting, rounded rim in RW. Globular pot with out-curved slightly beaded, flared, rounded rim in RSW. Globular pot with out turned beaded rim; shallow dish with featureless rim; shallow bowl/dish with beaded rim and deep bowl with incurved beaded rim in GW.

contd...

Index site	*Ware*	*Shapes (in brief)*	*Pl. No.*	*Corres. site*	*Ware*	*Pl. No.*	*Shapes*	*Remarks*
Do	Do	Jar-externally projecting rim(?)	Pl.IV.a. No.56	Do	Do	Pl. XXXVIII. a. No.3	Same as Padri Pl.IV.a. No.56	
Do	Do	Jar-vertical pointed rim.	Pl.IV.b. No.64	Do	Do	Pl. XXXVIII. a. No.5	Same as Padri Pl.IV.b. No.64	
Do	Do	Cup-disc base, flaring sides.	Pl.V.b. No.84	Do	Do	Pl. XXXVIII. a. No.9	Same as Padri Pl.V.b. No.84	
Do	RSW	Jar-internally flat ,slightly projecting rim.	Pl.I.b. No.12	Do	RSW	Pl. XXXVIII. b. No.10	Same as Padri Pl.I.b. No.12.	
Do	Do	Jar-out-turned and internally thickened rim.	Pl.I.b. No.11	Do	Do	Pl. XXXVIII. b. No.11	Same as Padri Pl.I.b. No.11	
Do	Do	Pot-flat projecting rim.	Pl.I.b. No.9	Do	Do	Pl. XXXVIII. b. No.12	Same as Padri Pl.I.b. No.9	
Do	GW	Jar-long out-turned and externally thickened rim.	Pl.VII.a. No.109	Do	GW	Pl. XXXVIII. b. No.16	Same as Padri Pl.VII.a. No.109	
Padri	RW	Jar-vertical externally thickened rim	Pl.IV.a. No.54	**Bharapur**	RW	Pl. XXXII.a. No.1	Same as Padri Pl.IV.a. No.54	New shapes are pot with beaded under-cut, out-curved beaded rim and jar with beaded, flared rim in RW. Jar without turned beaded rim; pot with flared, externally projecting, beaked rim; large shallow bowl with broad. Pot with beaked, out-curved beaded rim; shallow dish with externally projecting beaded rim, deep dish with externally projecting beaded rim and dish with featureless rim in RW. Pot with beaked, out-curved beaded rim; shallow dish with

contd...

Index site	*Ware*	*Shapes (in brief)*	*Pl. No.*	*Corres. site*	*Ware*	*Pl. No.*	*Shapes*	*Remarks*
								externally projecting beaded rim, deep dish with externally projecting beaded rim and dish with featureless rim in RW.
Do	Do	Jar-out-turned thickened rim.	Pl.IV.a. No.58	Do	Do	Pl. XXXII.a. No.4	Same as Padri Pl.IV.a. No.58	
Do	Do	Cup-disc base, flaring sides.	Pl.V.b. No.84	Do	Do	Pl. XXXII.a. No.5	Same as Padri Pl.V.b. No.84	
Do	RSW	Jar-beaked shaped rim.	Pl.II.a. No.20	Do	RSW	Pl. XXXII.a. No.9	Same as Padri Pl.II.a. No.20	
Do	Do	Jar-out-turned and pointed rim.	Pl.II.a. No.31	Do	Do	Pl. XXXII.b. No.11	Same as Padri Pl.II.a. No.31	
Do	Do	Jar-externally projecting beaked rim.	Pl.I.b. No.14	Do	Do	Pl. XXXII.b. No.13	Same as Padri Pl.I.b. No.14	
Do	Do	Pot-flat projecting rim.	Pl.I.b. No.9	Do	Do	Pl. XXXII.b. No.15	Same as Padri Pl.I.b. No.9	
Do	Do	Jar-externally out-turned rim.	Pl.IIa. No.27	Do	Do	Pl. XXXII.b. No.16	Same as Padri Pl.II.a. .No.27	
Do	Do	Small bowl/lid-short vertical rim.	Pl.II.b. No.37	Do	Do	Pl. XXXII.c. No.19	Same as Padri Pl.II.b. No.37	
Padri	RW	Jar with prominent externally projecting rim.	Pl.IV.a. No.60	**Hathab**	RW	Pl. XXXVI.a. No.2	Same as Padri Pl.IV.a. No. 60	New shapes are globular pot with externally beaded, flat rim; deep bowl with ring foot base and stem or part of finial of a vessel in RW. Jar with rounded thickened, beaded under-cut; pot with beaked rim; bowl with slightly

contd...

Index site	*Ware*	*Shapes (in brief)*	*Pl. No.*	*Corres. site*	*Ware*	*Pl. No.*	*Shapes*	*Remarks*
								out-curved and internally thickened rim and body sherd with wavy line in RSW. Jar with beaded under-cut rim and pot with out-curved beaded rim in GW.
Do	Do	Cup-disc base.	Pl.V.b. No.86	Do	Do	Pl. XXXVI.a. Nos.5 & 6	Same as Padri Pl.V.b. No.86	
Do	RSW	Jar-out-turned and slightly projecting rim.	Pl.II.a. No.31	Do	RSW	Pl. XXXVI.b. No.12	Same as Padri Pl.II.a. No.31	
Do	Do	Jar-out-turned and externally thickened rim.	Pl.II.a. No.26	Do	Do	Pl. XXXVI.b. No.13	Same as Padri Pl.II.a. No.26	
Do	GW	Globular Pot-flared out and externally thickened rim.	Pl.VII.a. No.110	Do	GW	Pl. XXXVI.d. No.24	Same as Padri Pl.VII.a. No.110	
Padri	RW	Lamp/lid-slightly flat out side, disc base.	Pl. VI.b. No.74	**Khadsa-liya**	RW	Pl. XXXIX.a. No.1	Same as Padri Pl. VI.b. No.74	New shapes are dish with featureless pointed rim; pot with externally projecting beaded rim in RW. Jar with externally projecting under-cut rim in RSW.
Do	Do	Cup-short pointed featureless rim.	Pl.V.a. No.74	Do	Do	Pl. XXXIX.a. No.2	Same as Padri Pl.V.a. No.74	
Do	Do	Cup-disc base.	Pl. V.a. No.84	Do	Do	Pl. XXXIX.a. No.3	Same as Padri Pl.V.a. No.84	
Do	Do	Jar-externally thickened rim, short vertical neck.	Pl.IV.b. No.67	Do	Do	Pl. XXXIX.a. No.6	Same as Padri Pl.IV.b. No.67	
Do	RSW	Jar-beaked shape rim, vertical neck.	Pl.II.a. No.20	Do	RSW	Pl. XXXIX.a. No.7	Same as Padri Pl.II.a. No.20	

contd...

Index site	*Ware*	*Shapes (in brief)*	*Pl. No.*	*Corres. site*	*Ware*	*Pl. No.*	*Shapes*	*Remarks*
Do	Do	Jar-externally out turned rim.	Pl.II.a. No.27	Do	Do	Pl. XXXIX.a. No.9	Same as Padri Pl.II.a. No.27	
Do	Do	Dish-internally beaked rim, ledge on exterior shoulder.	Pl.III.b. No.46	Do	Do	Pl. XXXIX.a. No.10	Same as Padri Pl.III.b. No.46	
Padri	RSW	Dish-internally beaked rim, ledge on exterior shoulder.	Pl.III.b. No.46	**Thalsar**	RSW	Pl. XLIV. a. No.3	Same as Padri Pl.III.b. No.46	Lid with round base in RW. Bowl with ring foot base, Jar with externally projecting beaked rim, Pot with flat projecting under-cut rim in RSW.
Do	RW	Cup-short featureless pointed rim.	Pl.V.a. No.74	Do	RW	Pl. XLIV. a. No.4	Same as Padri Pl.V.a. No.74	
Do	Do	Cup-featureless pointed rim.	Pl.V.a. No.71	Do	Do	Pl. XLIV.a No.5	Same as Pl.V.a. No.71	
Do	GW	Globular pot-flared out and externally thickened rim.	Pl.VII.a. No.110	Do	GW	Pl. XLIV.a. No.8	Same as Padri Pl.VII.a. No.110	
Do	Do	Jar-triangular rim.	Pl.VII.b. No.111.1	Do	Do	Pl. XLIV. a. No.10	Same as Padri Pl.VII.b. No.111.1	

Finally it can be said, on the basis of this comparative study that all the explored sites yielded more or less similar types of ceramic assemblages including their forms and fabric, as that of systematically excavated site of Padri. Apart from this, all the explored sites have also been yielded some new shapes. But it is very few. However, it could be said that, most of the explored Early Historic sites are contemporary with the excavated site of Padri.

Chapter 7

Conclusion

In the final chapter, thus, we can summarise briefly the results of the present study which we have already dealt in the preceding chapters. The Early Historic period of Gujarat in general and Saurashtra in particular was marked by a growth of large and small size towns such as Amreli, Akota and Valabhipur. This period is also marked by the growth of the entrepot along the western sea-board like Somnath, Nagara and Bharuch. Here foreign goods were exchanged for local products collected from the hinterland (Krishna Deva 1997: 140). The main theme of the present work is the Early Historic settlements which were located in the lower part of the Shetrunji river basin, i.e. in and around Padri and Hathab. Systematic excavation was carried out at the site of Padri which has yielded an Early Historic phase, dated 1st century B.C.-A.D. (Shinde 1992a and 1998). The climate of the region is semi-arid. What is interesting to note here is that there are no natural ports in this region but the southern tip provides suitable conditions for salt farming and the other parts of this region covered with black cotton soil, are favourable for dry farming. The major rivers in the district are Shetrunji, Gelo, Kalubhar and Padale and most of the rivers originate in the mountainous area. The annual precipitation of the district is between 500-800 mm. For establishing settlements some determinant factors are necessary such as availability of water, pasture land, fertile soil, natural resources and security. The study region provides ideal situation for the development of settlements.

Though most of the sites were located on both the banks of Shetrunji river, a good number of settlements were situated near the coast. These settlements could have played an important role in the economic organization during the Early Historic period. From the distribution of the sites it is clear that the sites were closely related to each other which is evident in the ceramic assemblage. It should be mentioned that the ceramic assemblage from different sites presents striking similarity in the surface treatment and shapes (Paul *et al.* 1997). The distribution of the settlements in the lower Shetrunji river basin confirms that most of the sites are nucleated and quite a number of sites formed linear pattern. Besides, the site size and inter-site distance analysis make it clear that all the sites were related together in a nexus comprising of small villages, fishing villages, agrarian-cum-fishing villages and regional centre. The regional centre played an important role. In the study region only one site called Hathab was identified as a regional centre on the basis of nature of the settlement, location and other factors like duration of the occupation, function and economic condition, etc. This particular site may have played an important role in the economic organization during the early part of Christian Era. The site of Hathab is mentioned as a port in the *Periplus of the Erythraean Sea* (Schoff 1912: 39-40). The discovery of some imported pottery such as the fragment of a Red Ware dish with green glaze on the interior of the body found at Bhalar resembling the BI Ware sherds of the Persian Gulf, suggests contacts with that region (Paul *et al.* 1997; Gupta 1997), Roman amphorae handles and Red Polished Ware sherds found at *Hathab, Alidhar, Bharapur, Bhegali, Dantrad, Katva, Pavti* and *Shilavadar* indicate the importance of this region from the trading point of view.

In the present study an attempt has also been made to analyze the demographic feature of every site. I studied on the basis of number of persons per hectare during the Early Historic period. For estimation of population we have applied Leshnik's method (Leshnik 1967). It should be mentioned that this method is not accurate but for the first time it has been applied in the study region and an attempt has been made in this regard.

Finally the sites at Padri, which were systematically excavated for over five seasons (Shinde 1992a; 1992b; 1994, 1996 and 1998), enabled us to propose chronology of the explored Early Historic settlements in this region. The characteristic features of the excavations at Padri are as follows:

1. From the detailed study of the ceramic assemblage of the Early Historic period four broad functional categories have been identified: a. cooking vessels; b. serving vessels (table ware); c. storage vessels and d. ritualistic vessels.
2. The Early Historic people at Padri were manufacturing shell objects on a large scale for the distribution purpose as the site has produced the evidences of finished bangles and by-products such as debitage, flakes and chips. It suggests that the site was a shell bangle manufacture centre as the raw material was easily accessible to the people because the site is located near the Gulf of Cambay in Saurashtra. It is interesting to note here, that the Saurashtra coast is one of the three coasts in India where (*"chankh/shankh"*) or conch shell is available.
3. The site yielded large number of beads of different materials. This also suggests that the people were very conscious about their ornamentation and had an aesthetic sense
4. The evidences of many kinds of household objects such as mullers, fishing hook, querns, knives, daggers, nails, chisel, hoe, pick, etc. suggest, that the Early Historic people were technologically advanced.
5. The site has produced quite a few structures. It has brought to light stone and mud structures in association with two plaques of Goddess *Lajjagauri*, one image each of Lord *Ganesa* and *Vishnu*. The floor and two mud platforms assume great significance in the light of the discovery of these figurines. This structure appears to have been place of worship, perhaps a temple of *Lajjagauri* (Shinde 1994). From the above discussion, it is clear that *Vishnuism* as well as *Saivism* were popular in this region during the Early Historic period.

6. The site has yielded quite a number of terracotta objects such as discs, human and animal figurines, wheels, ear-studs, boat-shaped motifs, toy pots and circular tablet with *Brahmi* inscription. This suggests that the peoples in this region knew several games and amused themselves in various ways.
7. The tortoise-shaped Roman copper lamp that has been found at the site shows contact with the Western world in this region during the Early Historic Period.
8. On the basis of occurrence of fishing hooks and others agricultural implements at the site it is assumed that fishing and agricultural activities must have played an important role in their subsistence pattern.

The important contribution of this work is that the data from the excavation at Padri was used for dating the Early Historic sites in this region precisely. Besides, for the first time an attempt has been made for the first time to study the pattern of Early Historic settlements, function of each settlement and interaction between the various settlements. Similar work will have to be extended in different parts of Saurashtra, so that the complete settlement system of the Early Historic period can be reconstructed. The data studied here by the author is subject to is several limitations. In order to overcome some of the problems a systematic excavation of the site of Hathab, a Regional centre in this area, will have to be undertaken.

Bibliography

Adams, R. M. 1961. Changing patterns of territorial organization in the central highlands Chiapas, Maxico. *American Antiquity*, 26(1): 341-360.

1965. *Land Behind Baghdad: A History of Settlement on the Diyala Plains.* Chicago: Chicago University press.

Agrawala, R. C. and V. L. Devalkar. 1970 Human Figurines on pottery handles from India and allied problems. *Dept. of Museum, Gujarat state, Ahmedabad.*

Agrawala, V. S. 1953. *India as known to Panini.* Lucknow: Lucknow University.

Allchin, F. R. 1995. *The Archaeology of South Asia: The Emergence of Cities and States.* pp.2-9 Cambridge: Cambridge University press.

1995. The Mauryan State and Empire. In *The Archaeology of Early Historic South Asia: The Emergence of Cities and States.* F.R. Allchin (ed.). Cambridge: Cambridge University press.

Ansari, Z. D. and M. S. Mate. 1966. *Excavations at Dwarka.* Poona.

Arkell, A. J. 1936. Cambay and the Bead Trade. *Antiquity* 10, pp.292-305

Beal, S. 1906. *Buddhist Records of the Western World,* Vol. II, London: Kegan paul, Trench, Trubner & Co. Ltd.

Bernard, V. J., Gachet and J-F. Salles. 1990. Apostilles en Marge de da ceramique des IVetv, in *Failaka 1986-88* (d' Yves Calvert and J. Gachet Eds.), pp. 241-284. Lyon: Travaux de la Maison De L' Orient., Fig.4

Bhan, K. K. 1983. *The Archaeology of Jamnagar District,* Gujarat. Unpublished Ph.D thesis, M.S.University of Baroda.

1986. Recent Explorations in the Jamnagar District of Saurashtra. *Man and Environment* 10:1-21, India

Bhan, S. 1979. Early Settlement in Haryana: A study of Urbanization. *Journal of Haryana Studies.* Vol.VIII, Nos.1-2:1-13.

Bharucha, A. M. 1997. *The Archaeology of the Settlements of the Kshatrapa period.* Unpublished Ph.D thesis, University of Poona.

Binford, L. R. 1964. A consideration of Archaeological Research Design. *American Antiquity.*29: 425-41.

Burgess, J. 1964. *Report of the Buddhist Caves Temples and their inscriptions.* Baranasi

Butzer, K. W. 1987. *Archaeology as human ecology: Method and theory for a contextual aproach.* Cambridge: Cambridge University press.

Chakrabarti, D. K. 1995. *The Archaeology of Ancient India.* Delhi: Oxford University press.

1995. Post Mauryan States of Mainland South Asia (c.185 A.D.-320). In *The Archaeology of Early Historic South Asia: The Emergence of cities and States.* F.R. Allchin (ed.), Cambridge: Cambridge University press.

Chakrabarti, S. 1977. *Prehistory of Bhavnagar District.* Unpublished Ph.D thesis, University of Poona.

Chang, K. C. 1958. Study of the Neolithic Social Grouping: Examples from New World. *American Anthropologist* 60: 298-334.

1962. A Typology of Settlement and Community pattern in some circumpolar societies. *Arctic Anthropology* 1: 28-41

Chattopadhaya, B. D. 1983. Political Process & Structure of polity. In Early Medieval India: Problems and Perspectives. *In Proceeding of the Indian National Congress, Burdwan, 44th session.*

Chaudhary, R. K. (ed.) 1983. *Inscriptions of Ancient India.* New Delhi: Menakshi Prokashan.

Chitalwala, Y. M. 1977. Harappan and Post Harappan Settlement Patterns in Saurashtra. *In Ecology and Archaeology of Western India.* (Agrawala, D.P. and B.M. Pande (ed.)). pp.93-98. Delhi: Concept Publishing Company.

1979. Harappan and Post Harappan Settlement Patterns in the Rajkot District of Saurashtra. In *Eassays in Indian Protohistory* (Agrawala, D.P. and D.K. Chakrabarti (ed.)), pp.113-121. Delhi: B.R. Publishing Corporation.

Chowdhary, S. N. 1961-62. A Bronze Statuette of Atlas from Shamalaji. *Journal of Oriental Institute, Baroda.*

Clark, D. L. 1972. A Provisional Model of an Iron Age Society and Its Settlement system. In *Models in Archaeology* (D.L. Clark ed.), pp. 801-869, London: Methuen.

Conigham, R. A. E. 1995. Dark Age or Continuum? An Archaeological analysis of the second emergence of Urbanism in South Asia. In *The Archaeology of Early Historic South Asia: The Emergence of Cities and States,* F.R. Allchin 1995. Cambridge: Cambridge University press.

Coomaraswamy, A. K. 1927. *History of Indian and Indonesian Art.* New York: Dover publication.

Coughlan 1956. *Notes on the Prehistoric and Early Iron in the Old World.* Oxford.

David Raju, B. 1985. *Neolithic Culture of Central Coastal Andhra, South India.* Unpublished Ph.D thesis, Nagarjuna University.

1990. The Settlement and Subsistence pattern of the Neolithic Culture of the Lower Krishna Valley. *Man and Environment* 15(2): 45-51.

Deo, S. B. and M. K. Dhavalikar 1968. *Paunar Excavation-1967.* Nagpur.

Desai, M. D. 1944-50. Some Roman Antiquities from Akota and Baroda. *Bulletin of the Baroda Museum and Picture Gallery*, VII (I-II),1949-50, Baroda.

Despande, C. D. 1948. *Western India: A Regional Geography*. Dharwar.

Deva, Krishna 1997. Historical Archaeology in India Since Independence. In *Him-Kanti: Archaeology, Art and History.* (Prof. K.P. Nautiyal Felicitation Volume)., B.M. Khanduri and Vinod Nautiyal (eds.). 1997. Delhi: Book India Publishing Co.

Dhavalikar, M. K. 1977b. Settlement Patterns at Inamgoan. *Man and Environment* 1: 46-5

1978b. Settlement Archaeology of Inamgaon. *Puratattava* 8: 44-54.

1979c. Early Farming Cultures of India. In *Essays in Indian Protohistory* (D.P. Agrawal ed.), Delhi.

1983. Towards an Ecological Model for Chalcolithic Cultures. Paper presented at the seminar on *Recent Advance in Indian Archaeology*, Pune

1984. Chalcolithic Cultures: A Socio-Economic Perspective, *Puratattava* 13-14: 68-80.

Dhavalikar, M. K. and G. L. Possehl. 1974. Subsistence Pattern of an Early Farming Communities of Western India. *Puratattva* 7: 39-46

Dhavalikar, M. K., Ravel, M. R., and Chitawala, Y. L. 1996. *Kuntasi: A Harappan Emporium on West Coast.* Deccan College: Pune.

Dikshit, M. G. 1968. *Excavations at Kaundinyapura*. Bombay.

Erdosy, G. 1988. *Urbanization in Early Historic India*. England: BAR International Series 430.

Fedden, I. 1884. The Geology of Khathiawar-Peninsula in Gujarat., *Memoir of the Geological Survey of India.* 21:2

Flaming, A. 1971. Territorial patterns in Bronze Age. *Proceedings of Prehistoric Society* 37:138-166.

Flannery, K. V. 1972. The Origins of Village as a Settlement type in Mesoamerican and the near East: A comparative Study. In *Man, Settlement and Urbanism*. pp.23-53 (eds. Ucko, P.J., R. Tringham and D.W. Dimbleby). London: Duckworth.

1976. *The Early Mesoamerican Village*. London: Academic press.

Fletcher, R. 1977. Settlement Studies (Micro and semi-micro). *Spatial Archaeology*. pp. 47-162 (ed. D.L. Clark). London: Academic press.

Foote, R. B. 1916. *The Foote collection of Indian Prehistoric and Protohistoric Antiquities: Notes on their Ages and distribution*. Madras: Government of India.

Gadre, A. S. 1947. *Archaeology of Baroda (1934-1947)*. Baroda: Baroda State press.

Ghose, A 1952. The Rajputana Desert: Its Archaeological aspect. *Bulletin of the National Institute of Sciences of India* 1: 37-42

1989. *Enclyclopaedia of Indian Archaeology* Vol.2. Delhi: Munshiram Monoharlal Publishers.

Gordon, D. H. 1943. Early Indian Terracottas. *Journal of the Indian Society of Oriental Art*: 11.

Govindan, P. R., V. S. Lele and S. N. Rajaguru. 1965. Quaternary Formation of Lower Hiron Valley, Saurashtra, Western India. *Bulletin of the Deccan College Post Graduate and Research Institute* 35:1-2, 123-137.

Gupta, Sunil 1997. *Roman Egypt to Peninsular India: Archaeological Patterns of Trade (1st century B.C. to 3rd century A.D.),* Unpublished Ph.D Thesis, University of Pune.

Haque, M. 1992. *Pre and Protohistoric Settlement Pattern of the Middle and Lower Ganga Valley.* Unpublished Ph.D thesis, University of Poona.

Hassan, F. A. 1978. Demographic archaeology. In Schiffer, M.B. (ed.) *Advance in Archaeological Method and Theory.* pp.49-103. London: Academic press.

Hegde, K. T. M. 1975. Iron Metallurgy. In *Excavations at Dhatva.* Baroda.

Heras, H 1990. The Origin of the Round Proto-Indian Seals discovered in Sumer. In B. Anderson and J. Correia- Afonso (eds.), *H. Heras Indological Studies* 44-62. New Delhi: Promilla and Co; in colaboration with Bombay Heras Institute of Indian History and Culture. (Originally published in *The B,B and C. I Railway Annual,* 1938

Hill, J. N. 1966. A Prehistoric Community in Eastern Arizona. *South Western Journal of Anthropology* 22: 9-30.

1970. Broken K. Pueblo: Prehistoric Social Organization. *Anthropological papers of the University of Arizona.* No.18

Houston, J. M. 1953. *A Social Geography of Europe.* London.

IAR. **1953-58; 1960-68; 1972-73; 1979-81.** ***Indian Archaeology-A Review.*** Annual Bulletine of the Archaeological Survey of India, New Delhi.

Jairath, V. K. 1986. *Archaeology of the Northern Part of Bhavnagar District, Gujarat State upto 15th century A.D.* Unpublished Ph.D thesis, M.S. University, Baroda.

Joshi, J. P. and Madhu Bala. 1982. Manda- A Harappan site in Jammu and Kashmir. In *Harappan Civilization: A Contemporary Perspectives,* pp.185-196 (ed. G.L. Possehl) New Delhi: Oxford-IBH.

Kielhorn, F. 1905-06. Junagadh Rock Inscription of Rudradaman. *Epigraphia Indica* VIII: 36-49.

King, L. J. 1961. A multivariate analysis of spacing of urban settlements in the United States. *Annals of the Association of American Geographers.* 51:222-33.

Koiso, M. 1994. *The analysis of pottery of Kuntasi in Relation with others Harappan Sites.* Unpublished Ph.D dissertation, University of Poona.

Lahiri, N. 1992. *The Archaeology of Indian Trade Routes upto c. 200 B.C.: Resource Use, Resource Access and Lines of Communication.* p.387. Delhi: Oxford University Press.

Lal, B. B. 1948. Sisupalgarh 1848: an Early Historic Fort in Eastern India. pp.62-105, *Ancient India* Vol. 5

Lal, M. 1984. *Settlement History and Rise of Civilization in Ganga-Yamuna Doabs From 1500 B.C. to 300 A.D.).* Delhi: B.R. Publishing Corporation.

Lele, V. S. 1972. *Late Quaternary History of Bhadar Valley, Saurashtra.* Unpublished Ph.D thesis, University of Poona.

Leshnik, L. 1967. The system of dry farming in the west Nimad district of Central India. *Journal of the South Asian Institute.* 56-74

1968. Prehistoric Exploration in North Gujarat and parts of Rajasthan. *East and West* 18. Nos.3-4

Majumdar, M. R. 1960. *Chronology of Gujarat.* Baroda.

Majumder, R. C. 1954. *The Classical Age.* Bombay.

Malik, Arun. S. 1996. *A Preliminary studies in the Settlement patterns of Early Historic sites in Gujarat,* Unpublished M.A. dissertation, Dept. of Archaeology and Ancient History, M.S. University, Baroda.

Margabandhu, C. 1985. *Archaeology of the Satavahana-Kshatrapa Times,* Delhi: Sundeep publication.

Mehta, R. N. 1955. *Excavations at Timbarva,* Baroda.

Metha, R. N. 1968. *Excavation at Nagara,* Baroda.

1983. Urban Centres of Western India and the Western World, in *India and the West* (S. Deppert Ed.), pp.139-148. Delhi: Manohar Publishers.

Mehta, R. N., S. N. Chowdhary, K. T. M. Hegde and D. R. Shah. 1975. *Excavation at Dhatva,* Baroda.

Mehta, R. N. and S. N. Chowdhary. 1966. *Excavation at Devnimori,* Baroda.

1971. *Excavation at Jokha,* Baroda.

Mehta, R. N. and A. J. Patel. 1967. *Excavation at Shamalaji,* Baroda.

Mirashi, V. V. 1981. *The History and Inscriptions of the Satavahanas and the Western Kshatrapas.* Bombay.

Misra, V. N. , Vasant Shinde, R. K. Mohanty, Kurush Dalal, Anup Mishra, Lalit Pandey and Jeevan Kharakwal. 1995. Excavations at Balathal: Their contribution to the Chalcolithic and Iron Age cultures of Mewar, Rajasthan. pp.57-80. *Man and Environment.* XX(1).

Momin, K. N. 1974. Chalcolithic settlements in Bhalbara, Taluka Cambay, Gujarat. *Journal of the M.S. University of Baroda (Humanities).* 1974, 20 (1)-21(1), 1971-72: 57-63.

1976a. The Chalcolithic settlement in Kaira District, Gujarat State. *Journal of the M.S. University of Baroda.* 22(1)-23(1): 54-56.

1976b. The Chalcolithic settlements in Bhalbara, Taluka Cambay, Gujarat. In U.V. Singh (ed.), *Archaeological congress and Siminar*: 1972, 51-54. Kurukshetra: B.N. Chakrabarti University.

1979. *Archaeology of Kheda District (Gujarat) upto 1500 A.D.* Unpublished Ph.D thesis, M.S. University of Baroda.

1984. Villages Harappans in Kheda District of Gujarat. In B.B.Lal and S.P. Gupta (eds.) *Frontiers of the Indus Civilization*, 231-234. New Delhi: Books & Books.

Mookerji, R. K. 1928. *Asoka.* Oxford.

Nanavati, J. M., Mehta, R. N. and Chowdhary, S. N. 1971. *Somnath-1956*, Baroda.

Nanavati, J. M. 1962. Ivory figurines from Probhas Patan. *Journal of the Madhya Pradesh Itihasa Parishad,* vol.4, pp.57-61.

Nikam, N. A. and Richard Mokeon. (eds.) 1959. *The Edicts of Asoka*, Bombay.

Naraian, L. A. 1974. *A Study in the technique and Bone Tool making at Chirand and their Probable use.* Patna: Nilima Publications.

Orton, N. P. 1991. Red Polished Ware in Gujarat: A Catalogue of Twelve Sites. In Begly, Vimla and Richard Daniel De Puma (eds.), pp.46-81.*The Ancient Sea Trade.* Madision: Wisconsin.

Paddayya, K. 1982. *The Acheulian Culture of the Hunagi Valley (Peninsular India) : A Settlement System Perspective.* Poona: Deccan College Post Graduate and Research Institute.

Pandya, Suman. 1973. *Ethno Archaeological Study of Harappan and Post Harappan Culture of Saurashtra.* Unpublished Ph.D. thesis, University of Poona.

Parikh, R. T. 1977. *Archaeology of Banaskantha District.* Unpublished Ph.D. Dissertation, M.S. University of Baroda.

Parkar, A. J. 1973. Under water Archaeology For Roman Trade in The Western Mediterranean. In D.J. Blackman 1973, *Marine Archaeology. Proceedings of the Twenty third Symposium of the Coastal Research Society.* London: Butterworth.

Parson, J. R. 1971. *Prehistiric Settlement Patterns in the Taxcoco Region. Memoir No.*3. An Arbor: University of Michigan, Museum of Anthropology.

Paul, A. B., B. Tripathi and V. Shinde. 1997. New Archaeological Discoveries in the Lower Shetrunji River Basin, Bhavnagar District, Gujarat. In *Him-kanti: Archaeology, Art and History.* pp.53-63. (Prof. K.P.Nautiyal Felicitation Vol., B.M. Khanduri and Vinod Nautiyal eds.), New Delhi: Book India Publishing Co.

2000. The Settlements and Subsistence Pattern of the Early Historic Culture in the Shetrunji River Basin, Bhavnagar District, Gujarat, *Puratattva* 30: 99-109, Bulletin of the Indian Archaeological Society, New Delhi,

Peterson, W. 1975. A demographer's view of Prehistoric demography. *Current Anthropology.*16

Possehl, G. L. 1977. Variation and Changes in the Indus Civilization: A study of rehistoric Gujarat with special reference to the Post Urban Harappan. Unpublished Ph.D. thesis, University of Chicago.

1980. *Indus Civilization in Saurashtra.* New Delhi: B.R. publishing corporation.

Puri, B. N. 1965. *India under the Kushanas,* Bombay: Bharatiya Vidya Bhawan.

Rao, K. N., C. J. George and K. S. Ramasastri. 1972 *Agroclimatic Classification of India.* Meteorological Monograph, Indian Meteorological Department, Poona, p.5

Rao, S. R. 1959. *Indian Archaeology-A Review.*1958-59: 18-19

1963. Excavations at Rangpur and other explorations in Gujarat. *Ancient India.* 18-19 (1962-1963) : 5-207

1966. Excavations at Amreli: A Kshatrapa-Gupta town. *Bulletin of the Baroda Museum and Picture Gallery,* XVIII, Baroda.

Ray, H. P. 1986. *Monastery and Guild: Commerce under the Satavahanas.* Delhi: Oxford University Press.

Renfrew, C. 1972. Patterns of population growth in Pre-historic Aegean. In *Man, Settlement and Urbanism.* pp.383-99, (eds. Ucko, P.J., R.Tringham and D.W. Dembleby).

Rhyd, Hanna 1959. *Rangmahal, The Swedish Archaeological Expedition To India.* Lund: Sweden.

Rouse, I. 1972. Settlements Patterns in Archaeology. In *Man, Settlement and Urbanism* (eds. Ucko, P.J., R. Tringham and D.W. Dimbleby), London: Duckwoth. pp.95-107.

Sanders, W.T. 1956. The Central Mexican Symbiotic region: A Study in Prehistoric Settlement Patterns. In *Prehistoric Settlement Patterns in New World*, (Willey, G.R. ed.), pp.115-127, Viking Fund Publication in Anthropology No.23

1965. *The Cultural Ecology of the Teotihuacan Valley.* University Park: Pennsylvania State University.

Sankalia, H. D. 1941. *The Archaeology of Gujarat (Including Kathiawar)*, Bombay: Natwal lal & Co.

1965 Early Stone Age in Saurashtra, Gujarat. In *Miscelanea Homena at Abata Heuri Breuil, II*: 327-346. Bercelona: Institute de Prehistoria

1987. *Prehistoric and Historic Archaeology of Gujarat.* Delhi: Munshiram Manoharlal publishers.

Sankalia, H. D. and S. B. Deo 1955. *Report on the Excavations at Nasik and Jorwe*, 1950-51. Poona.

Sankalia, H. D., B. Subbarao, and S. B. Deo 1958. *The Excavations at Maheshwar and Navdatoli* (1952-53). Poona.

Sankalia, H. D., S. B. Deo., Z. D. Ansari and Sophie Ehrhrdt 1960. *From History to Prehistory at Nevasa* (1954-55). Poona.

Sankalia, H. D., S. B. Deo and Z. D. Ansari 1969. *Excavations at Ahar* (Timbarvati) 1961-62. Poona.

Sarkar, D. C. 1942. *Selected Inscriptions.* Vol.1. No.50:160, Calcutta.

Sarma, I. K. 1980. *Coinage of the Satavahana Empire.* New Delhi.

Sastri, N. A. 1957. *Comprehensive history of India.* Vol.II.

Sastry, V. V. Krishna 1983. *The Proto and Early Historical Cultures of Andhra Pradesh.* The Govt. of Andhra Pradesh, Hyderabad.

Schoff, W. H. 1912. *The Periplus of the Erythraean Sea.* London: Longmans, Green and Co., Bombay and Calcutta.

Sears, W. T. 1961. The study of social and religious system in North American Archaeology. *Current Anthropology.* 2: 223-246.

Sharma, R. S. 1987. *Urban Decay in India* (c.300-1000 A.D.) Delhi: Munshiram Monoharlal publishers.

Shinde, V. S. 1984. *Early Settlement in the Central Tapi Basin.* Unpublished Ph.D. thesis, University of Poona.

1990. The Malwa Culture in Maharastra: A study of Settlement and Subsistence Patterns. *Man and Environment* XV (2):53-60.

1992a. Excavations at Padri-1990-91: A preliminary Report. *Man and Environment*, XVII (1): 79-86.

1992b. Padri and the Indus Civilization. *South Asian Studies* 8: 55-66.

Shinde, V. S 1994a. Early Harappan phase in Gujarat with special Reference to Padri. *World Archaeology* Unpublished volume, New Delhi.

1994b. The Earliest Temple of Lajjagauri? The Recent Evidence from Padri in Gujarat, *East and West.* ISMEO, 44-Nos.2-4: 481-485.

1996. A Preliminary Report of the second season Excavation at Padri. In *Krsna Smrti, Studies in Indian Art and Archaeology.*(Prof. K.D.Bajapai Commemoration volume), R.K. Sharma and R.C. Agrawal (ed.) New Delhi: Aryan Book International. 40-45

1998. Pre-Harappan Padri Culture in Saurashtra: The Recent Discovery. *South Asian Studies,* 14: 173-182.

Shinde, V. S. and Bhagat-Kar, S. 1992c. Padri Ware: A New painted Ceramic found in the Harappan Levels at Padri in Gujarat. *Man and Environment* XVII(2): 105-110.

Sing, Purushottam. 1994. *Excavation at Narhan* (1984-89). Delhi: B.R. Publishing Corporation.

Sonawane, V. H. 1974. Explorations in the Panchmahal District, A preliminary note. *Journal of the M.S. University of Baroda.* 20(1)-21(1), 1971-72: 53-56.

1988. Some Remarkable Sculptures of Lajjagauri from Gujarat. *Lalit kala,* Journal of Oriental Art. No.23: 27-35.

Subbarao, B. 1953. *Baroda through the Ages,* Baroda.

1958. *The Personality of India: Pre and Protohistoric foundation of India and Pakistan.* Baroda: M.S. University of Baroda.

Subbarao B. and Mehta, R. N. 1955. Excavations at Vadnagar, *Journal of the Baroda Museum,* IV, Baroda.

Sundarrajan 1967. *Indian Archaeology-A Review.* 1963-64: 86

Tarn, W. W. 1951. *The Greeks in Bactria and India.* Cambridge.

Thomas, E. T. 1996. *Harappan Civilization in Saurashtra: A Study of Cultural Transformation from Mature to Late phase.* Unpublished Ph.D. thesis, University of Poona.

Tolstoy, P. and S. K. Fish 1973. *Excavations at Coapexco,* 1973. New York: Queens College.

Trigger, B. G. 1963. Settlement as an aspect of Iroquoion adaptation at the time of contact. *American Anthropologist.* 65: 86-101

1967. Settlement Archaeology-Its goal and promise. *American Antiquity.* 32: 149-160

1968. The Determinants of Settlement Patterns. In *Settlement Archaeology* (Chang, K.C.(eds.)) Palo Alto. National Press.

Tringham, Ruth 1972. Introduction: Settlement Pattern and Urbanization. In *Man, Settlement and Urbanism* (ed. Ucko, P.J., Ruth Tringham and G.W. Dimbleby). pp.IXX-XXVII. London: Duckworth.

Trivedi, R. K. (ed.) 1969. *Gujarat State Gazetteers, Bhavnagar District.* Ahmedabad.

Vats, M. S. 1936. Trial Excavations at Rangpur, Limbdi State, Kathiawar. *Annual Report of the Archaeological Survey of India* 1934-35.

Virji, K. J 1952. *Ancient History of Saurashtra.* Konkon Institute of Arts and sciences, Bombay.

Vogt, E. Z. 1956. An Appraisal of Prehistoric Settlement Patterns in the New World. In *Prehistoric Settlement Patterns in the New World.* (Willey, G.R. ed). Viking Fund Publication in Anthropology. No.23, pp.173-183.

Wadia, D. N. 1944. *Geology in India*. London: Macmillan and Co., third edition.

Wallace, R. 1888. *India in 1887*. Edinburgh: Oliver and Boyd: Twee dale court.

Warmington, E. H. 1974. *The Commerce Between the Roman Empire and India*. Delhi: Munshi Monoharlal.

Wheeler, Sir, R. E. M. 1946. Aricamedu: An Indo-Roman Trading Station on the East Coast of India. *Ancient India*, Vol.2: 22

Willey, G. R. 1953. Prehistoric Settlement Patterns in the Viru Valley, Peru. *Bureau of American Ethnology,* Bulletin 155, Washington D.C.: Smithsonian Institute.

Willey, G. R., W. R. Bullard, J. B. Glass and J. C. Gifford 1965. Prehistoric Maya Settlement Pattern in Belize Valley. *Papers of Peabody Museum*, No. 54, Harward University.

Index

U

V

W

Y

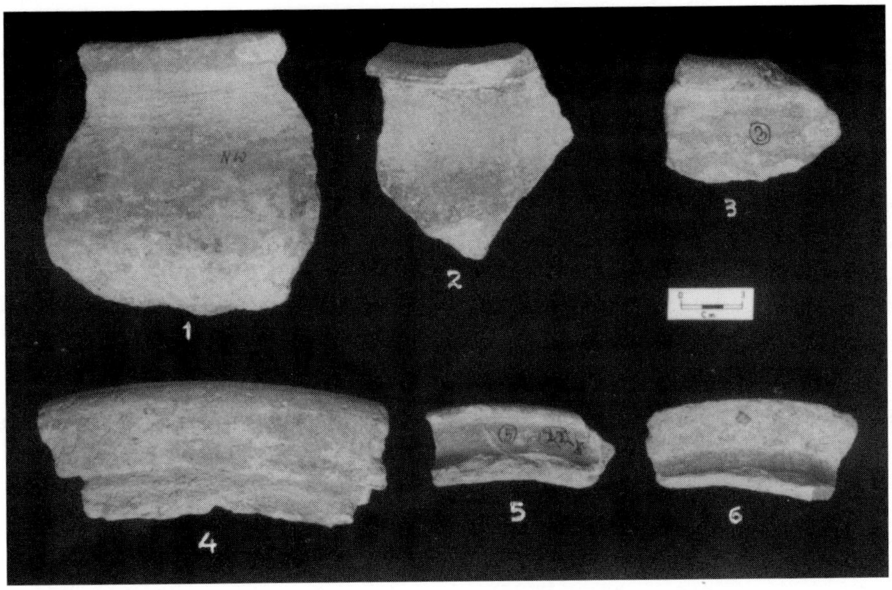

Pl. I-a: Red-Slipped Ware:
Nos.1-6-Jars.

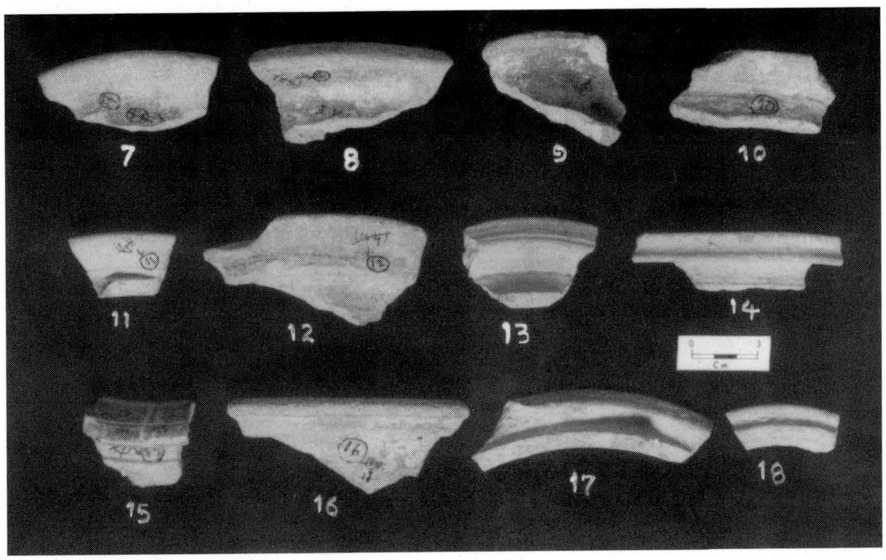

Pl. I-b: Red-Slipped Ware:
Nos.7-18-Jars.

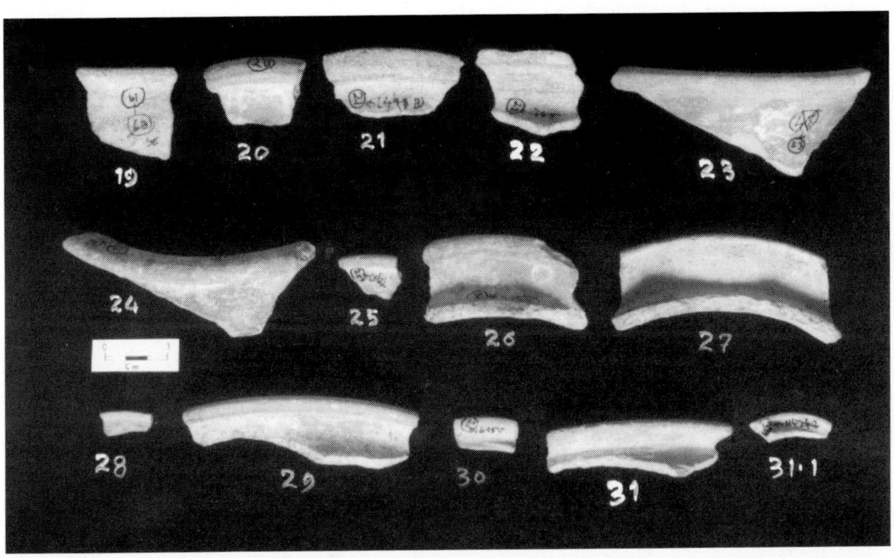

Pl. II-a: Red-Slipped Ware:
No.19-Pot, Nos.20-24-Jars,
Nos. 25, 28-Pots, Nos.26-27,
29-31- Jars, Nos.31.1-Pot.

Pl. II-b: Red-Slipped Ware: No.32-Pot, No.33-Jar, Nos.34-37-Bowls.

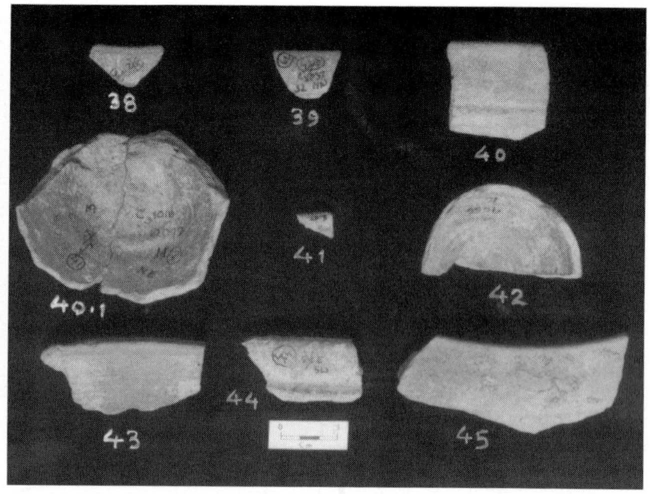

Pl. III-a: Red-Slipped Ware: Nos.38-42-Bowls, Nos.43-45-Basins,

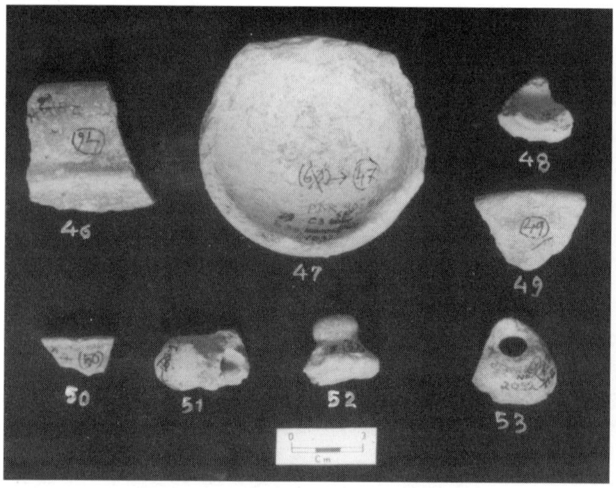

Pl. III-b: Red-Slipped Ware: No.46-Dish, No.47-Jar, Nos.48-49-Lids, No.50-Flare stand, Nos.51-53-Spouts.

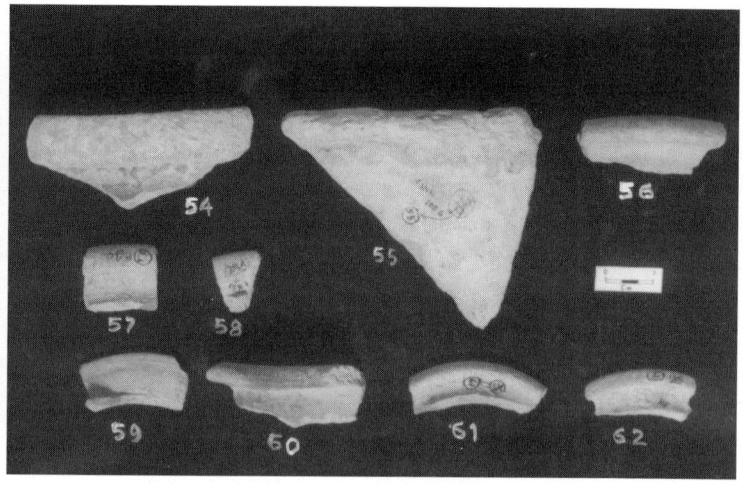

Pl. IV-a: Red Ware: Nos.54-62-Jars.

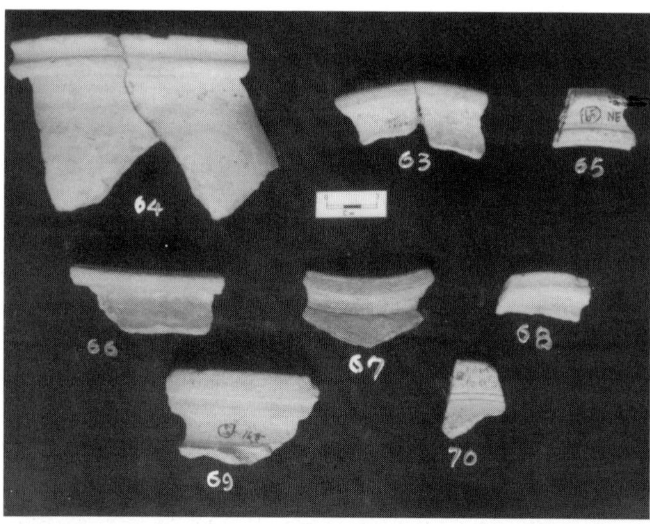

Pl. IV-b: Red Ware: No.63-Pot, Nos.64-65-Jars, No.66-Pot, Nos.67-69-Jars, No.70- Unascertained vessel.

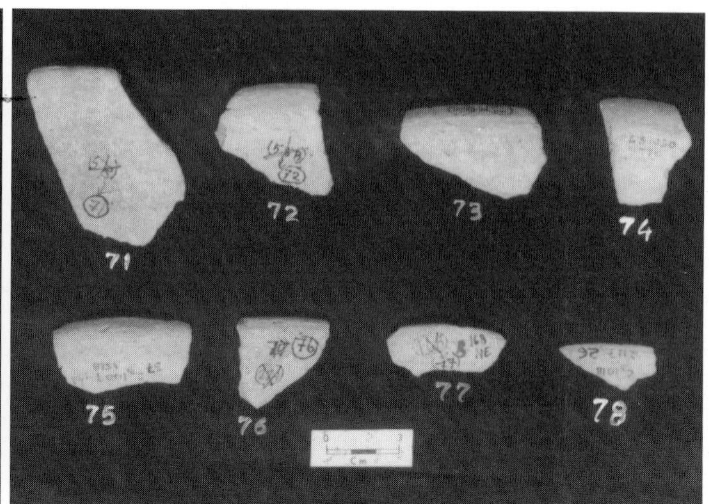

Pl. V-a: Red Ware: Nos.71-78-Cups.

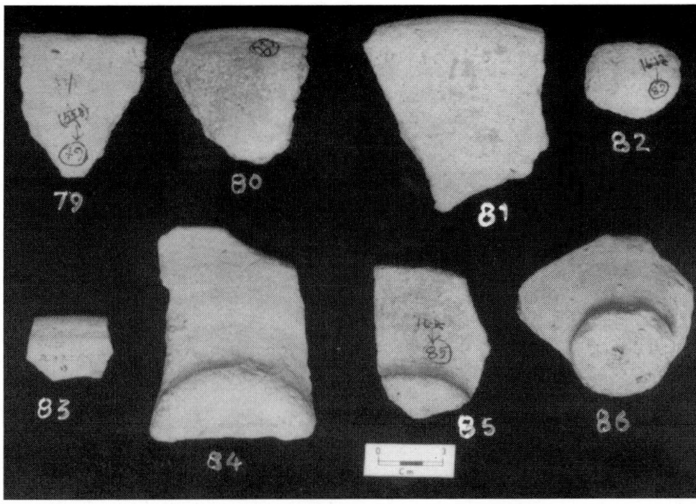

Pl. V-b: Red Ware: Nos.79-86-Cups.

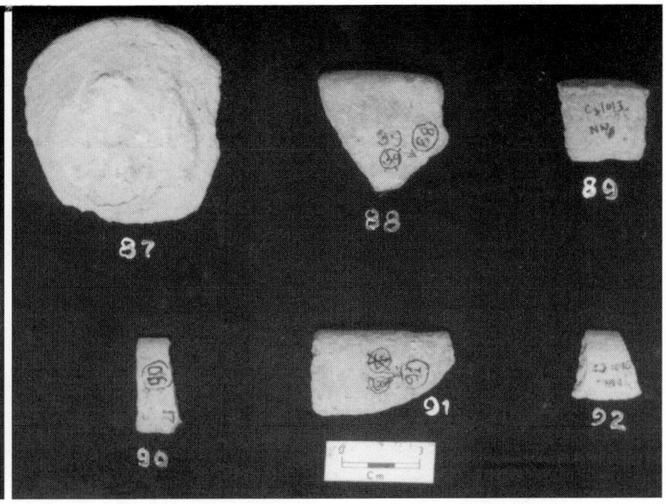

Pl. VI-a: Red Ware: Nos.87-92-Saucers.

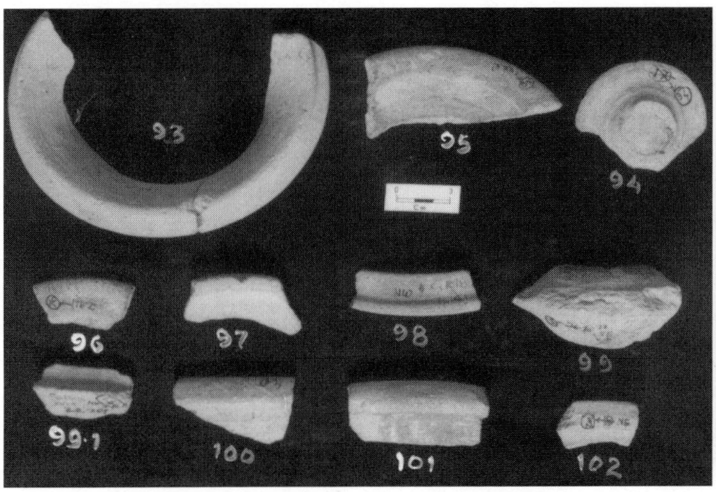

Pl. VI-b: Red Ware: Nos.93-99.1-Lids, Nos.100-101-Basins, No.102-Dish/basin.

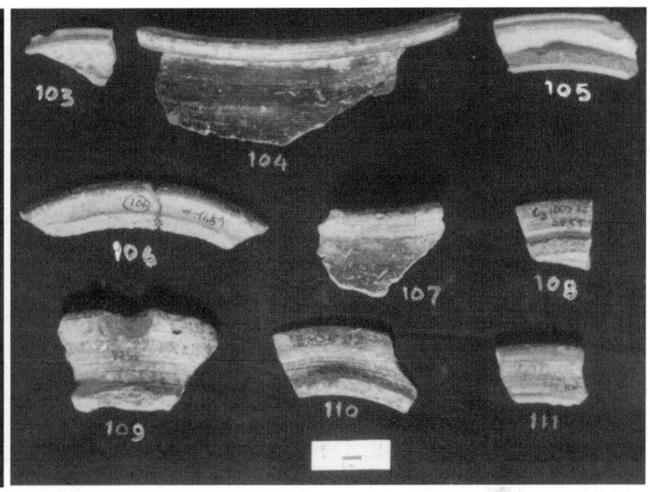

Pl. VII-a: Grey Ware: No.103-Pot, Nos.104-109-Jars, No.110-Globular pot, No.111-Jar.

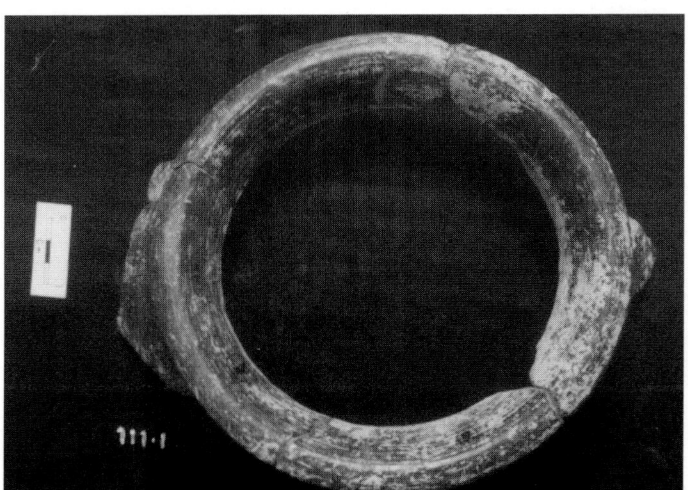

Pl. VII-b: Grey Ware: No.111.1-Jar.

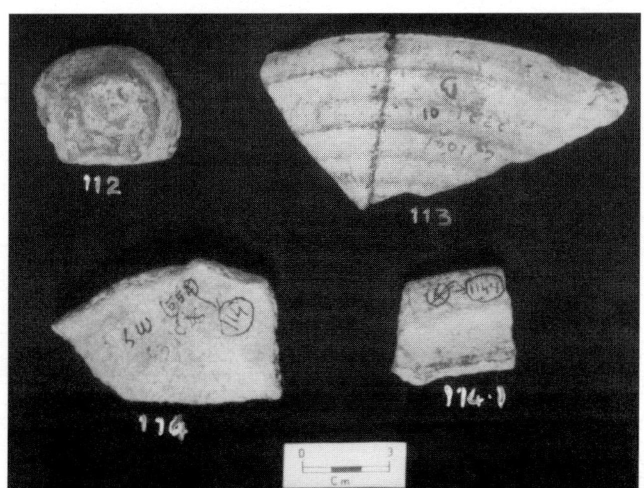

Pl. VIII-a: Grey Ware: No.112-Lamp , No.113-Bowl, No.114-Lid,- No.114.1-Unascertain vessel.

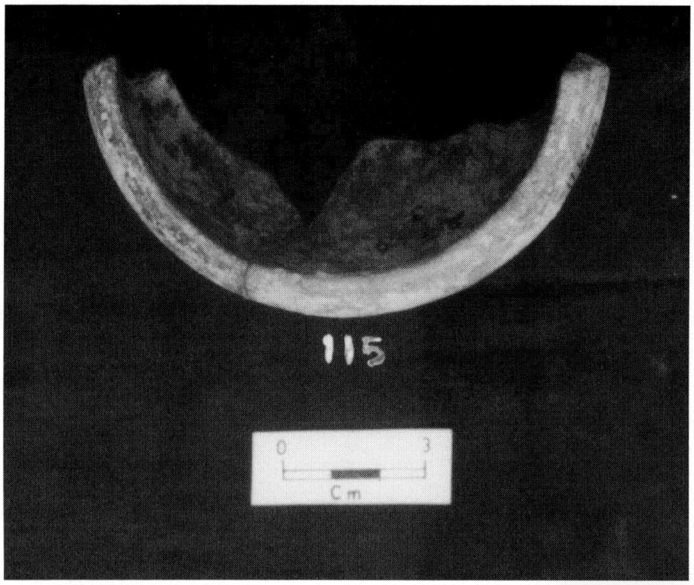

Pl. VIII-b: Black-and-Red Ware:
No.115-Bowl.

Pl. IX. Nos.1-19-Shell bangles,
No. 20- Copper bangle

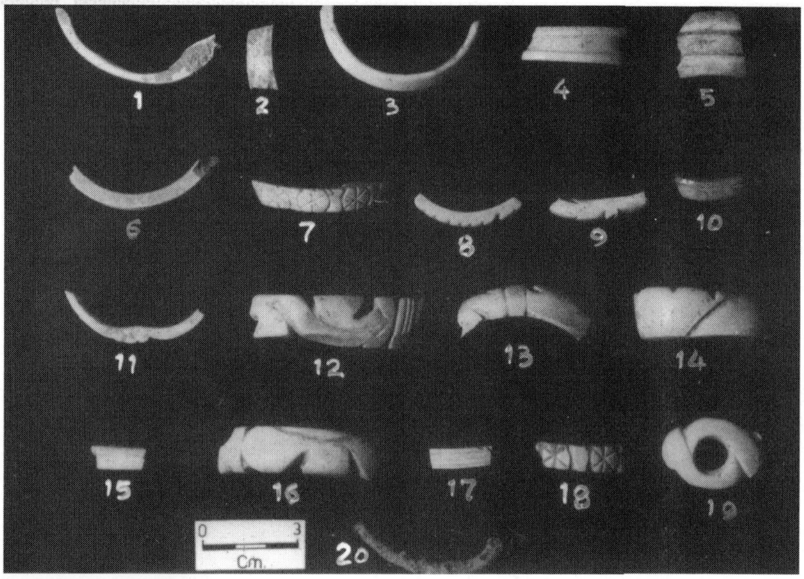

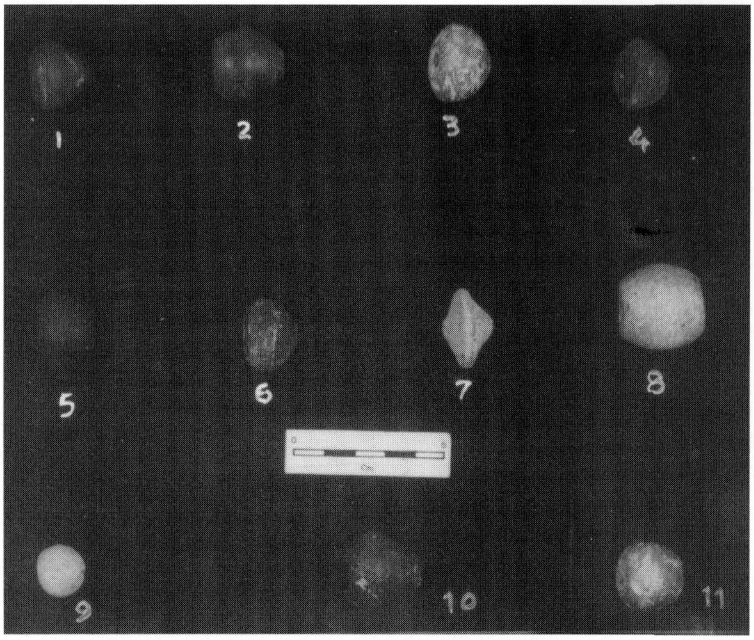

Pl. X-a: Nos.1-11-Terracotta beads

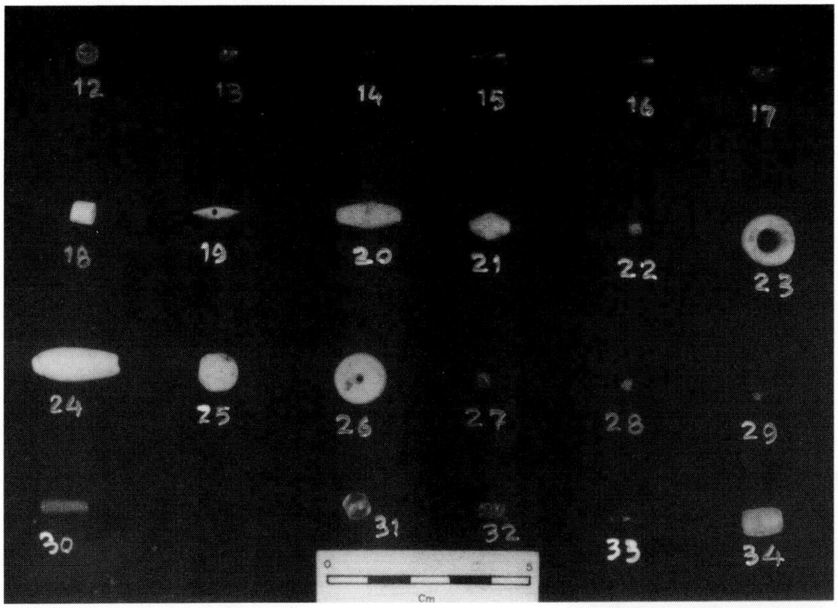

Pl. X-b: Nos.12-17-Carnelian beads, Nos.18-26-Shell beads, Nos.27-30-Glass beads, No.31-Crystal bead, No.32-Lapis-lazuli bead, No.33-Chert bead, No.34-Agate bead.

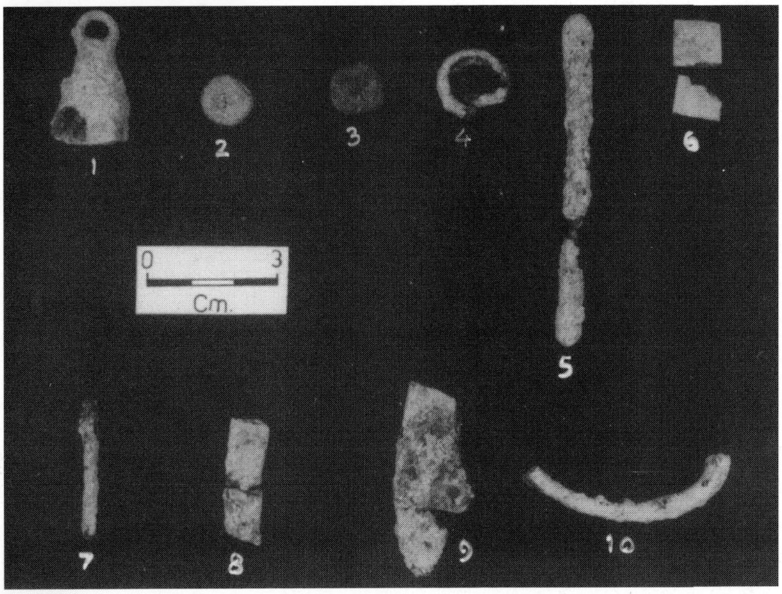

Pl. XI-a:
Nos.1-10-Copper objects.

Pl. XI-b: Roman copper lamp

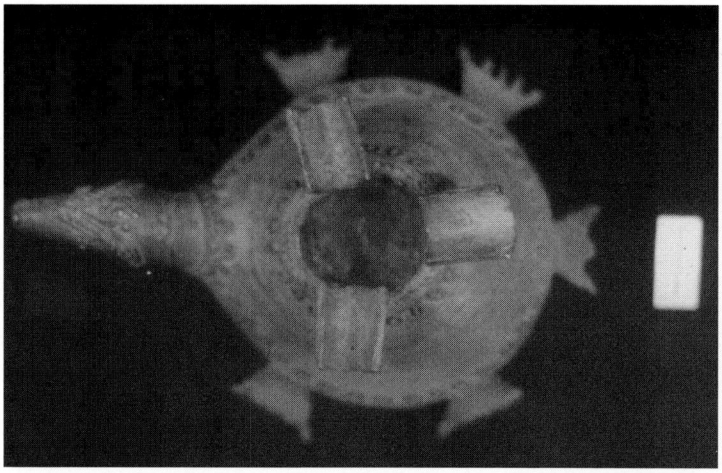

Pl. XI-c: Modern ash-tray resembling the copper lamp from Padri.

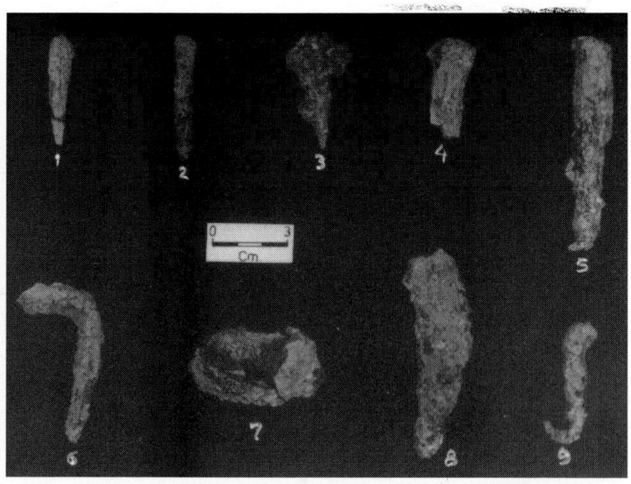

Pl. XII-a: Iron objects: Iron objects: Nos. 1-4-Nails.

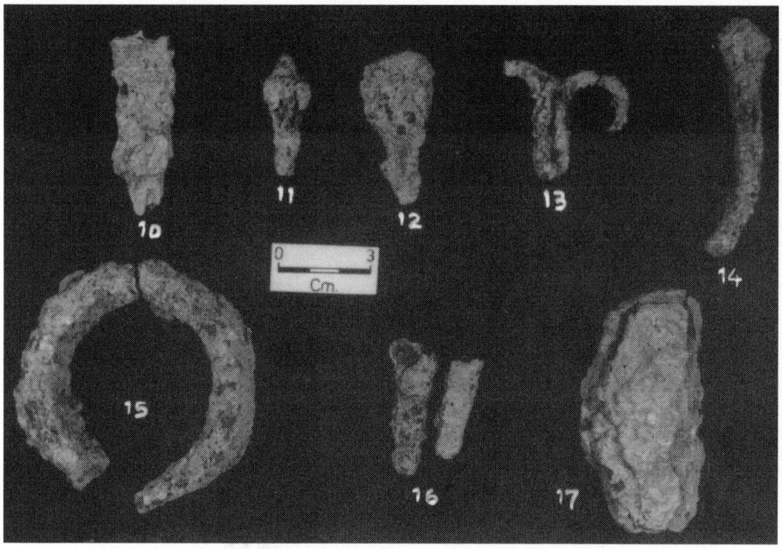

Pl. XII-b: Iron objects: No.10-Knife, No.11-Pendulum, No.12-Arrowhead, No.13-Door chain, No.14-Knife, No.15-Bangle, No.16-Clamp(?), No.17-Dagger.

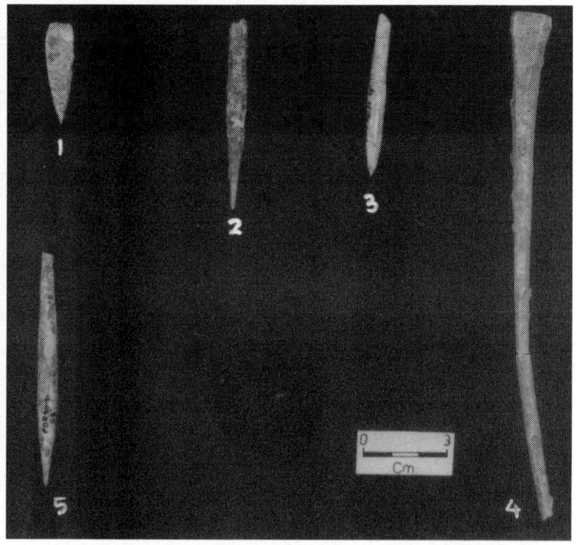

Pl. XIII: Bone objects: No.1-Arrowhead, No.2-4-Points, No.5-Arrowhead.

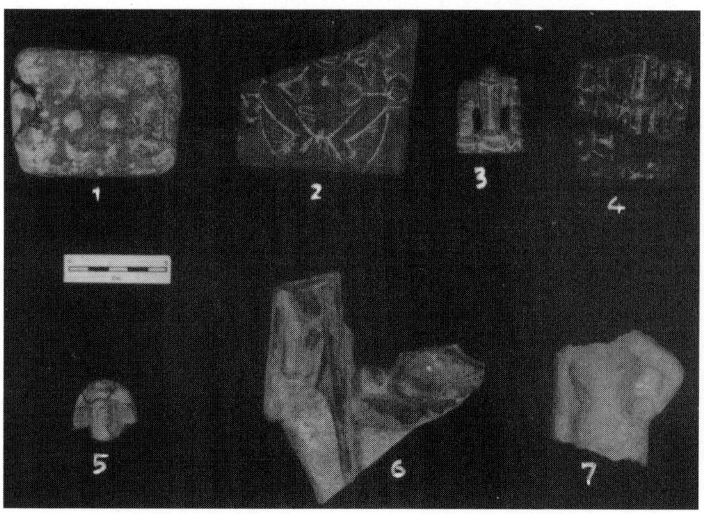

Pl. XIV-a: No.1-Terracotta Lajjagauri figurine, No.2-Lajjagauri figurine in stone, No.3-Vishnu figurine in stone, No.4-Lower portion of a deity, No.5-Sand stone head of Lord Ganesa, No.6-An unidentified stone figurine, No.7-Terracotta female figurine.

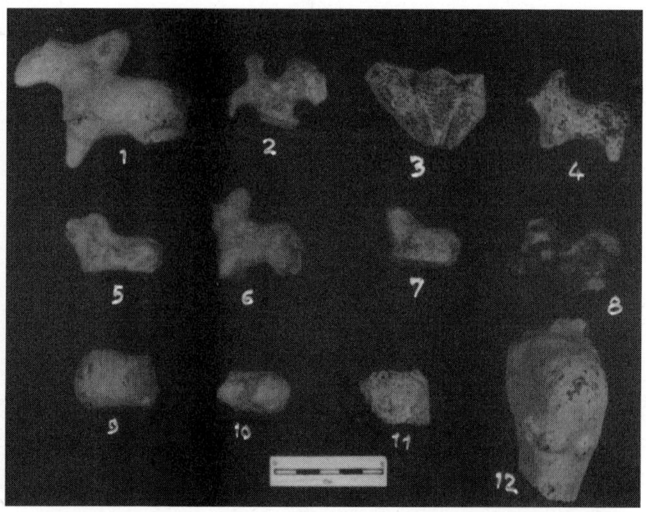

Pl. XIV-b: No.1-Terracotta bull figurine, No.2-An unidentified stone figurine, No.3-A terracotta yoni portion of Lajjagauri figurine, Nos.4-7-Terracotta bull figurines. No.8-Terracotta figurine-shaped spout, No.9-Terracotta bull figurine, No.10-Terracotta head of a bird, No.11-Terracotta bull figurine, No.12-Terracotta head of a elephant.

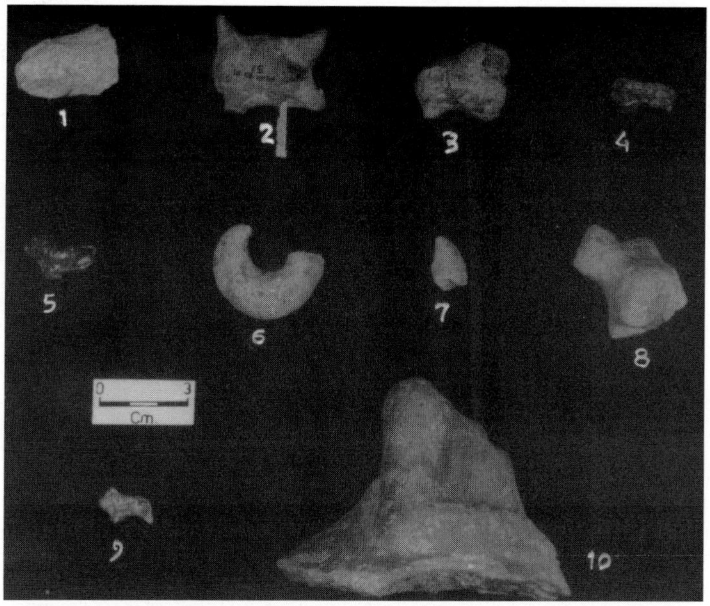

Pl. XIV-c: No.1-Terracotta head of a bird, No.2-A hand made terracotta torso. No.3-Terracotta bull figurine, Nos.4-5-Terracotta dog figurines, No.6-Terracotta ring fragment, No.7-Terracotta horn fragment.No.8-Terracotta bull figurine, No.9-A miniature terracotta bull figurine. No.10-A fragment of terracotta human figurine.

Pl. XIV-d: Nos.1-2-Terracotta boat-shaped motifs.

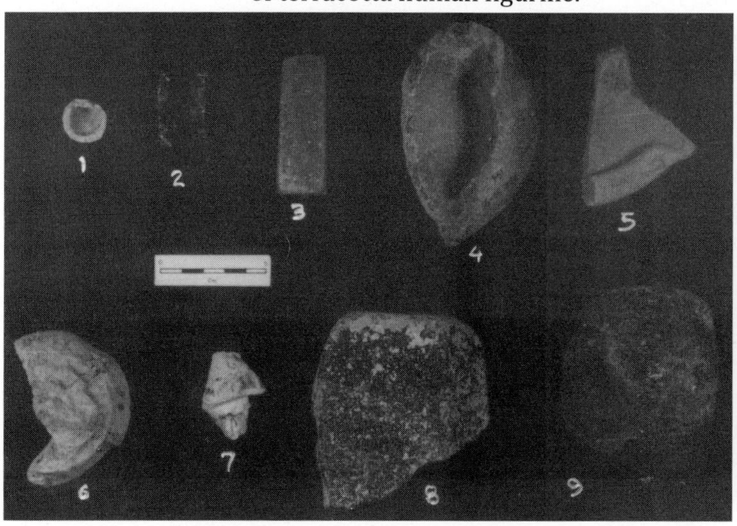

Pl. XV-a: No.1-A small clay toy pot, No.2-Black jasper weight, No.3-Dolorite weight. No.4-Pottery lamp, No.5-Pottery lamp, No.6-Basalt potter's dabbar, No.7-Fragment of columellar, No.8-Basalt mullar, No.9-Rubber stone.

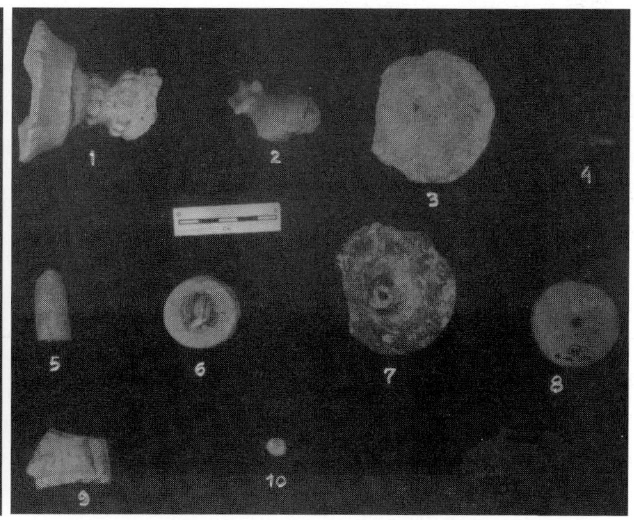

Pl. XV-b: No.1-Terracotta incense burner, No.2-Terracotta lid finial, No.3-Terracotta crucible, No.4-Fragment of terracotta incense burner, No.5-Fragment of a terracotta gamesmen, No.6-Terracotta circular base of a goblet, Nos.7-8-Terracotta wheel, No.9-Fragment of terracotta incense burner, No.10 Ground shell.

Pl. XV-c: No.1-Used shell, No.2-Terracotta stopper, No.3-Terracotta ball, No.4-Stone ball, No.5-Fragment of hammer stone, No.6-Terracotta ball, No.7-Chert flake, No.8-Fragment of white glass.

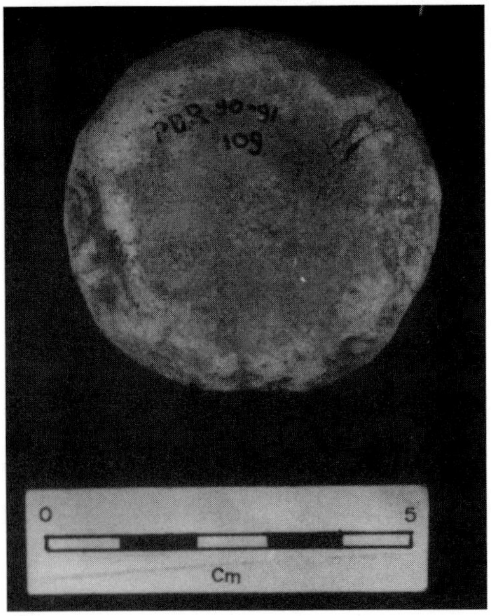

Pl. XV-d: Terracotta tablet with Brahmi inscription.

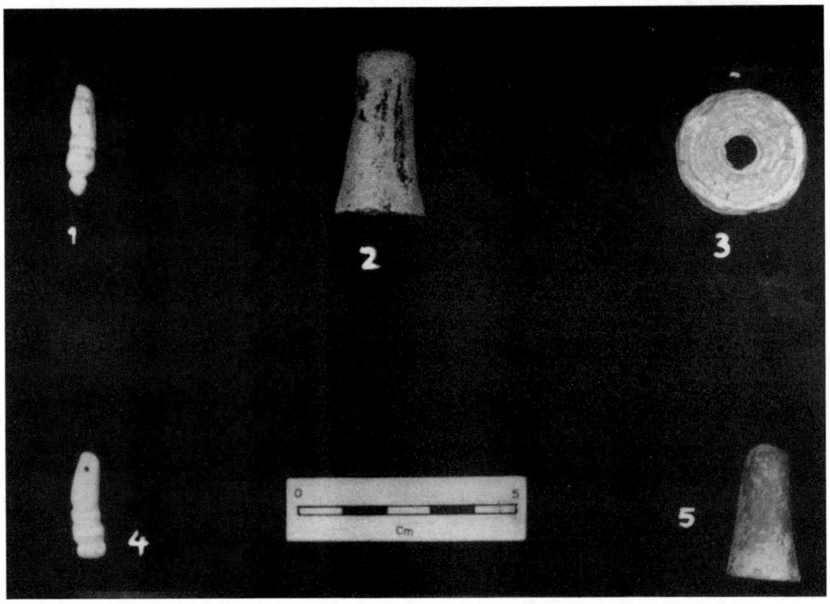

Pl. XVI: No.1-Shell pendant, No.2-Terracotta stopper, No.3-Shell pendant, No.4-Shell pendant, No.5-Terracotta stopper.

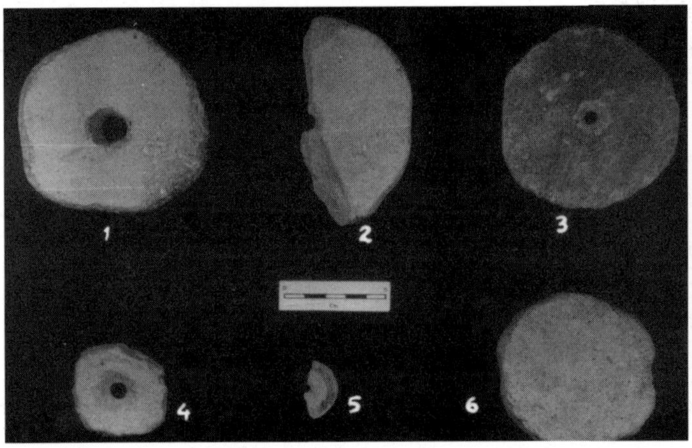

Pl. XVII-a: Nos.1-5-Terracotta discs, No.6-Stone disc.

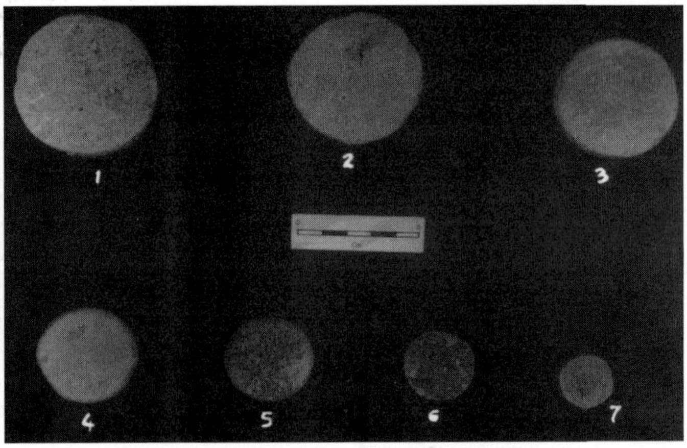

Pl. XVII-b: Nos.1-7-Terracotta discs.

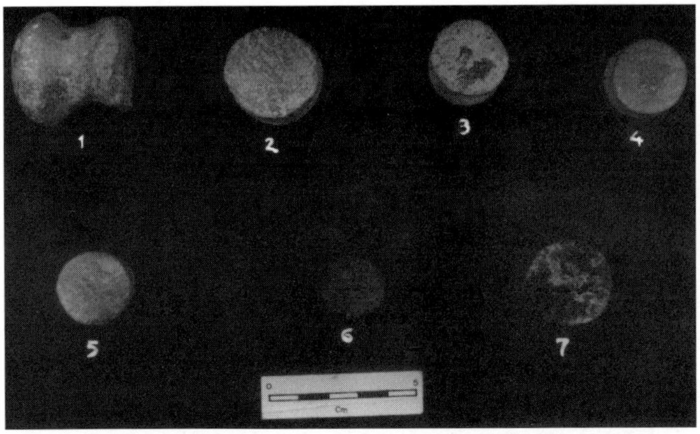

Pl. XVIII: Nos.1-7- Terracotta ear-stud.

Pl. XIX-a: Early Historic site at Bandi-Rohil.

Pl. XIX-b: Early Historic site at Begali.

Pl. XX-a: Early Historic site at Bhalar.

Pl. XX-b: Early Historic site at Bharapur/Juno Timba.

Pl. XXI-a: Early Historic site at Chopra.

Pl. XXI-b: Early Historic site at Dakana.

Pl. XXII-a: Early Historic site at Dantrad.

Pl. XXII-b: Early Historic site at Devalia.

Pl. XXIII-a: Early Historic site at Gorkhi.

Pl. XXIII-b: Early Historic site at Hathab.

Pl. XXIV-a: Early Historic site at Ichhora.

Pl. XXIV-b-Early Historic site at Katva.

Pl. XXV-a: Early Historic site at Khadsaliya.

Pl. XXV-b: Early Historic site at Padri.

Pl. XXVI-a: Early Historic site at Pavti.

Pl. XXVI-b: Early Historic site at Phulsar.

Pl. XXVII-a: Early Historic site at Piparla.

Pl. XXVII-b: Early Historic site at Shilavadar.

Pl. XXVIII-a: Early Historic site at Saltanpur.

Pl. XXVIII-b: Early Historic site at Thalsar.

Pl. XXIX-a: Early Historic site at Timbana.

Pl. XXIX-b: Early Historic site at Valavadar.

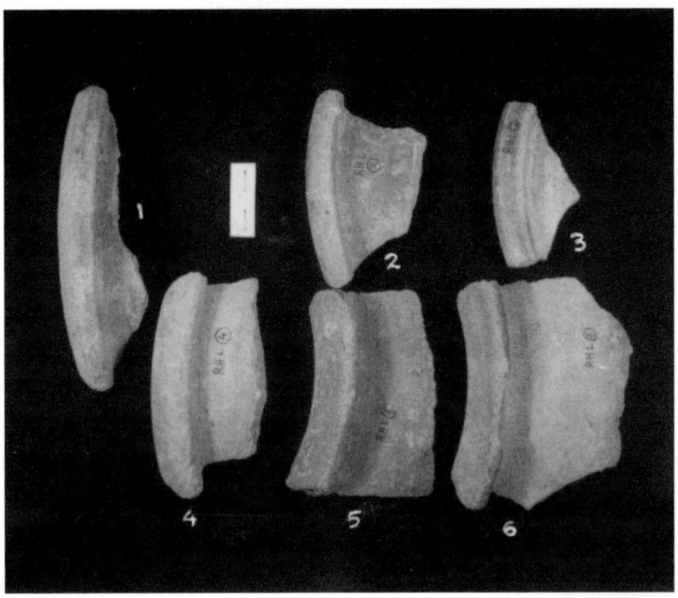

Pl. XXX-a: Red-Slipped Ware: Nos.1-3-Jars, Nos.4-6-Pots.

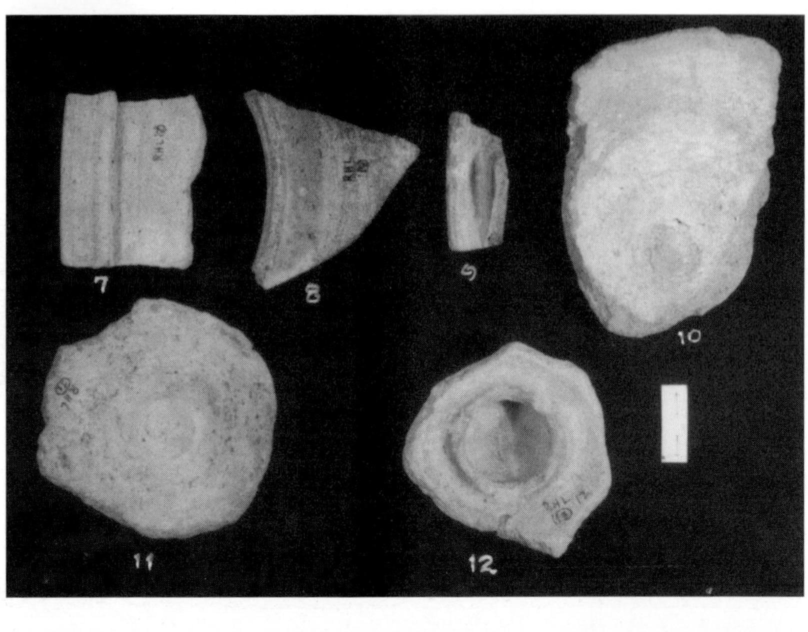

Pl. XXX-b: Red Ware: No.7-Jar, Grey Ware: No.8-Jar, No.9-Pot, Red Ware: Nos.10-11-Cups, No.12- Lid.

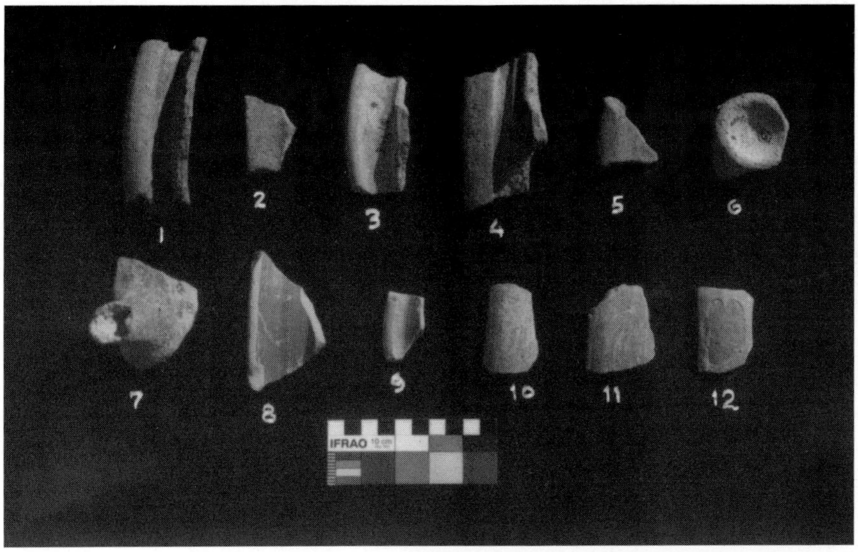

Pl. XXXI-a: Red-Slipped Ware: No.1-Jar, Red Ware: No.2-Pot, |Red-Slipped Ware: No.3-Jar. Grey Ware: No.4-Pot, No.5-Dish. Red-Slipped Ware: No.6-Spout, No.7-Lamp-on-stand. Red Polished Ware: Nos.8-9- Jars, Nos.10-12- Bowls.

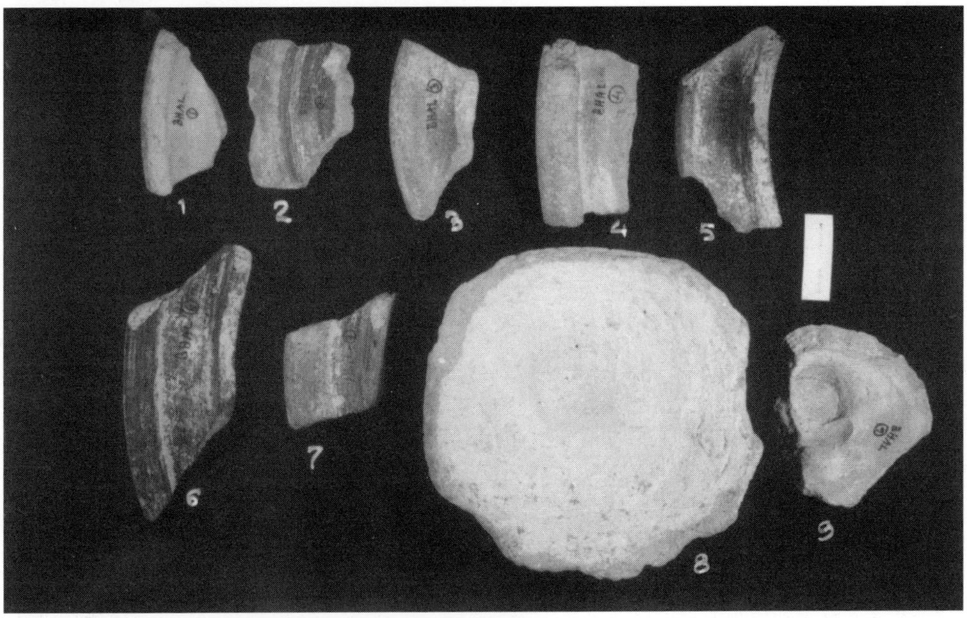

Pl. XXXI-b: Red-Slipped Ware: No.1-Pot, No.2-Jar, Nos.3-5-Pots, Grey Ware: No.6-Jar, No.7-Pot. Red Ware: Nos.8-9-Cups.

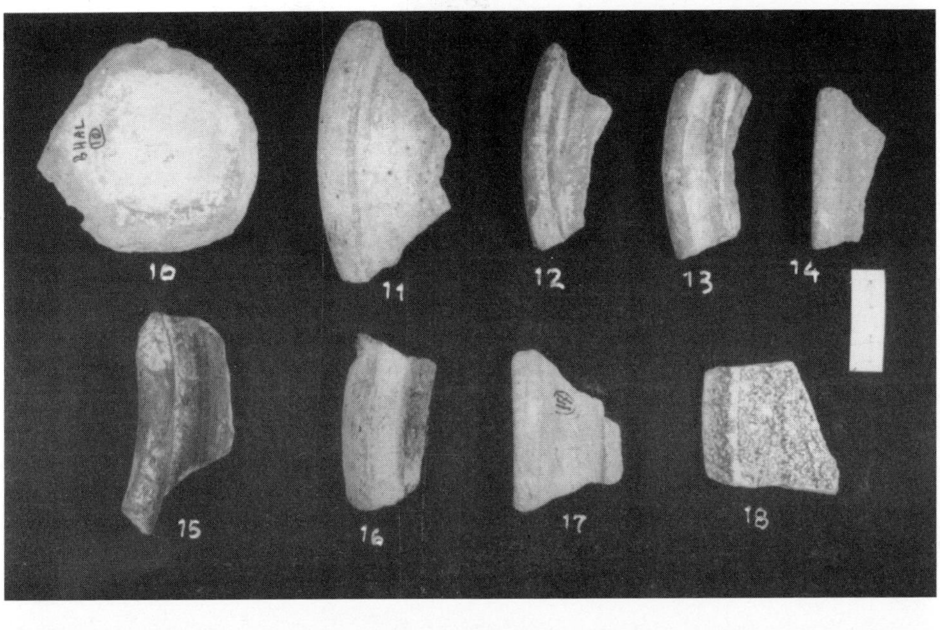

Pl. XXXI-c: Red Ware: No.10-Cup, Red-Slipped Ware: Nos.11-13-Pots. No.14-Saucer, Grey Ware: Nos. 15-16-Pots, Red Ware: No. 17-Pot, No.18-Dish.

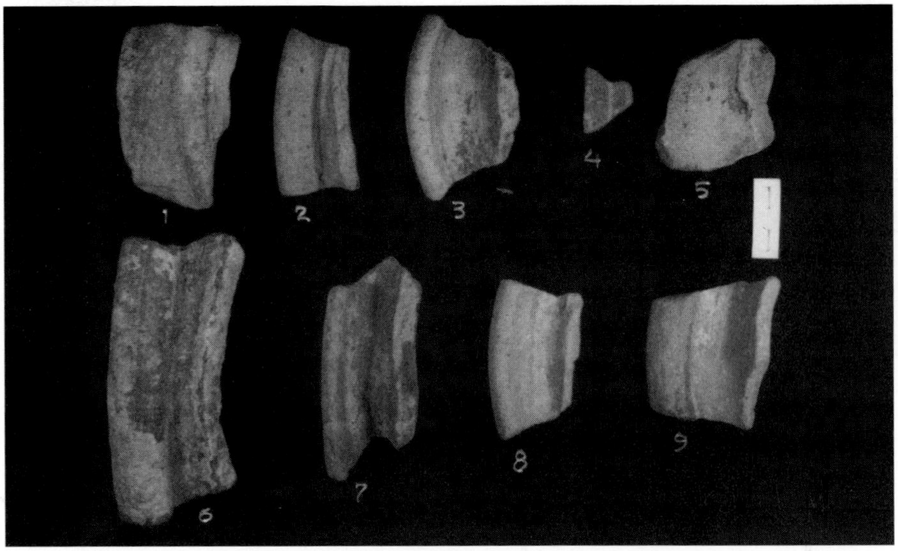

Pl. XXXII-a: Red Ware: No.1-Jar, Nos.2-3-Pots, No.4-Jar, No. 5-Cup, Nos.6-7-Jars. Red-Slipped Ware: Nos.8-9-Jars.

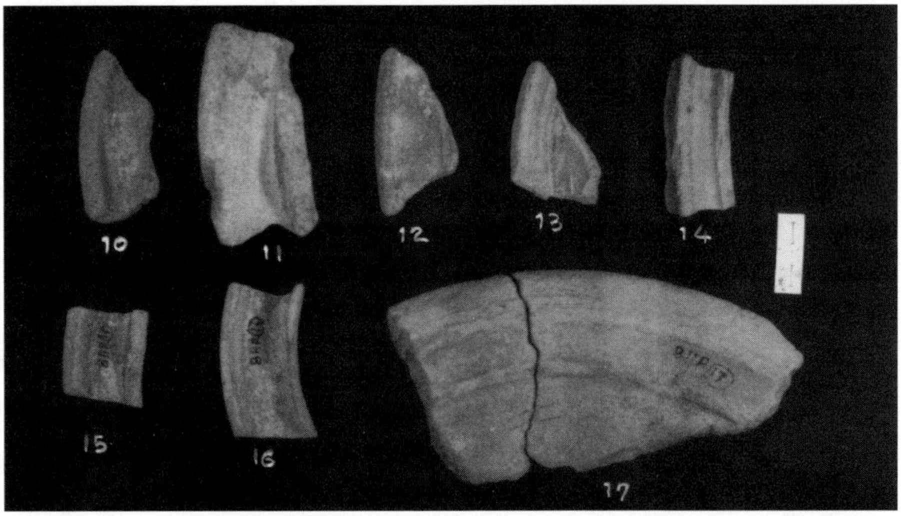

Pl. XXXII-b: Red-Slipped Ware: No.10-Pot, No.11-Jar, No.12- Pot, No.13-Jar, Nos.14-15-Pots, No.16-Jar, No.17-Bowl.

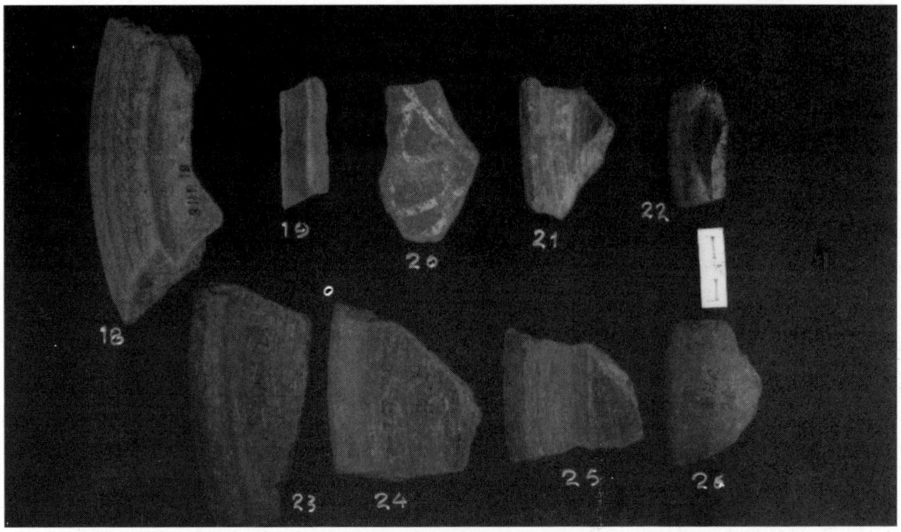

Pl. XXXII-c: Red-slipped Ware: No.18-Basin, No.19-Lid/bowl, No.20-Painted Sherd, Grey Ware: Nos.21-22-Pots, No.23-26-Dishs.

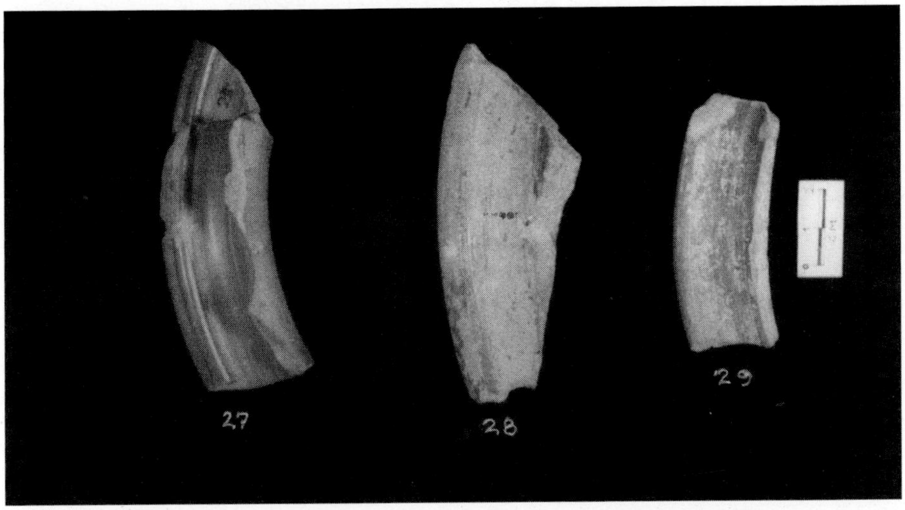

Pl. XXXII-d: Red Polished Ware: No.27-Jar, Nos.28-29-Bowls.

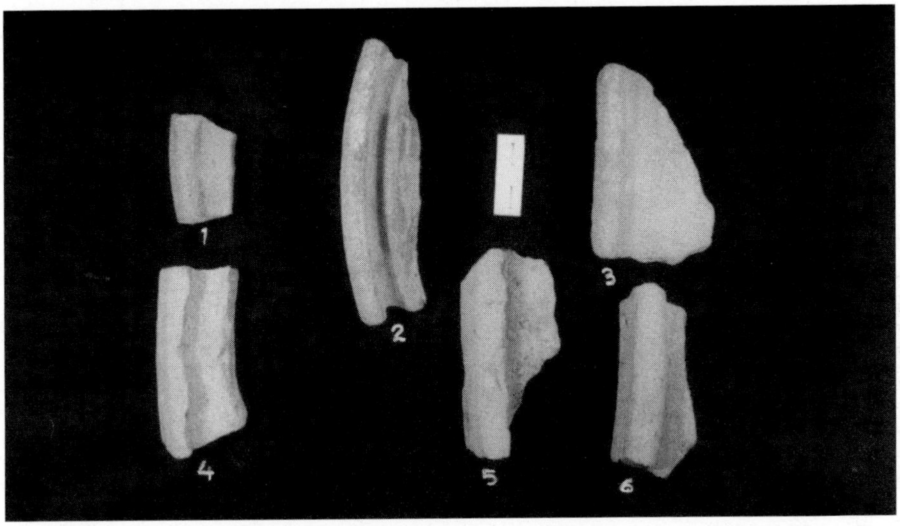

Pl. XXXIII-a: Red-Slipped Ware:Nos.1-3-Jars, Red Ware: No.4-Jar, Red-Slipped Ware: No.5-Jar, Red Ware: No.6-Jar

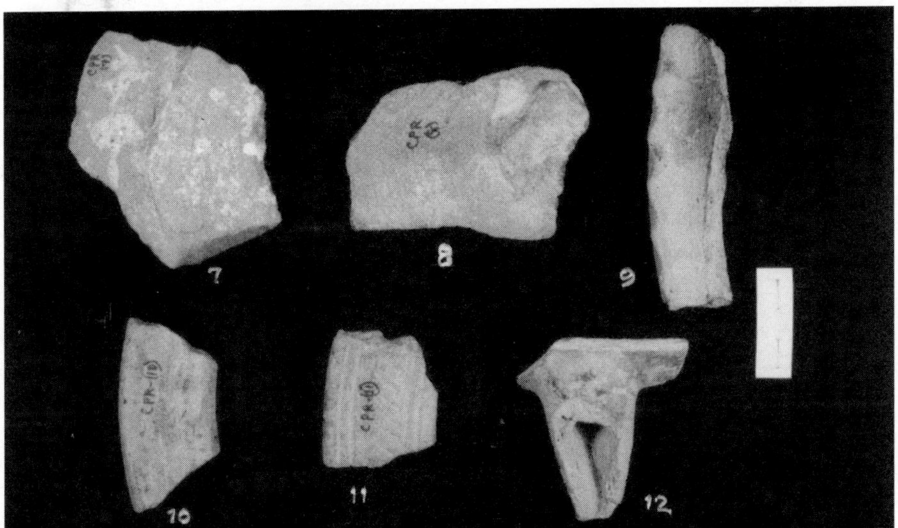

Pl. XXXIII-b: Red Ware: No.7-Cup, Grey Ware: No.8-Bowl, No.9-Unascertained vessel, No.10-Basin, No.11-Dish, No.12-Spout.

Pl. XXXIV-a: Red-Slipped Ware: Nos.1-3-Jars, No.4-Pot,
Nos. 5-6-Jars, Nos. 7-8-Pots, Nos.9-10-Cups.

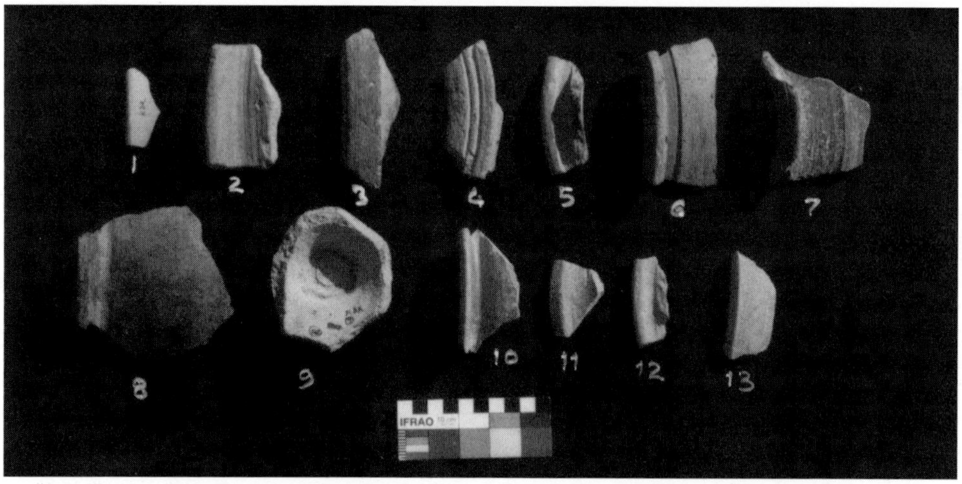

Pl. XXXIV-b: Red-Slipped Ware: No.1-Pot, No.2-Dish, Grey Ware:
Nos.3-4-Basins, Nos.5-6-Jars, No.7-Pot, No.8-Jar, Red Ware: No.9-Saucer,
Red Polished Ware: Nos.10-11-Jars, Nos.12- 13-Bowls.

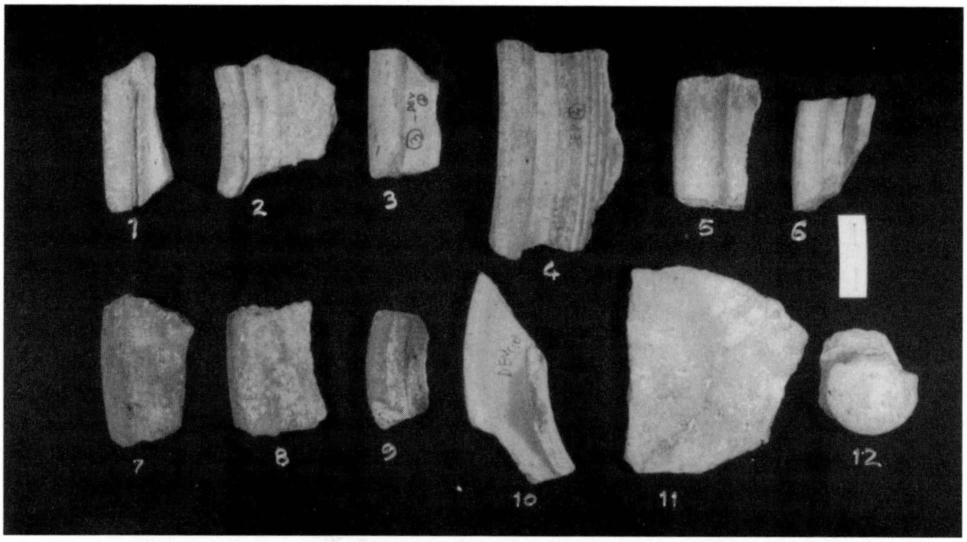

Pl. XXXV-a: Red-Slipped Ware: No.1-Pot, Red Ware: Nos.2-3-Jars,
Red-Slipped Ware: No.4-Jar, Grey Ware: No.5-Dish, No.6-Jar, Nos.7-8,
Dishes, Nos.9-10-Jars, Red Ware: No.11-Bowl, No.12-Dish-on-stand.?

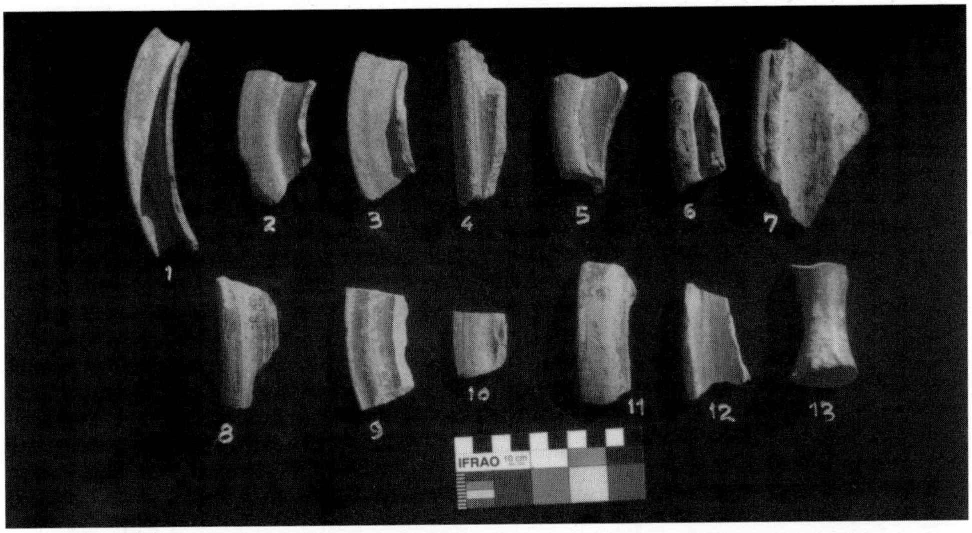

Pl. XXXV-b: Red-Slipped Ware: No.1-Pot, Nos.2-3-Jars, No.4-Pot, No.5-Jar, No.6- Pot, Nos.7-8-Dish, Red Polished Ware: No.9-Jar, Nos.10-11-Bowls, No.12-Jar- No.13-Sprinkler.

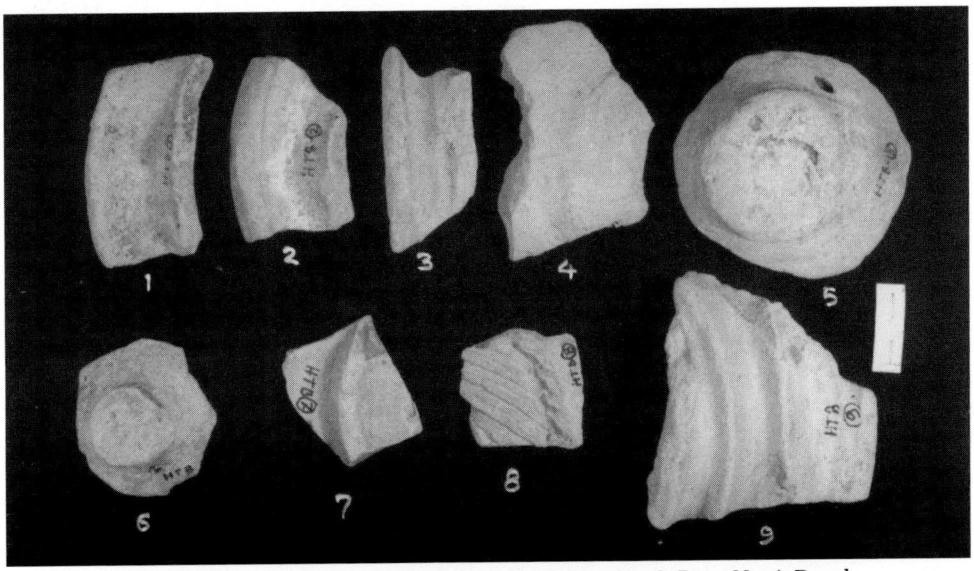

Pl. XXXVI-a: Red Ware: No.1-Pot, No.2-Jar, No.3-Pot, No.4-Bowl, Nos.5-6-Cups, No.7-Bowl, Nos.8-9-Uncertain sherds.

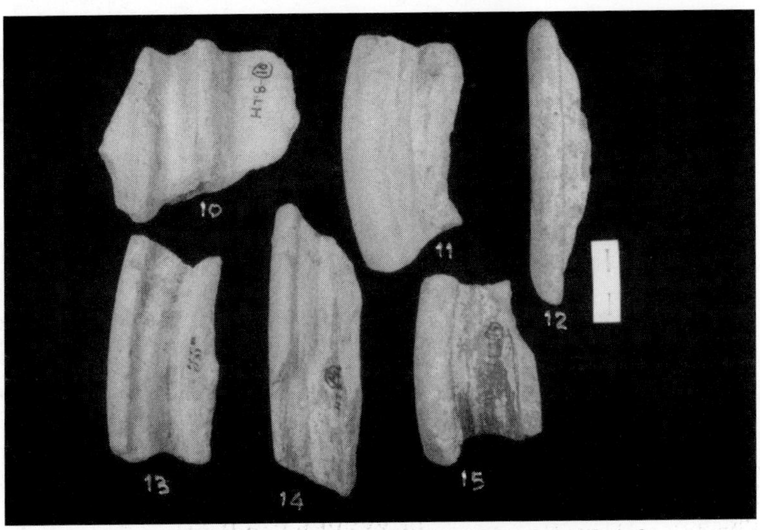

Pl. XXXVI-b: Red Ware: No.10-Uncertain sherd, Red-Slipped Ware: Nos. 11-13-Jars, No.14-Pot, No.15-Jar.

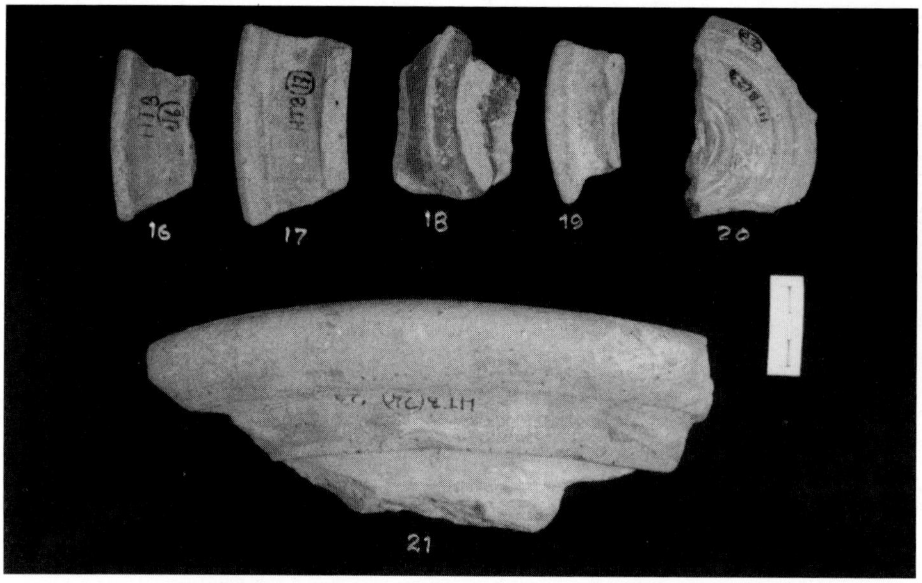

Pl. XXXVI-c: Red-slipped Ware: No. 16-Bowl, No.17- Jar, Nos.18-19-Uncertain sherds, No. 20-Lid- No. 21-Jar

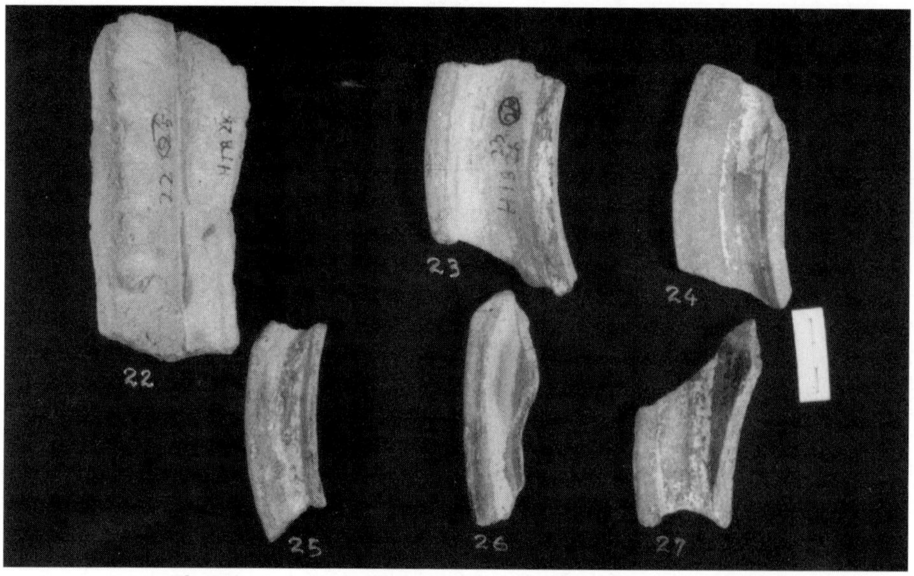

Pl. XXXVI-d: Red-slipped Ware: No.22-Uncertain sherd, Grey Ware: Nos.23-24-Jars, No.25 –Pot, No.26-Handi, No.27-Pot.

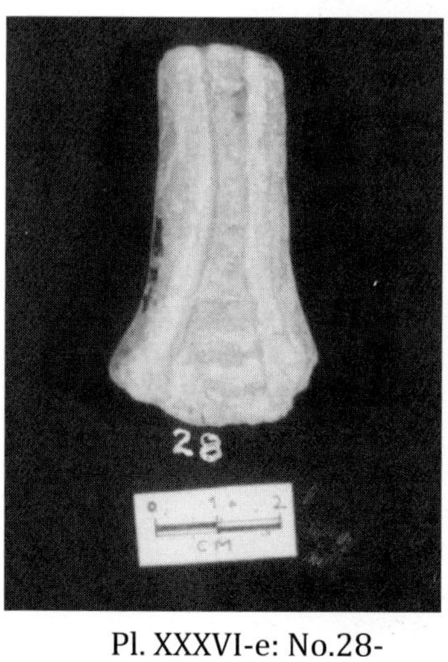

Pl. XXXVI-e: No.28- Amphorae handle sherd.

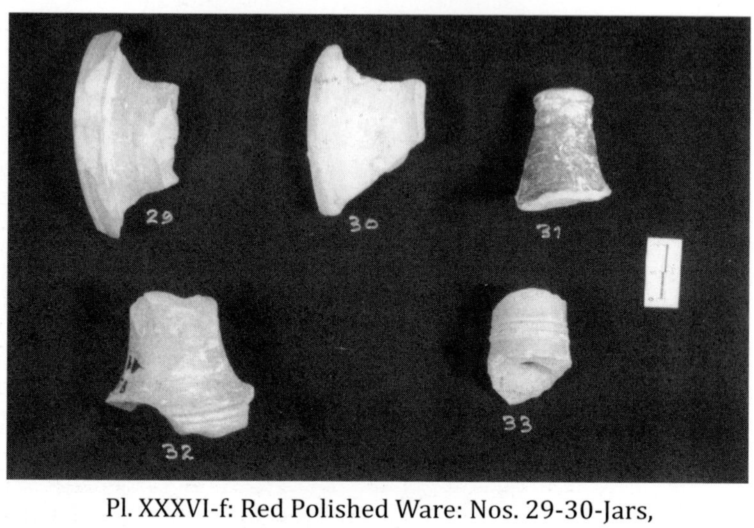

Pl. XXXVI-f: Red Polished Ware: Nos. 29-30-Jars, Nos.31-33-Spout/ basins.

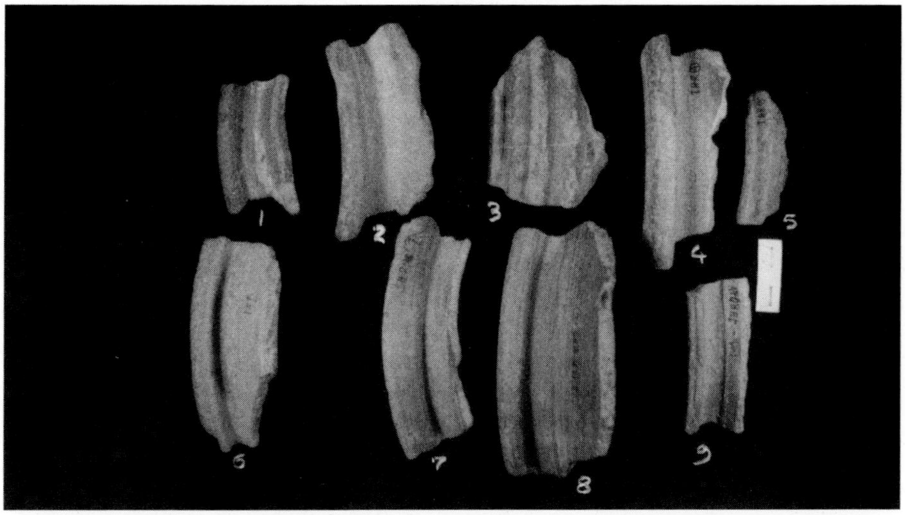

Pl. XXXVII-a: Red-Slipped Ware : Nos.1-2- Jars, No.3-Dish, No.4-Pot, No.5-Cup, Nos. 6-7-Jars, No.8-Pot, Red Ware: No.9-Jar.

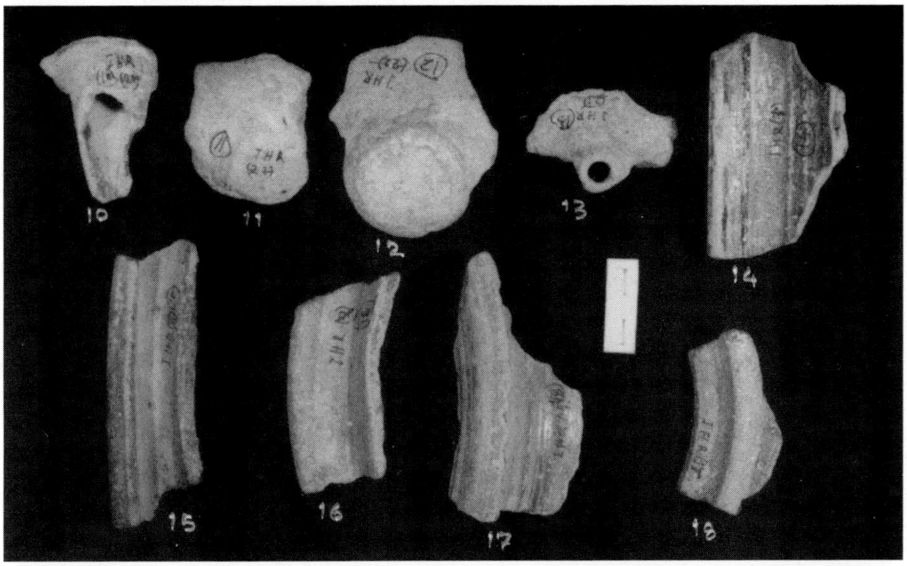

Pl. XXXVII-b: Red-Slipped Ware: No. 10-Conical spout, Nos.11-12-Bowls, No. 13-Spout, Grey Ware: No. 14-Jar, No.15-Pot, No.16-Jar, Nos. 17-18-Pots.

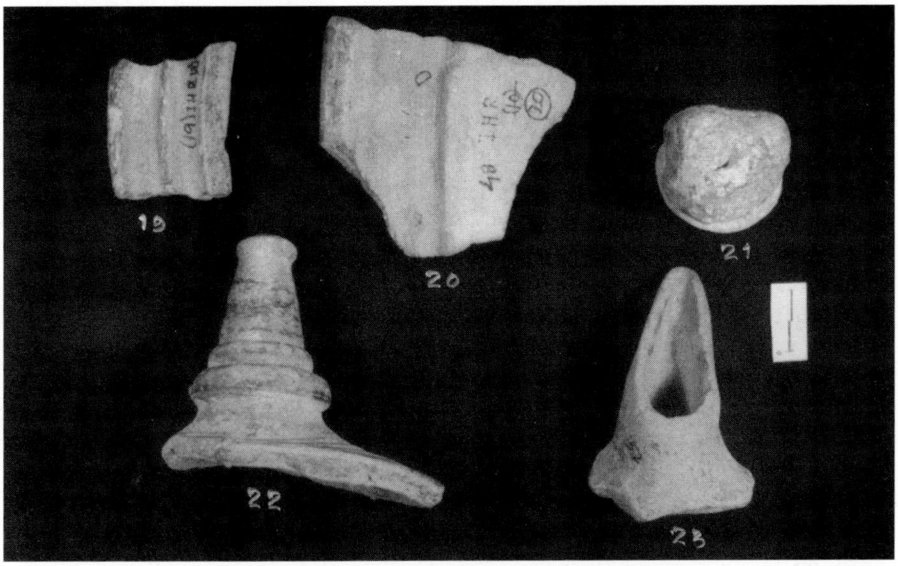

Pl. XXXVII-c: Grey Ware: No19-Pot, No.20-Dish, No. 21-Dish-on-stand?, No.22-Lid, No.23-Spout.

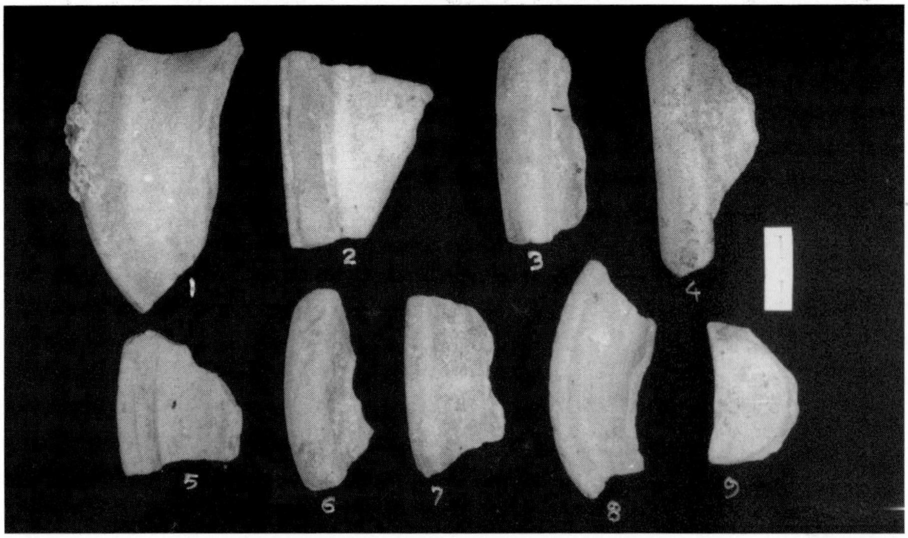

Pl. XXXVIII-a: Red Ware: Nos.1-6-Jars,
Red-Slipped Ware: Nos.7-8-Pots, Red Ware: No.9-Cup.

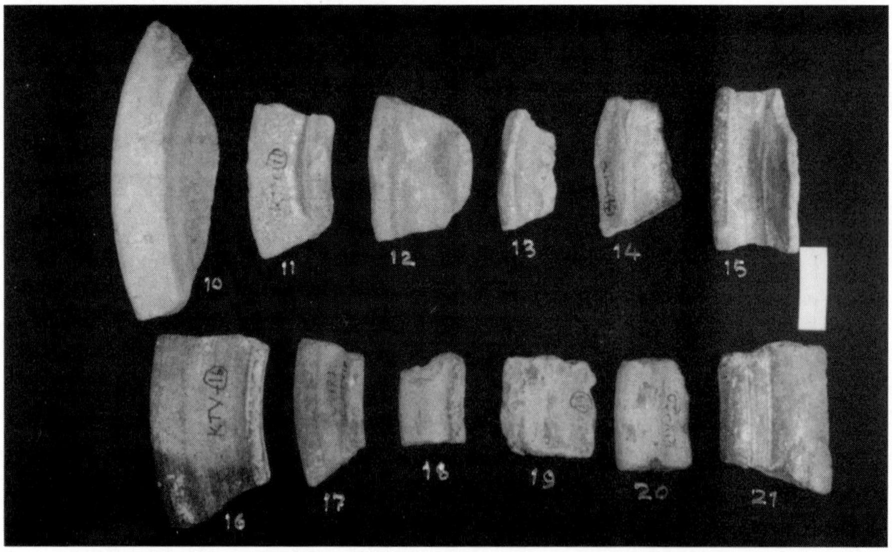

Pl. XXXVIII-b: Red-Slipped Ware: Nos.10-11-Jars, Nos.12-13, Pots,
No. 14-Basin, Grey Ware: Nos.15-18-Pots, No.19-Dish,
No.20-Bowl/dish, No.21-Bowl.

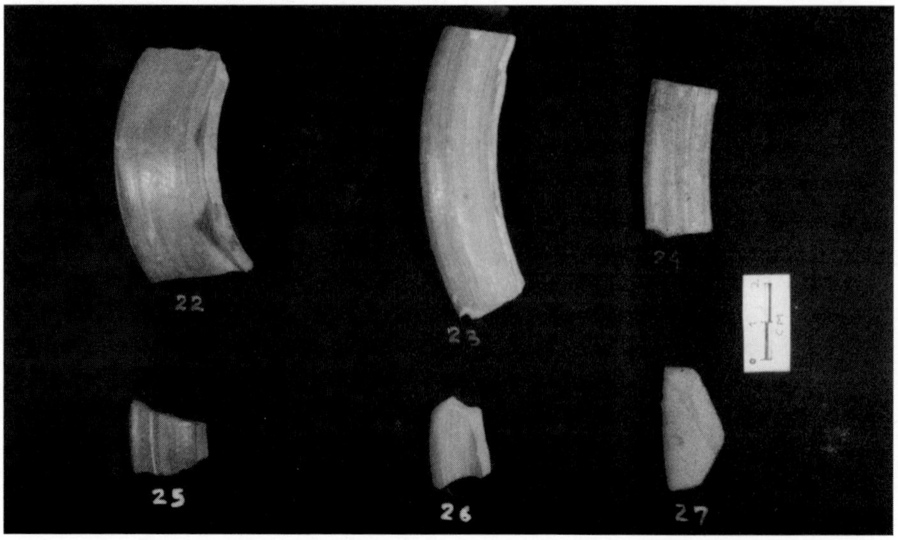

Pl. XXXVIII-c: Red Polished Ware: Nos.22-26-Jars, **No.**27-Bowl.

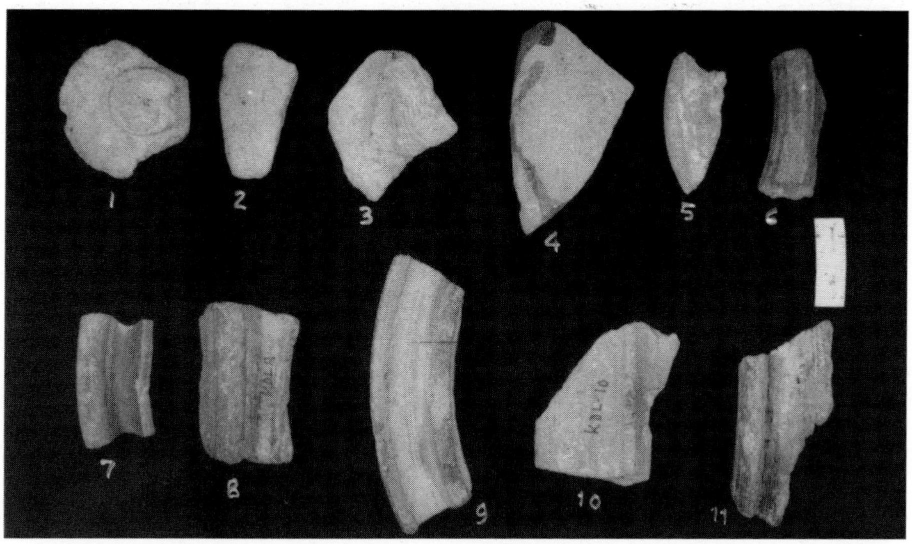

Pl. XXXIX-a: Red Ware: No. 1-Lamp/lid, Nos.2-3-Cups, No.4-Dish, No.5-Pot, No.6-Jar, Red-Slipped Ware: Nos.7-9-Jars, No.10-Dish, No.11-Jar.

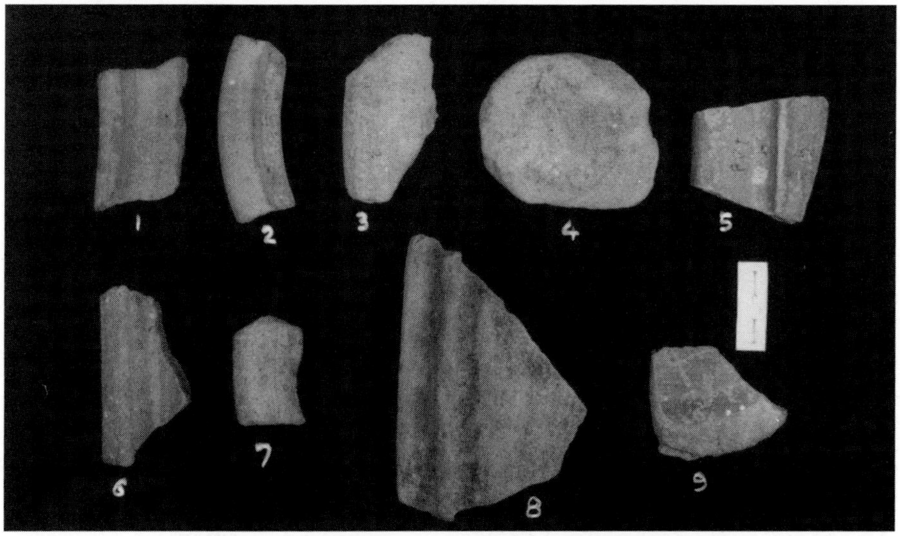

Pl. XXXIX-b: Red Ware: Nos.1-2-Jars, Nos.3-4-Cups, Red-Slipped Ware: Nos.5-Dish, No.6-Pot, No.7-Jar, No. 8-Bowl, No.9-Painted sherd.

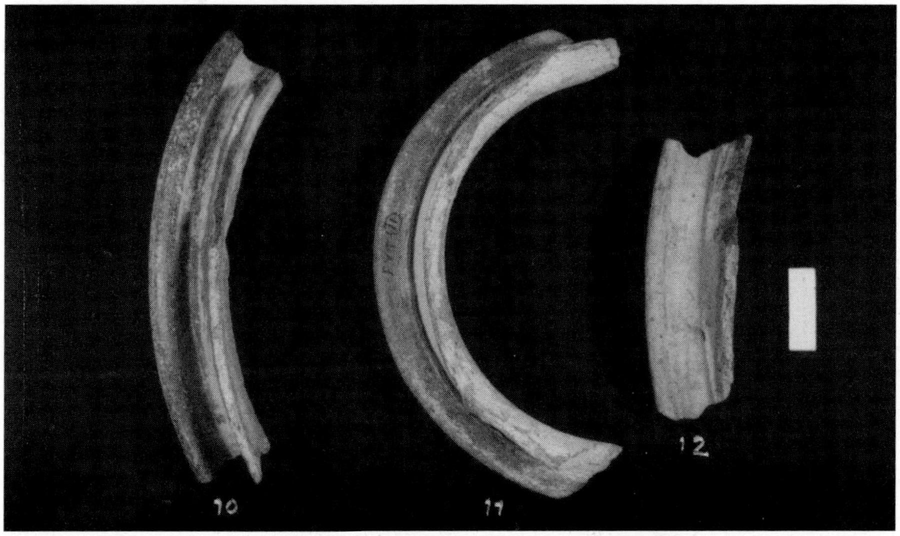

Pl. XXXIX-c: Grey Ware: Nos.10-12-Jars.

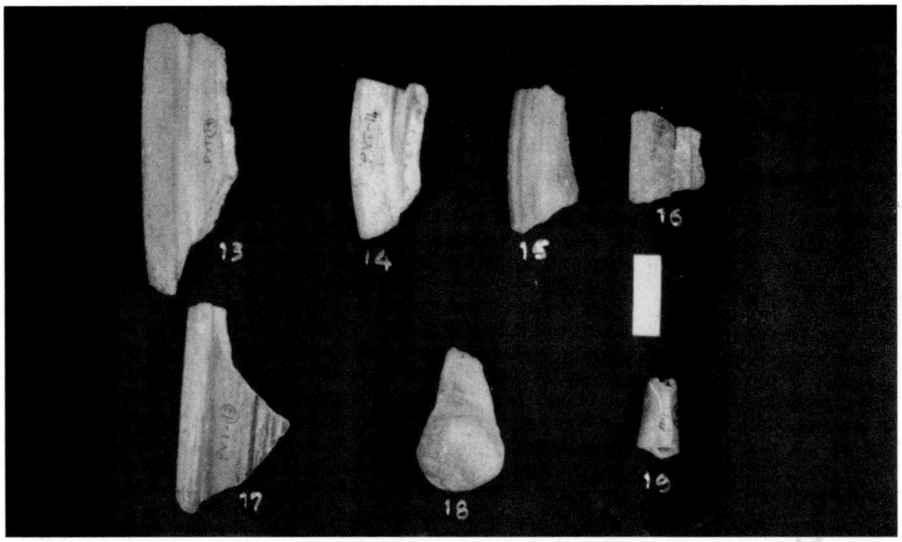

Pl. XXXIX-d: Grey Ware: Nos.13-14-Pots, No.15- Jar, No.16-Pot, No.17-Dish, No.18-Bowl, No.19-Conical spout.

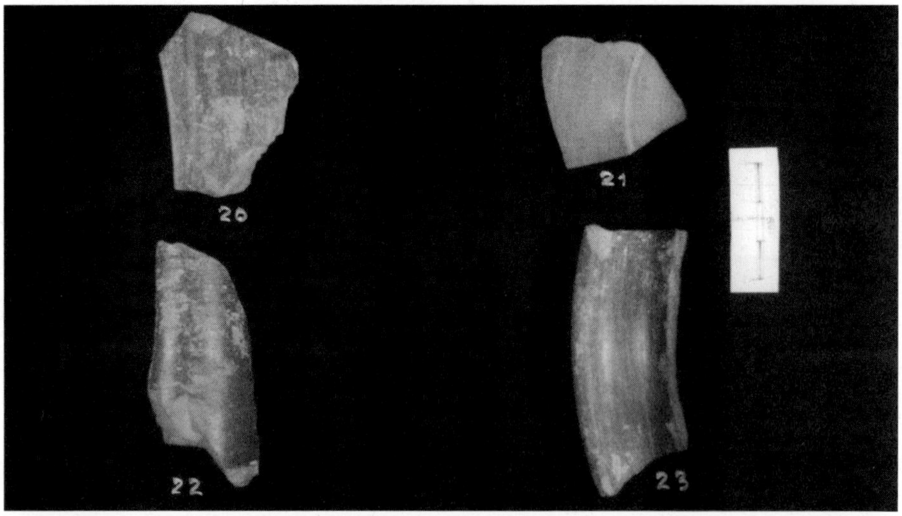

Pl. XXXIX-e: Red Polished Ware: Nos.20-21-Bowls, No.22-Sprinkler, No.23-Jar.

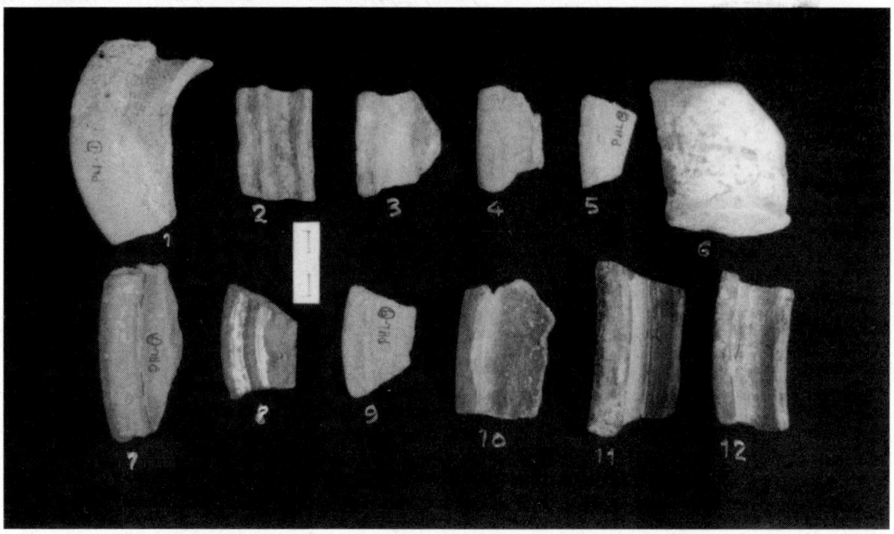

Pl. XL-a: Red-Slipped Ware: No.1-Pot, Red Ware: Nos.2-3 –Jars, Red-Slipped Ware: No.4-Jar, RedWare: Nos.5-6-Cups, Red-Slipped Ware: No.7-Jar, No.8-Pot, No.9-Basin, No.10-Bowl/lid, Grey Ware: Nos.11-12-Pots.

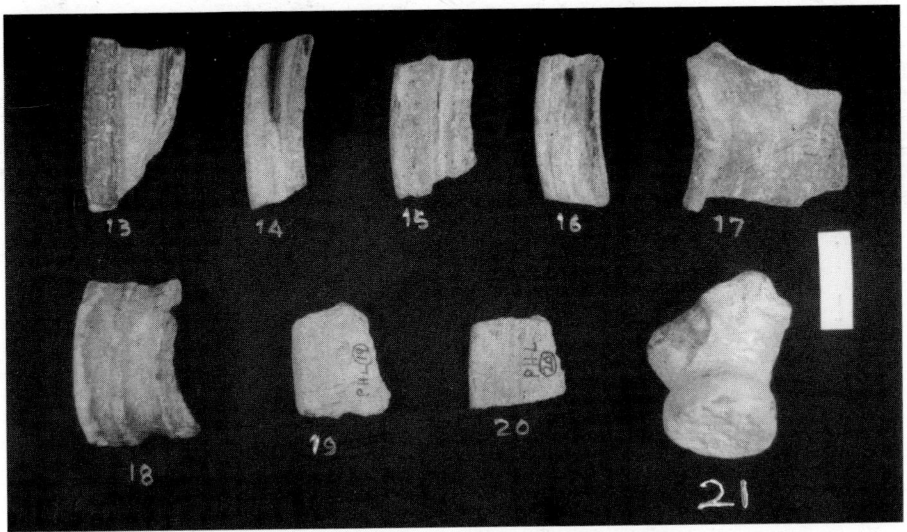

Pl. XL-b: Grey Ware: No.13-Pot, No.14-Jar, No.15-Pot, No.16- Jar, No.17-Pot, No.18-Uncertain vessel, No.19-Dish, Nos.20-21-Bowls.

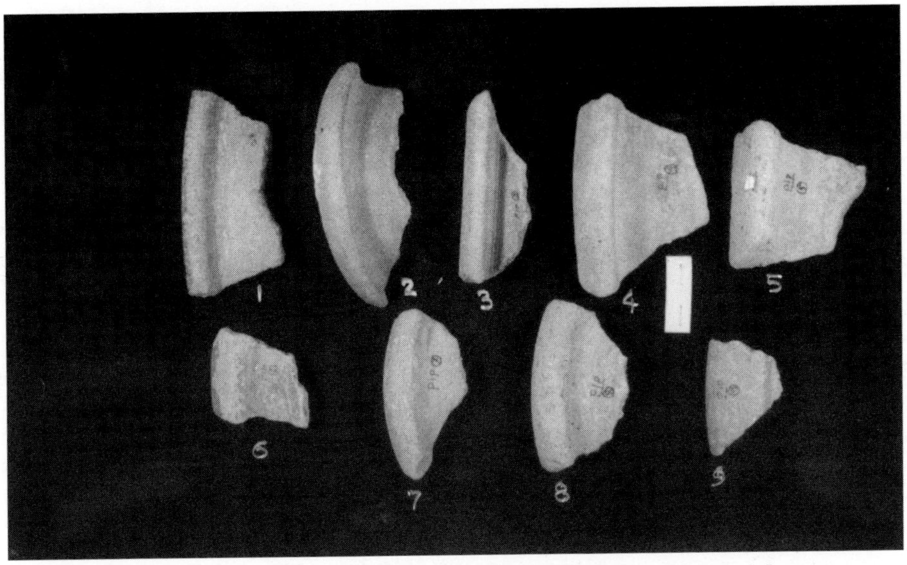

Pl. XLI-a: Red-Slipped Ware: No.1-Dish, No.2-Pot, Nos.3-4-Jars, Nos.5-8-Pots, No.9-Uncertain vessel.

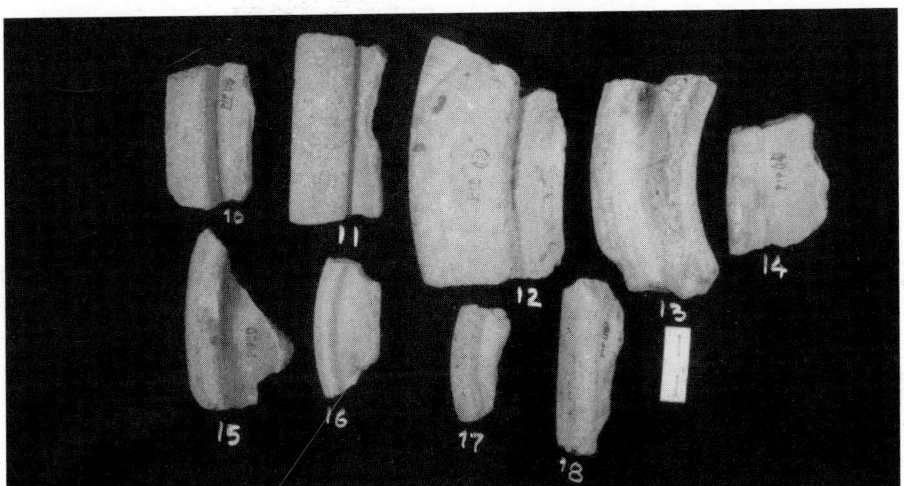

Pl. XLI-b: Red Ware: No.10-Jar, Red-Slipped Ware: No.11-Pot, Nos.12-14-Jars, No.15- Pot, Red Ware: No.16-Pot, Red-Slipped Ware: No.17-Pot, Grey Ware: No.18-Jar.

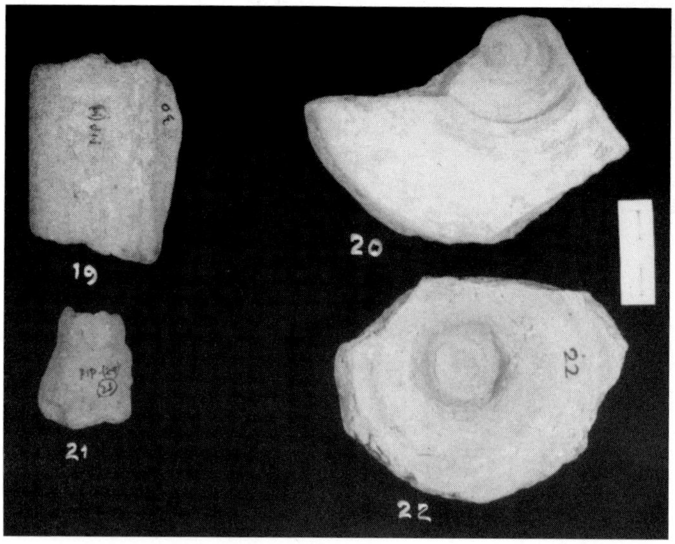

Pl. XLI-c: Red-Slipped Ware: No.19-Dish, Red Ware: No.20-Lid, Red-Slipped Ware: No.21-Spout, Red Ware: No.22-Bowl.

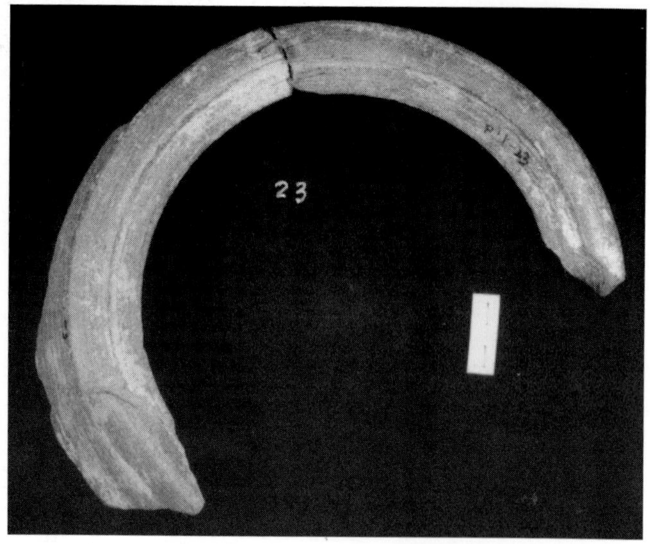

Pl. XLI-d: Grey Ware: No.23-Jar.

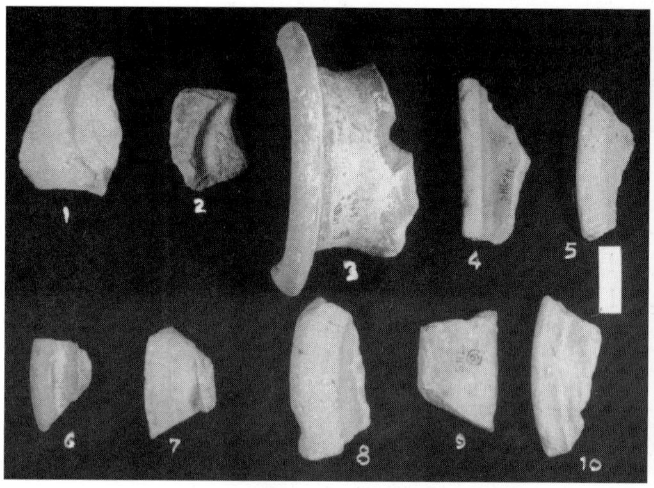

Pl. XLII-a: Red Ware: No.1-Cup, No.2-Lid, Red-Slipped Ware: Nos.3-4-Jars, No.5-Bowl, No.6-Pot, Nos.7-8-Jars, No.9-Bowl, No.10- Jar.

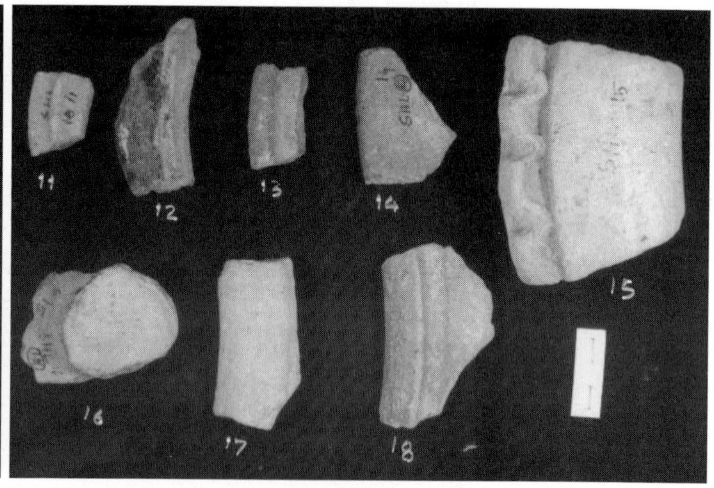

Pl. XLII-b: Red-Slipped Ware: No.11-Pot, Grey Ware: No.12- Pot, No.13-Jar, No 14-Bowl, Red Ware: No.15-Dish, No.16-Bowl, Red-Slipped Ware: Nos.17-18-Bowls.

Pl. XLII-c: Red Polished Ware: No.19-Dish, No.20- Bowl.

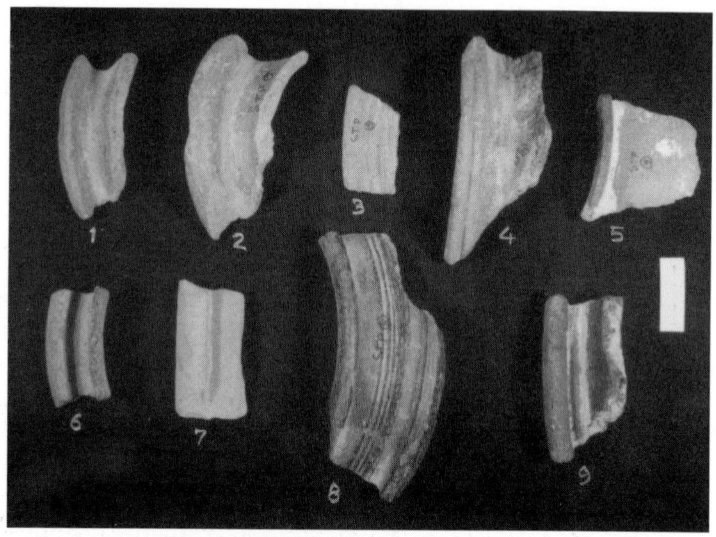

Pl. XLIII-a: Red-Slipped Ware: Nos.1-6-Pots, Red Ware: No.7-Jar, Grey Ware: No.8-Bowl, No.9-Pot.

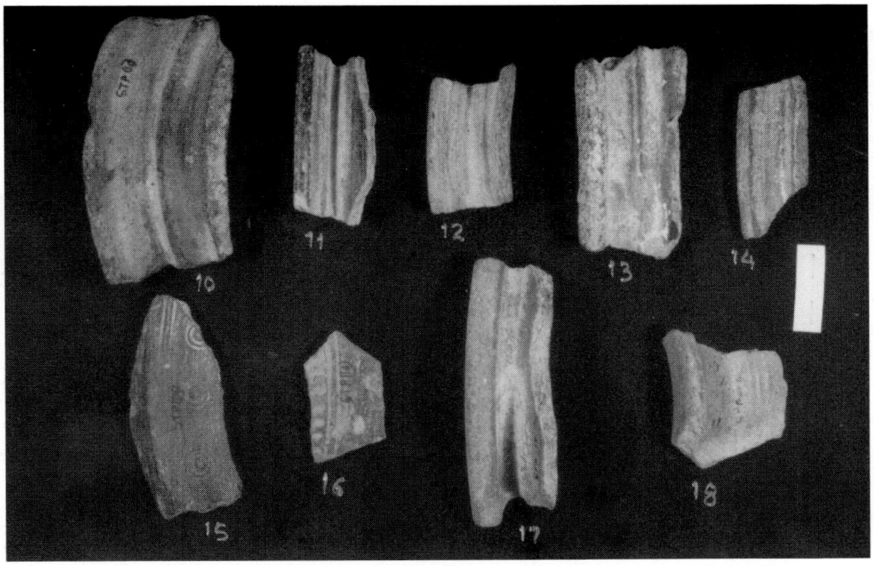

Pl. XLIII-b: Grey Ware: Nos.10-11-Pots, No.12-Jar, Nos.13-14-Pots, No.15-Bowl, No.16-Stamped body sherd, No. 17-Pot, No.18-Jar.

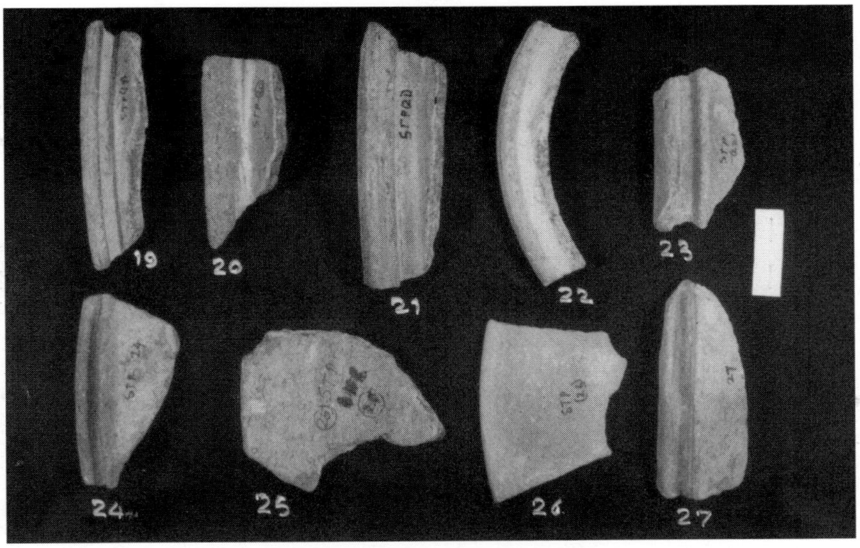

Pl. XLIII-c: Grey Ware: Nos.19-22-Pots, Nos.23-24-Dishes, Red-Slipped Ware: Nos. 25-27-Dishes.

Pl. XLIII-d: Red-Slipped Ware: Nos.28-29-Spouts, Grey Ware: No.30-Bowl, No.31-Lid, Red Ware: No.32-Saucer, No.33-Stamped body sherd, Red -Slipped Ware: No.34-Painted body sherd, Red Ware: No.35-Perforated disc base.

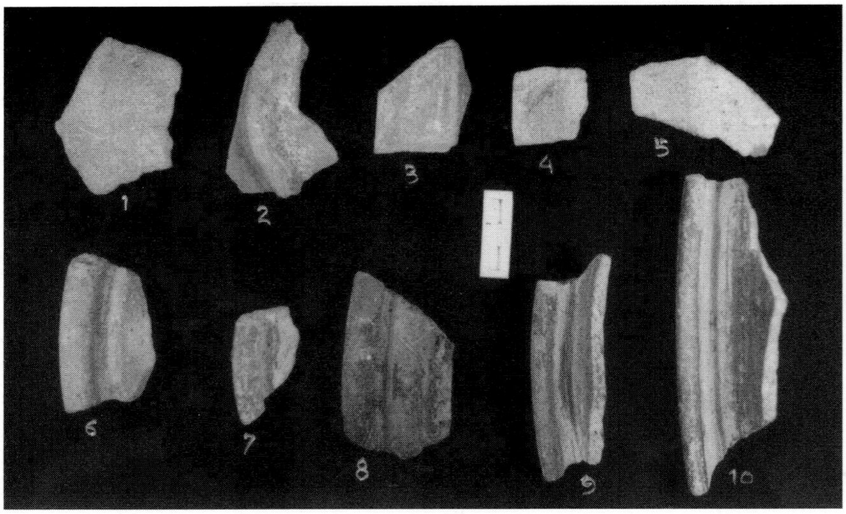

Pl. XLIV-a: Red Ware: No.1- Lid, Red-Slipped Ware: No.2- Bowl, No.3-Dish, Red Ware: Nos.4-5-Cups, Red-Slipped Ware: No.6-Jar, No.7-Pot, Grey Ware: No.8-Pot, Nos.9-10-Jars.

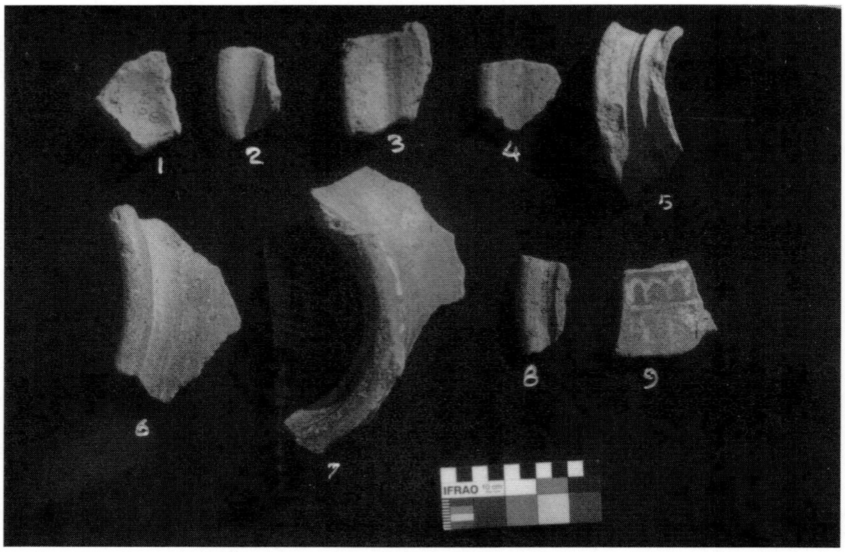

Pl. XLIV-b: Red Ware: No.1-Cup, No.2-Pot, Nos.3-4-Dish, Red-Slipped Ware: No.5-Pot, No.6-Jar, Grey Ware: Nos.7-8-Jars, Red Slipped Ware: No.9-Painted body sherd.

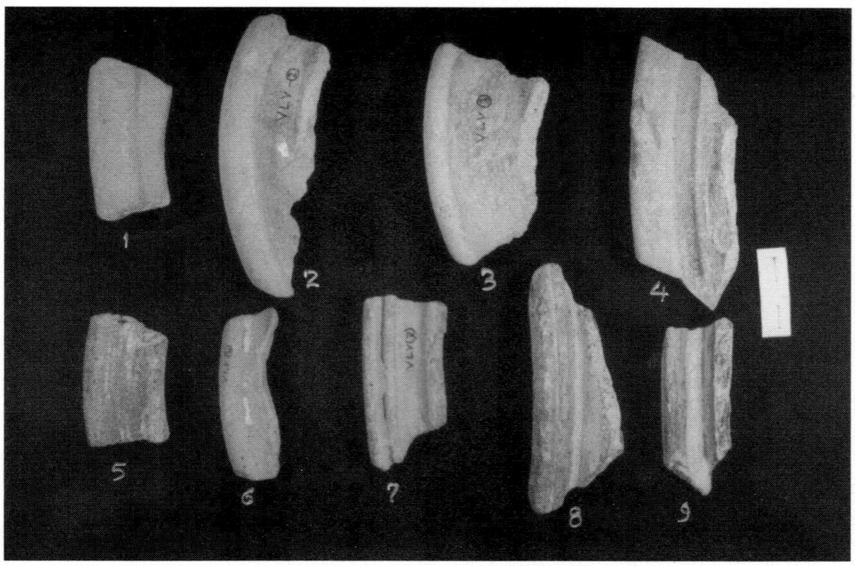

Pl. XLV-a: Red-Slipped Ware: No.1-Dish, Nos.2-3-Pots, Nos.4-5-Jars, No.6-Pot, Grey Ware: Nos.7-8-Jars, No.9-Pot.

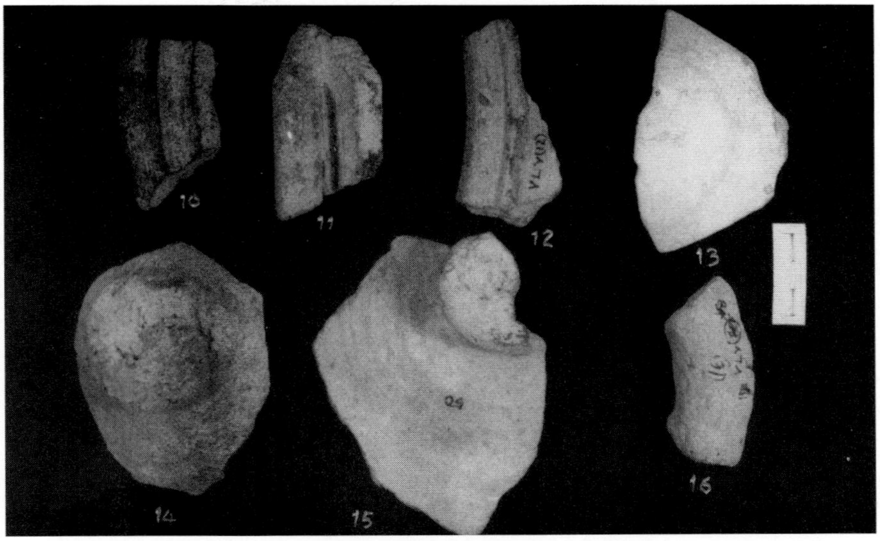

Pl. XLV-b: Grey Ware: No.10-Jar, No.11-Pot, No.12-Basin, No.13-Bowl, Red Ware: No.14-Bowl, Grey Ware: No.15-Bowl, Red Ware: No.16-Handle of a vessel.

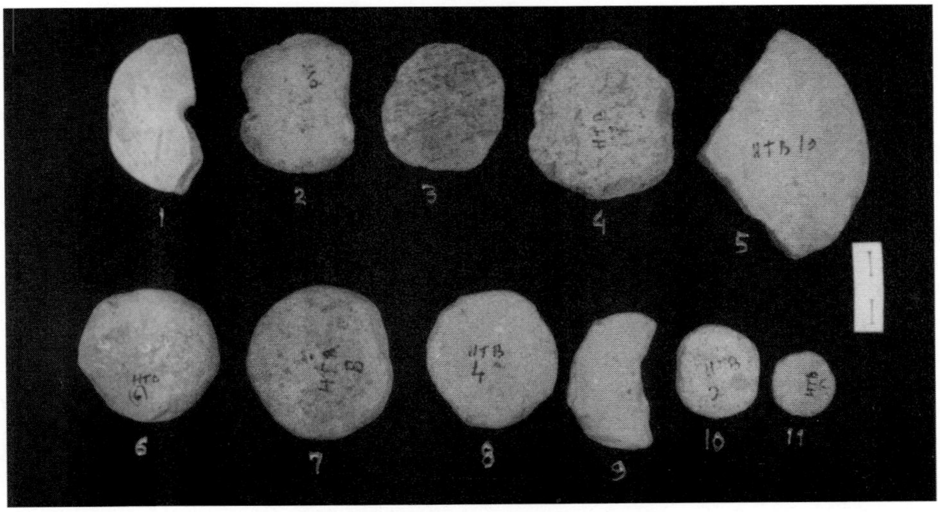

Pl. XLVI-a: No. 1-A fragment of perforated potsherd disc found at Valavadar, No.2-A circular terracotta disc found at Pavti, No.3-A circular potsherd disc found at Saltanpur, No.4-A unperforated terracotta disc found at Hathab, No.5-A fragment of terracotta disc found at Hathab, Nos.6-11-Unperforated terracotta discs found at Hathab.

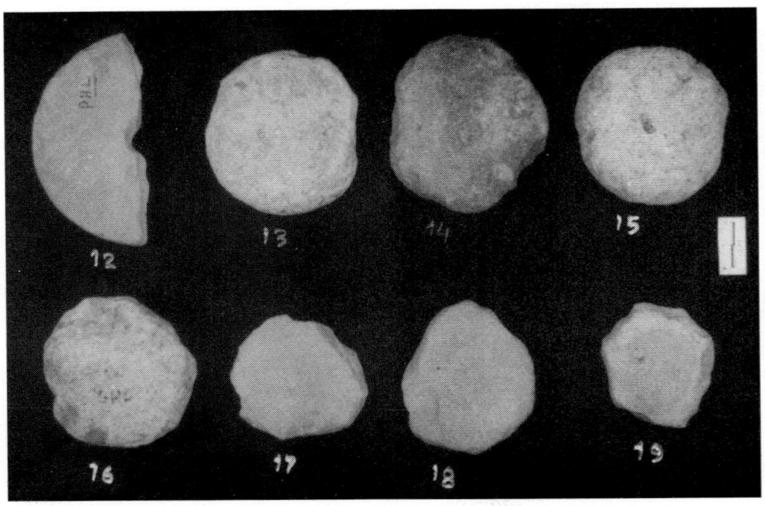

Pl. XLVI-b: No.12-A perforated terracotta disc found at Phulsar, No.13-A circular terracotta disc found at Gorkhi, No.14-A circular potsherd disc found at Ichhora, No.15-A circular terracotta disc found at Piparla, No16-A circular terracotta disc found at Shilavadar, Nos.17-18-Unperforated potsherd discs found at Saltanpur, No.19-A circular terracotta disc found at Bhegali.

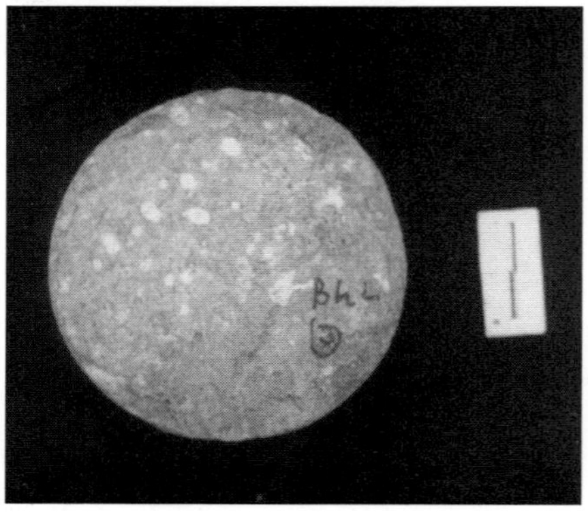

Pl. XLVII-a: Red ware: Sand stone muller found at Bhegali.

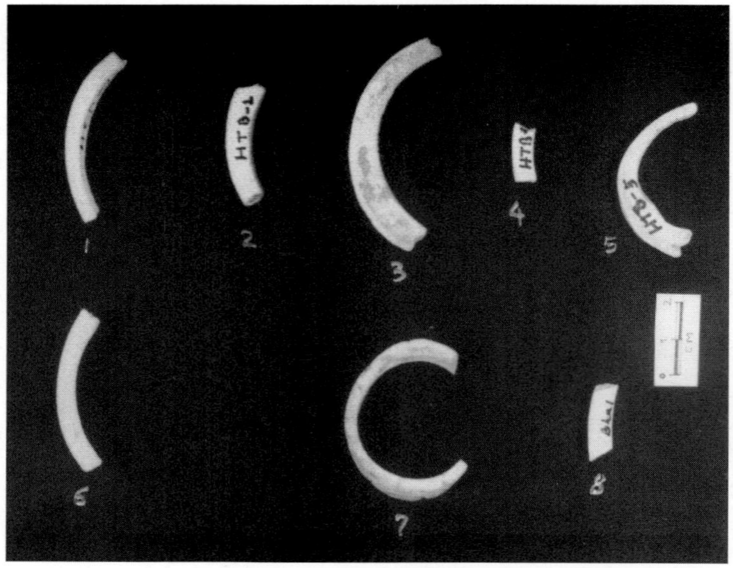

Pl. XLVII-b: Nos.1-2-Fragments of shell bangle found at Hathab, No.3-Shell bangle found at Piparla, Nos.4-6-Fragments of shell bangle found at Hathab, No.7-Fragment of Shell bangle found at Pavti, No.8-Shell bangle found at Bhalar.

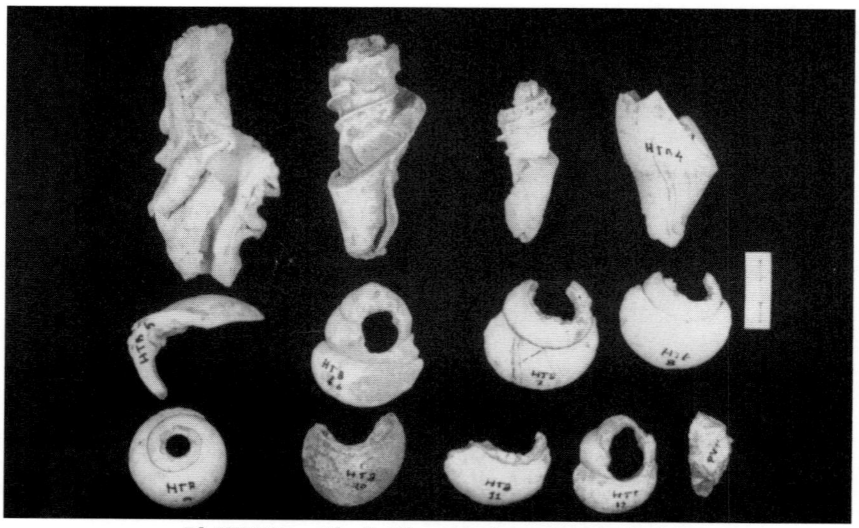

Pl. XLVIII-a: Shell dibatage found at Hathab.

Pl. XVIII-b: No.1-Used shell found at Hathab, Nos.2-3-Used shell found at Chopa, No.4-Used shell found at Piparla, No.5-Used shell found at Saltanpur.

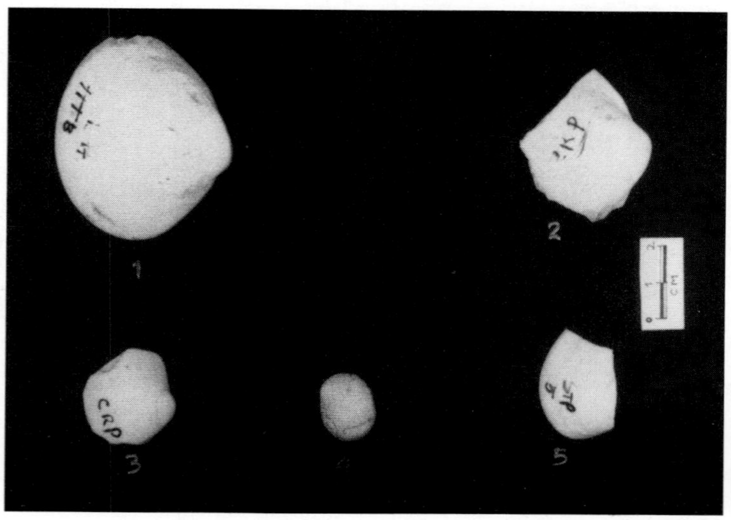

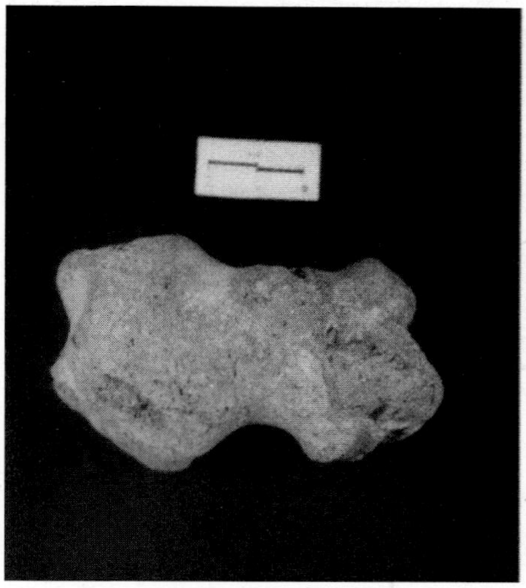

Pl. XLIX-a:Terracotta animal figurine found at Bhegali.

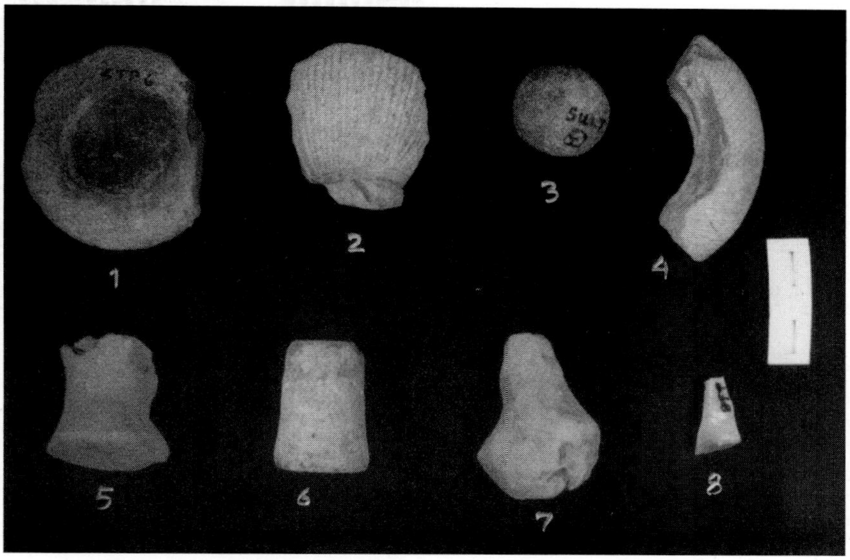

Pl. XLIX-b: No.1-Terracotta lamp found at Saltanpur, No.2-Decorated terracotta bell found at Pavti, No.3-Stone ball found at Saltanpur, No.4-Fragment of terracotta bell found at Phulsar, No.5-Terracotta stopper found at Saltanpur, No.6-Terracotta stopper found at Piparla, No.7-Fragment of unidentified figurine found at Katva, No.8-Agates flake found at Piparla.

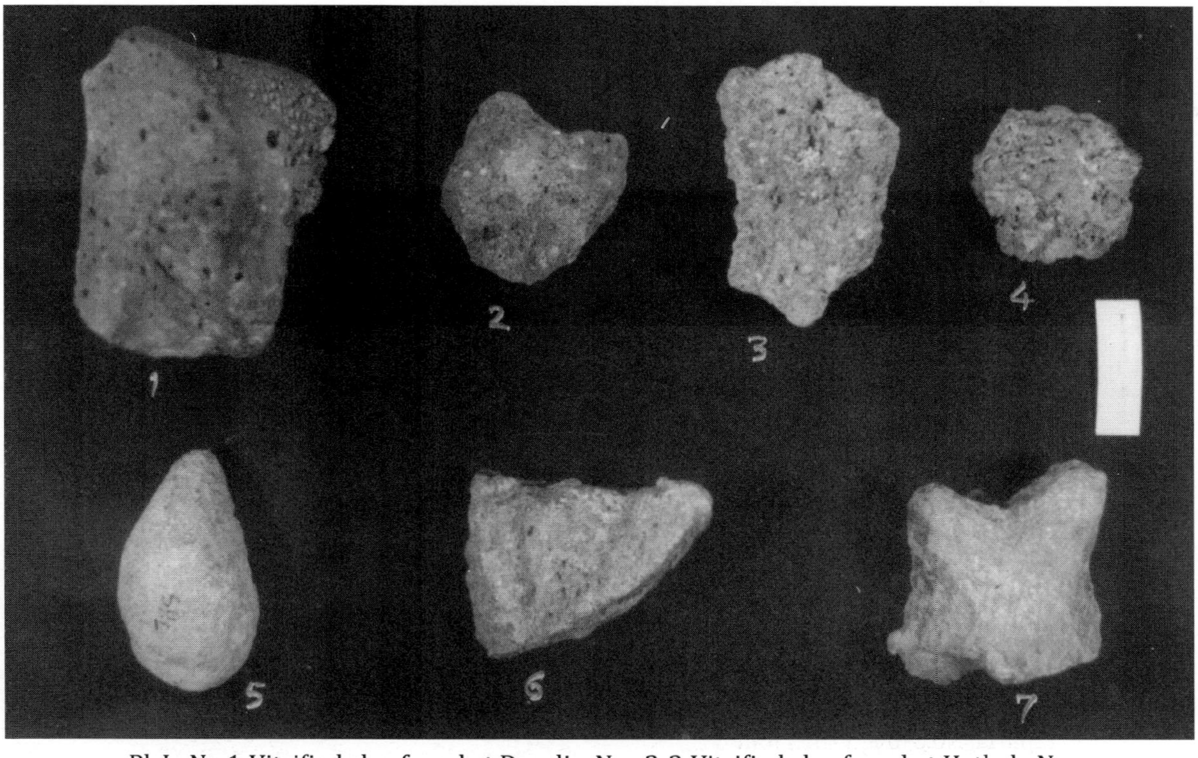

Pl. L: No.1-Vitrified clay found at Devalia, Nos.2-3-Vitrified clay found at Hathab, No. 4-Iron slag found at Saltanpur, No.5-Unidentified stone object found at Shilavadar, No.6-Fragment of iron object found at Bharapur, No.7-Iron slag found at Phulsar.

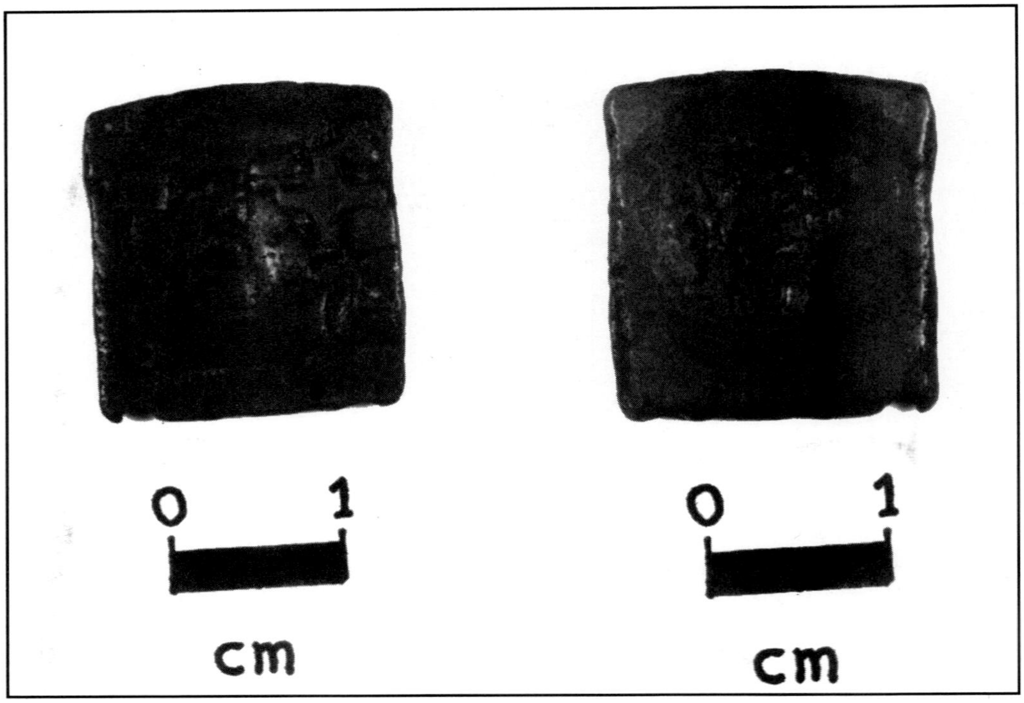

Pl. LI a & b: Punch marked copper coin found at Hathab.

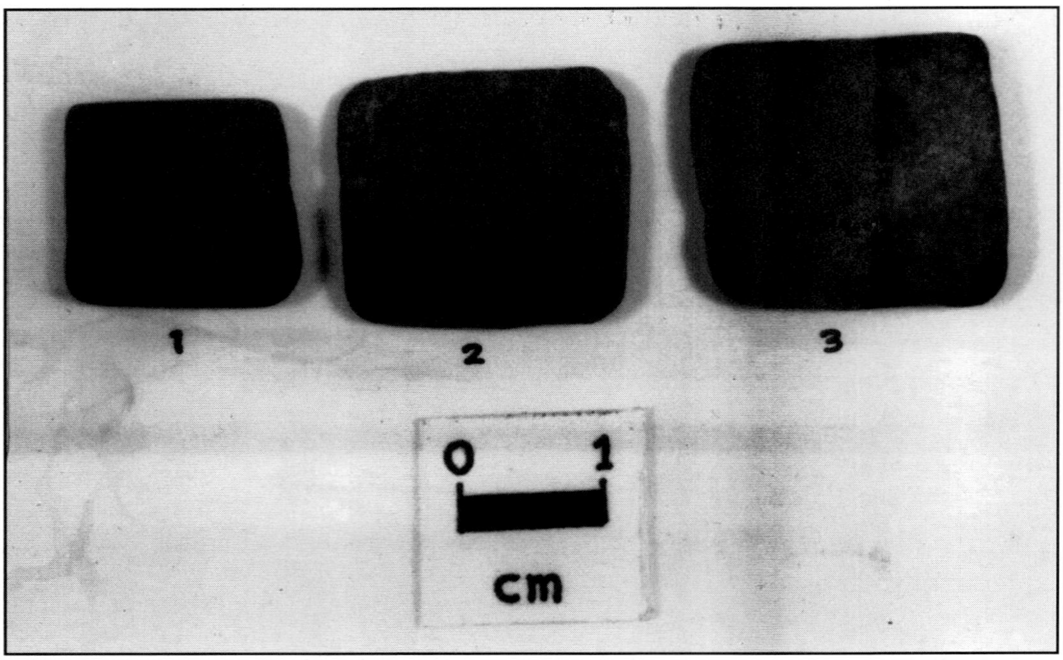

Pl. LII: Nos.1-3- Punch marked copper coins found at Hathab.